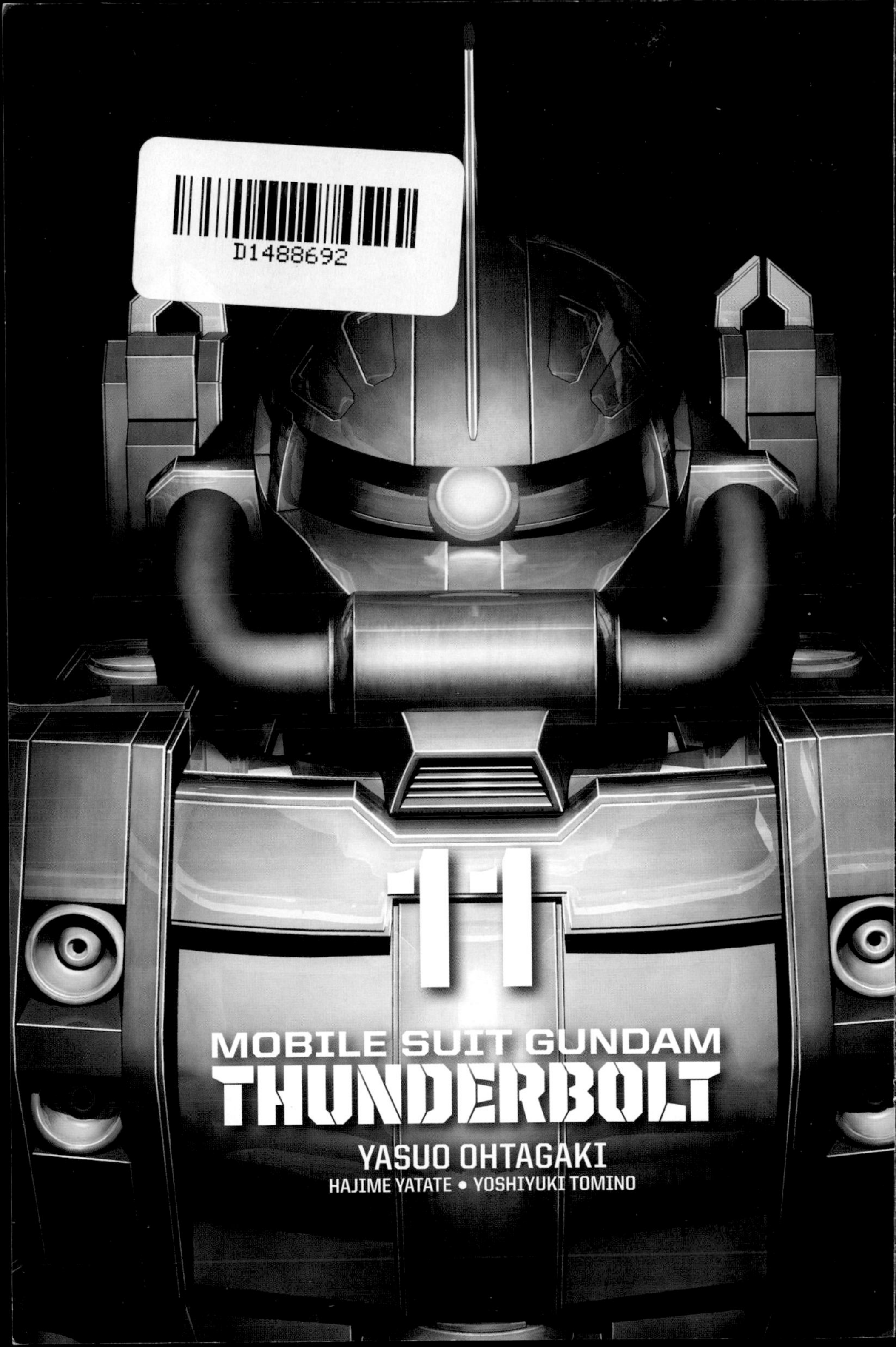

11

MOBILE SUIT GUNDAM THUNDERBOLT

YASUO OHTAGAKI

HAJIME YATATE • YOSHIYUKI TOMINO

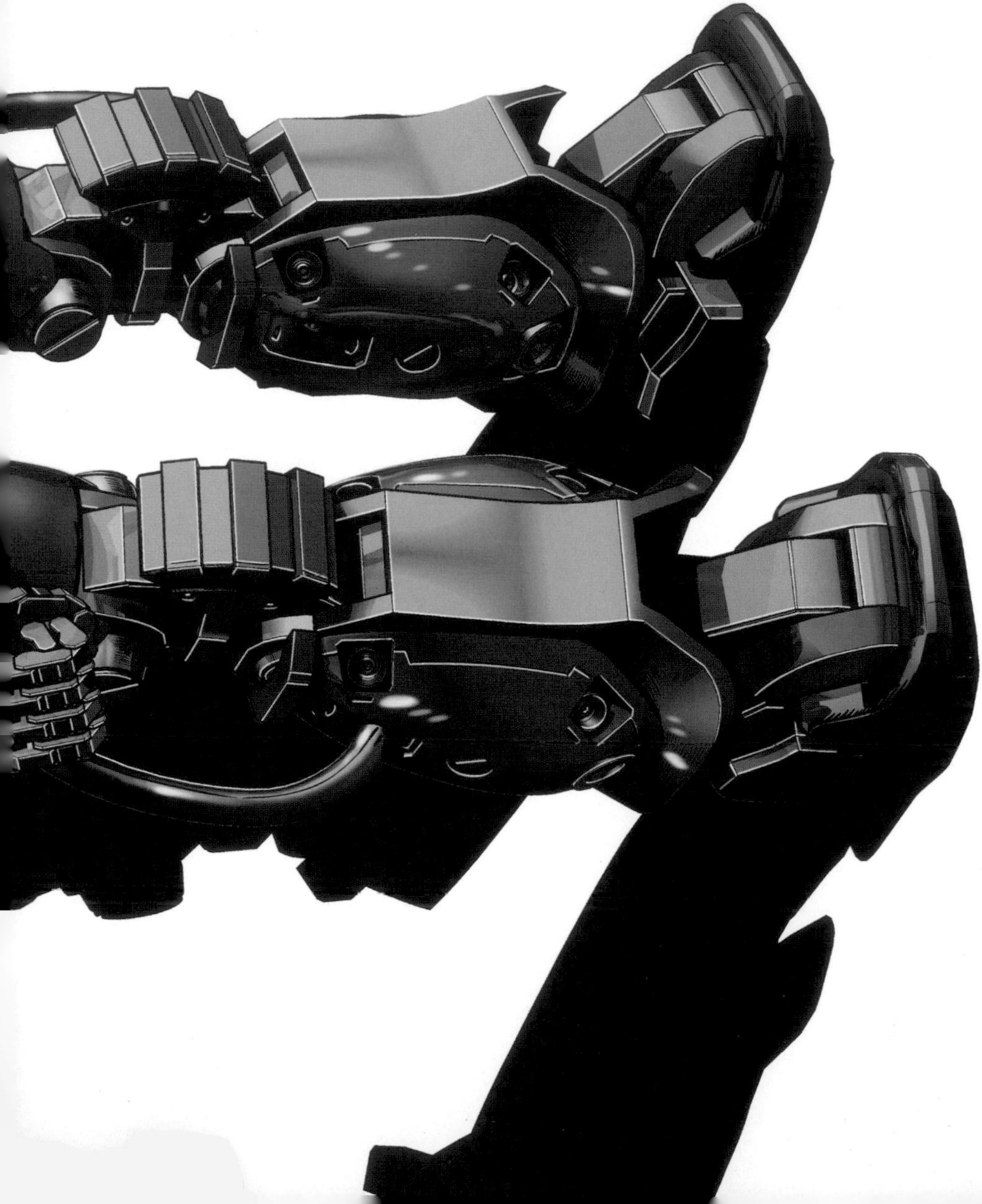

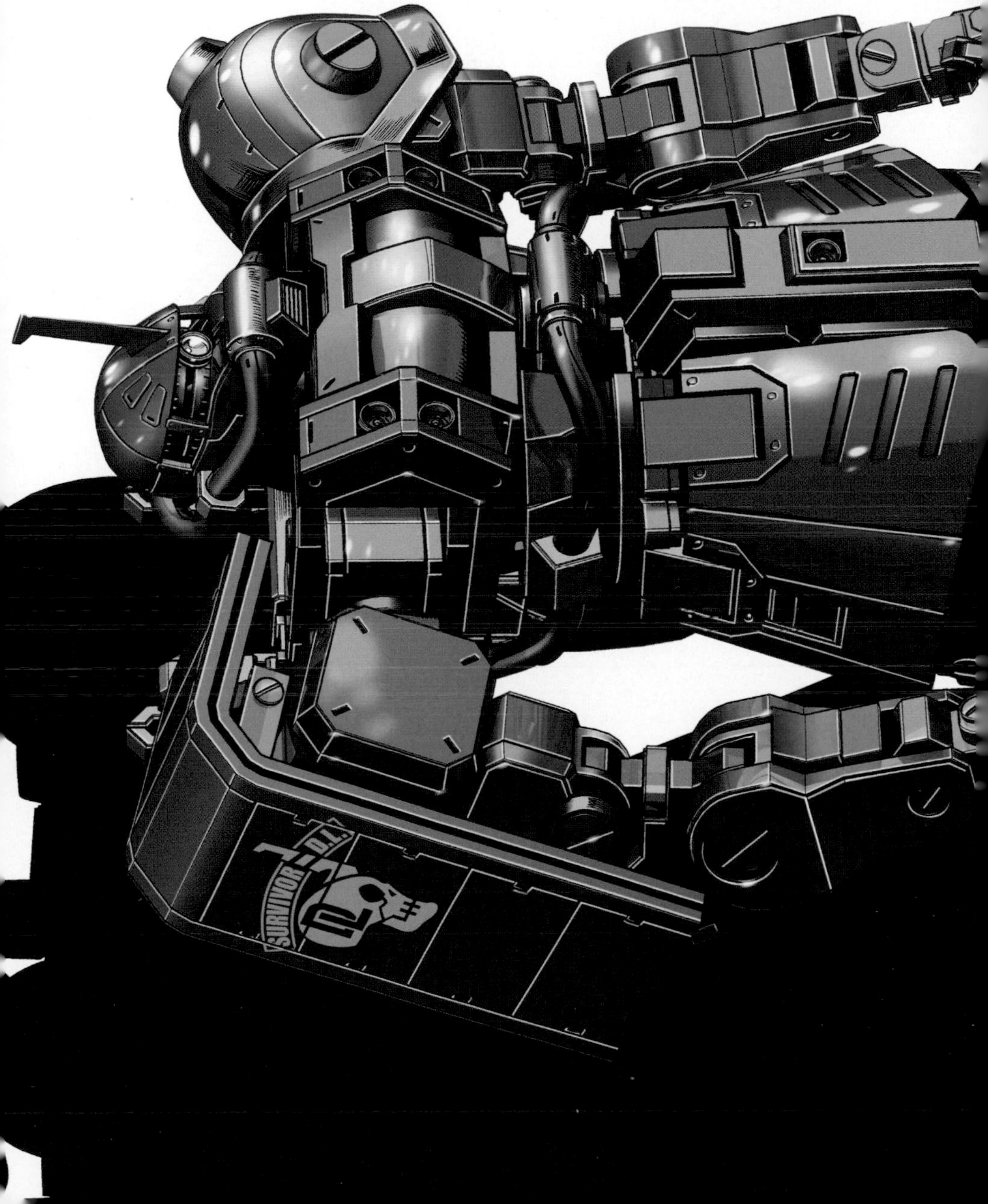
SURVIVOR
D.L.

MOBILE SUIT GUNDAM
THUNDERBOLT
11

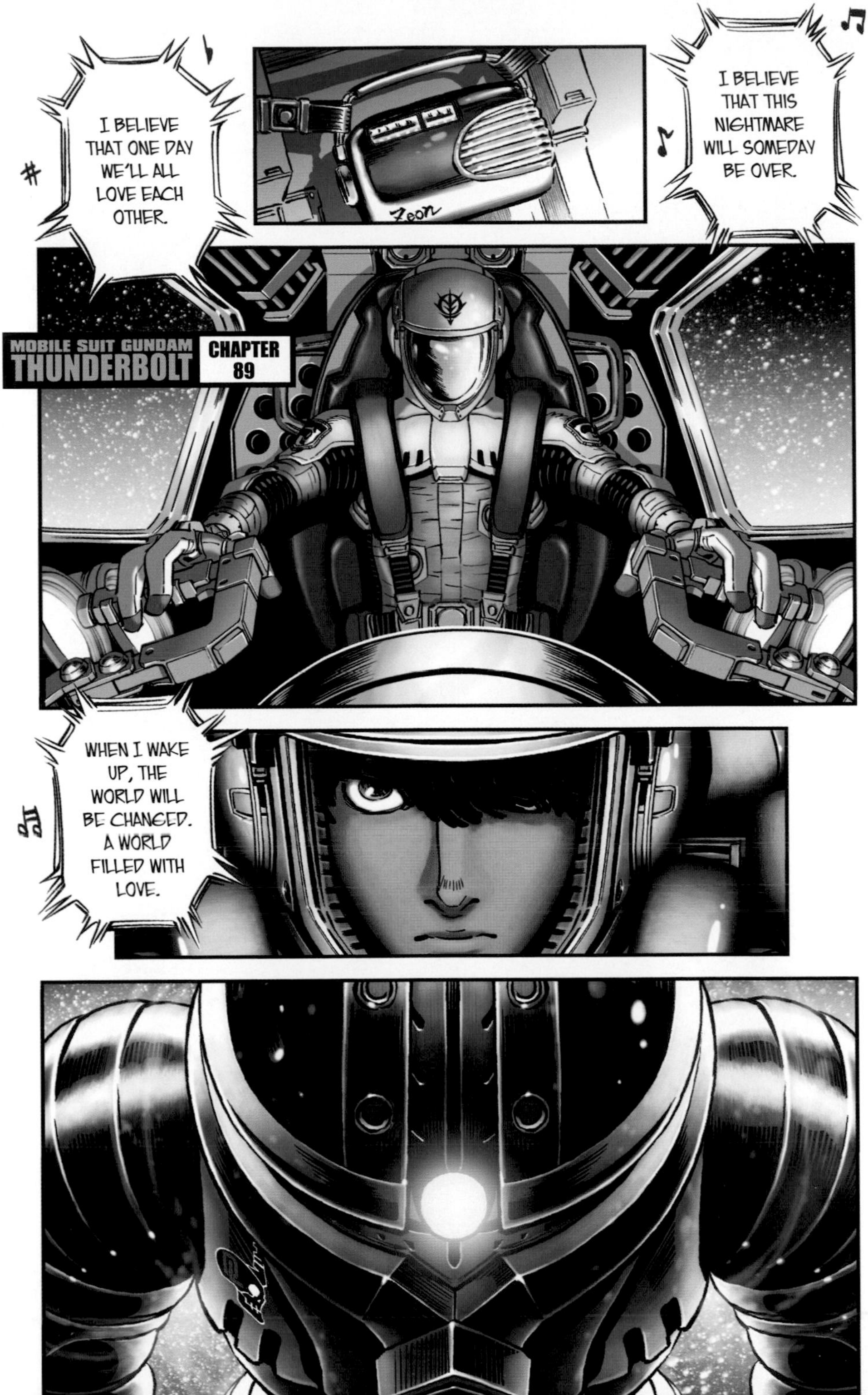
I BELIEVE THAT THIS NIGHTMARE WILL SOMEDAY BE OVER.
Zeon
I BELIEVE THAT ONE DAY WE'LL ALL LOVE EACH OTHER.
MOBILE SUIT GUNDAM THUNDERBOLT
CHAPTER 89
WHEN I WAKE UP, THE WORLD WILL BE CHANGED. A WORLD FILLED WITH LOVE.

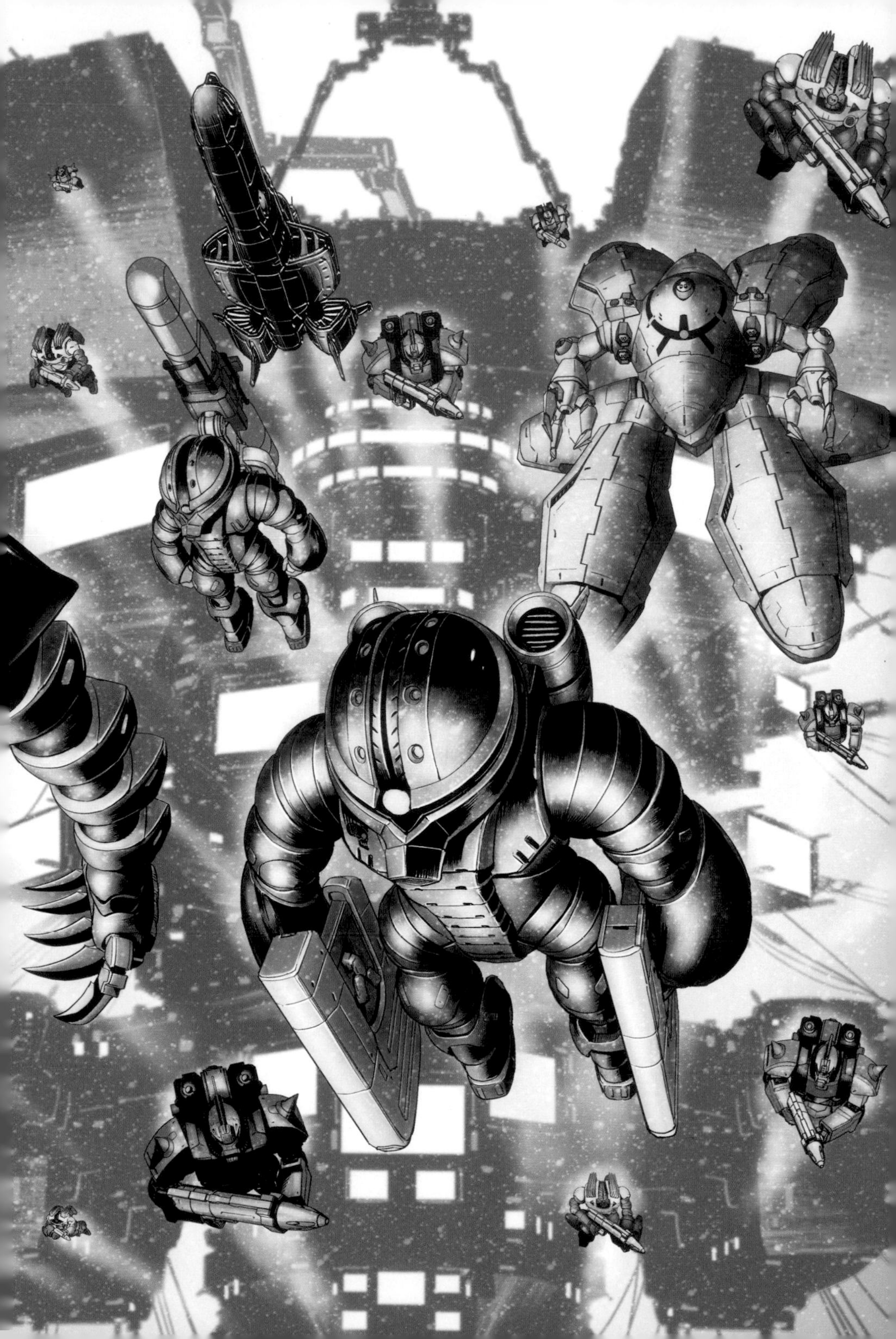

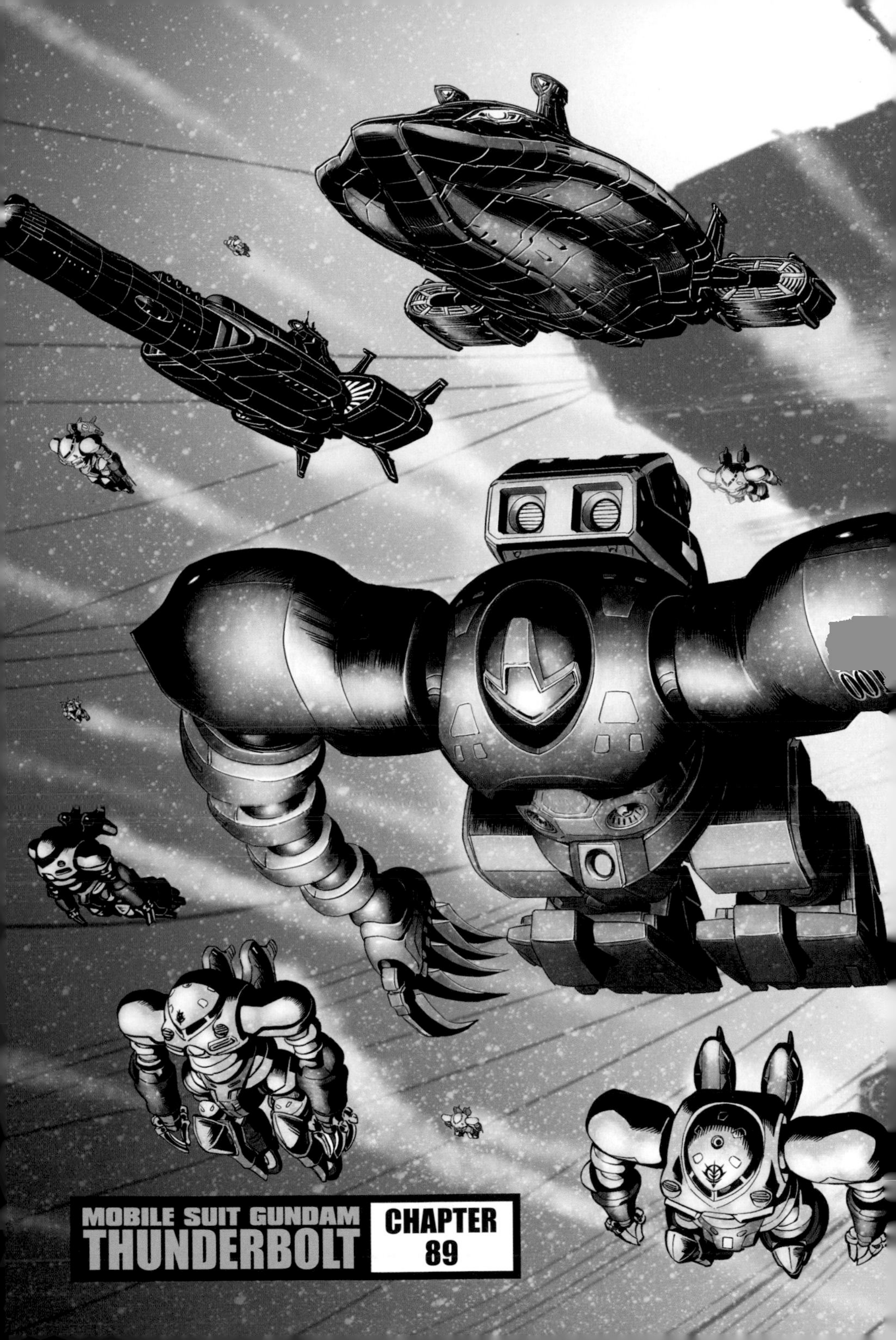
MOBILE SUIT GUNDAM
THUNDERBOLT
CHAPTER
89

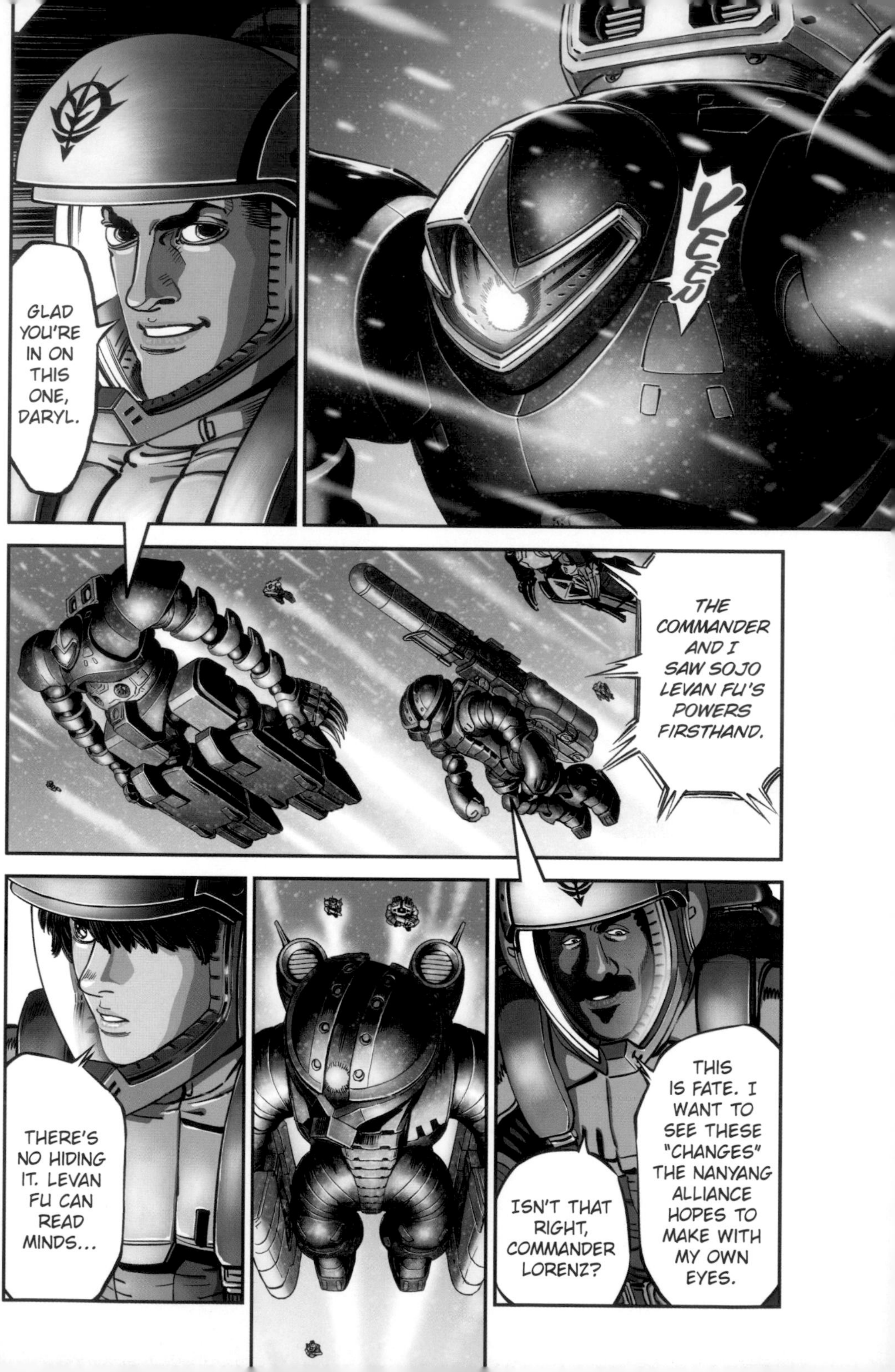
VEEN
GLAD YOU'RE IN ON THIS ONE, DARYL.
THE COMMANDER AND I SAW SOJO LEVAN FU'S POWERS FIRSTHAND.
THIS IS FATE. I WANT TO SEE THESE "CHANGES" THE NANYANG ALLIANCE HOPES TO MAKE WITH MY OWN EYES.
ISN'T THAT RIGHT, COMMANDER LORENZ?
THERE'S NO HIDING IT. LEVAN FU CAN READ MINDS...

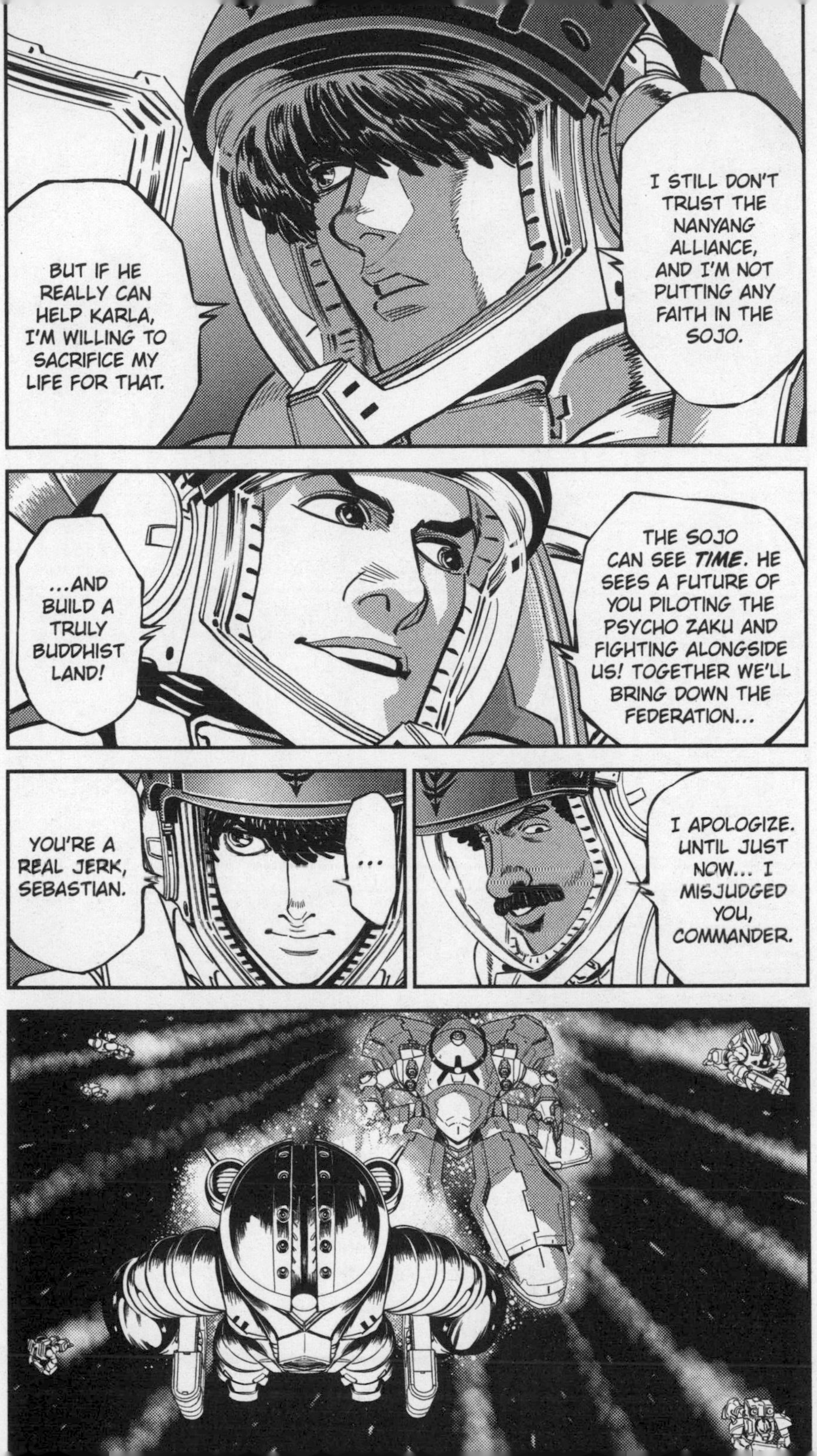
I STILL DON'T TRUST THE NANYANG ALLIANCE, AND I'M NOT PUTTING ANY FAITH IN THE SOJO.
BUT IF HE REALLY CAN HELP KARLA, I'M WILLING TO SACRIFICE MY LIFE FOR THAT.
THE SOJO CAN SEE TIME. HE SEES A FUTURE OF YOU PILOTING THE PSYCHO ZAKU AND FIGHTING ALONGSIDE US! TOGETHER WE'LL BRING DOWN THE FEDERATION...
...AND BUILD A TRULY BUDDHIST LAND!
I APOLOGIZE. UNTIL JUST NOW... I MISJUDGED YOU, COMMANDER.
...
YOU'RE A REAL JERK, SEBASTIAN.

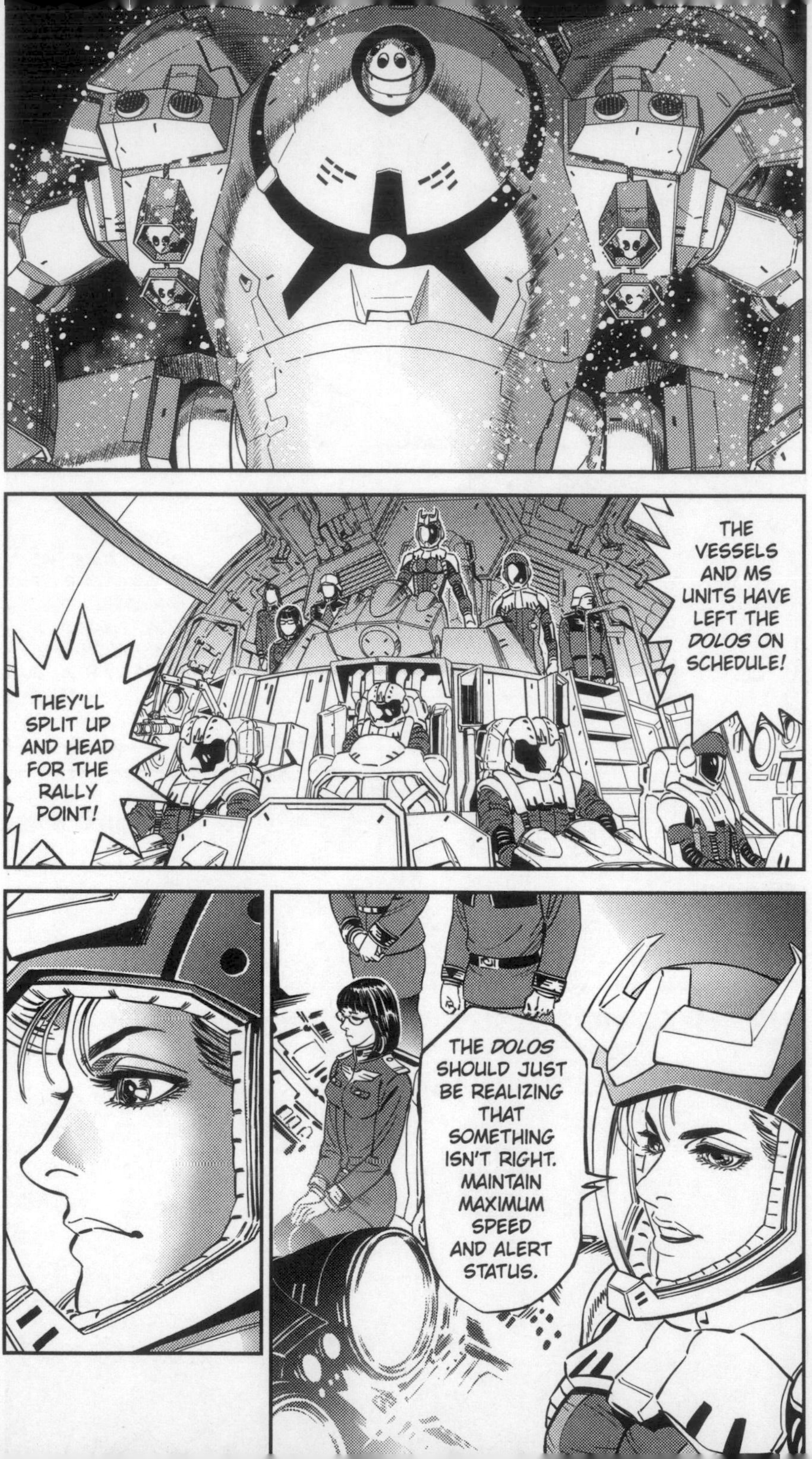
THE VESSELS AND MS UNITS HAVE LEFT THE *DOLOS* ON SCHEDULE!
THEY'LL SPLIT UP AND HEAD FOR THE RALLY POINT!
THE *DOLOS* SHOULD JUST BE REALIZING THAT SOMETHING ISN'T RIGHT. MAINTAIN MAXIMUM SPEED AND ALERT STATUS.

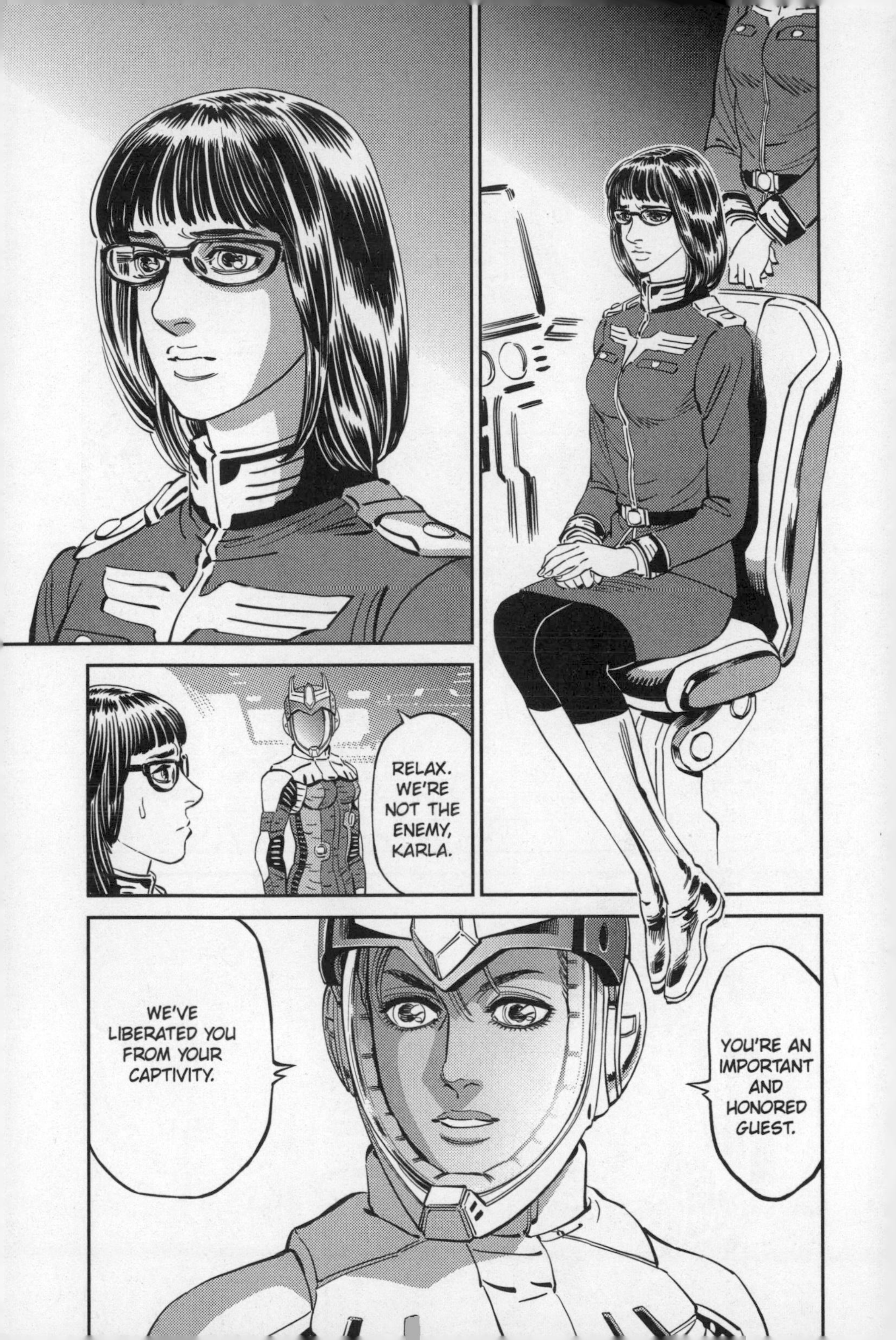
RELAX. WE'RE NOT THE ENEMY, KARLA.
YOU'RE AN IMPORTANT AND HONORED GUEST.
WE'VE LIBERATED YOU FROM YOUR CAPTIVITY.

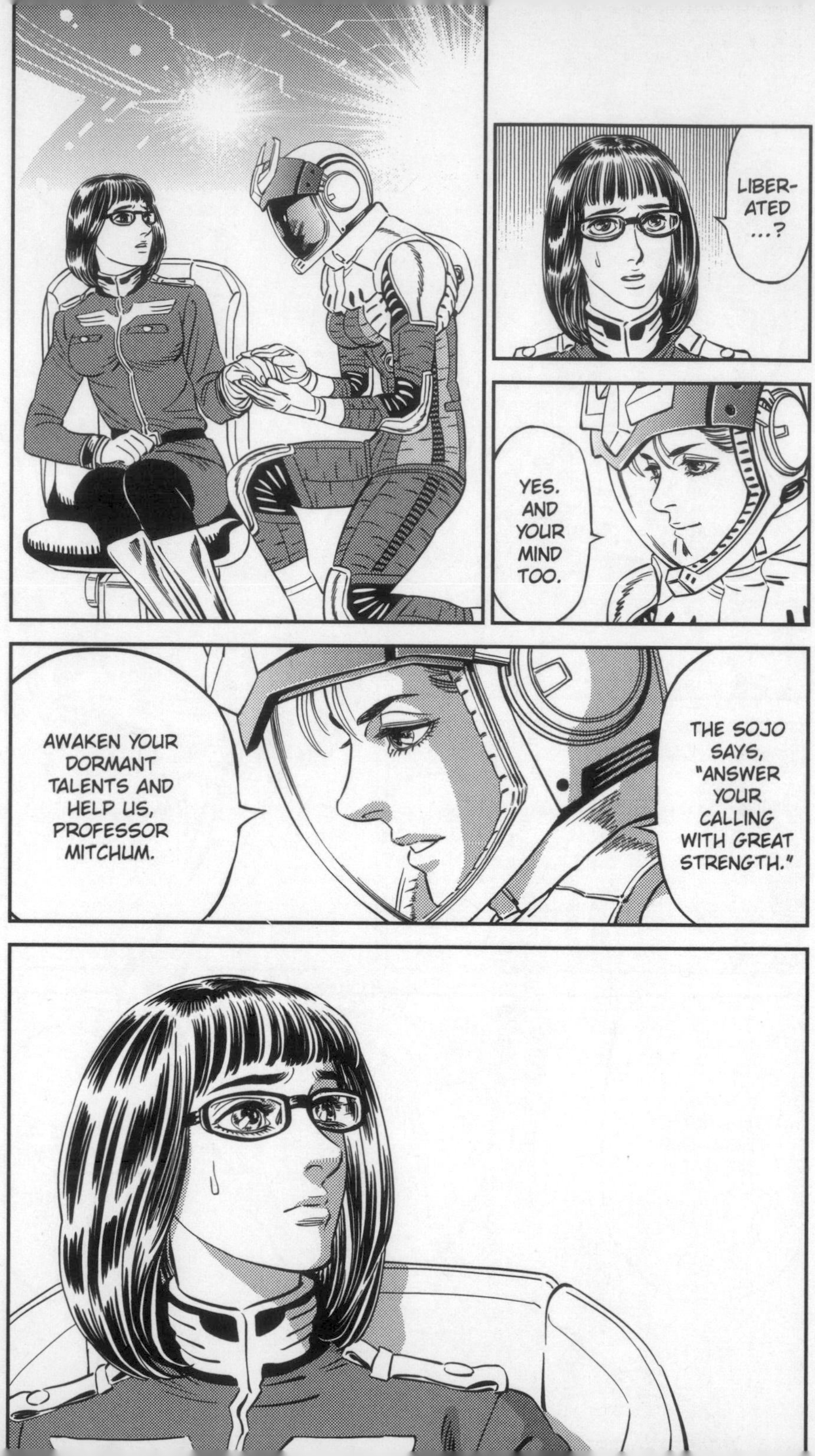
LIBER-ATED ...?
YES. AND YOUR MIND TOO.
THE SOJO SAYS, "ANSWER YOUR CALLING WITH GREAT STRENGTH."
AWAKEN YOUR DORMANT TALENTS AND HELP US, PROFESSOR MITCHUM.

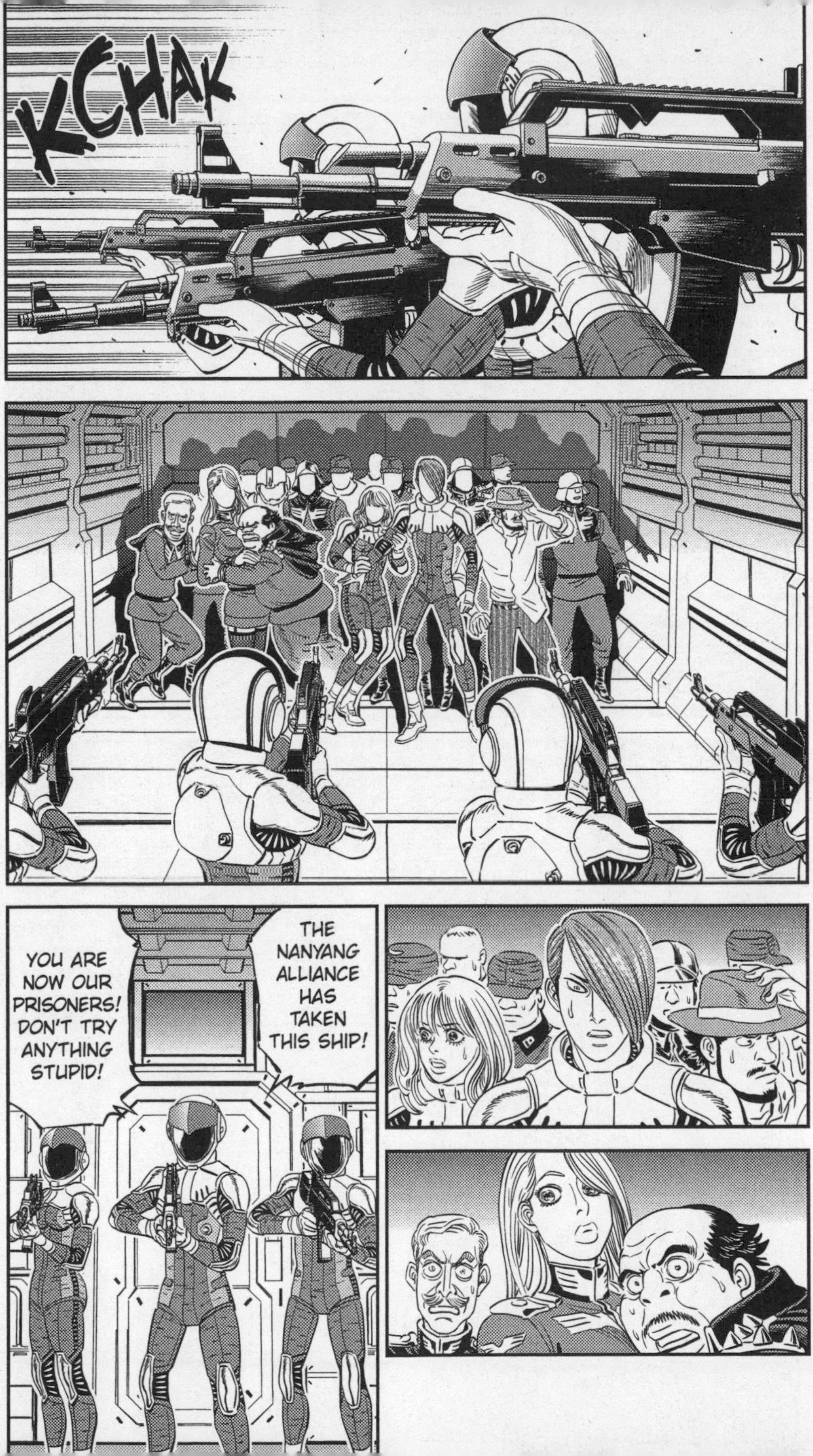
KCHAK
THE NANYANG ALLIANCE HAS TAKEN THIS SHIP!
YOU ARE NOW OUR PRISONERS! DON'T TRY ANYTHING STUPID!

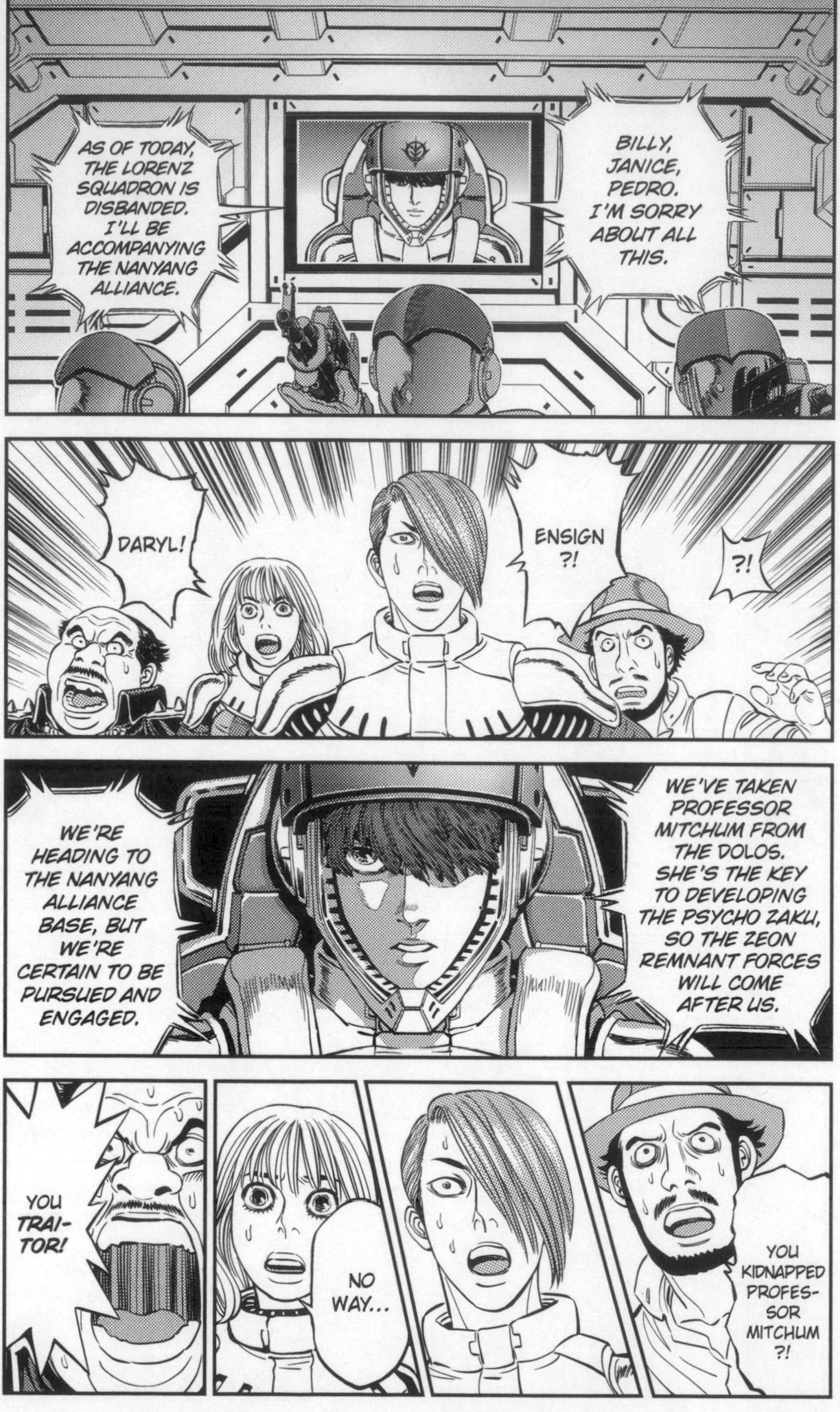
BILLY, JANICE, PEDRO. I'M SORRY ABOUT ALL THIS.
AS OF TODAY, THE LORENZ SQUADRON IS DISBANDED. I'LL BE ACCOMPANYING THE NANYANG ALLIANCE.
?!
ENSIGN ?!
DARYL!
WE'VE TAKEN PROFESSOR MITCHUM FROM THE DOLOS. SHE'S THE KEY TO DEVELOPING THE PSYCHO ZAKU, SO THE ZEON REMNANT FORCES WILL COME AFTER US.
WE'RE HEADING TO THE NANYANG ALLIANCE BASE, BUT WE'RE CERTAIN TO BE PURSUED AND ENGAGED.
YOU KIDNAPPED PROFES-SOR MITCHUM ?!
NO WAY...
YOU TRAI-TOR!

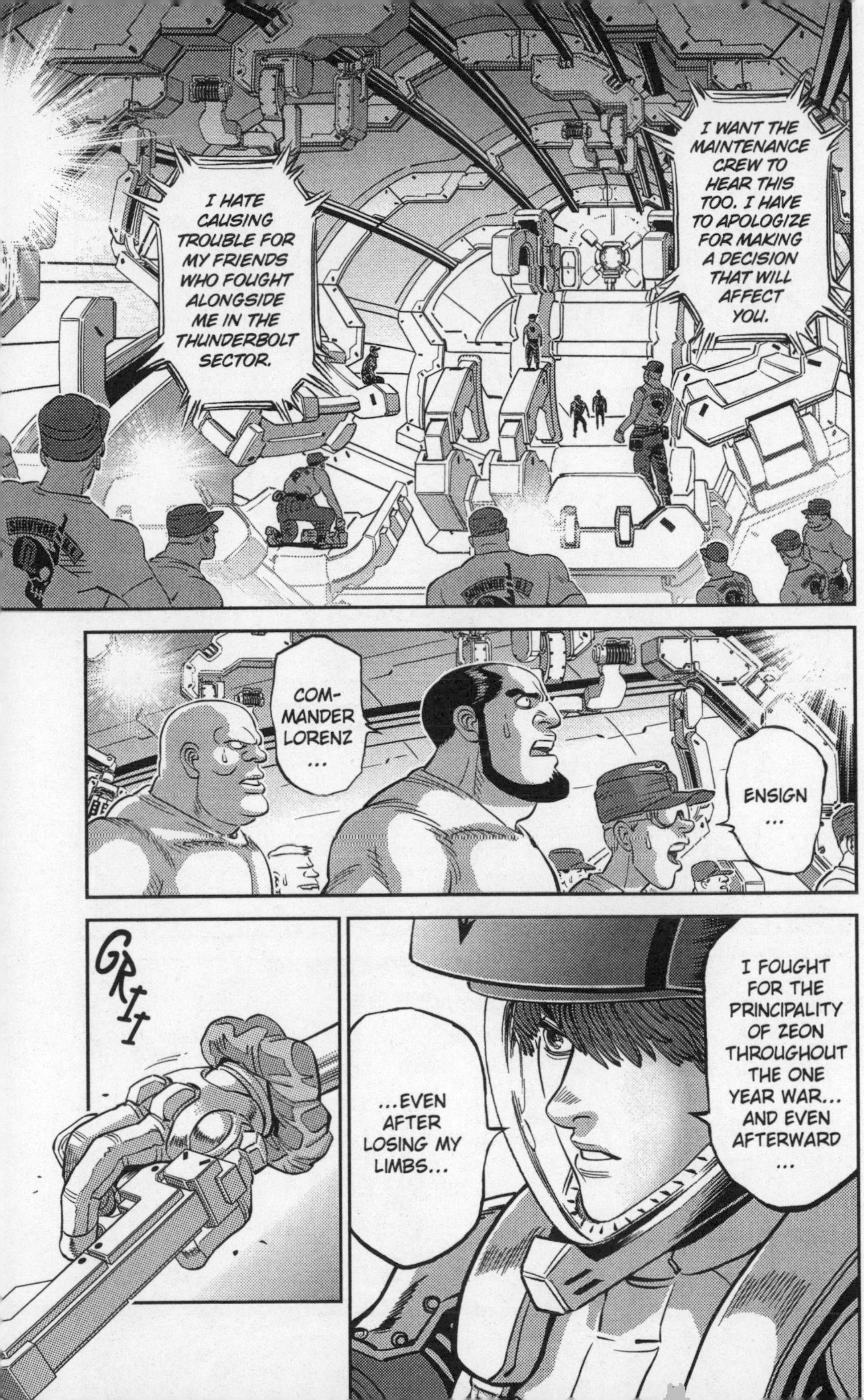
I WANT THE MAINTENANCE CREW TO HEAR THIS TOO. I HAVE TO APOLOGIZE FOR MAKING A DECISION THAT WILL AFFECT YOU.
I HATE CAUSING TROUBLE FOR MY FRIENDS WHO FOUGHT ALONGSIDE ME IN THE THUNDERBOLT SECTOR.
ENSIGN ...
COM-MANDER LORENZ ...
I FOUGHT FOR THE PRINCIPALITY OF ZEON THROUGHOUT THE ONE YEAR WAR... AND EVEN AFTERWARD ...
...EVEN AFTER LOSING MY LIMBS...
GRII

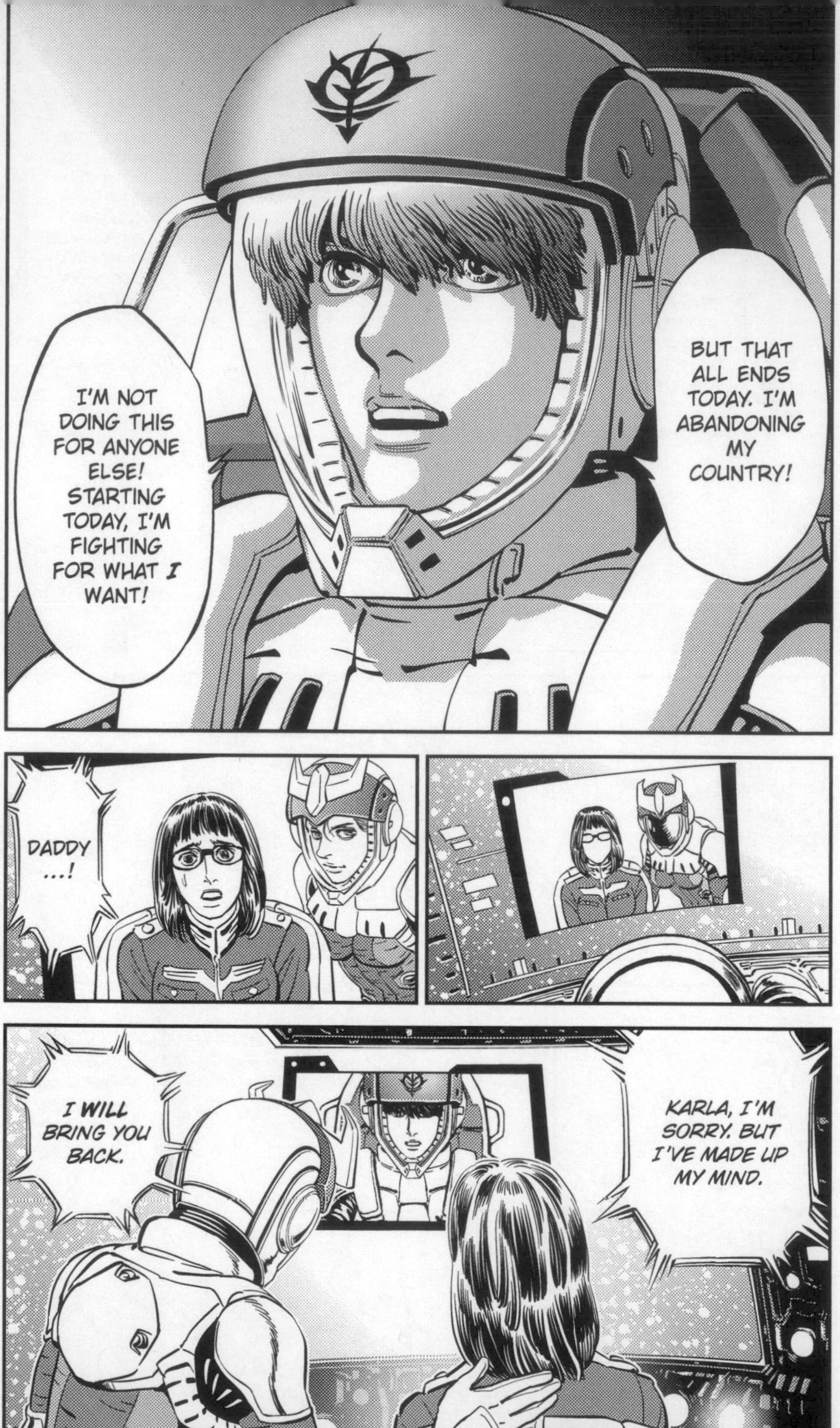
BUT THAT ALL ENDS TODAY. I'M ABANDONING MY COUNTRY!
I'M NOT DOING THIS FOR ANYONE ELSE! STARTING TODAY, I'M FIGHTING FOR WHAT *I* WANT!
DADDY ...!
KARLA, I'M SORRY. BUT I'VE MADE UP MY MIND.
I **WILL** BRING YOU BACK.

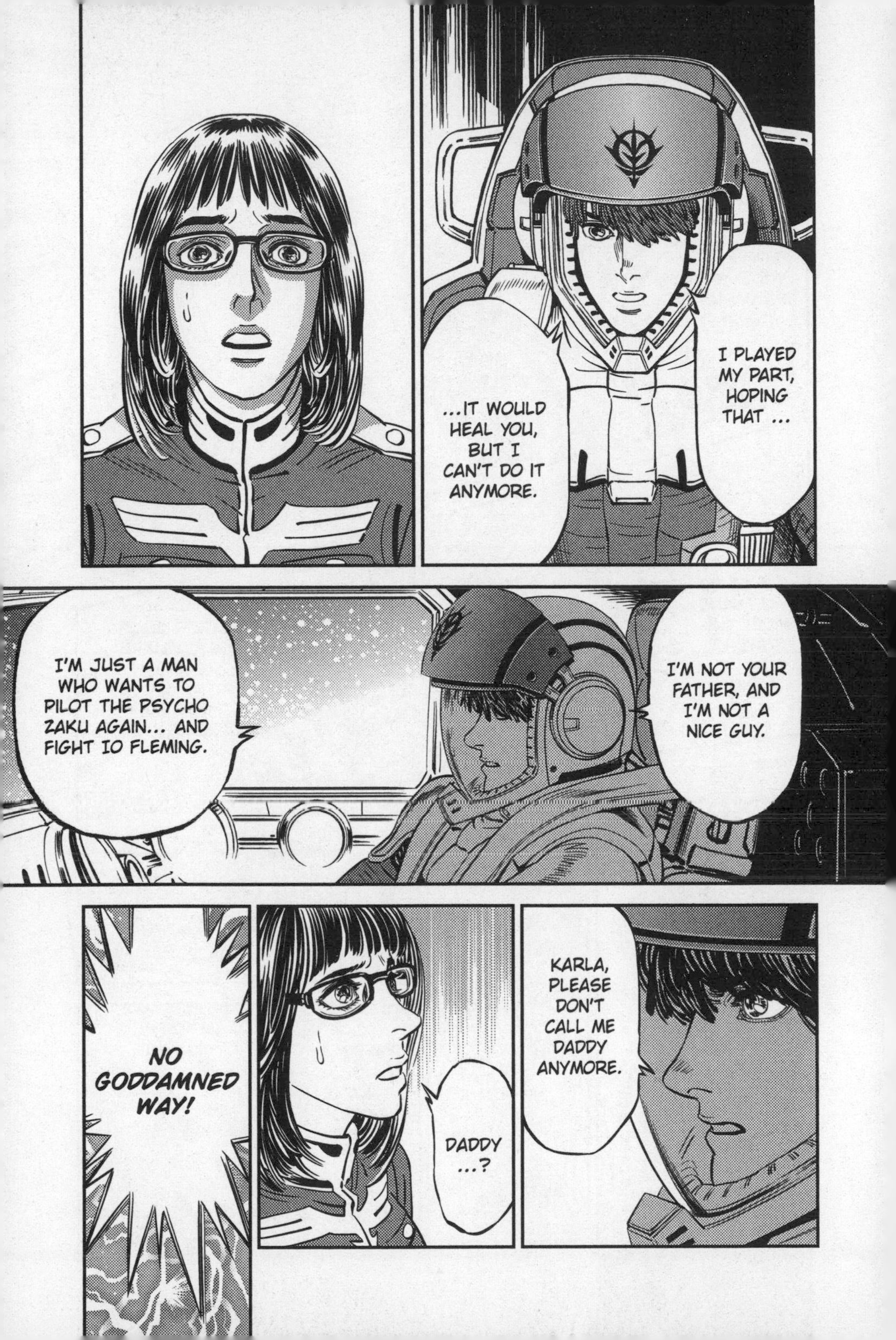
I PLAYED MY PART, HOPING THAT ...
...IT WOULD HEAL YOU, BUT I CAN'T DO IT ANYMORE.
I'M NOT YOUR FATHER, AND I'M NOT A NICE GUY.
I'M JUST A MAN WHO WANTS TO PILOT THE PSYCHO ZAKU AGAIN... AND FIGHT IO FLEMING.
KARLA, PLEASE DON'T CALL ME DADDY ANYMORE.
DADDY ...?
NO GODDAMNED WAY!

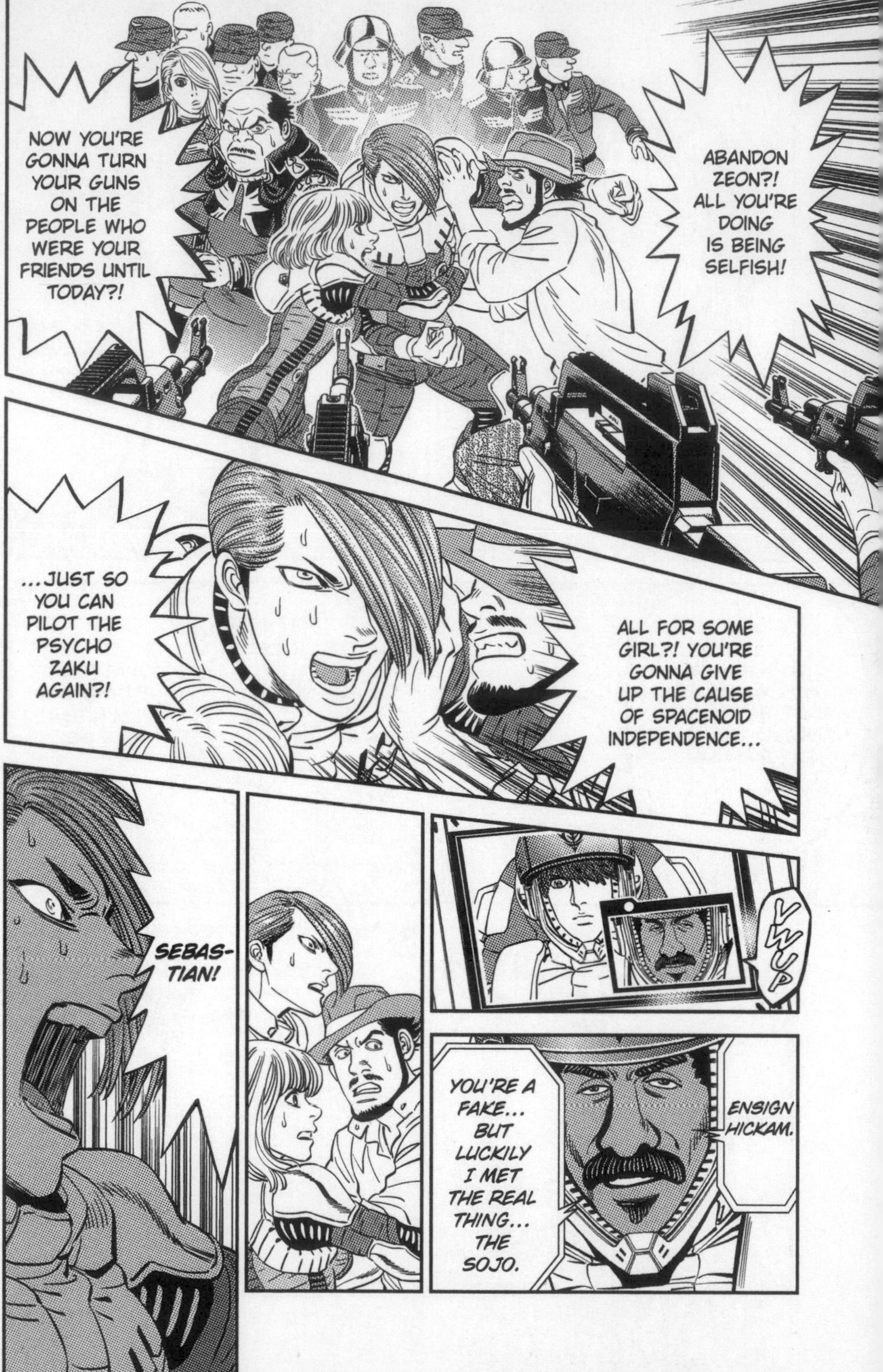
ABANDON ZEON?! ALL YOU'RE DOING IS BEING SELFISH!
NOW YOU'RE GONNA TURN YOUR GUNS ON THE PEOPLE WHO WERE YOUR FRIENDS UNTIL TODAY?!
ALL FOR SOME GIRL?! YOU'RE GONNA GIVE UP THE CAUSE OF SPACENOID INDEPENDENCE...
...JUST SO YOU CAN PILOT THE PSYCHO ZAKU AGAIN?!
VWUP
ENSIGN HICKAM.
YOU'RE A FAKE... BUT LUCKILY I MET THE REAL THING... THE SOJO.
SEBAS-TIAN!

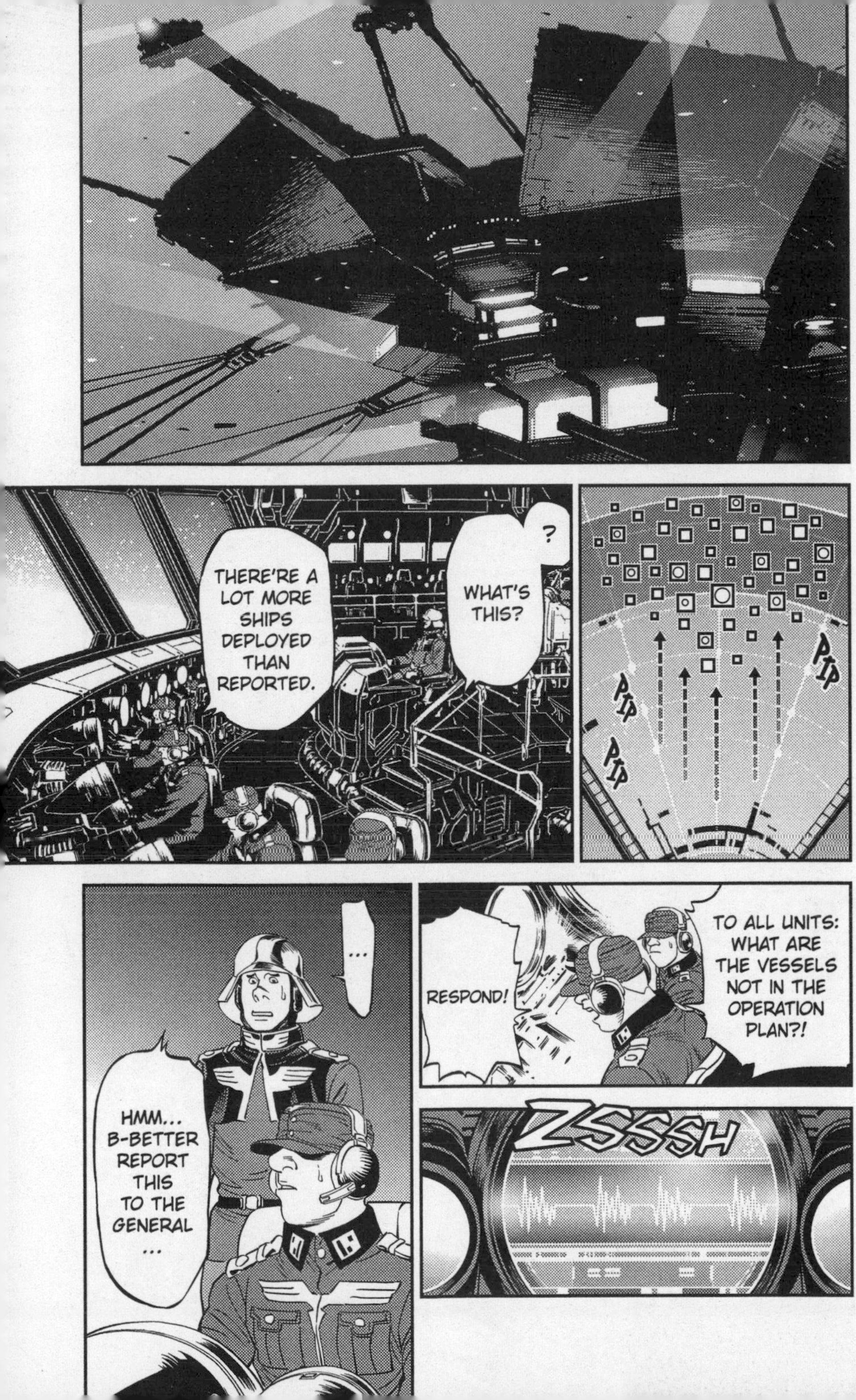
PIP
PIP
PIP
?
WHAT'S THIS?
THERE'RE A LOT MORE SHIPS DEPLOYED THAN REPORTED.
TO ALL UNITS: WHAT ARE THE VESSELS NOT IN THE OPERATION PLAN?!
RESPOND!
ZSSSH
...
HMM... B-BETTER REPORT THIS TO THE GENERAL ...

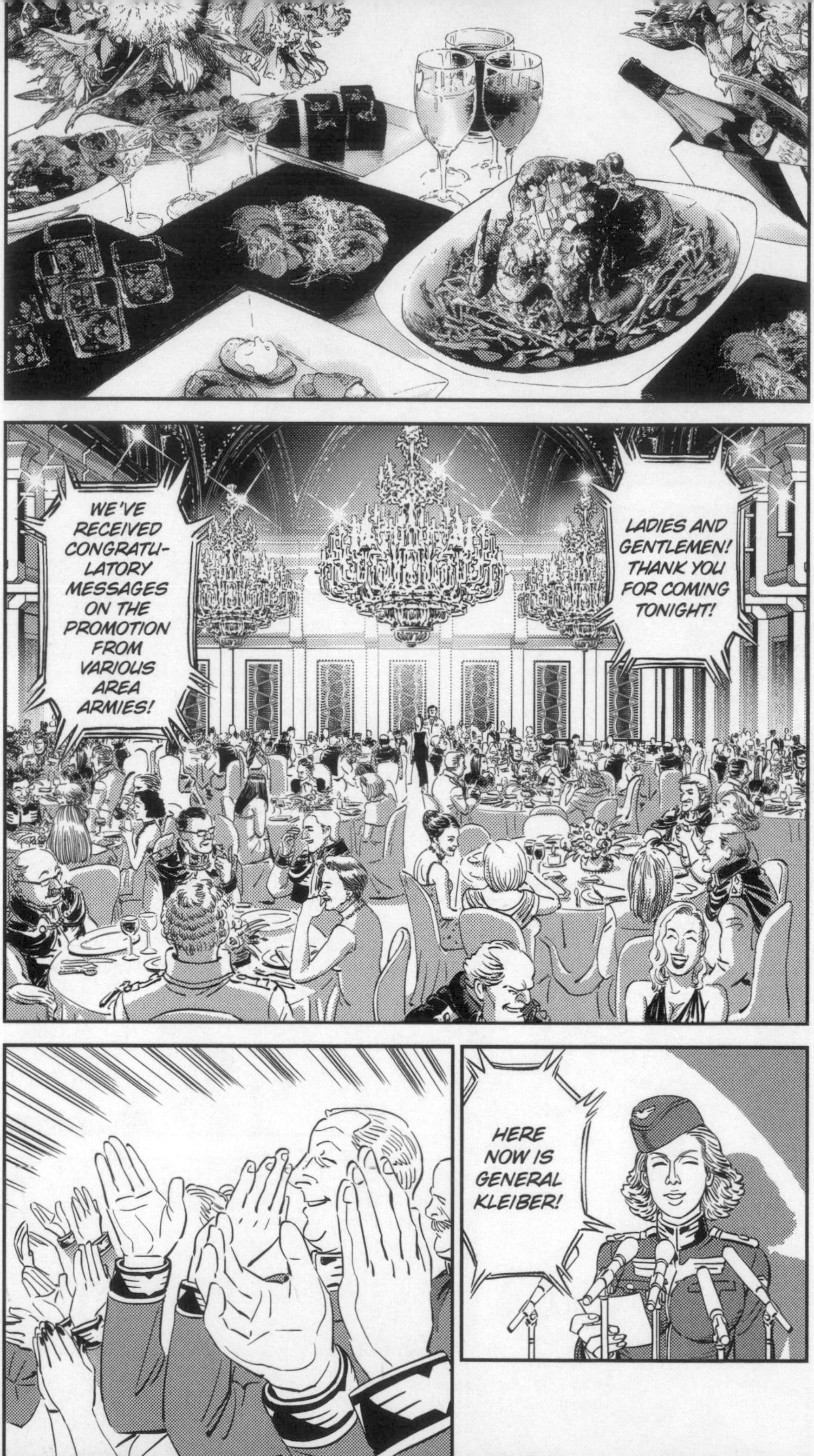
LADIES AND GENTLEMEN! THANK YOU FOR COMING TONIGHT!
WE'VE RECEIVED CONGRATU-LATORY MESSAGES ON THE PROMOTION FROM VARIOUS AREA ARMIES!
HERE NOW IS GENERAL KLEIBER!

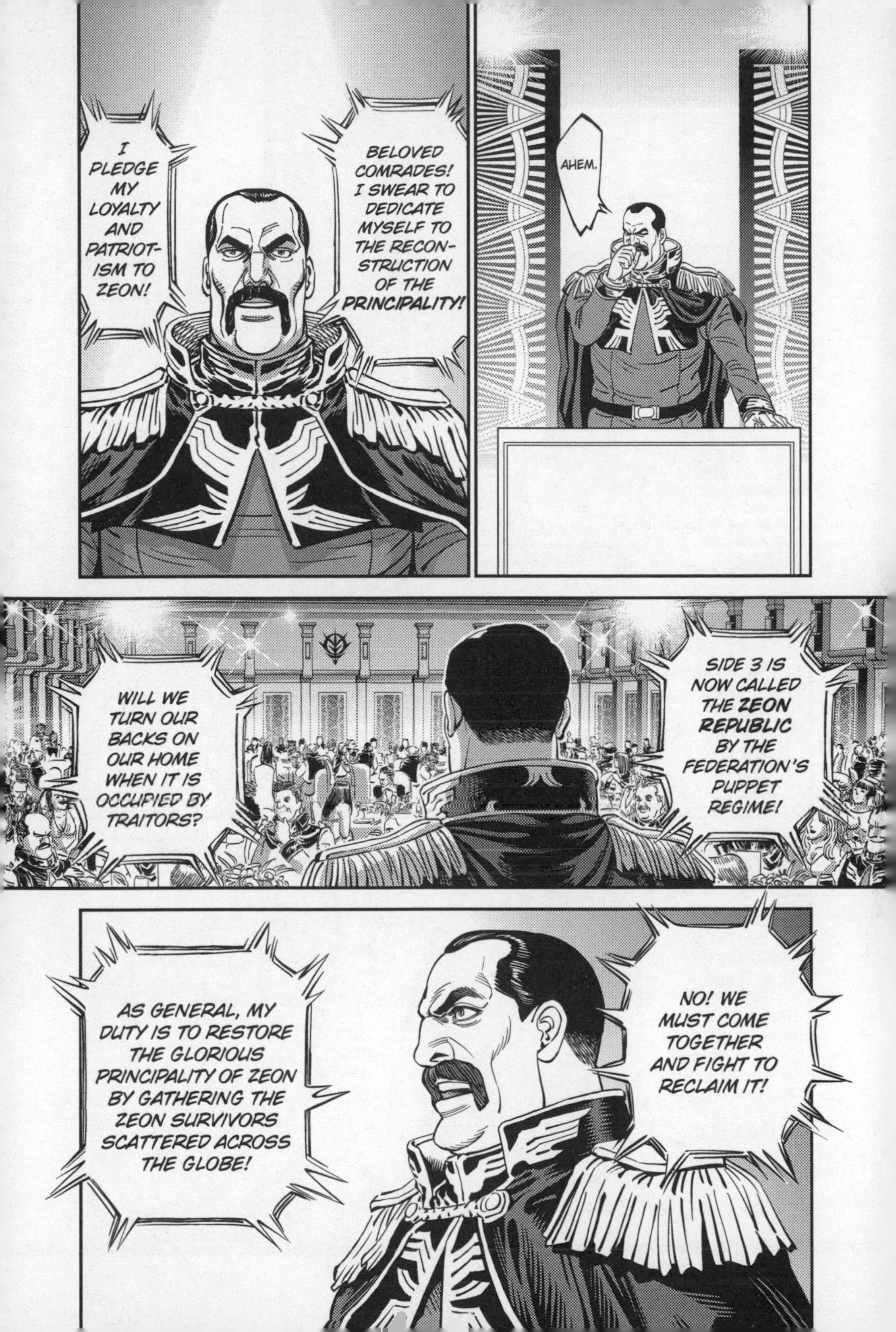
AHEM.
BELOVED COMRADES! I SWEAR TO DEDICATE MYSELF TO THE RECONSTRUCTION OF THE PRINCIPALITY!
I PLEDGE MY LOYALTY AND PATRIOTISM TO ZEON!
SIDE 3 IS NOW CALLED THE ZEON REPUBLIC BY THE FEDERATION'S PUPPET REGIME!
WILL WE TURN OUR BACKS ON OUR HOME WHEN IT IS OCCUPIED BY TRAITORS?
NO! WE MUST COME TOGETHER AND FIGHT TO RECLAIM IT!
AS GENERAL, MY DUTY IS TO RESTORE THE GLORIOUS PRINCIPALITY OF ZEON BY GATHERING THE ZEON SURVIVORS SCATTERED ACROSS THE GLOBE!

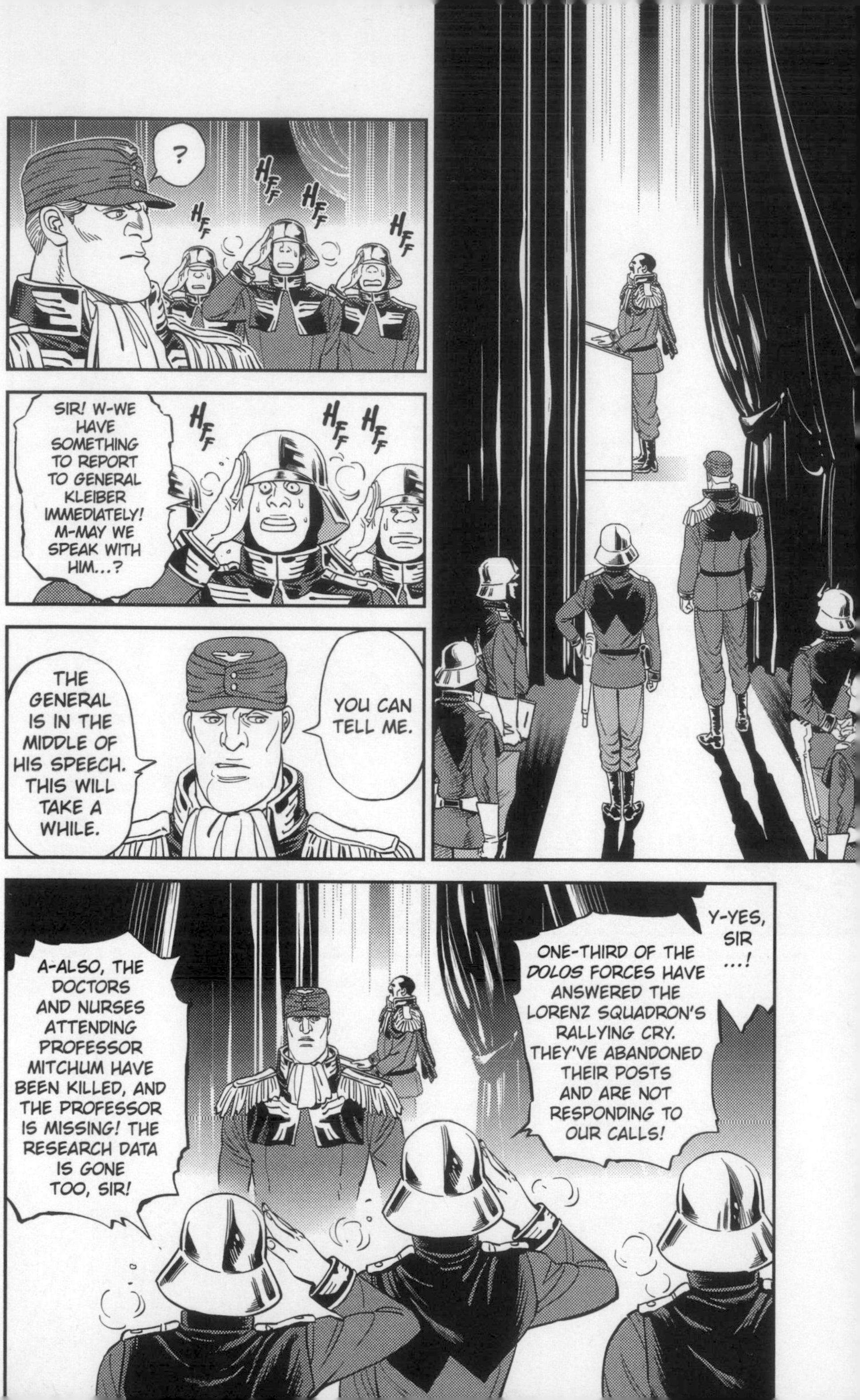
?
HFF HFF HFF HFF
SIR! W-WE HAVE SOMETHING TO REPORT TO GENERAL KLEIBER IMMEDIATELY! M-MAY WE SPEAK WITH HIM...?
HFF HFF HFF
YOU CAN TELL ME.
THE GENERAL IS IN THE MIDDLE OF HIS SPEECH. THIS WILL TAKE A WHILE.
Y-YES, SIR ...!
ONE-THIRD OF THE *DOLOS* FORCES HAVE ANSWERED THE LORENZ SQUADRON'S RALLYING CRY. THEY'VE ABANDONED THEIR POSTS AND ARE NOT RESPONDING TO OUR CALLS!
A-ALSO, THE DOCTORS AND NURSES ATTENDING PROFESSOR MITCHUM HAVE BEEN KILLED, AND THE PROFESSOR IS MISSING! THE RESEARCH DATA IS GONE TOO, SIR!

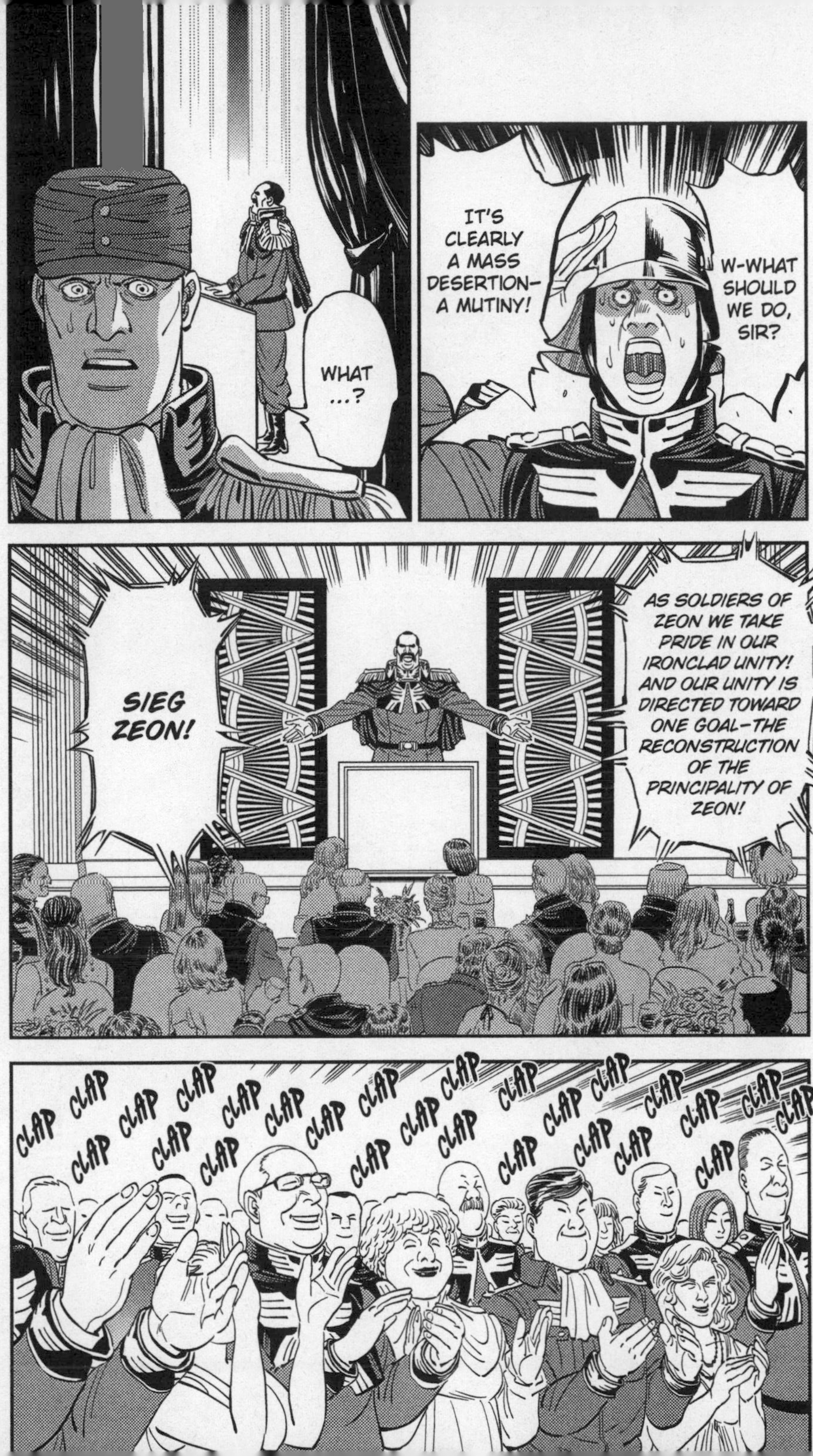
IT'S CLEARLY A MASS DESERTION— A MUTINY!
W-WHAT SHOULD WE DO, SIR?
WHAT ...?
AS SOLDIERS OF ZEON WE TAKE PRIDE IN OUR IRONCLAD UNITY! AND OUR UNITY IS DIRECTED TOWARD ONE GOAL—THE RECONSTRUCTION OF THE PRINCIPALITY OF ZEON!
SIEG ZEON!
CLAP CLAP CLAP CLAP CLAP CLAP CLAP CLAP CLAP CLAP CLAP CLAP CLAP CLAP CLAP CLAP CLAP CLAP CLAP CLAP CLAP CLAP CLAP CLAP CLAP CLAP

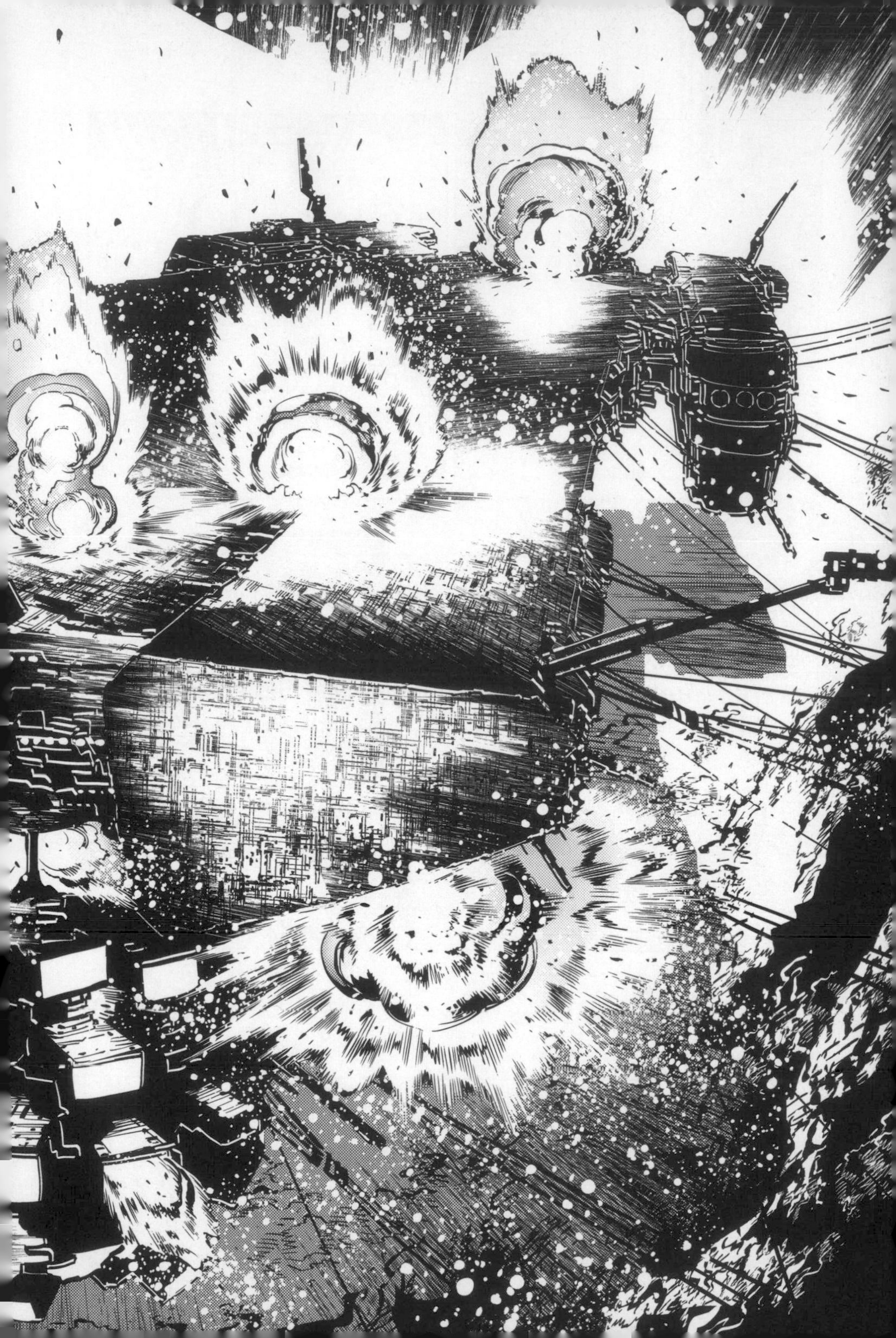

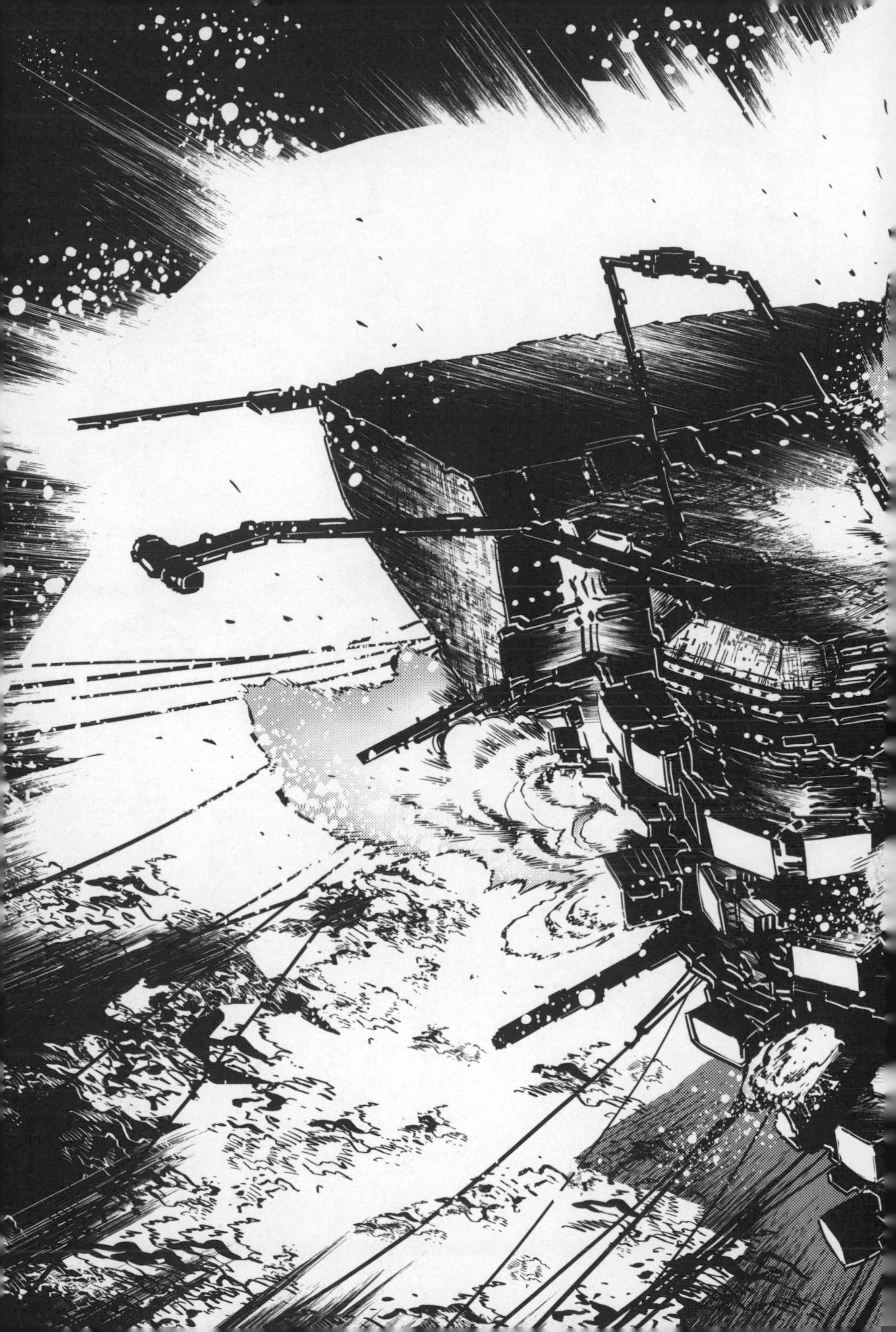

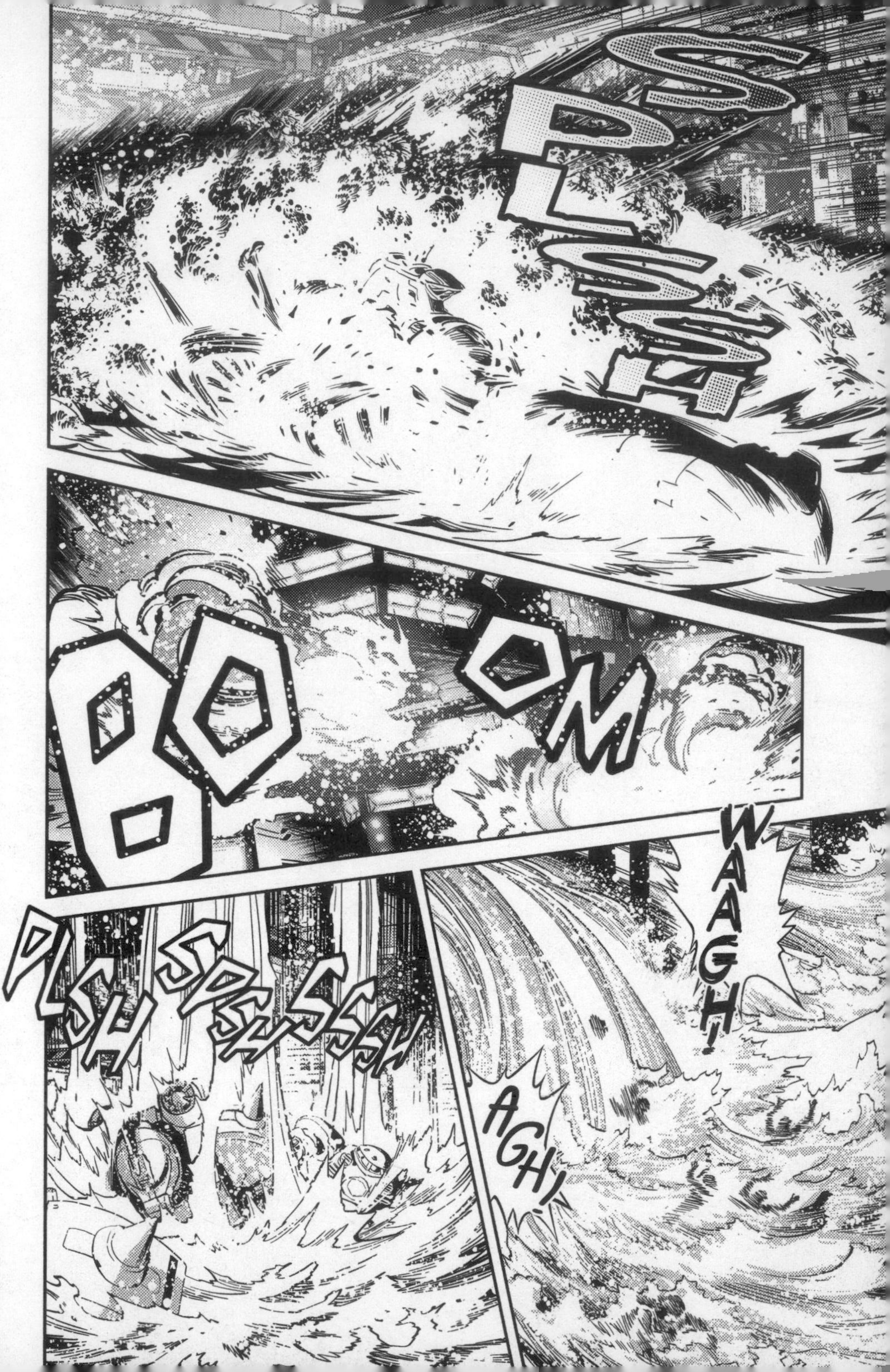
SPLASH
BOOOM
WAAGH!
AGH!
SPSHSSSH
PLSH

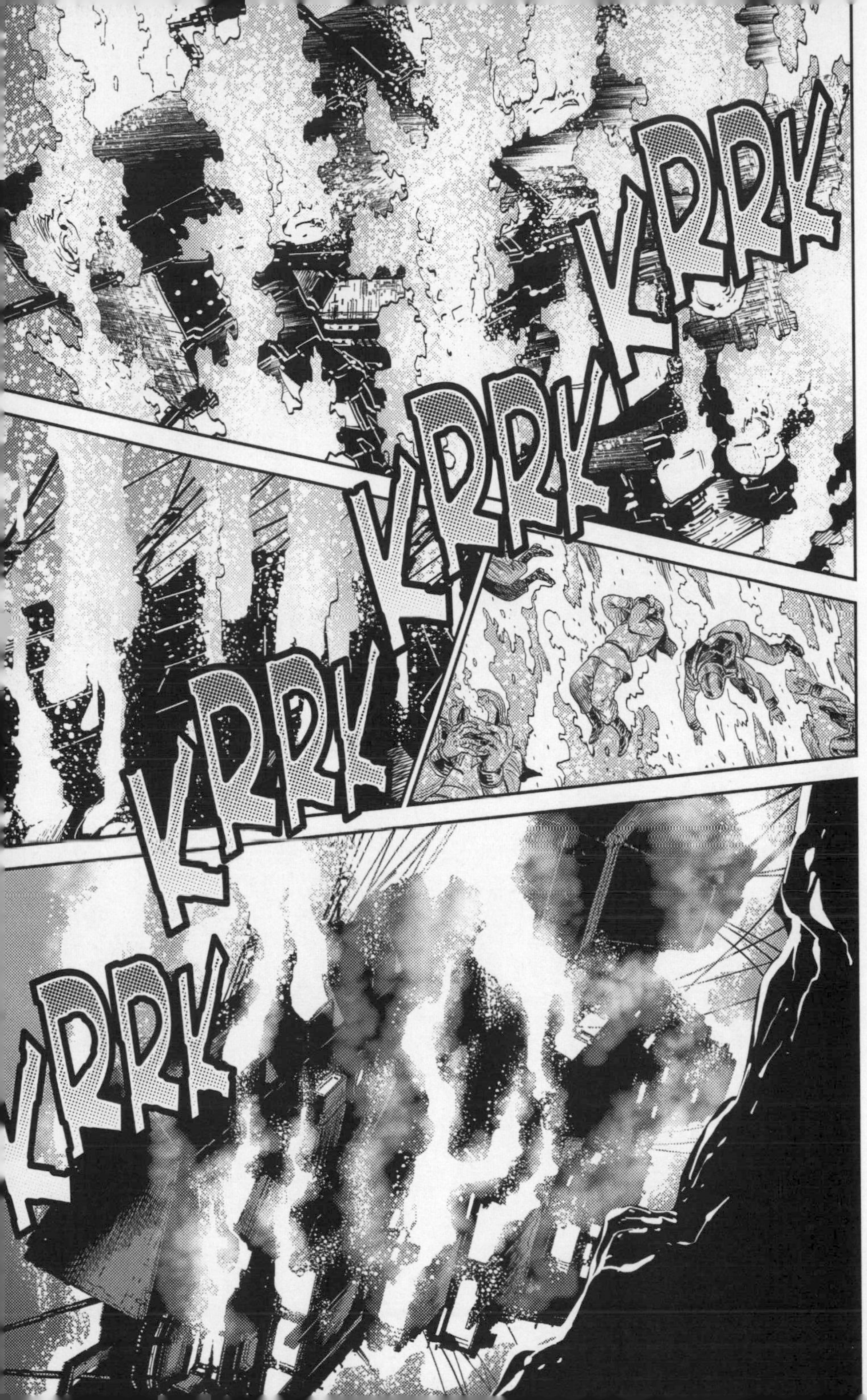
KRRK
KRRK
KRRK
KRRK

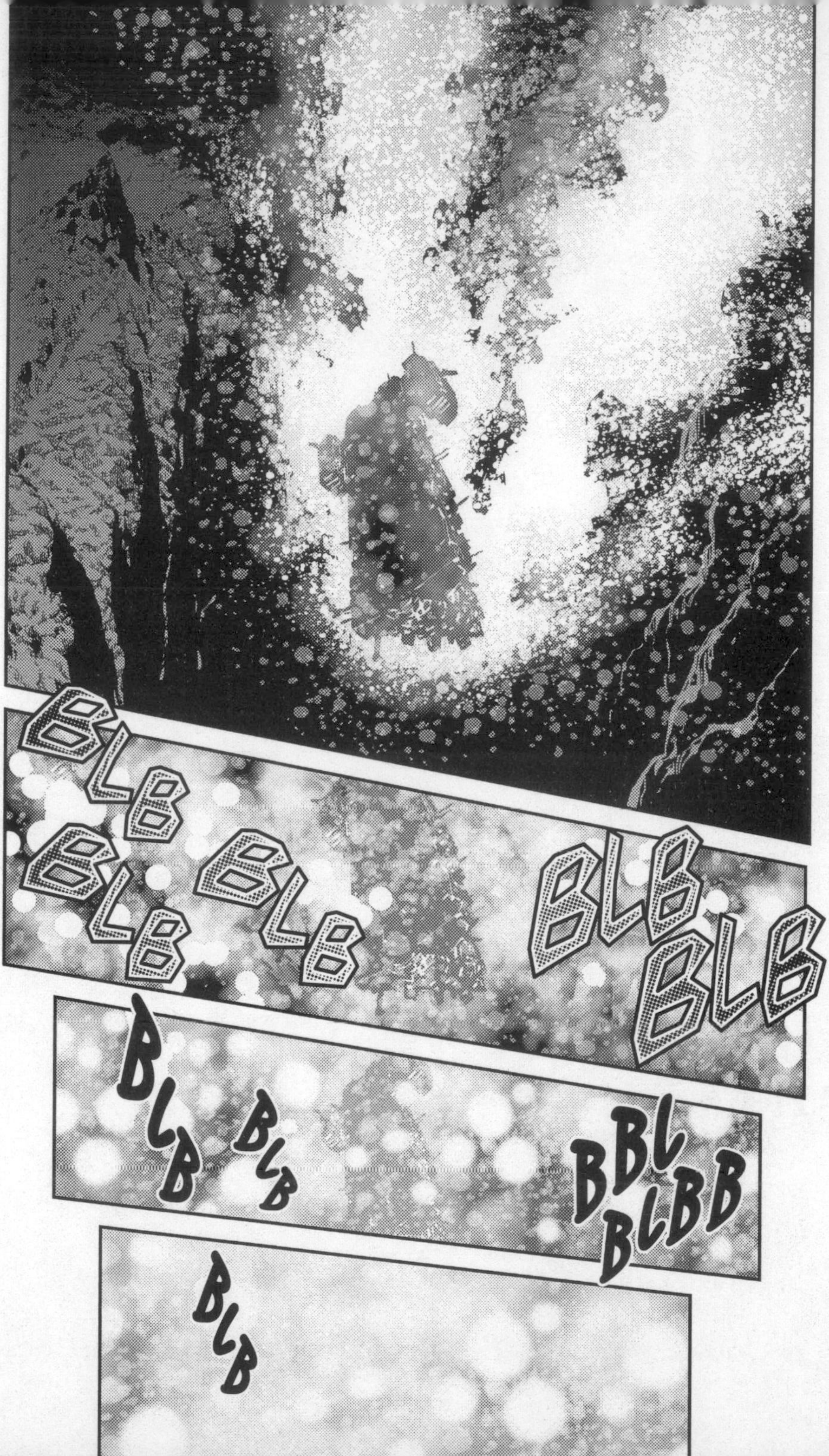
BLB
BLB
BLB
BLB
BLB
BLB
BBL
BLBB
BLB
BLB
BLB

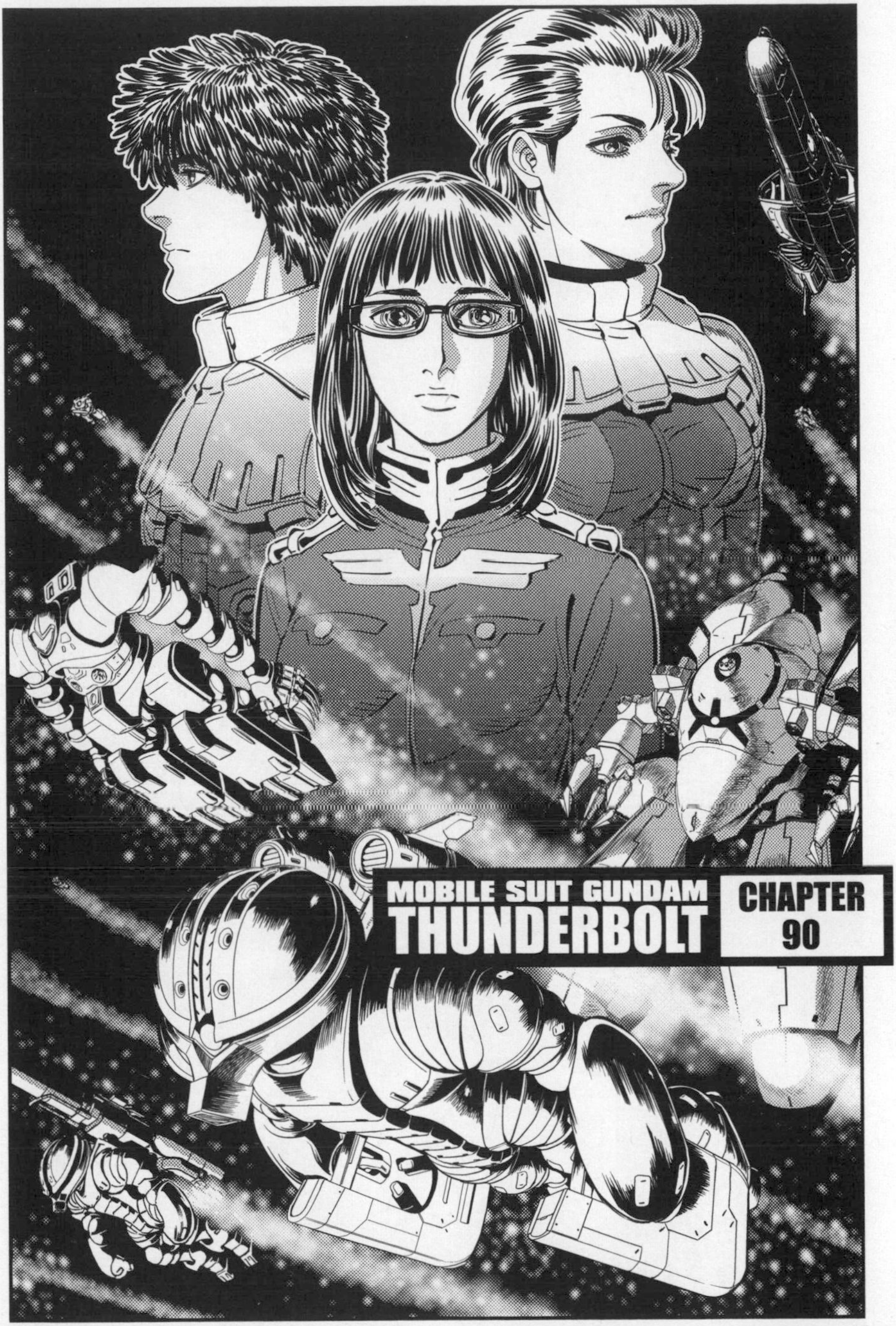
MOBILE SUIT GUNDAM
THUNDERBOLT
CHAPTER
90

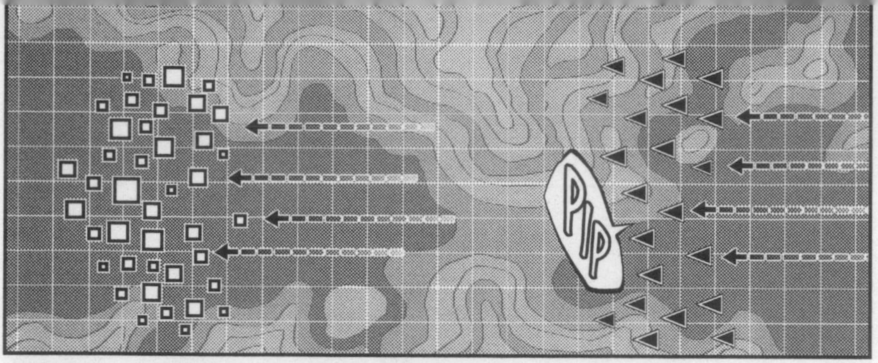
PIP

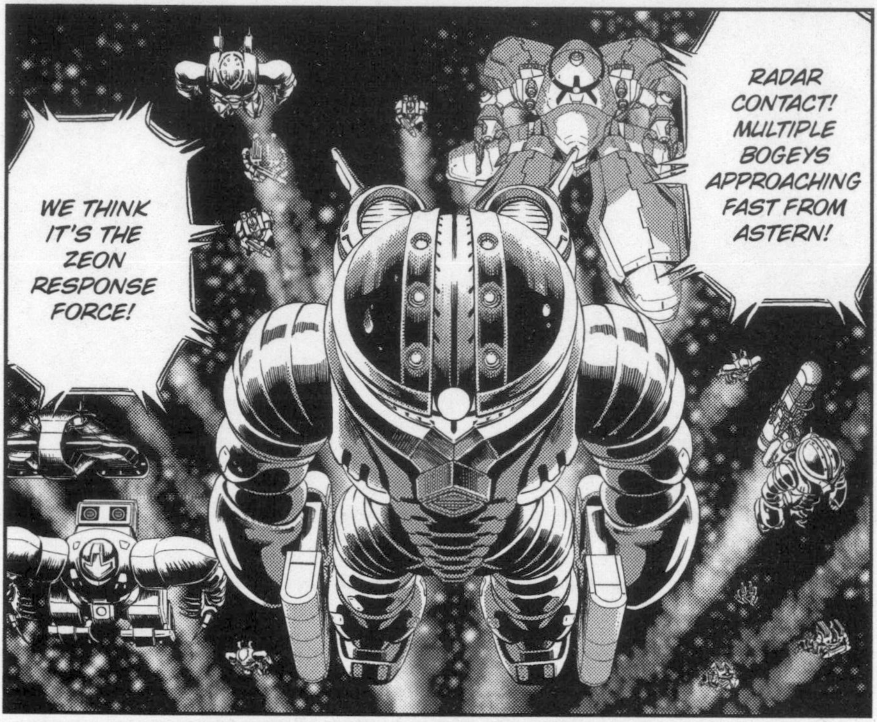
RADAR CONTACT! MULTIPLE BOGEYS APPROACHING FAST FROM ASTERN!
WE THINK IT'S THE ZEON RESPONSE FORCE!

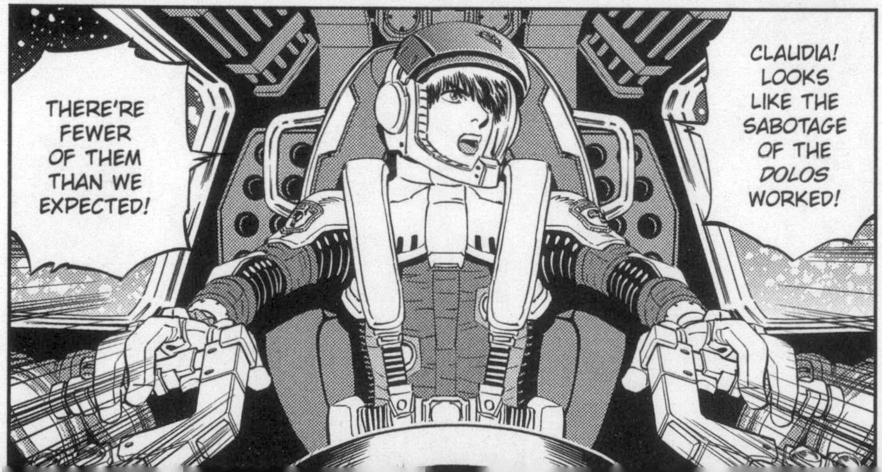
CLAUDIA! LOOKS LIKE THE SABOTAGE OF THE *DOLOS* WORKED!
THERE'RE FEWER OF THEM THAN WE EXPECTED!

ATTEN-
TION,
ALL HANDS
...

THE ENEMY IS
APPROACHING
AT MAXIMUM
SPEED! THE MF
ZOCK AND OUR
SUBMERSIBLES
AREN'T FAST
ENOUGH TO
SHAKE THEM!

THEY'LL BE
WITHIN RANGE IN
APPROXIMATELY
20 MINUTES.
WE'LL BE
FORCED TO
ENGAGE THEM!
I WANT THE MS
UNITS READY TO
INTERCEPT!

SO
THEY'RE
HERE.

AS
PREDIC-
TED.

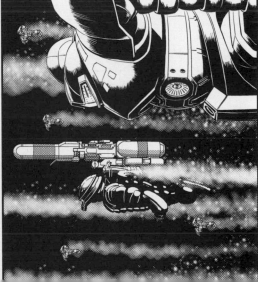

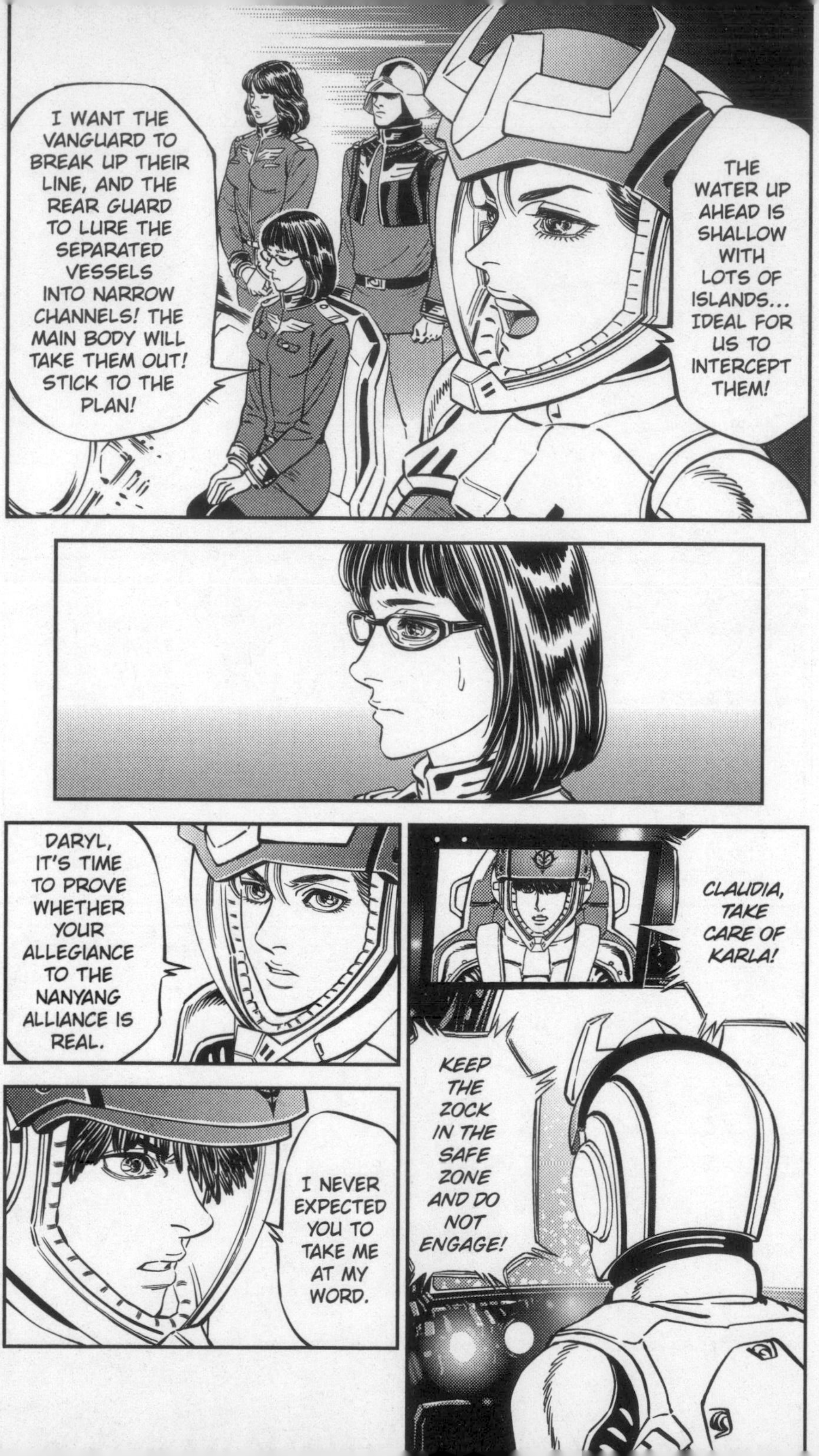
THE WATER UP AHEAD IS SHALLOW WITH LOTS OF ISLANDS... IDEAL FOR US TO INTERCEPT THEM!
I WANT THE VANGUARD TO BREAK UP THEIR LINE, AND THE REAR GUARD TO LURE THE SEPARATED VESSELS INTO NARROW CHANNELS! THE MAIN BODY WILL TAKE THEM OUT! STICK TO THE PLAN!
CLAUDIA, TAKE CARE OF KARLA!
KEEP THE ZOCK IN THE SAFE ZONE AND DO NOT ENGAGE!
DARYL, IT'S TIME TO PROVE WHETHER YOUR ALLEGIANCE TO THE NANYANG ALLIANCE IS REAL.
I NEVER EXPECTED YOU TO TAKE ME AT MY WORD.

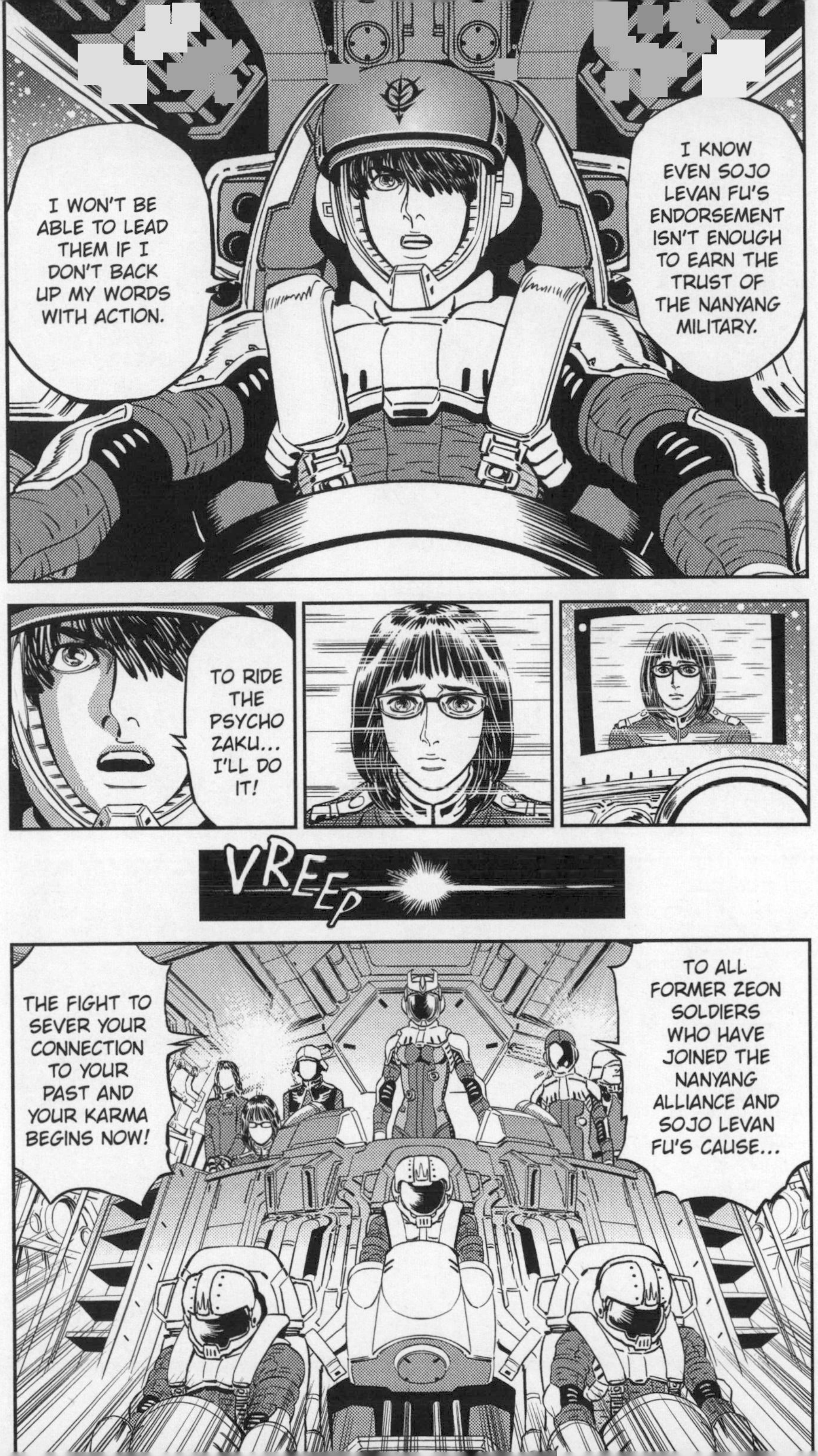
I KNOW EVEN SOJO LEVAN FU'S ENDORSEMENT ISN'T ENOUGH TO EARN THE TRUST OF THE NANYANG MILITARY.
I WON'T BE ABLE TO LEAD THEM IF I DON'T BACK UP MY WORDS WITH ACTION.
TO RIDE THE PSYCHO ZAKU... I'LL DO IT!
VREEP
TO ALL FORMER ZEON SOLDIERS WHO HAVE JOINED THE NANYANG ALLIANCE AND SOJO LEVAN FU'S CAUSE...
THE FIGHT TO SEVER YOUR CONNECTION TO YOUR PAST AND YOUR KARMA BEGINS NOW!

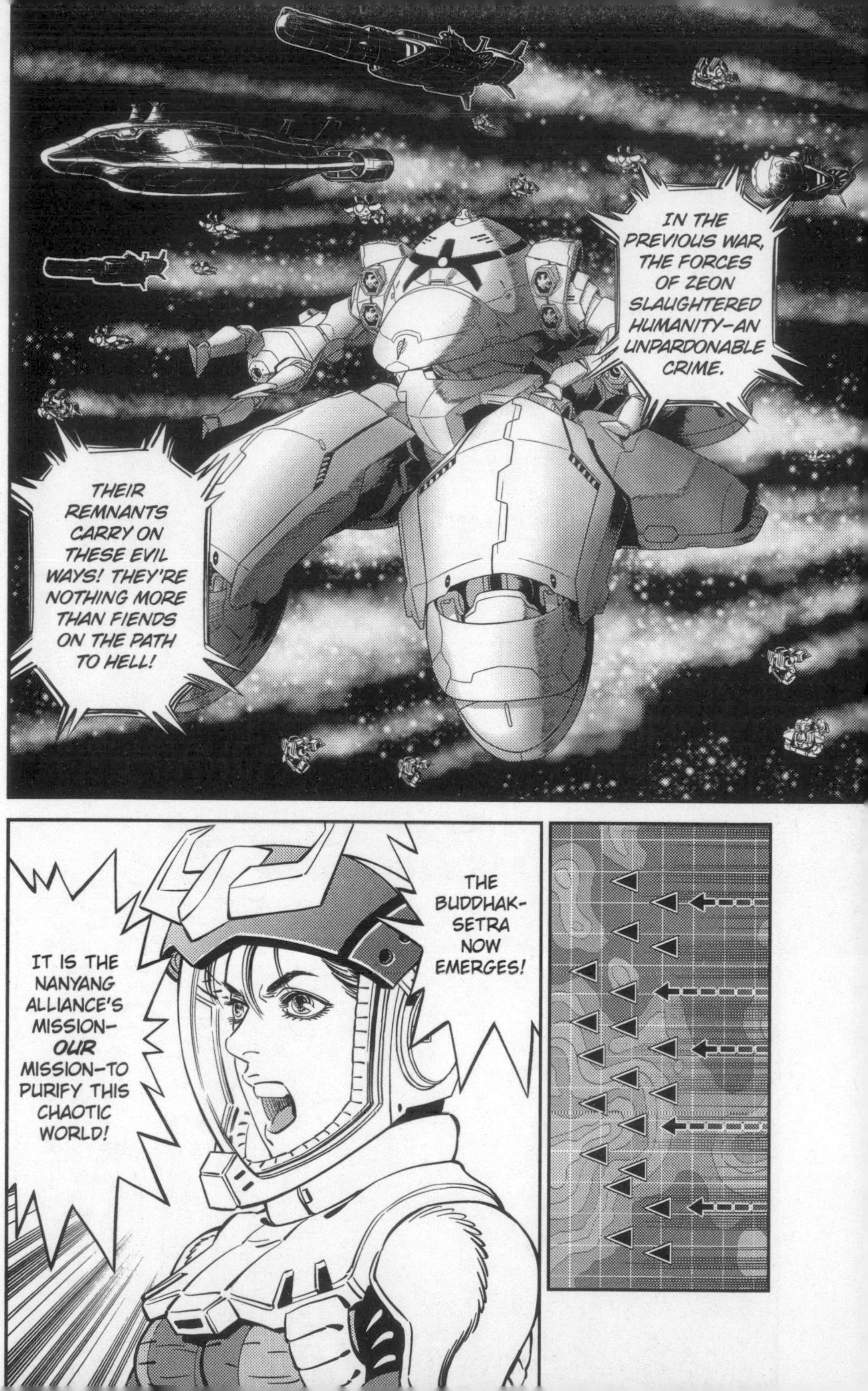
IN THE PREVIOUS WAR, THE FORCES OF ZEON SLAUGHTERED HUMANITY—AN UNPARDONABLE CRIME.
THEIR REMNANTS CARRY ON THESE EVIL WAYS! THEY'RE NOTHING MORE THAN FIENDS ON THE PATH TO HELL!
THE BUDDHAK-SETRA NOW EMERGES!
IT IS THE NANYANG ALLIANCE'S MISSION—**OUR** MISSION—TO PURIFY THIS CHAOTIC WORLD!

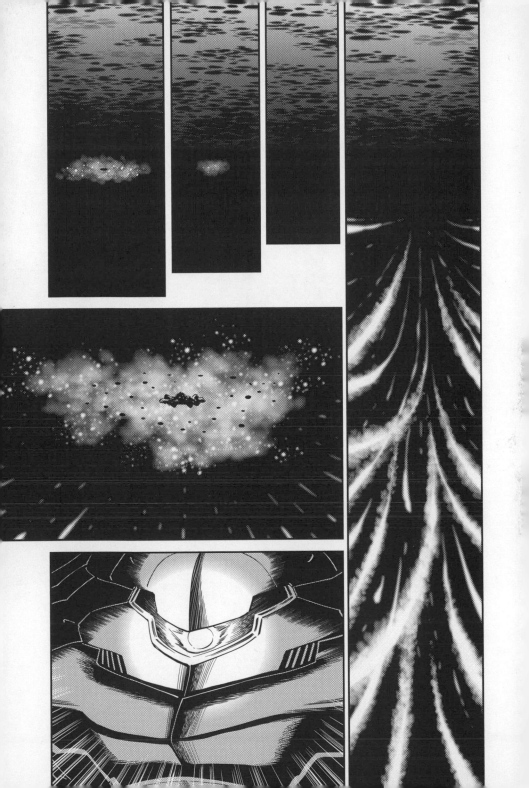

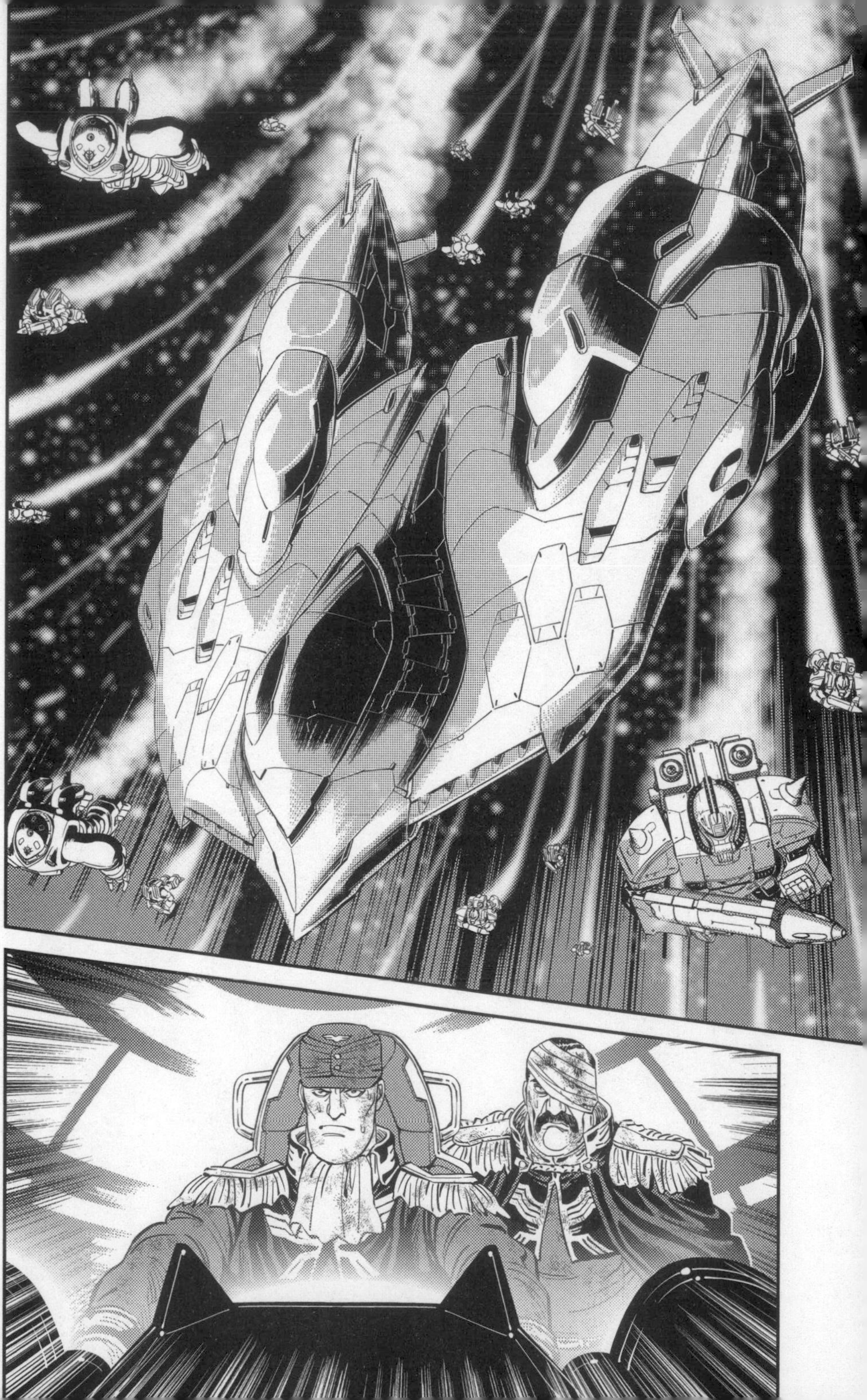

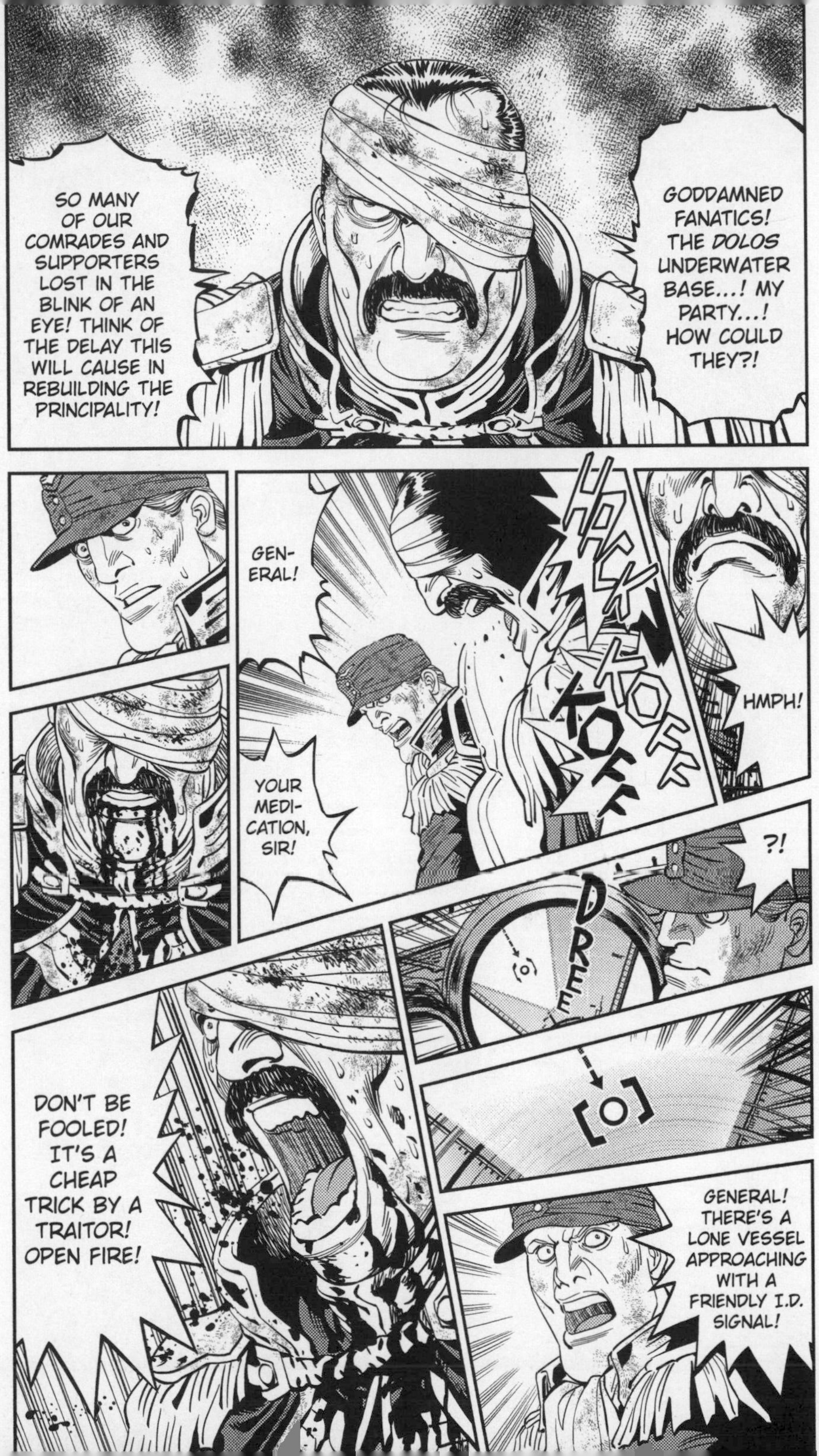
GODDAMNED FANATICS! THE *DOLOS* UNDERWATER BASE...! MY PARTY...! HOW COULD THEY?!
SO MANY OF OUR COMRADES AND SUPPORTERS LOST IN THE BLINK OF AN EYE! THINK OF THE DELAY THIS WILL CAUSE IN REBUILDING THE PRINCIPALITY!
HMPH!
HACK KOFF KOFF
GEN-ERAL!
YOUR MEDI-CATION, SIR!
?!
DREE
[o]
GENERAL! THERE'S A LONE VESSEL APPROACHING WITH A FRIENDLY I.D. SIGNAL!
DON'T BE FOOLED! IT'S A CHEAP TRICK BY A TRAITOR! OPEN FIRE!

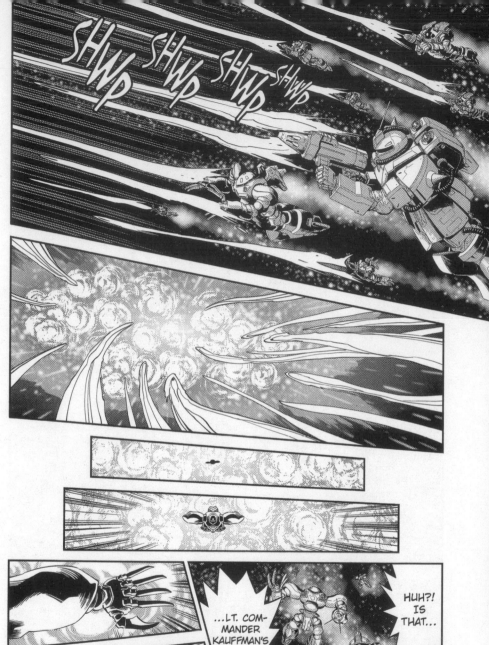

SHWP SHWP SHWP SHWP

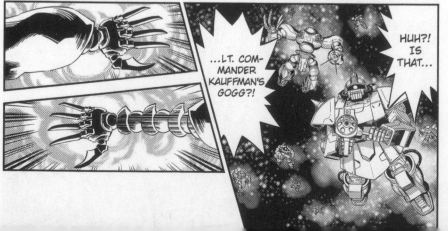

...LT. COMMANDER KAUFFMAN'S GOGG?!

HUH?! IS THAT...

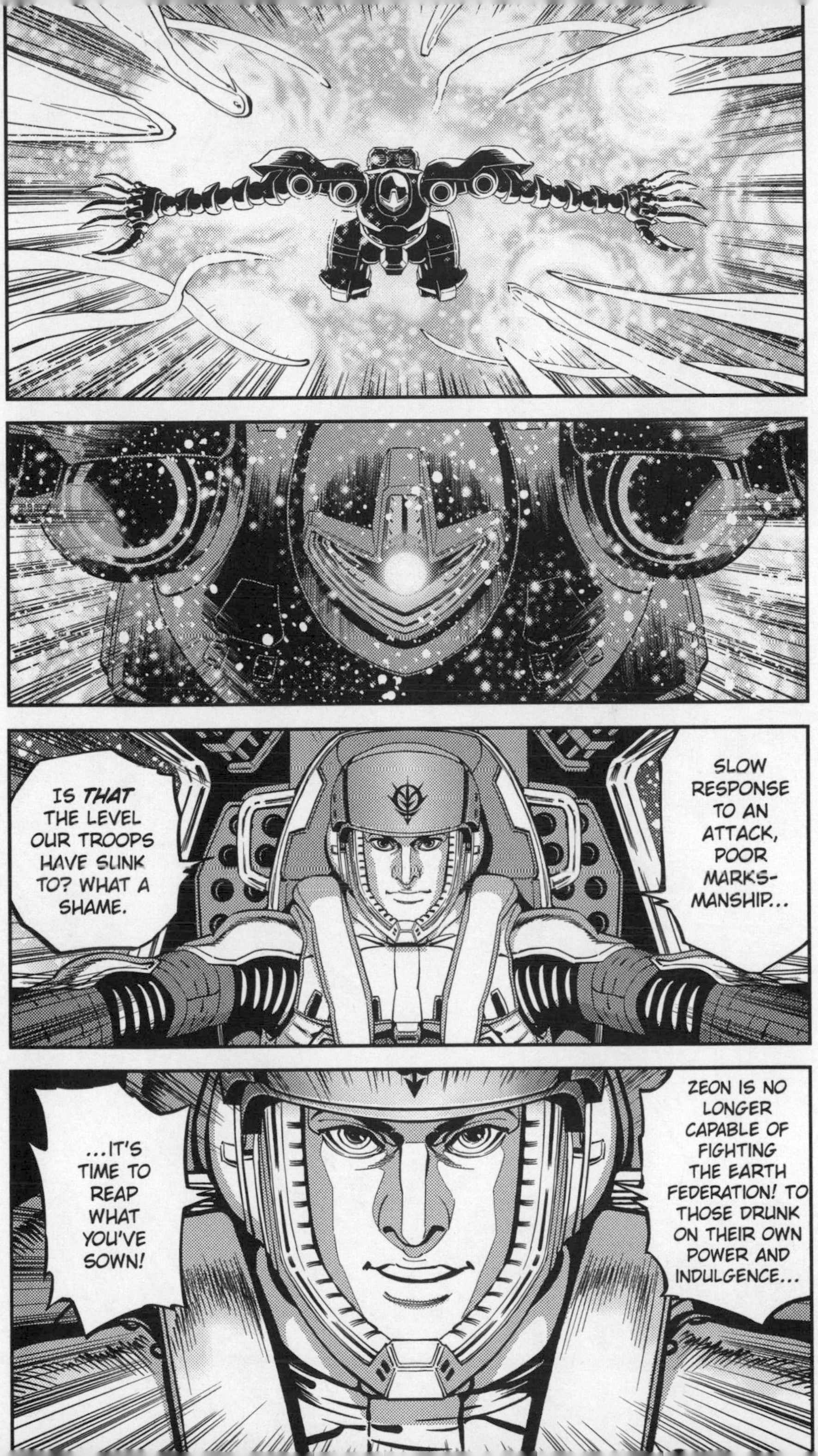
SLOW RESPONSE TO AN ATTACK, POOR MARKS-MANSHIP...
IS *THAT* THE LEVEL OUR TROOPS HAVE SUNK TO? WHAT A SHAME.
ZEON IS NO LONGER CAPABLE OF FIGHTING THE EARTH FEDERATION! TO THOSE DRUNK ON THEIR OWN POWER AND INDULGENCE...
...IT'S TIME TO REAP WHAT YOU'VE SOWN!

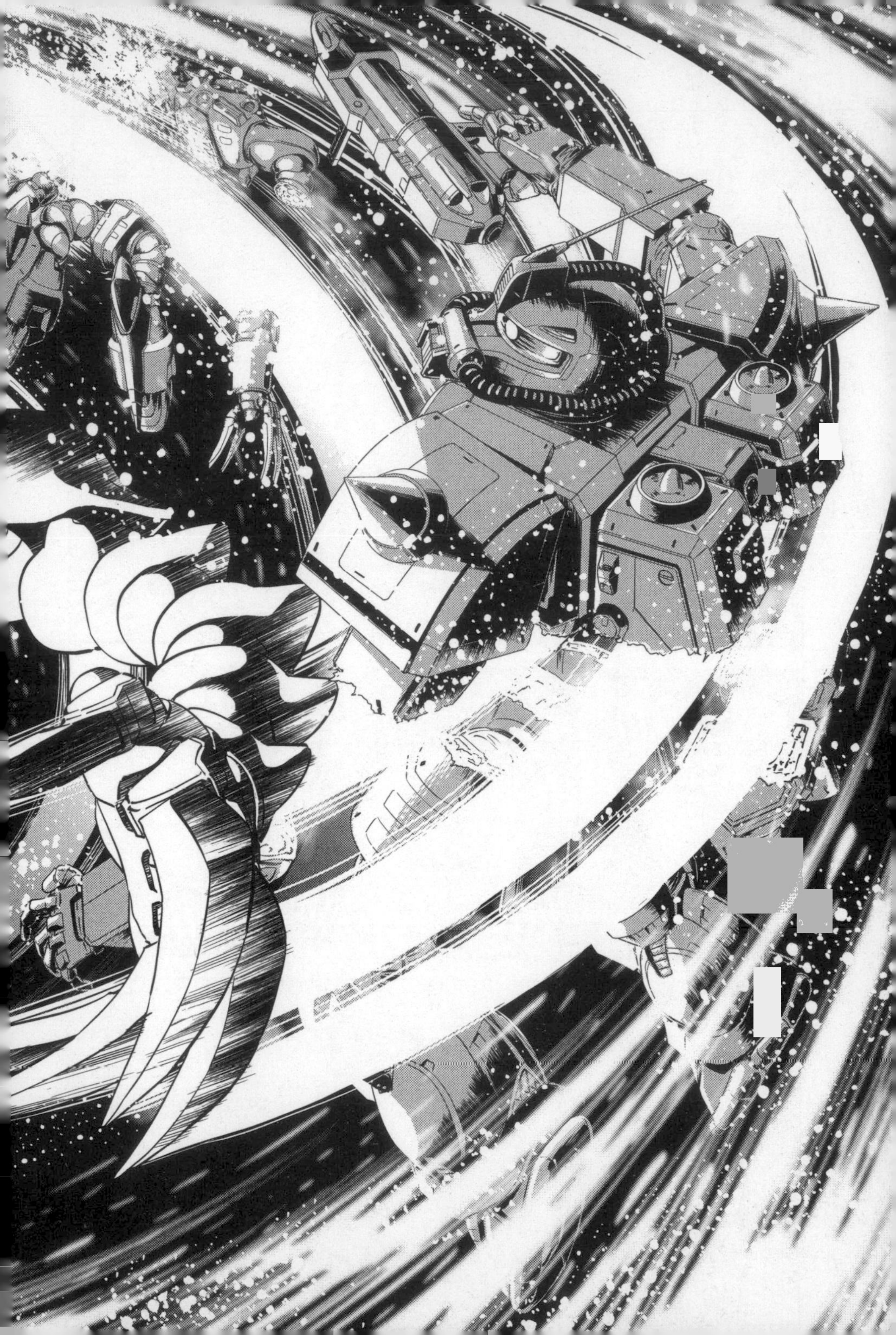

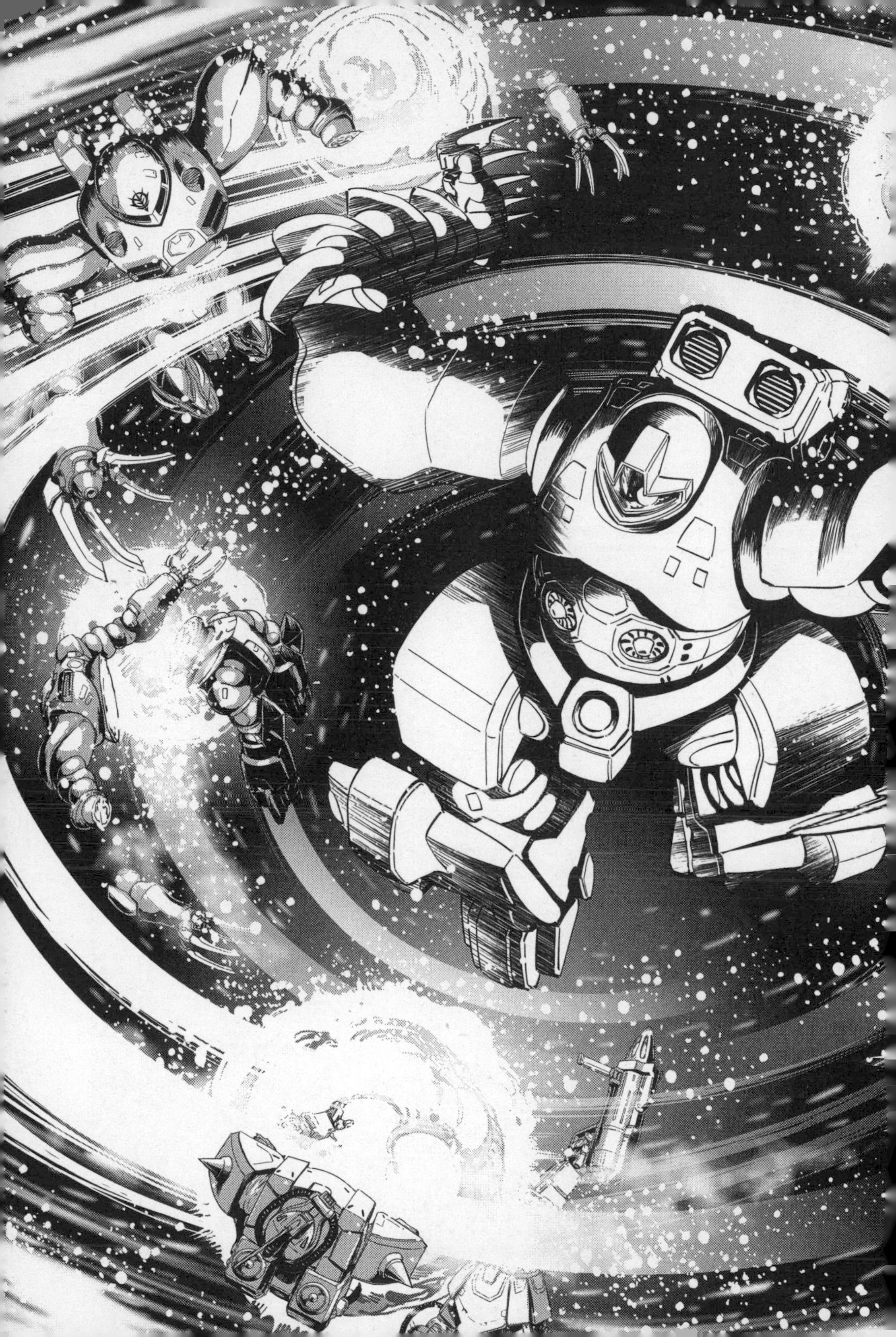

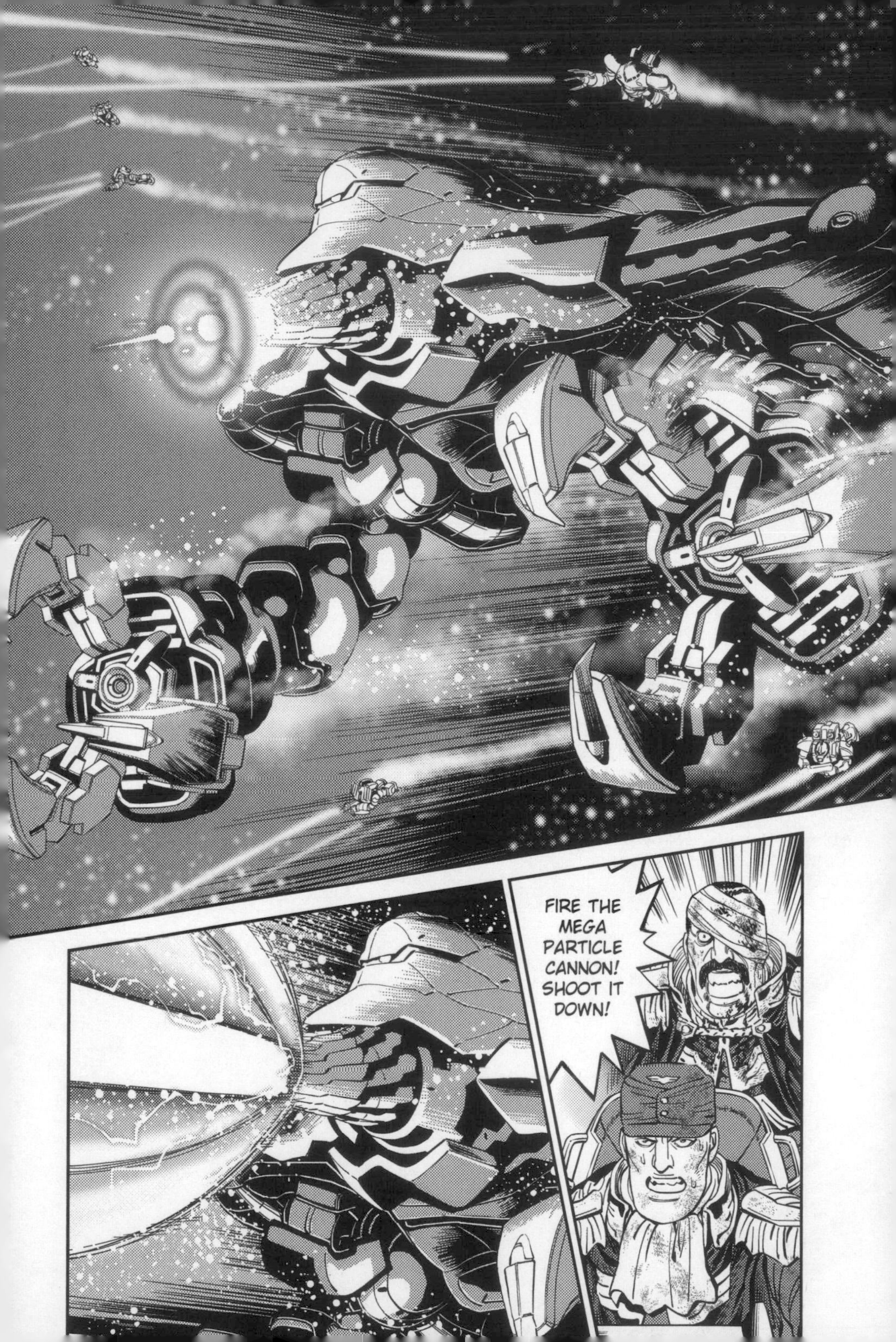
FIRE THE MEGA PARTICLE CANNON! SHOOT IT DOWN!

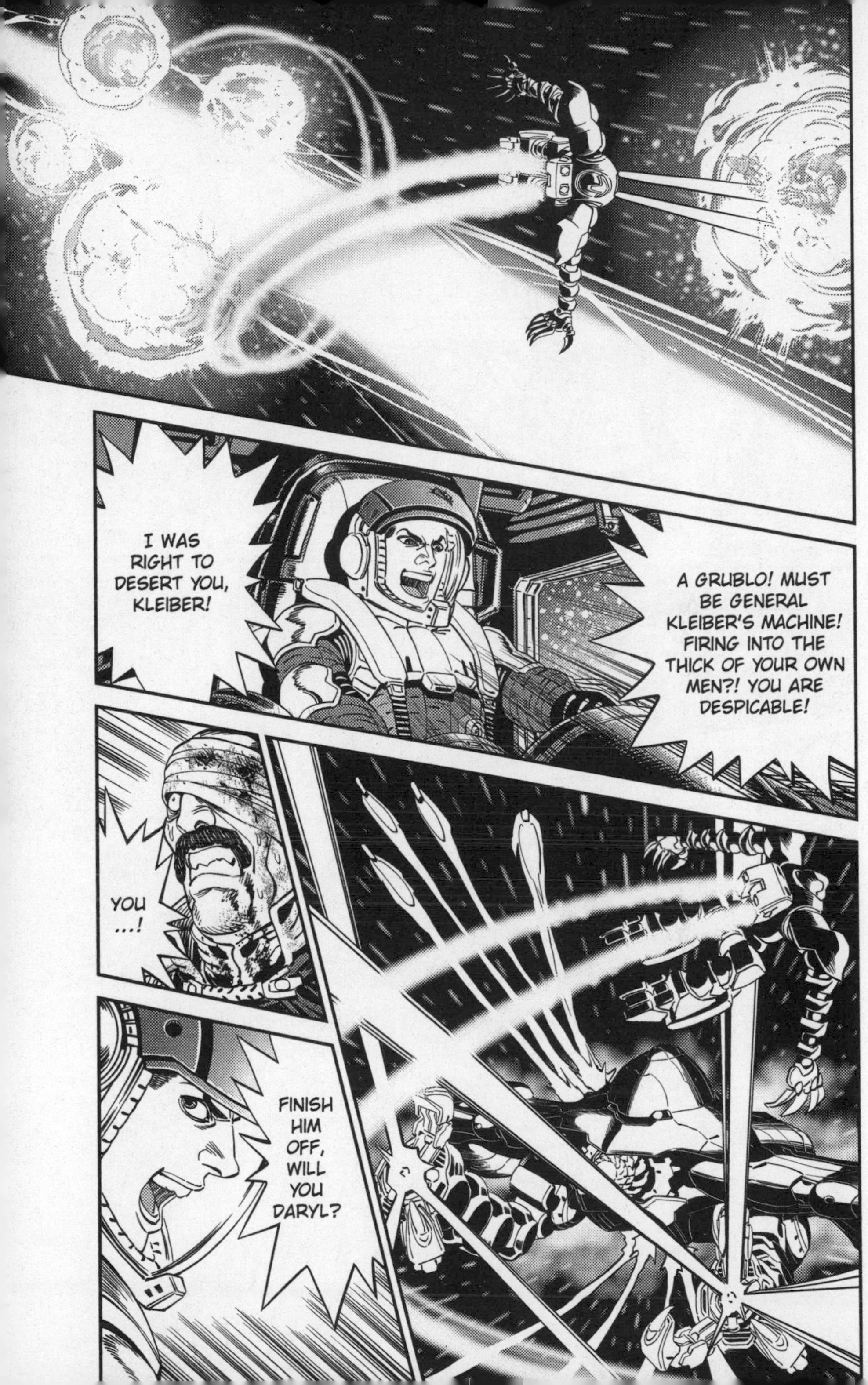
A GRUBLO! MUST BE GENERAL KLEIBER'S MACHINE! FIRING INTO THE THICK OF YOUR OWN MEN?! YOU ARE DESPICABLE!
I WAS RIGHT TO DESERT YOU, KLEIBER!
YOU ...!
FINISH HIM OFF, WILL YOU DARYL?

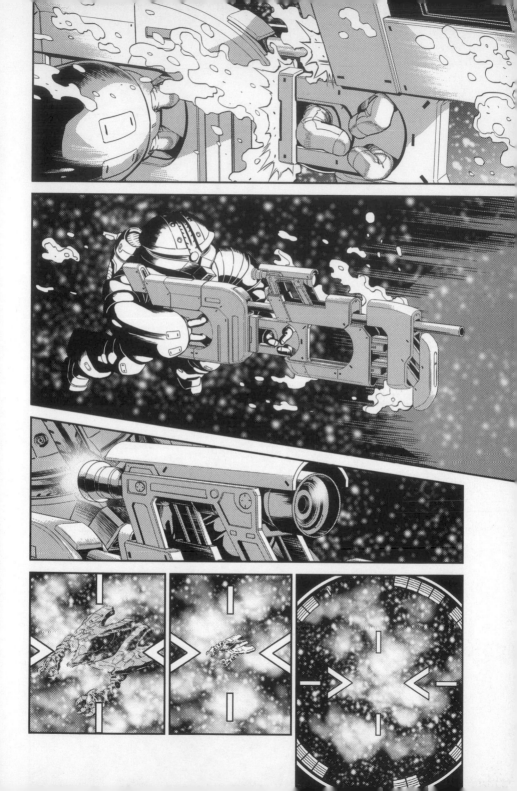

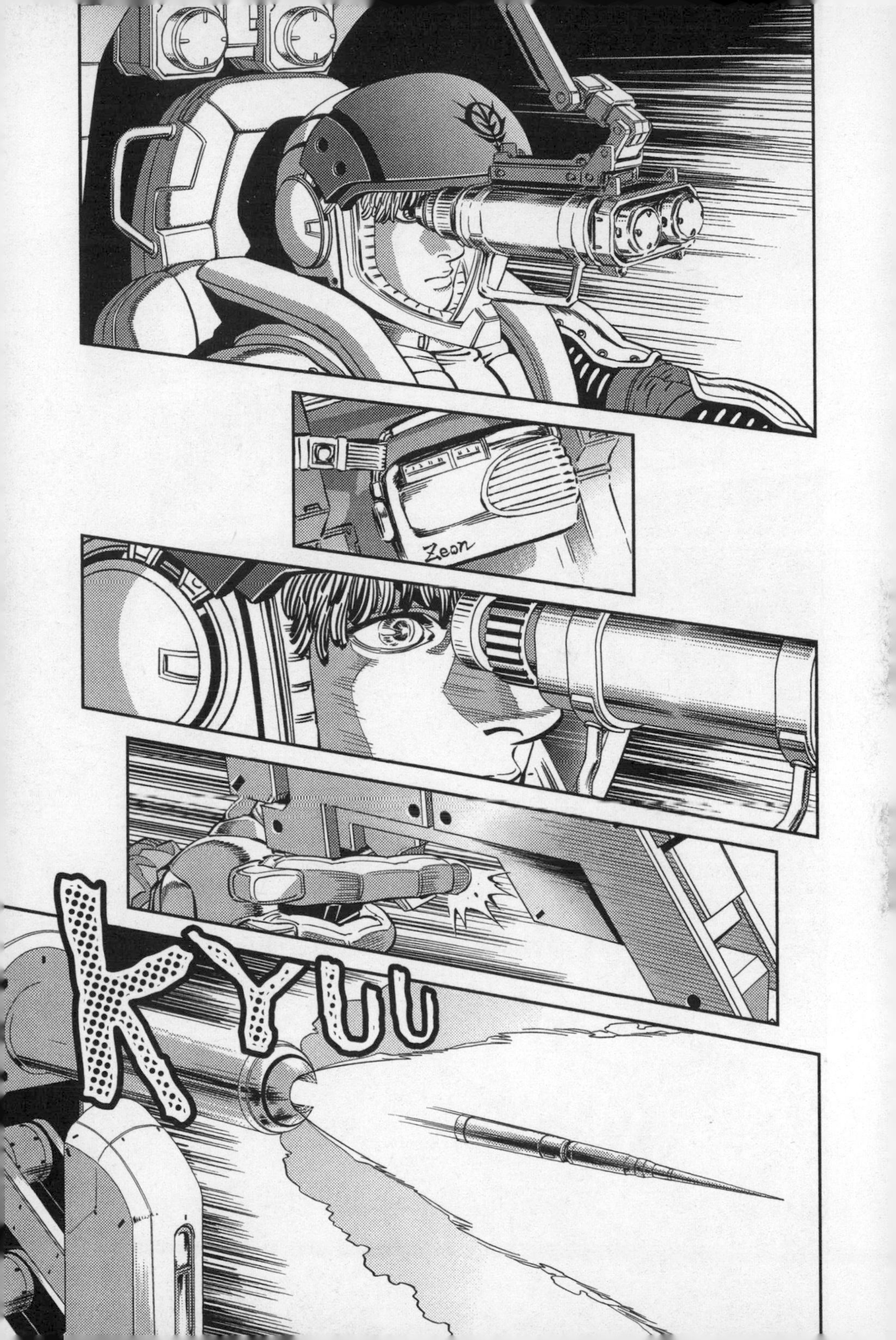
Zeon
KYUU

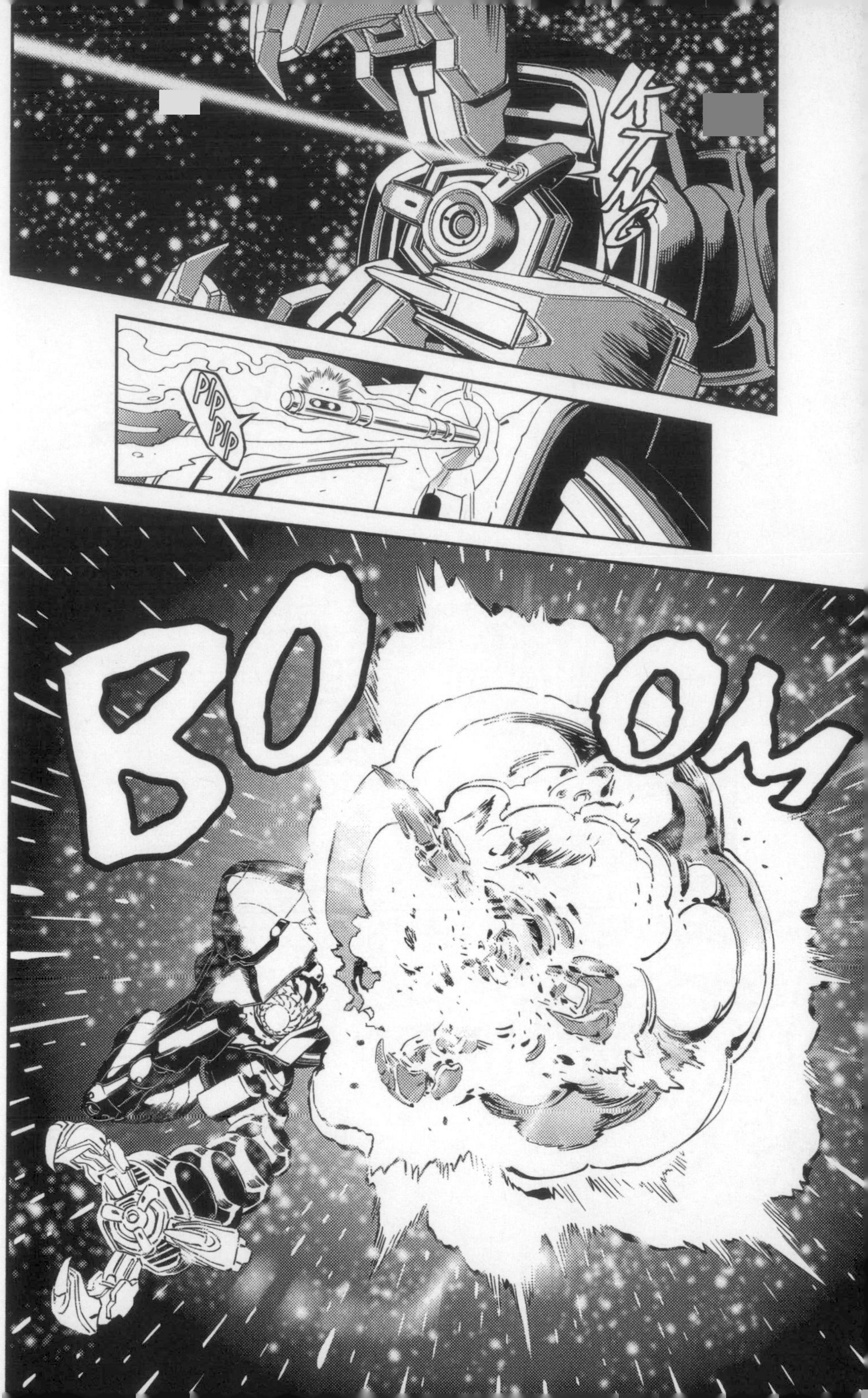
KTING
PIP PIP
BOOM

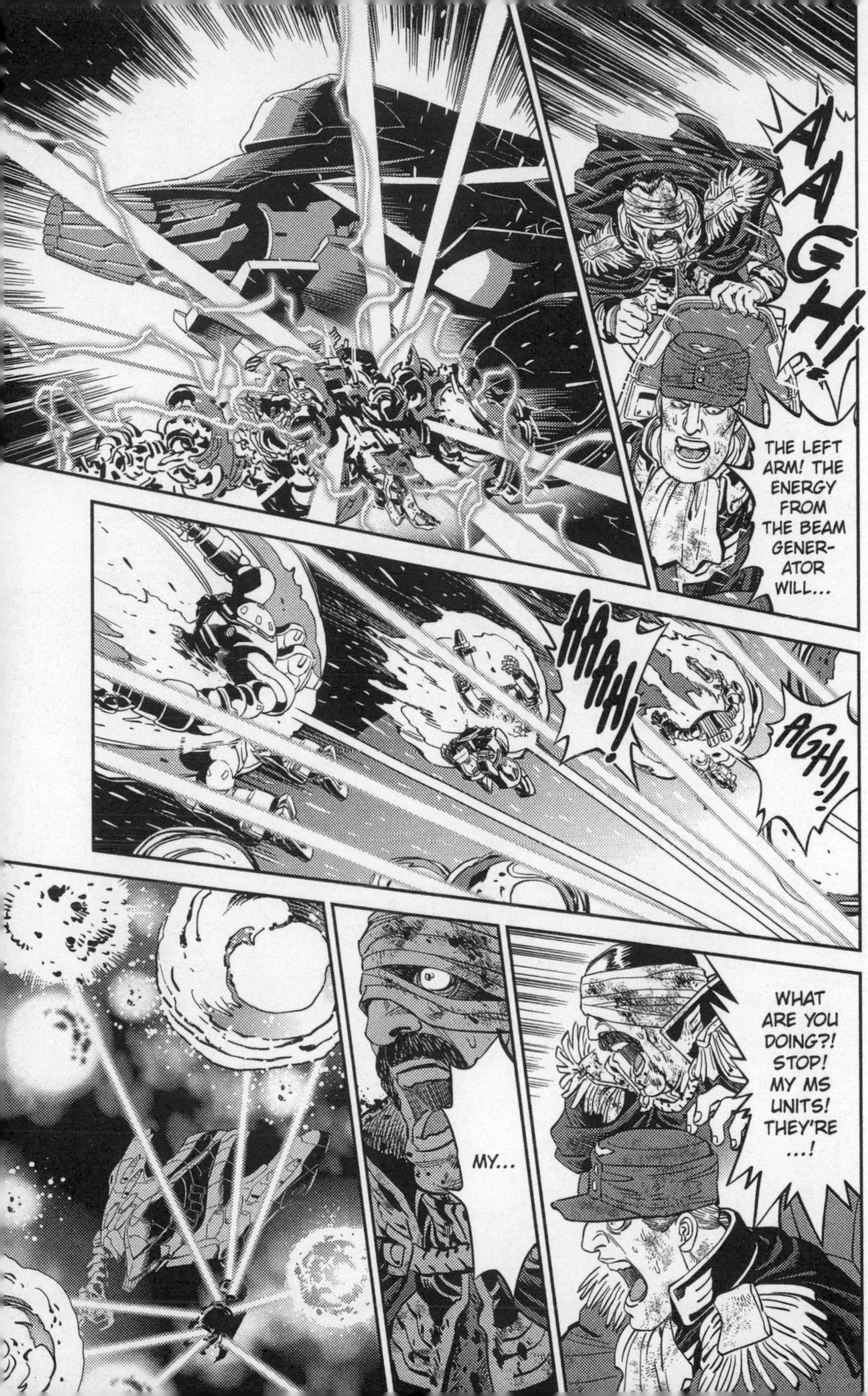
AAGH!
THE LEFT ARM! THE ENERGY FROM THE BEAM GENERATOR WILL...
AAAAH!
AGH!!!
WHAT ARE YOU DOING?! STOP! MY MS UNITS! THEY'RE ...!
MY...

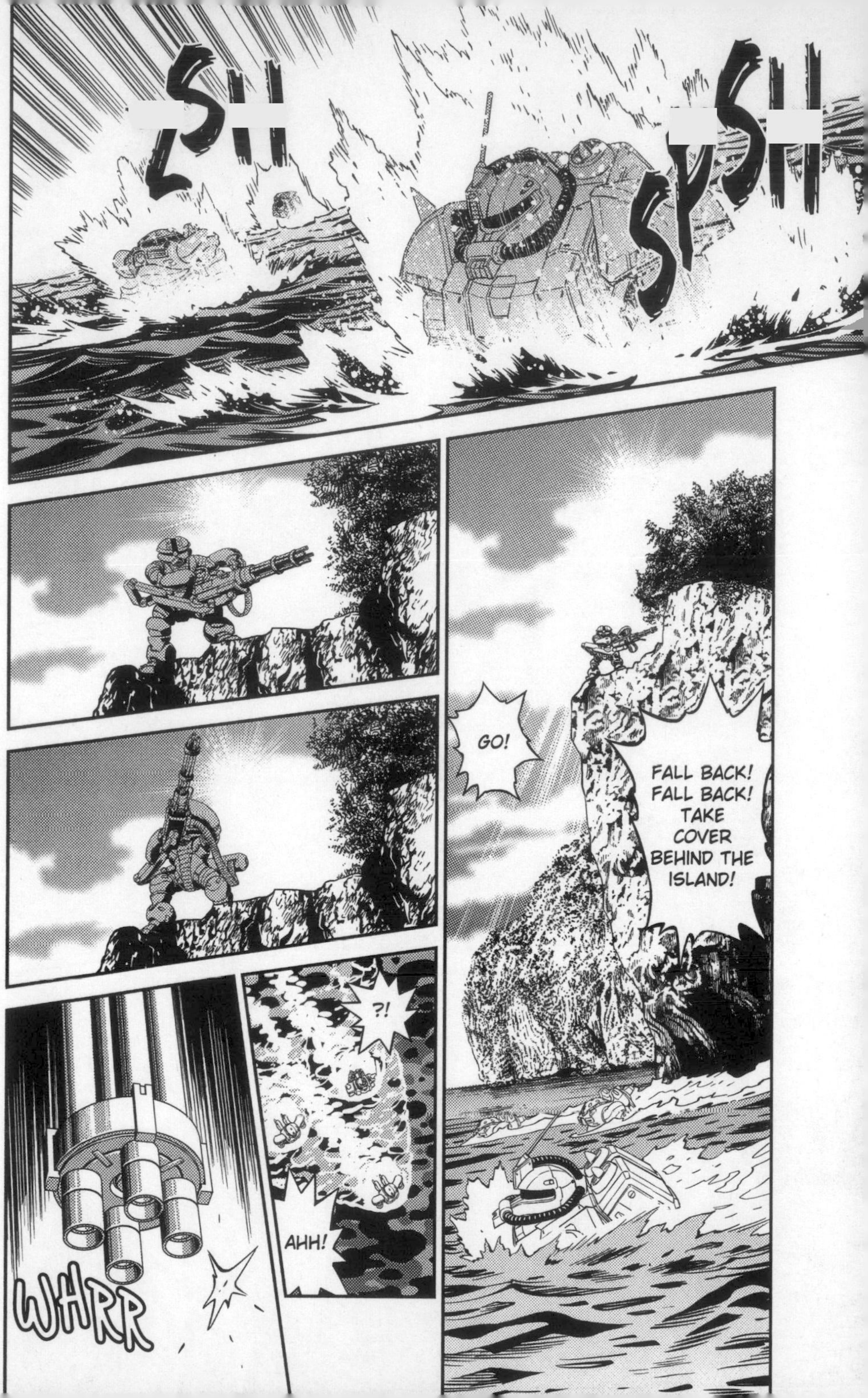
SPSH
SH
FALL BACK! FALL BACK! TAKE COVER BEHIND THE ISLAND!
GO!
?!
AHH!
WHRR

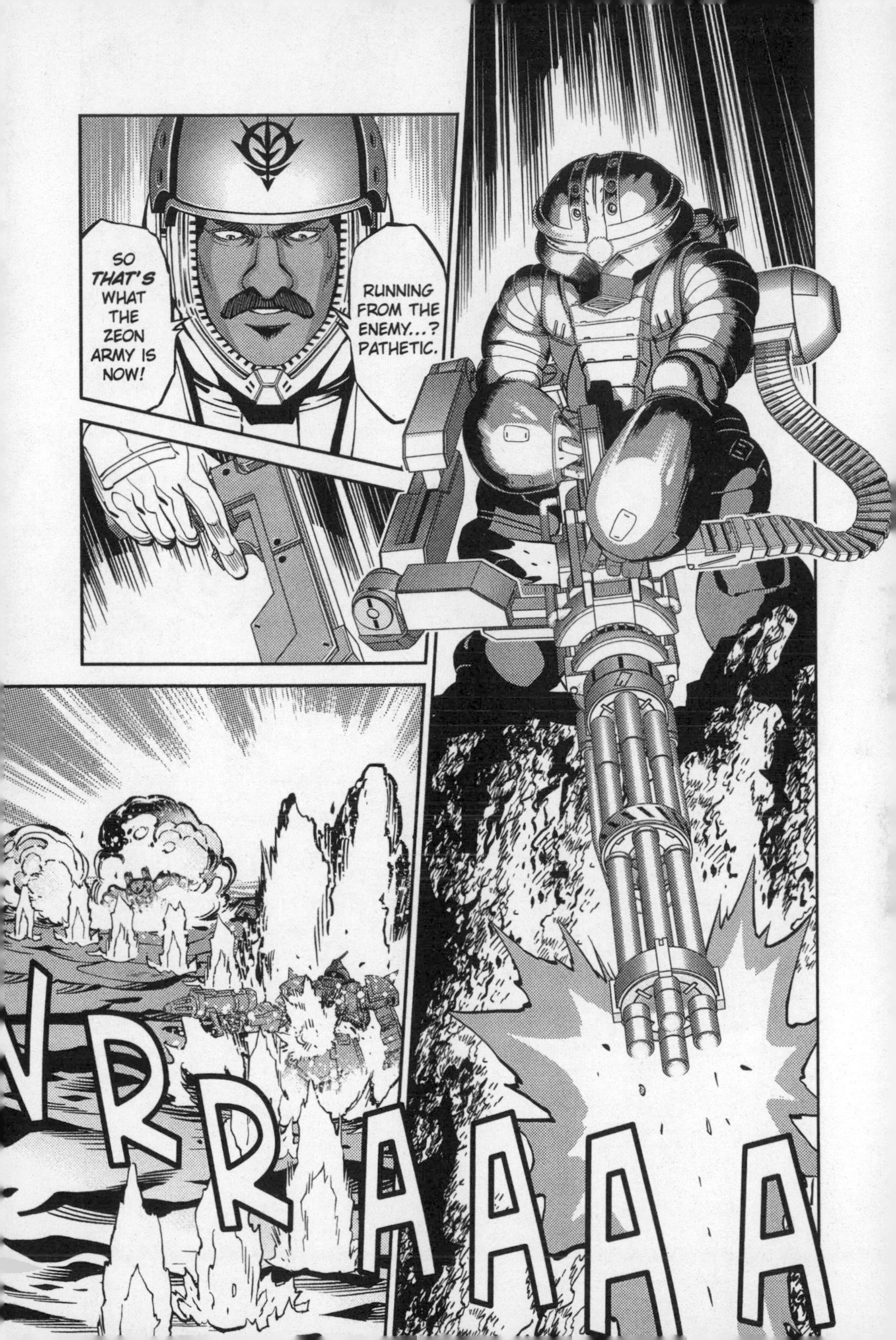
RUNNING FROM THE ENEMY...? PATHETIC.
SO *THAT'S* WHAT THE ZEON ARMY IS NOW!
NRRAAAA

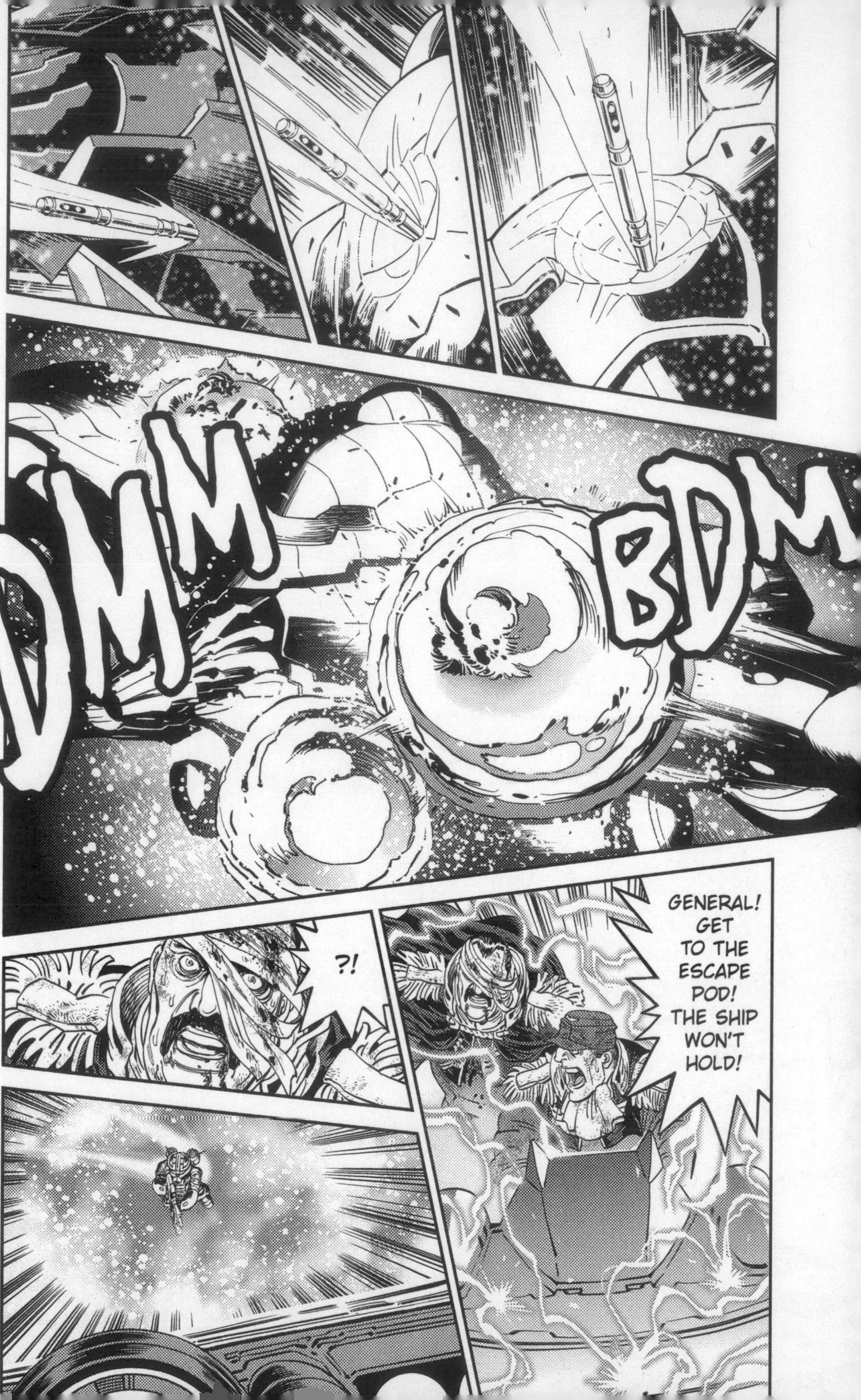
BDM
DMM
GENERAL! GET TO THE ESCAPE POD! THE SHIP WON'T HOLD!
?!

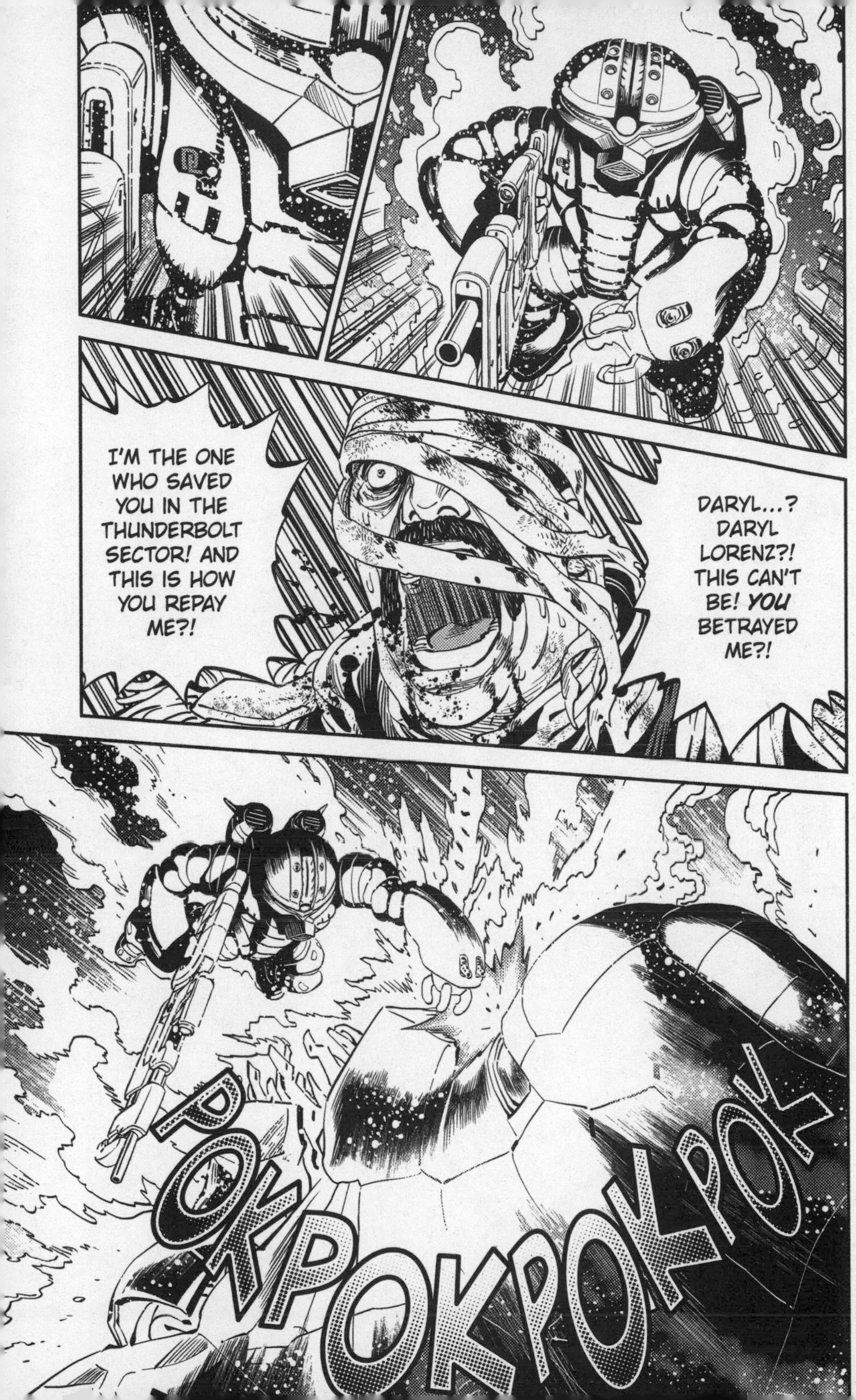
DARYL...? DARYL LORENZ?! THIS CAN'T BE! *YOU* BETRAYED ME?!
I'M THE ONE WHO SAVED YOU IN THE THUNDERBOLT SECTOR! AND THIS IS HOW YOU REPAY ME?!
POKPOKPOKPOK

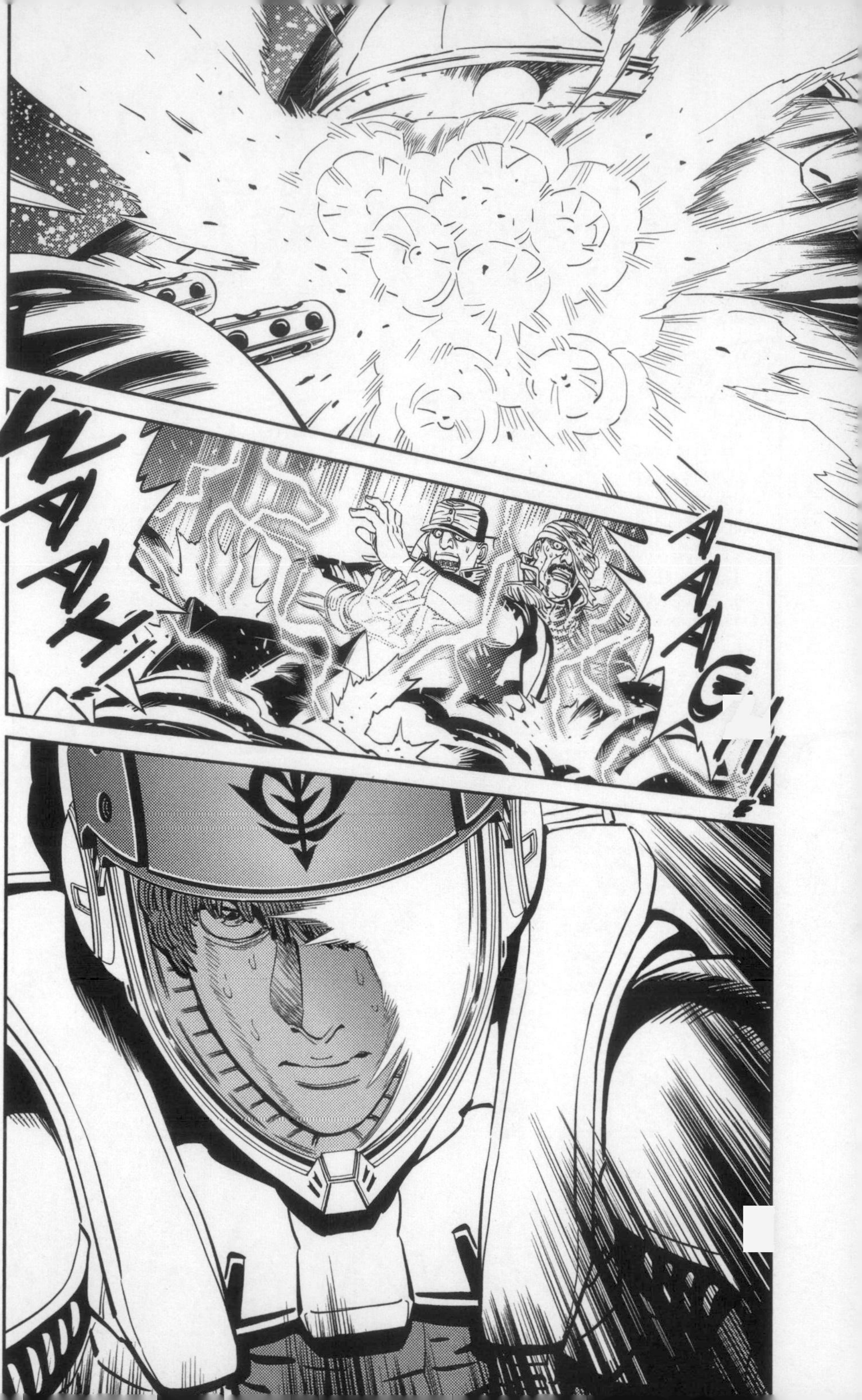
AAAG!!
WAAH!!

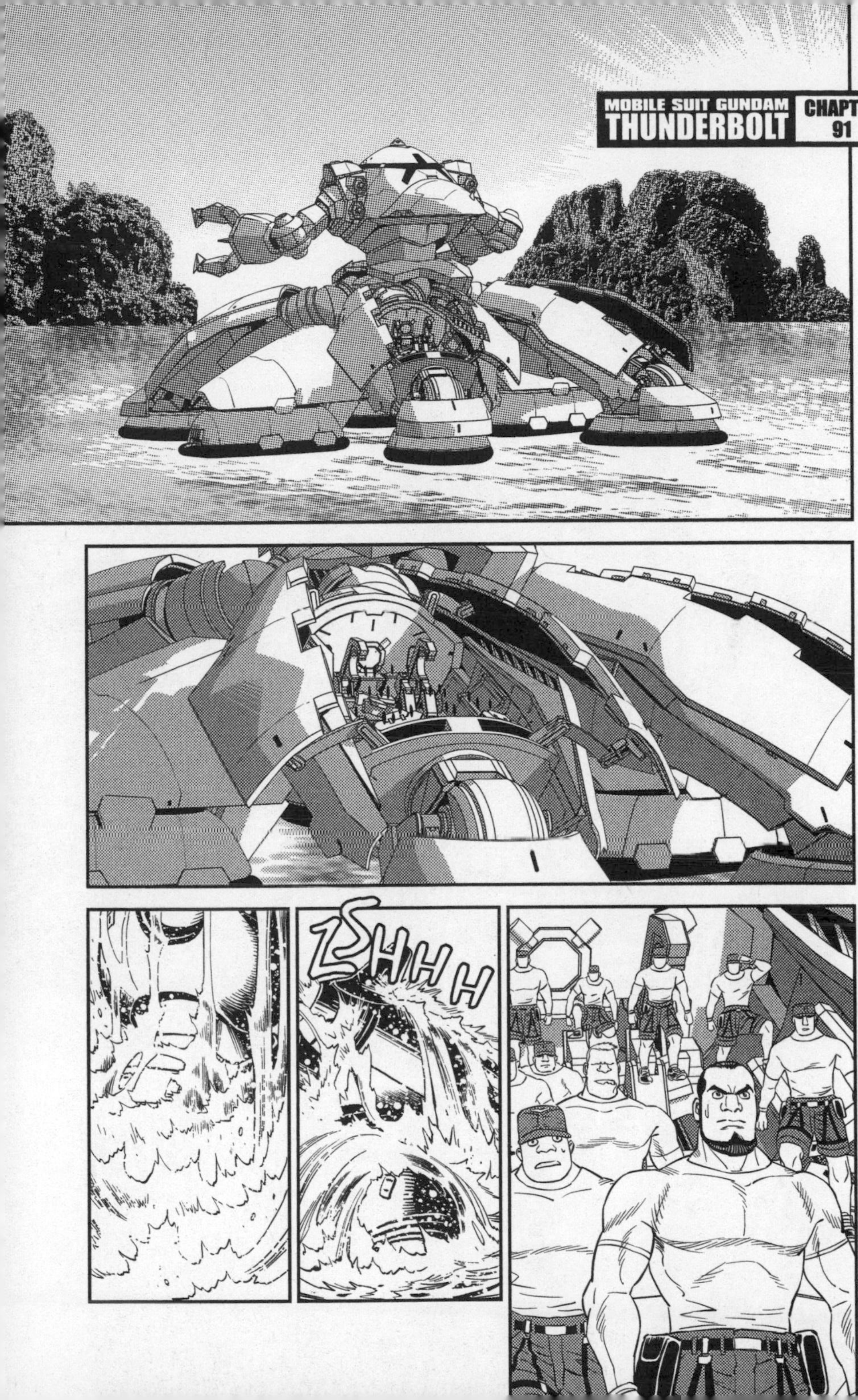
MOBILE SUIT GUNDAM
THUNDERBOLT
CHAPTER
91
ZSHHHH

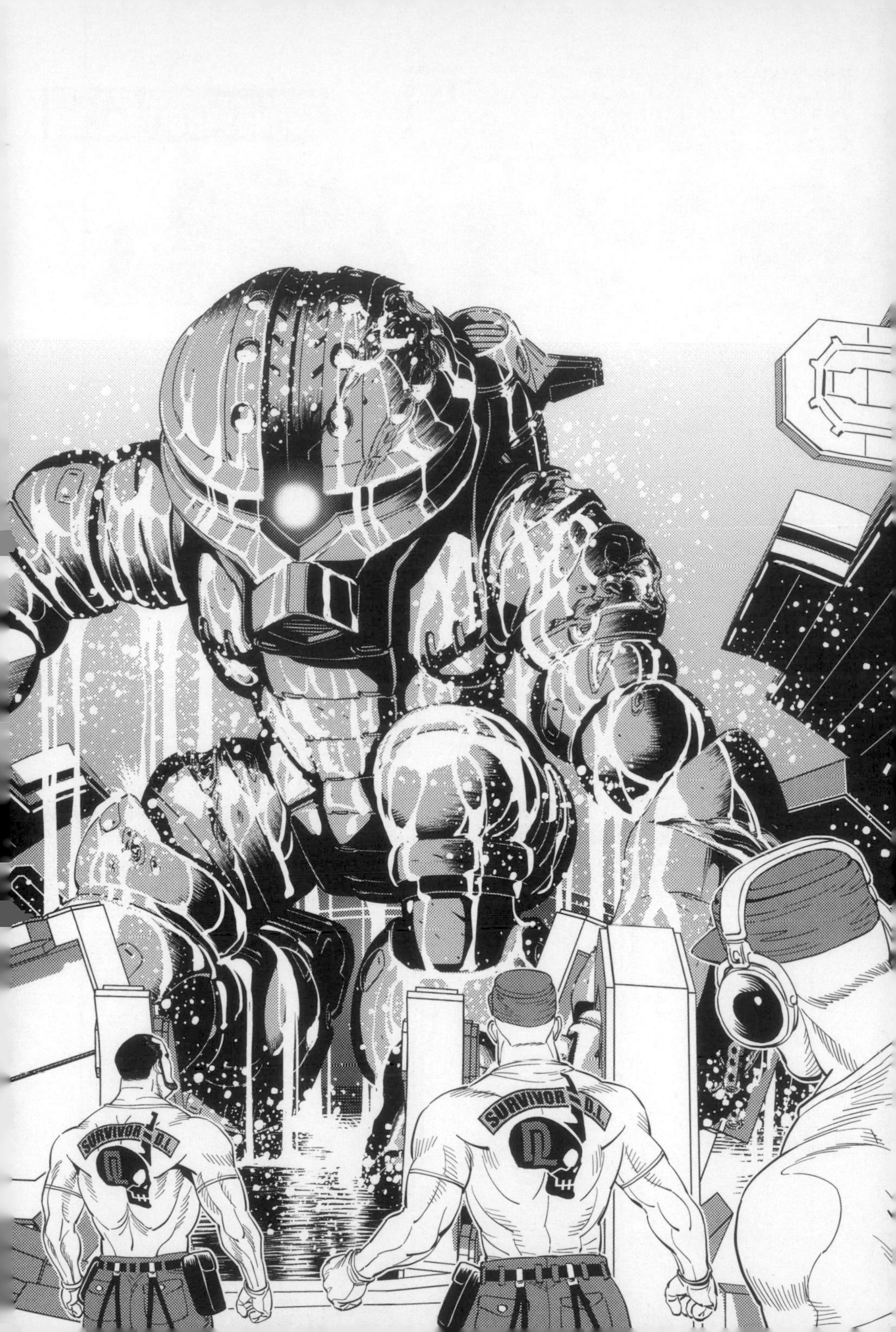
SURVIVOR D.I.
SURVIVOR D.I.

MOBILE SUIT GUNDAM THUNDERBOLT

CHAPTER 91

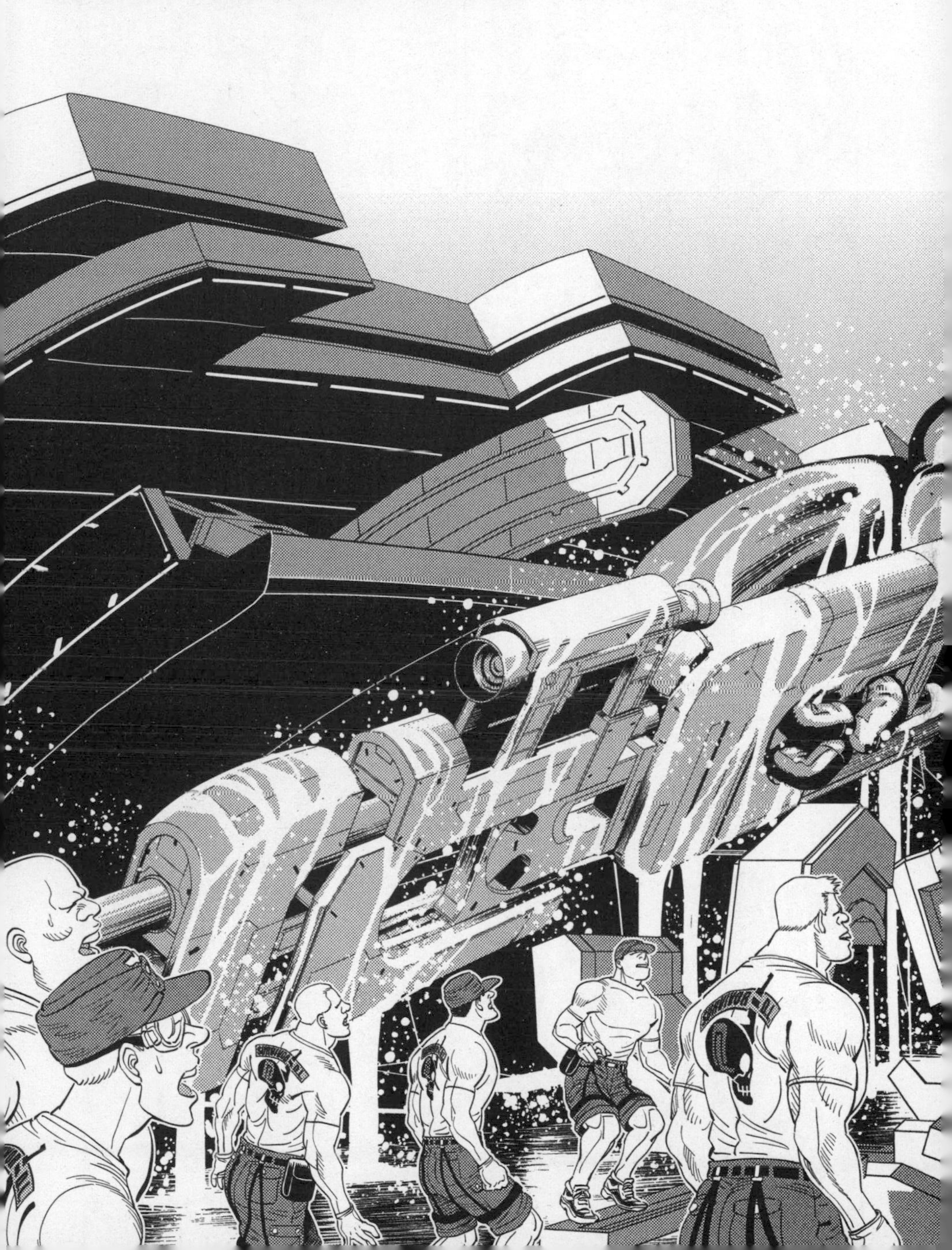

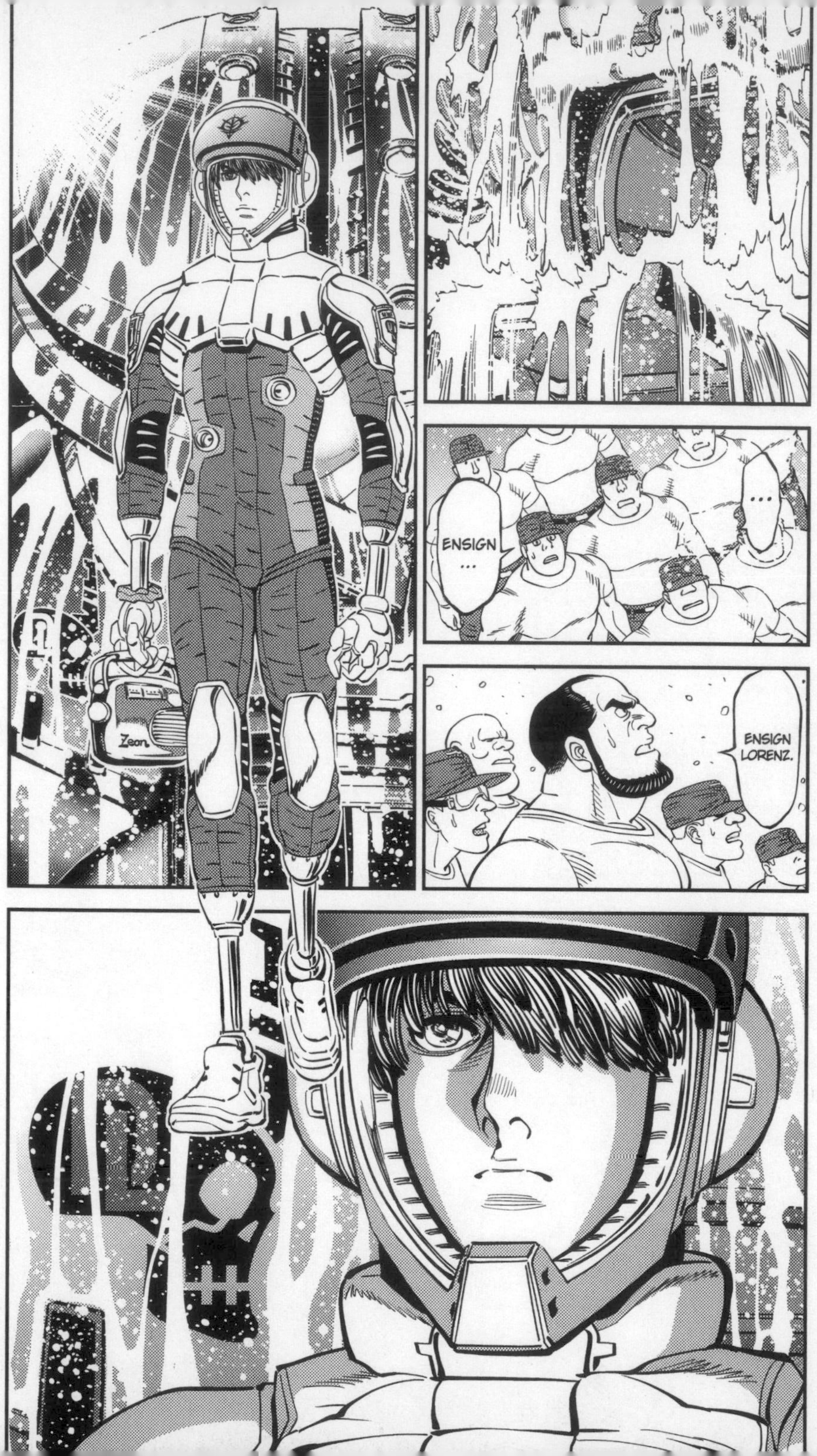
...
ENSIGN ...
ENSIGN LORENZ.
Zeon

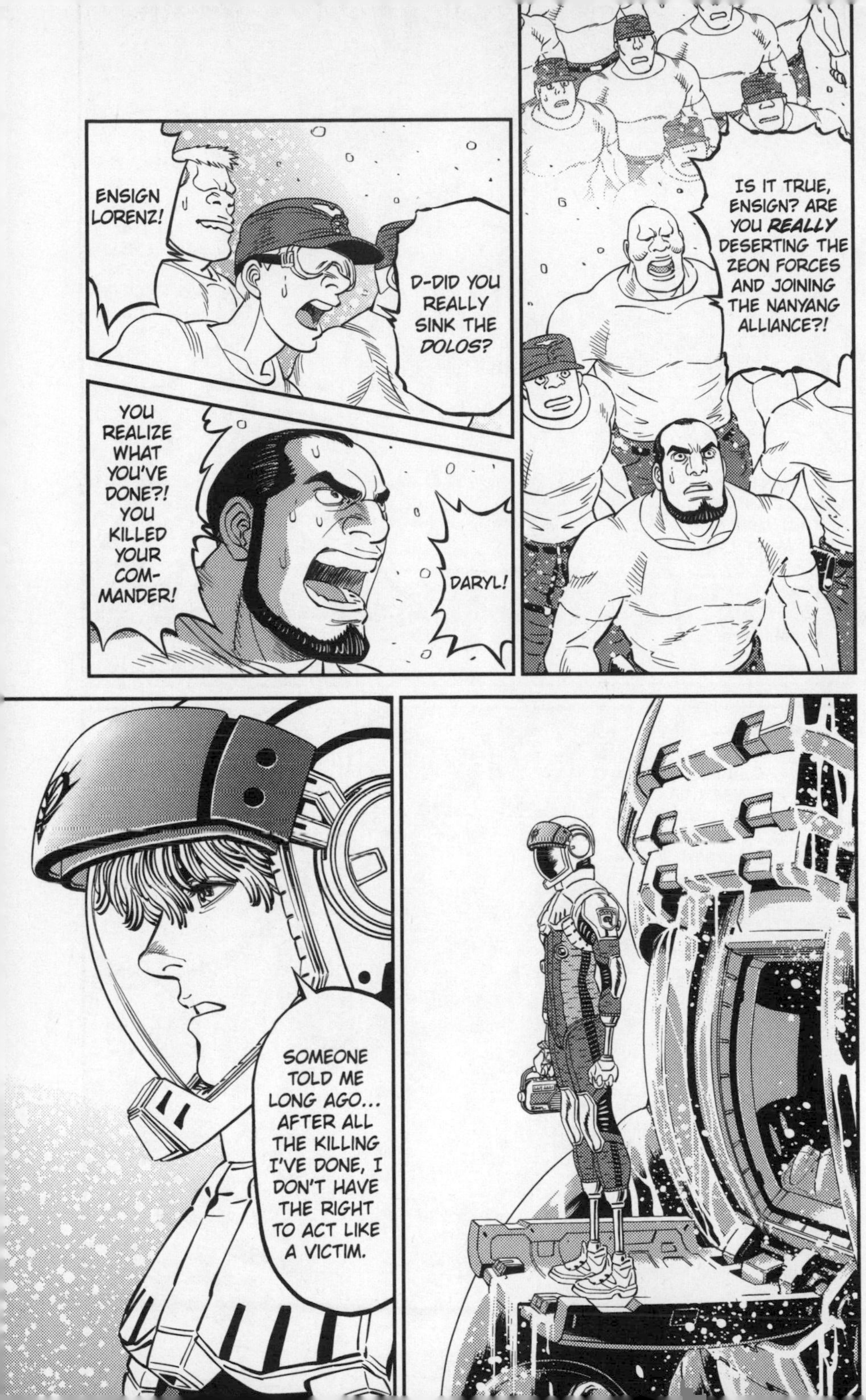
IS IT TRUE, ENSIGN? ARE YOU *REALLY* DESERTING THE ZEON FORCES AND JOINING THE NANYANG ALLIANCE?!
ENSIGN LORENZ!
D-DID YOU REALLY SINK THE *DOLOS*?
DARYL!
YOU REALIZE WHAT YOU'VE DONE?! YOU KILLED YOUR COM-MANDER!
SOMEONE TOLD ME LONG AGO... AFTER ALL THE KILLING I'VE DONE, I DON'T HAVE THE RIGHT TO ACT LIKE A VICTIM.

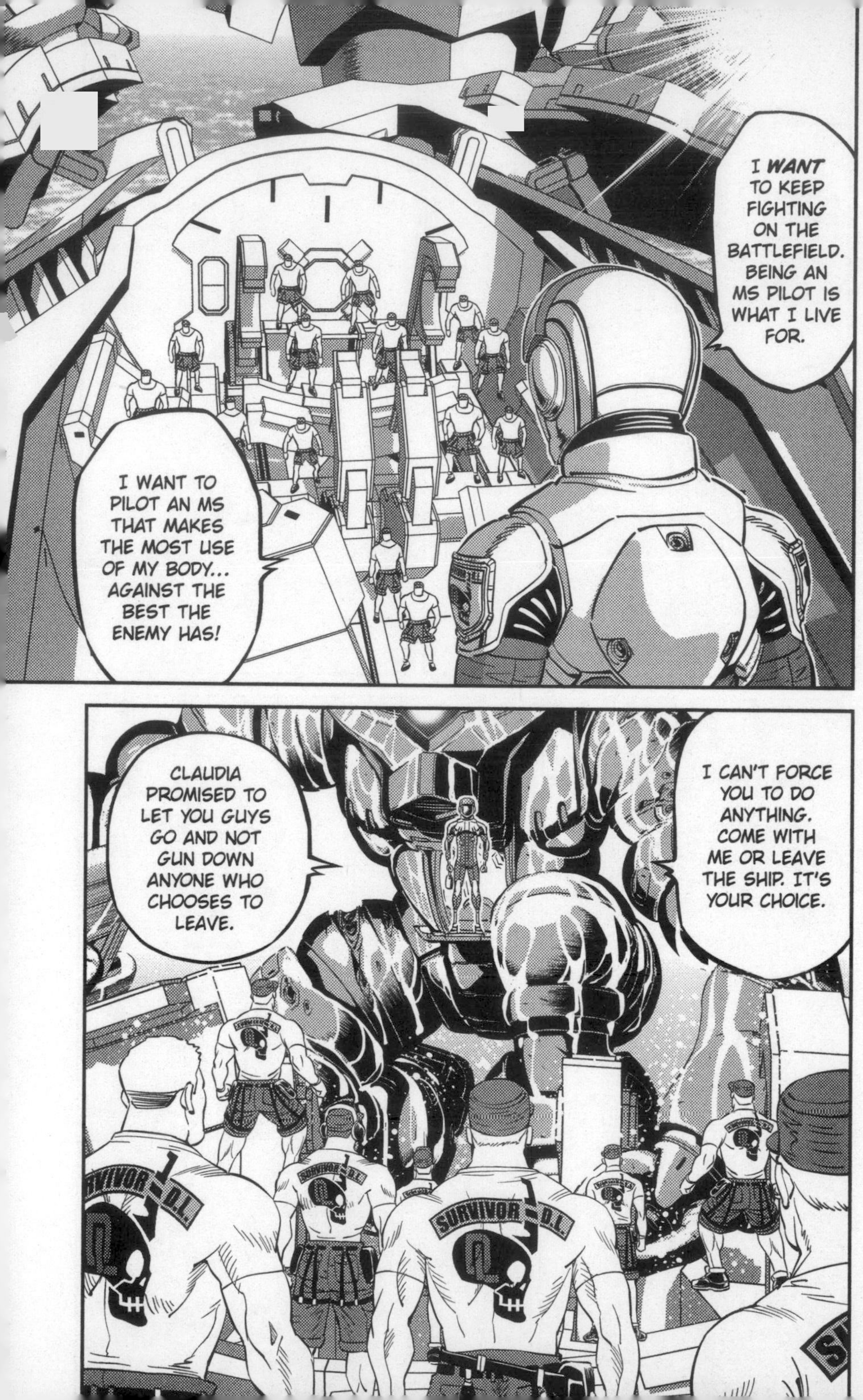
I *WANT* TO KEEP FIGHTING ON THE BATTLEFIELD. BEING AN MS PILOT IS WHAT I LIVE FOR.
I WANT TO PILOT AN MS THAT MAKES THE MOST USE OF MY BODY... AGAINST THE BEST THE ENEMY HAS!
I CAN'T FORCE YOU TO DO ANYTHING. COME WITH ME OR LEAVE THE SHIP. IT'S YOUR CHOICE.
CLAUDIA PROMISED TO LET YOU GUYS GO AND NOT GUN DOWN ANYONE WHO CHOOSES TO LEAVE.
SURVIVOR D.I.

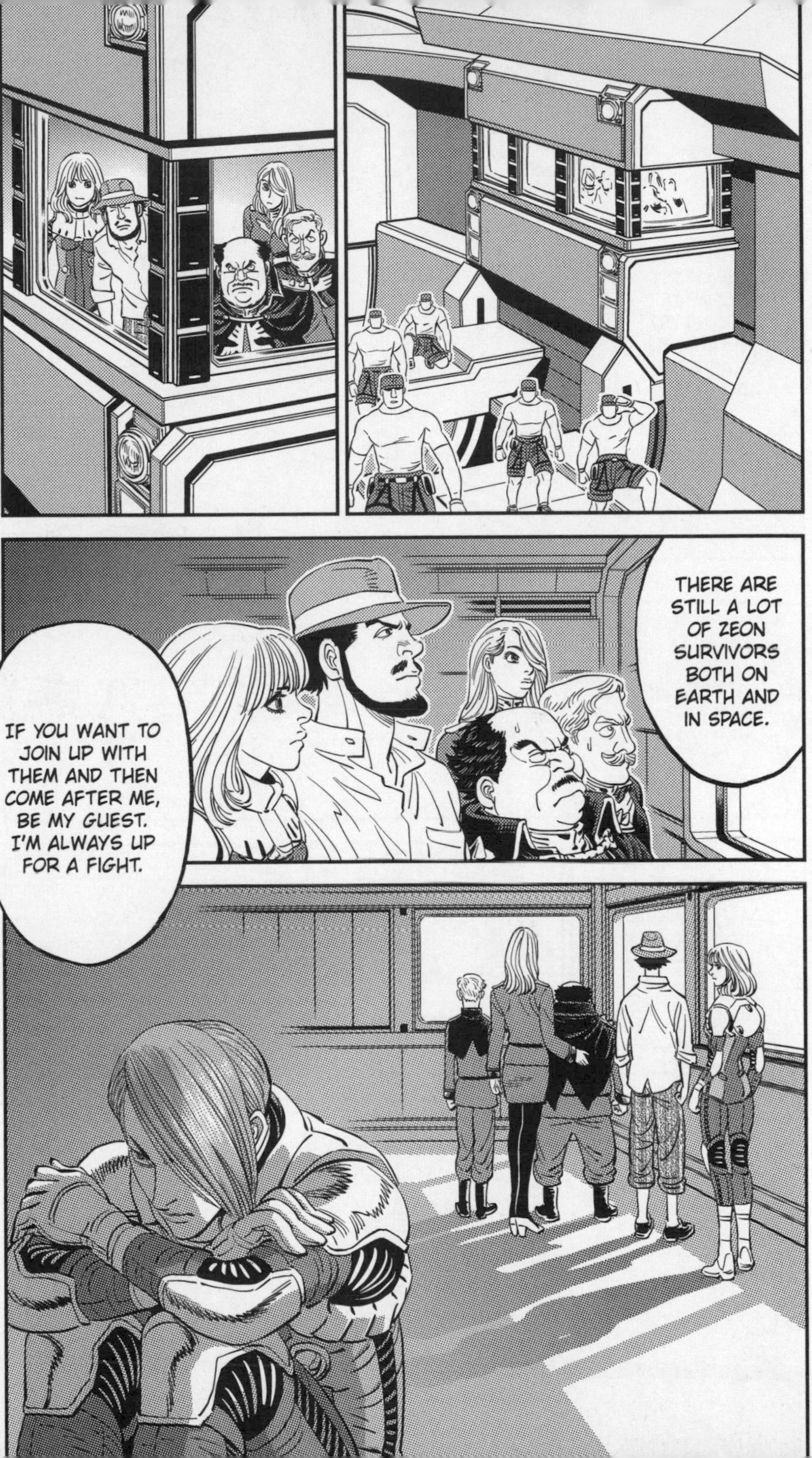
THERE ARE STILL A LOT OF ZEON SURVIVORS BOTH ON EARTH AND IN SPACE.
IF YOU WANT TO JOIN UP WITH THEM AND THEN COME AFTER ME, BE MY GUEST. I'M ALWAYS UP FOR A FIGHT.

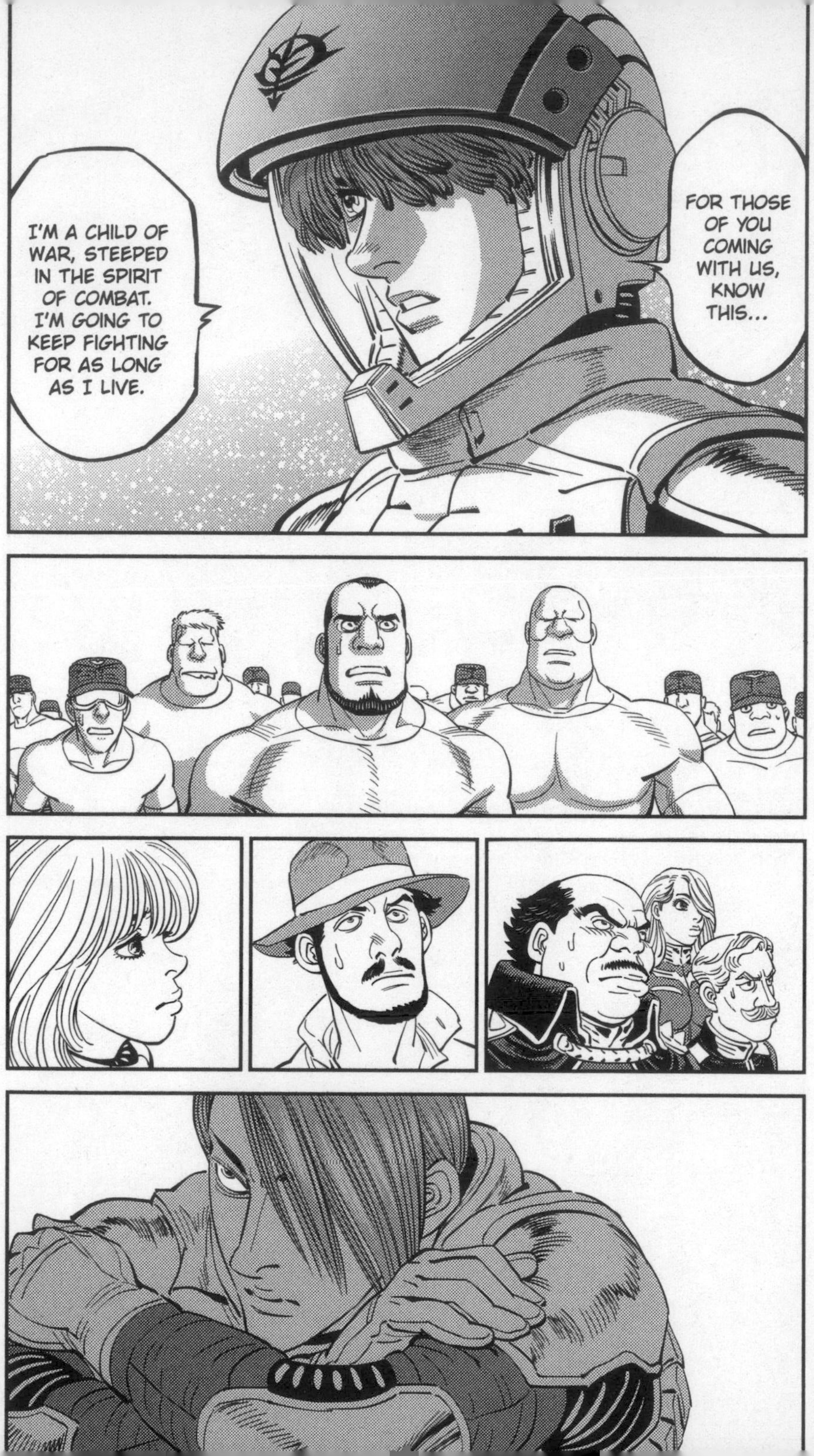
FOR THOSE OF YOU COMING WITH US, KNOW THIS...
I'M A CHILD OF WAR, STEEPED IN THE SPIRIT OF COMBAT. I'M GOING TO KEEP FIGHTING FOR AS LONG AS I LIVE.

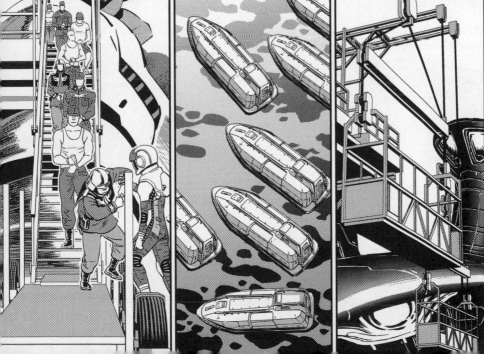

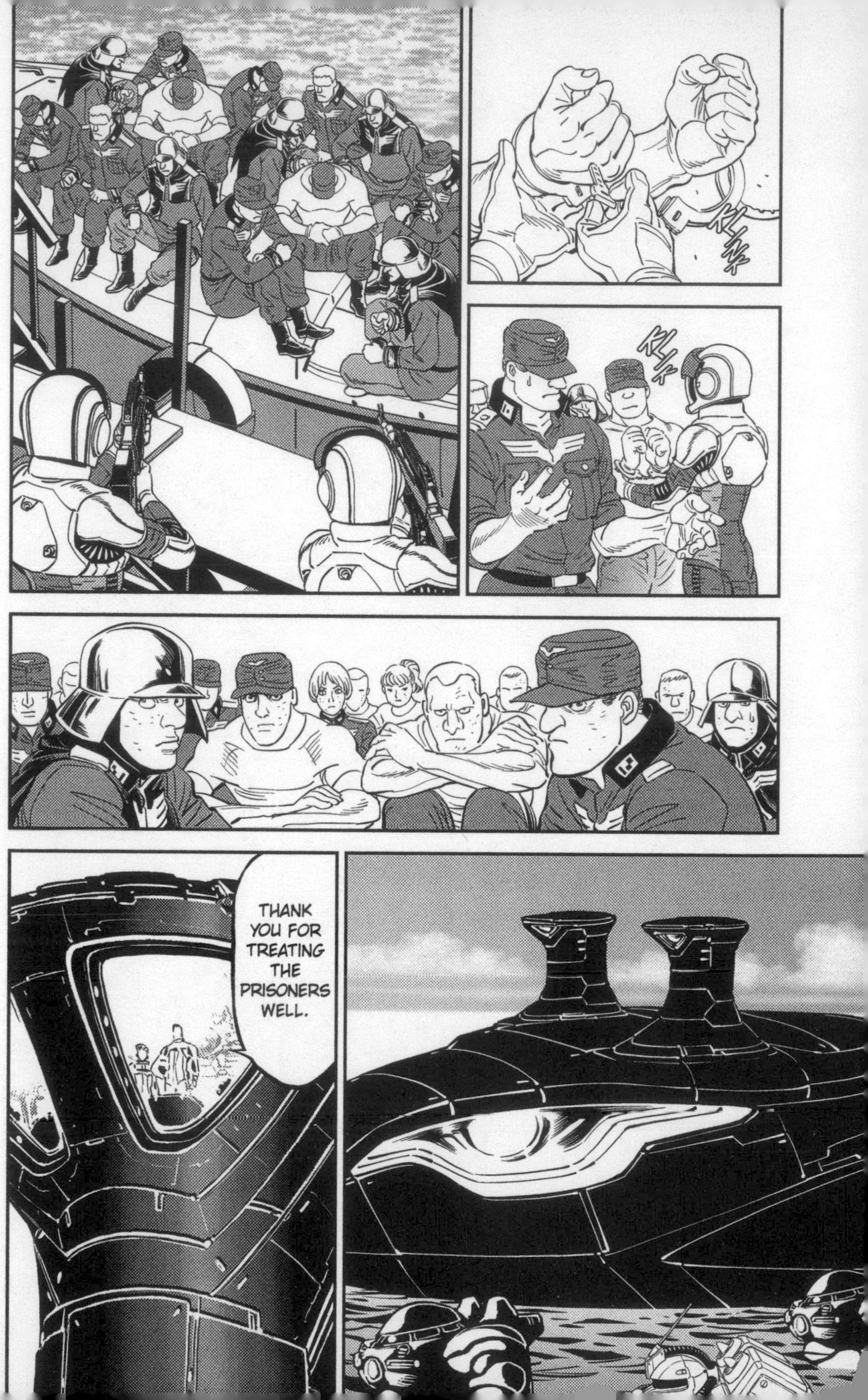
KLINK
KLIK
THANK YOU FOR TREATING THE PRISONERS WELL.

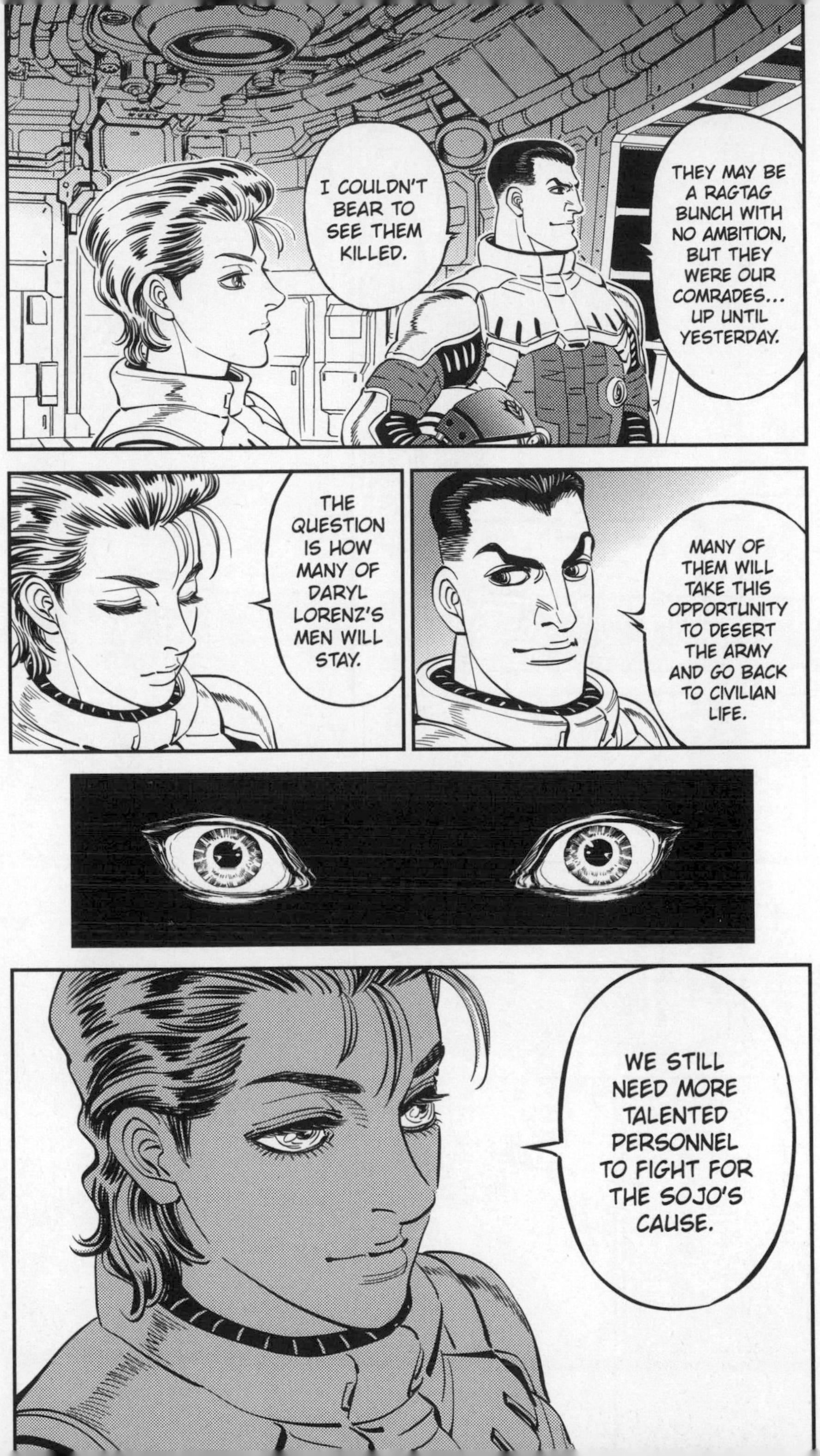
THEY MAY BE A RAGTAG BUNCH WITH NO AMBITION, BUT THEY WERE OUR COMRADES... UP UNTIL YESTERDAY.
I COULDN'T BEAR TO SEE THEM KILLED.
MANY OF THEM WILL TAKE THIS OPPORTUNITY TO DESERT THE ARMY AND GO BACK TO CIVILIAN LIFE.
THE QUESTION IS HOW MANY OF DARYL LORENZ'S MEN WILL STAY.
WE STILL NEED MORE TALENTED PERSONNEL TO FIGHT FOR THE SOJO'S CAUSE.

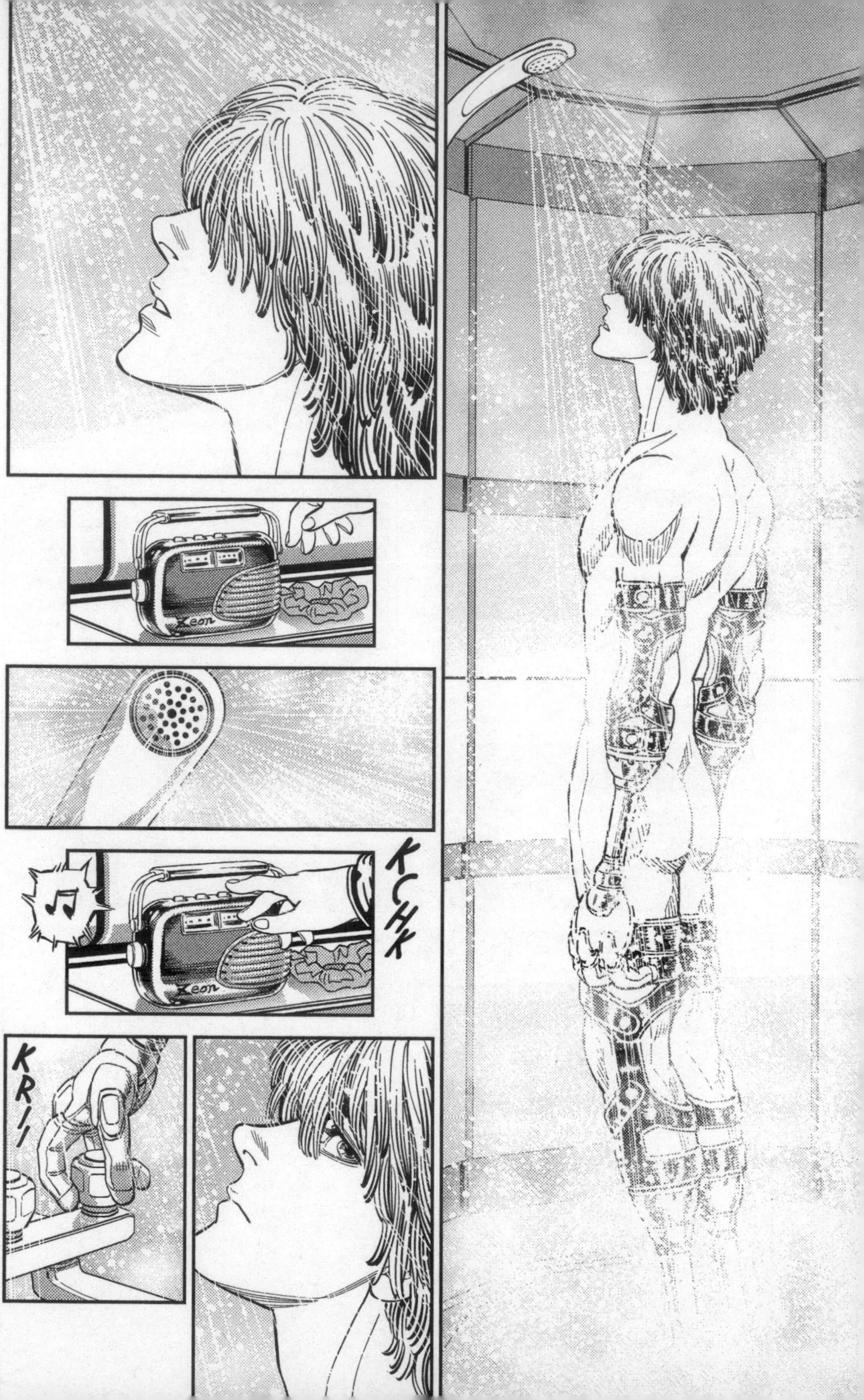
Xeon
KCHK
♪
Xeon
KRII

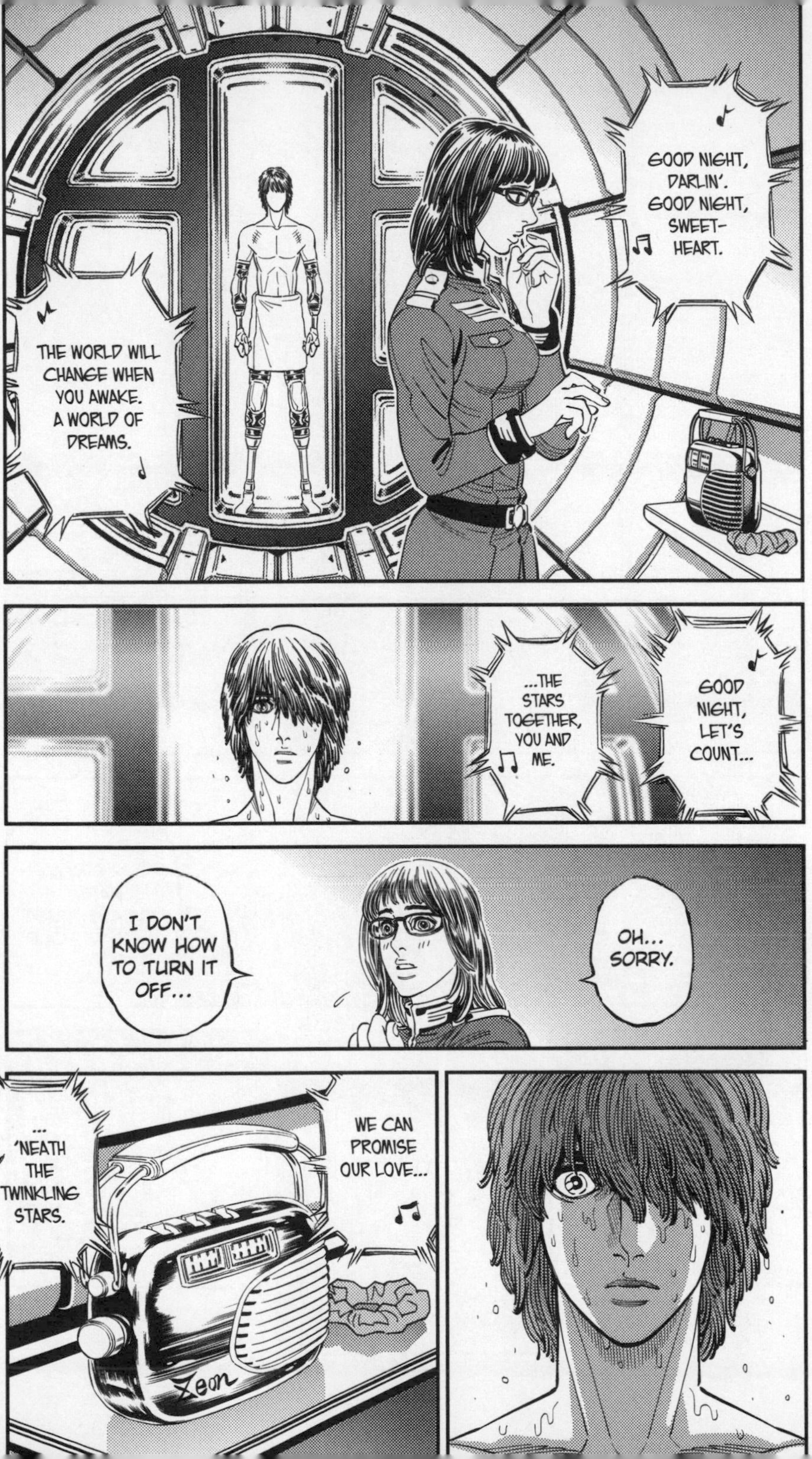
GOOD NIGHT, DARLIN'. GOOD NIGHT, SWEET-HEART.
THE WORLD WILL CHANGE WHEN YOU AWAKE. A WORLD OF DREAMS.
GOOD NIGHT, LET'S COUNT...
...THE STARS TOGETHER, YOU AND ME.
OH... SORRY.
I DON'T KNOW HOW TO TURN IT OFF...
WE CAN PROMISE OUR LOVE...
...'NEATH THE TWINKLING STARS.
Zeon

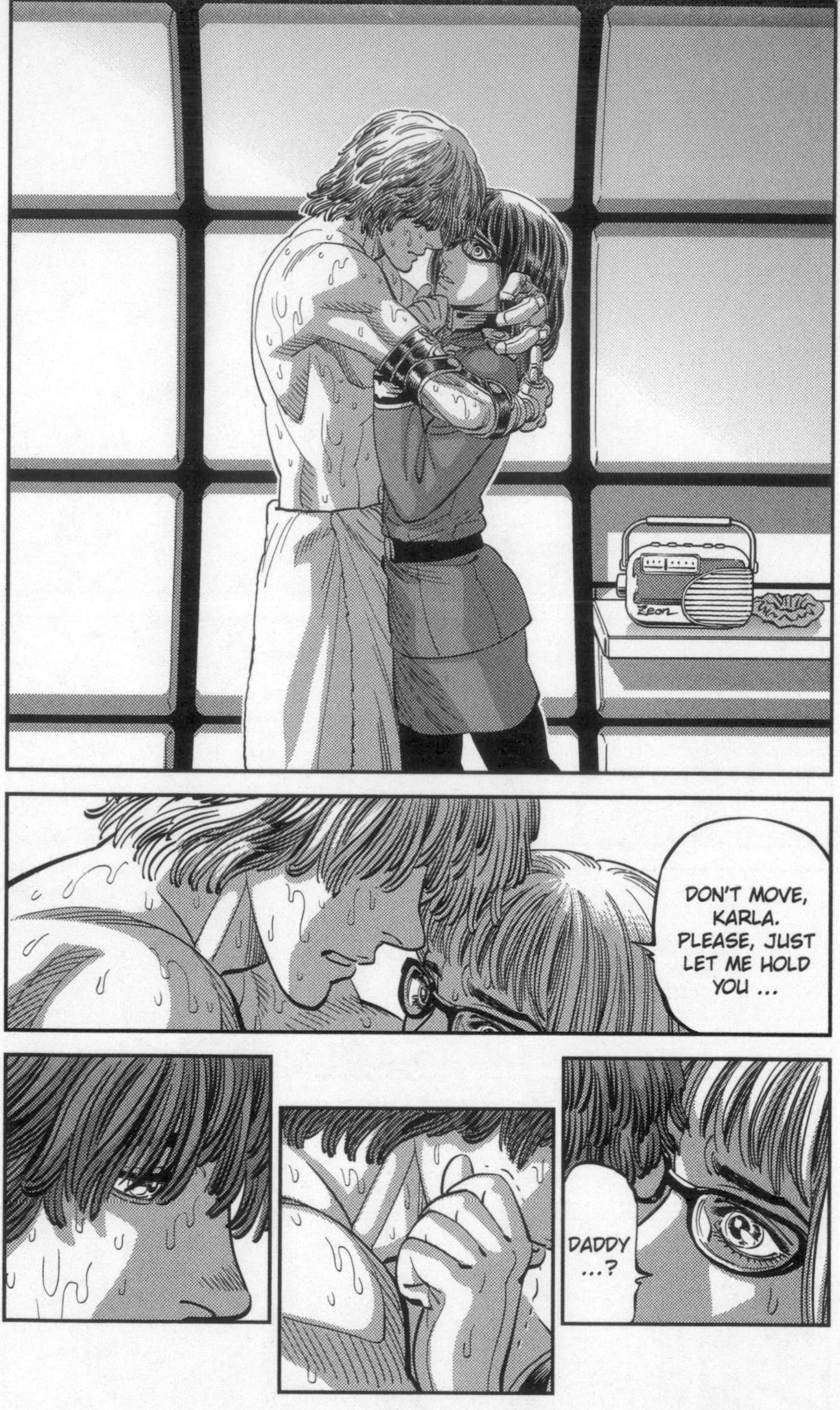
Zeon
DON'T MOVE, KARLA. PLEASE, JUST LET ME HOLD YOU ...
DADDY ...?

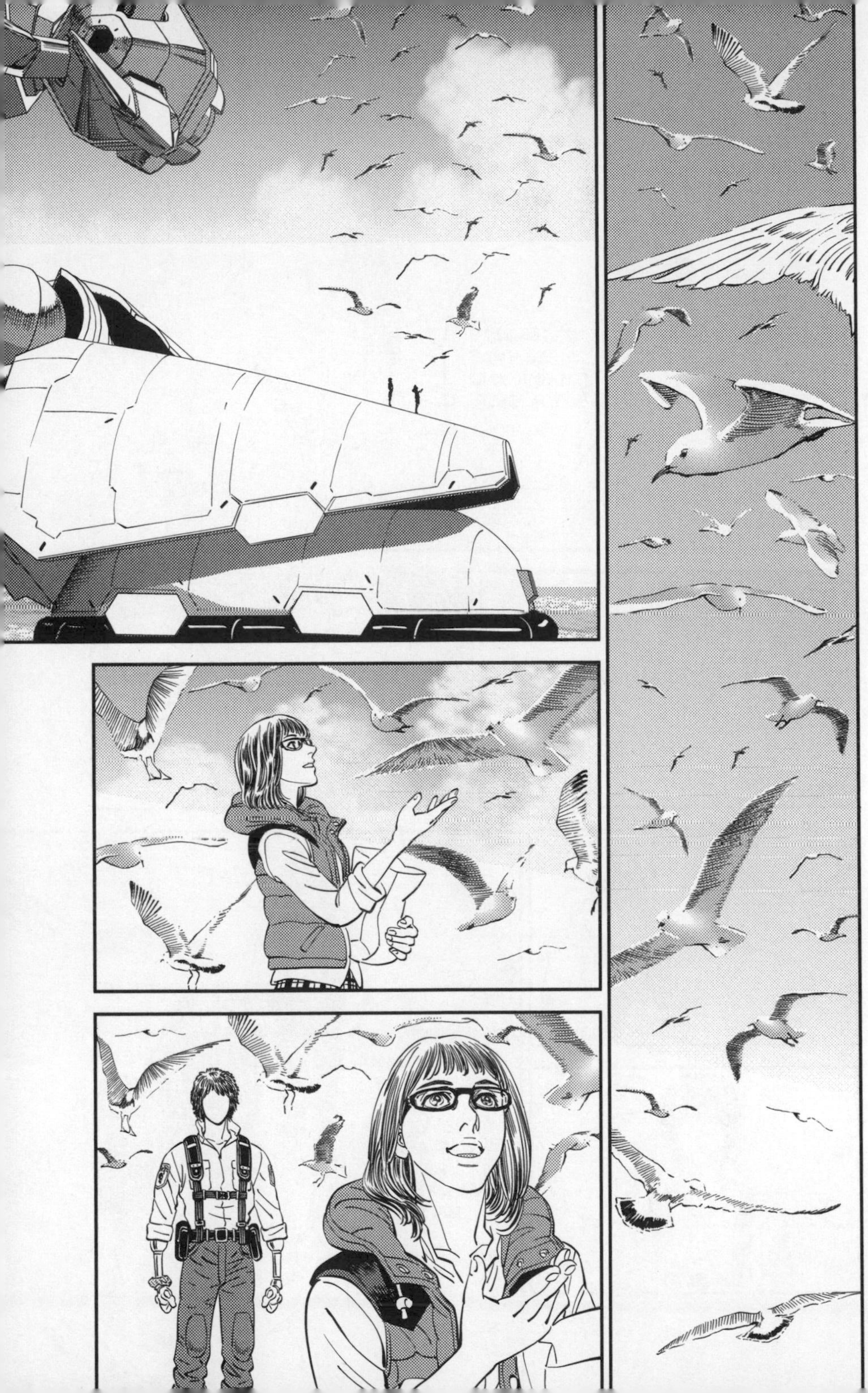

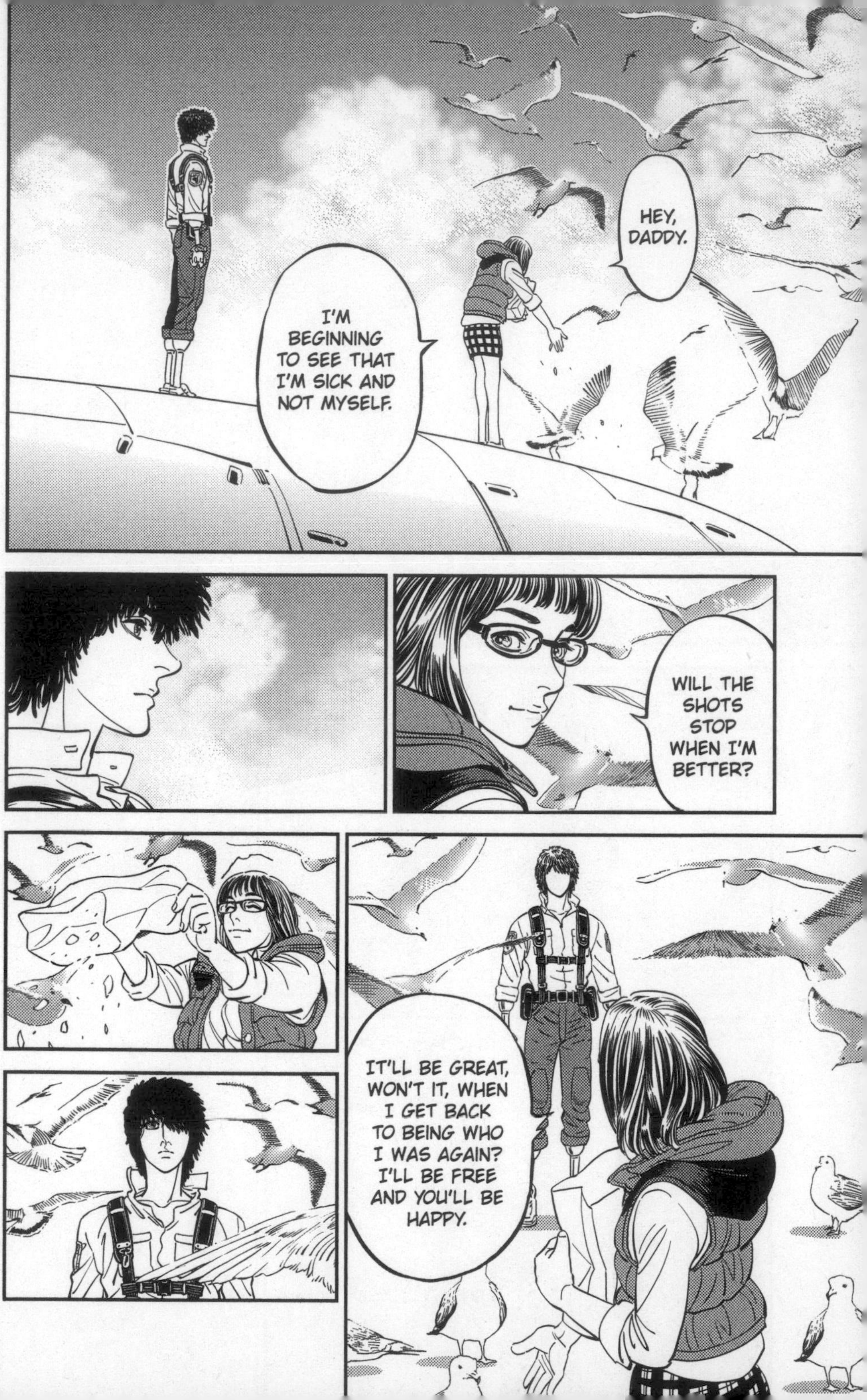
HEY, DADDY.
I'M BEGINNING TO SEE THAT I'M SICK AND NOT MYSELF.
WILL THE SHOTS STOP WHEN I'M BETTER?
IT'LL BE GREAT, WON'T IT, WHEN I GET BACK TO BEING WHO I WAS AGAIN? I'LL BE FREE AND YOU'LL BE HAPPY.

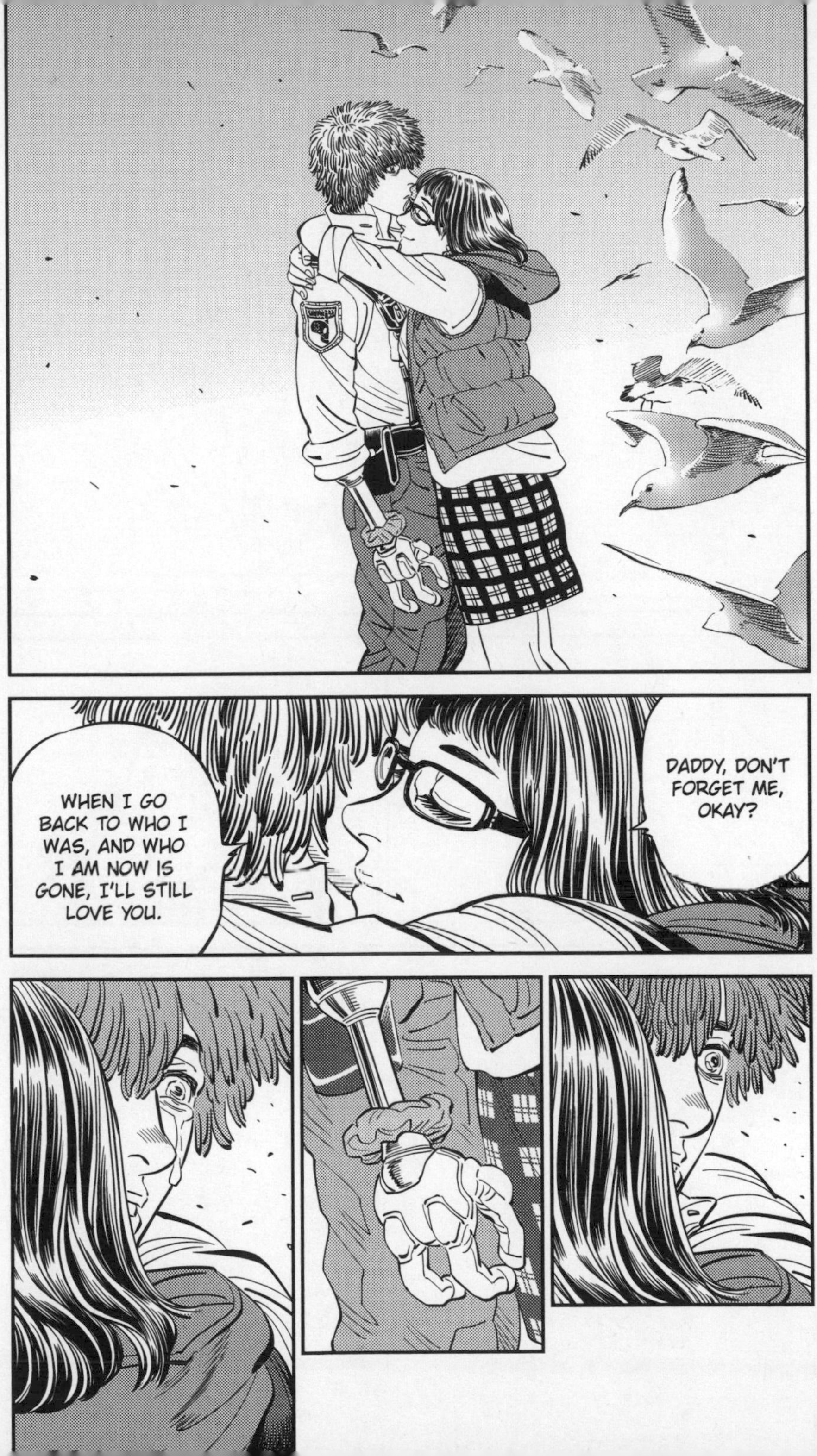
DADDY, DON'T FORGET ME, OKAY?
WHEN I GO BACK TO WHO I WAS, AND WHO I AM NOW IS GONE, I'LL STILL LOVE YOU.

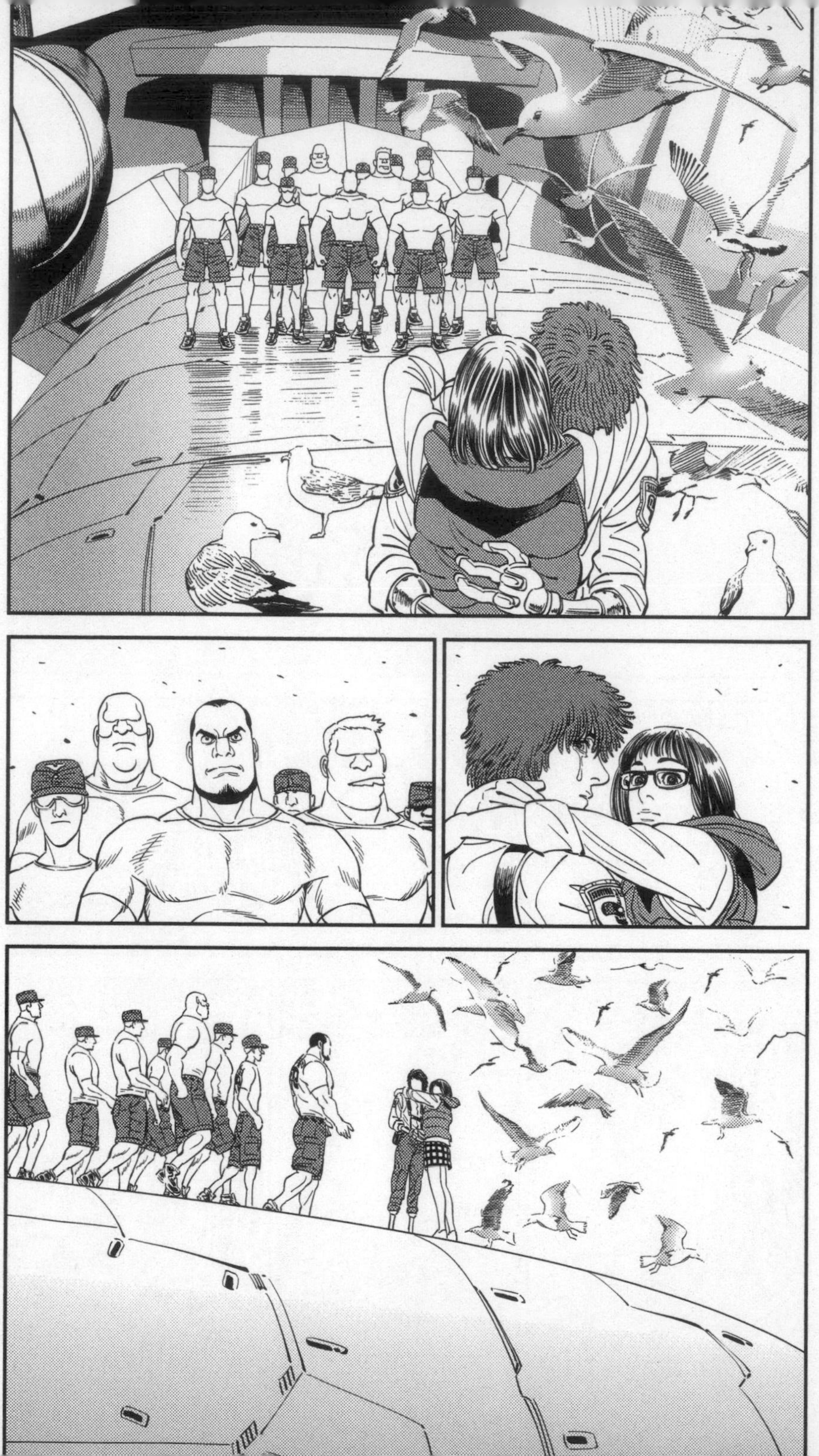

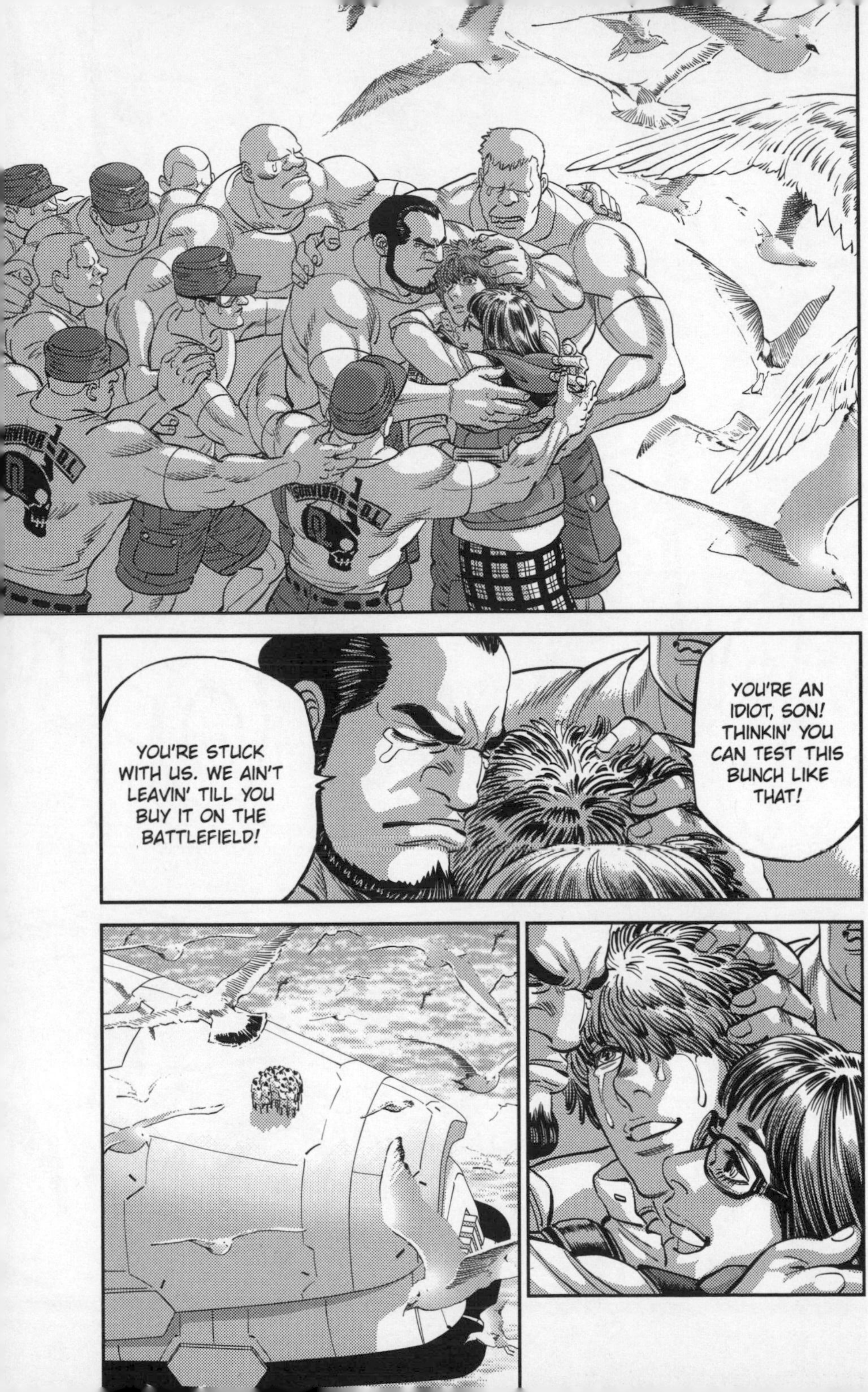
YOU'RE AN IDIOT, SON! THINKIN' YOU CAN TEST THIS BUNCH LIKE THAT!
YOU'RE STUCK WITH US. WE AIN'T LEAVIN' TILL YOU BUY IT ON THE BATTLEFIELD!

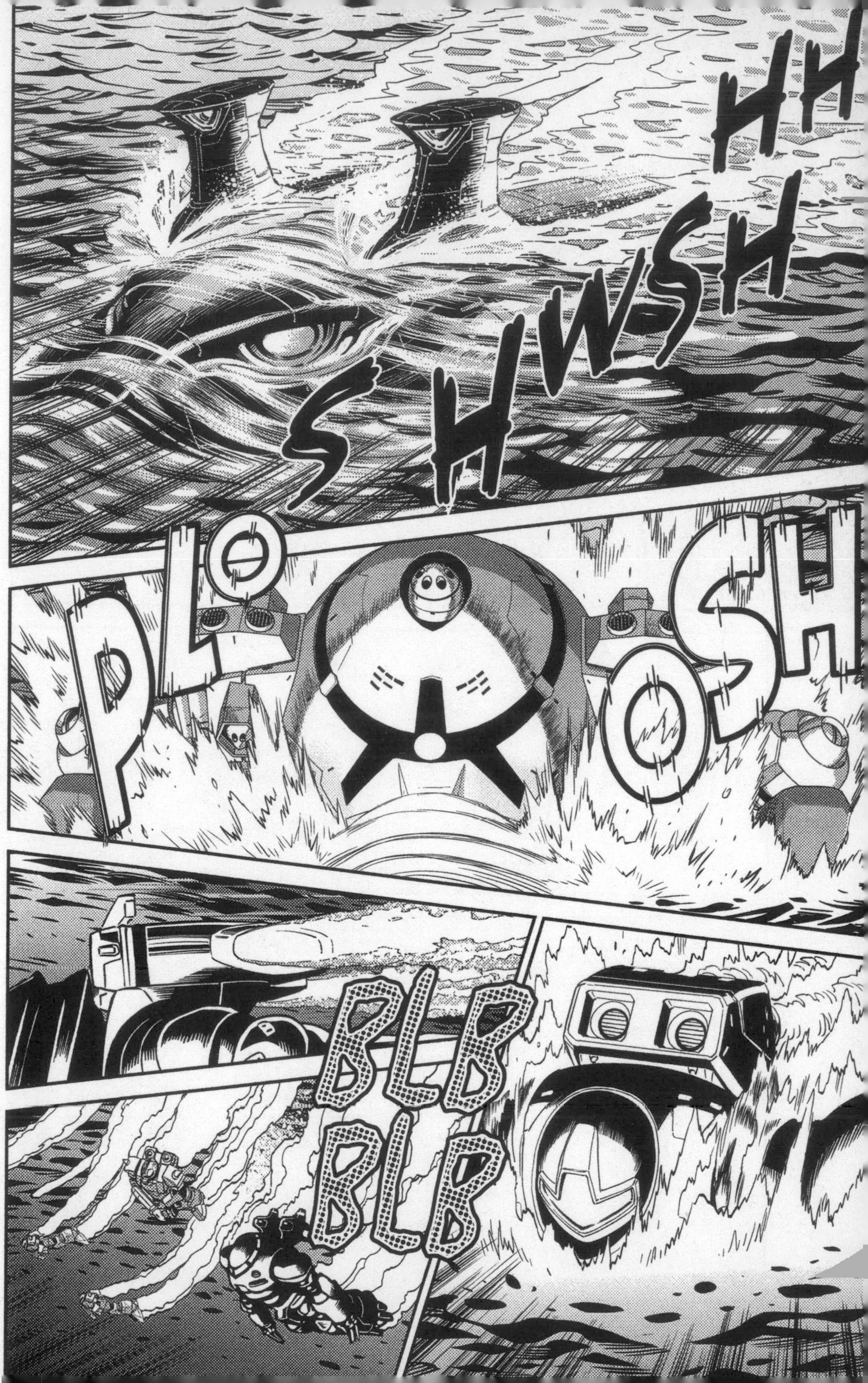
SHWSHHH
PLOOSH
BLB
BLB

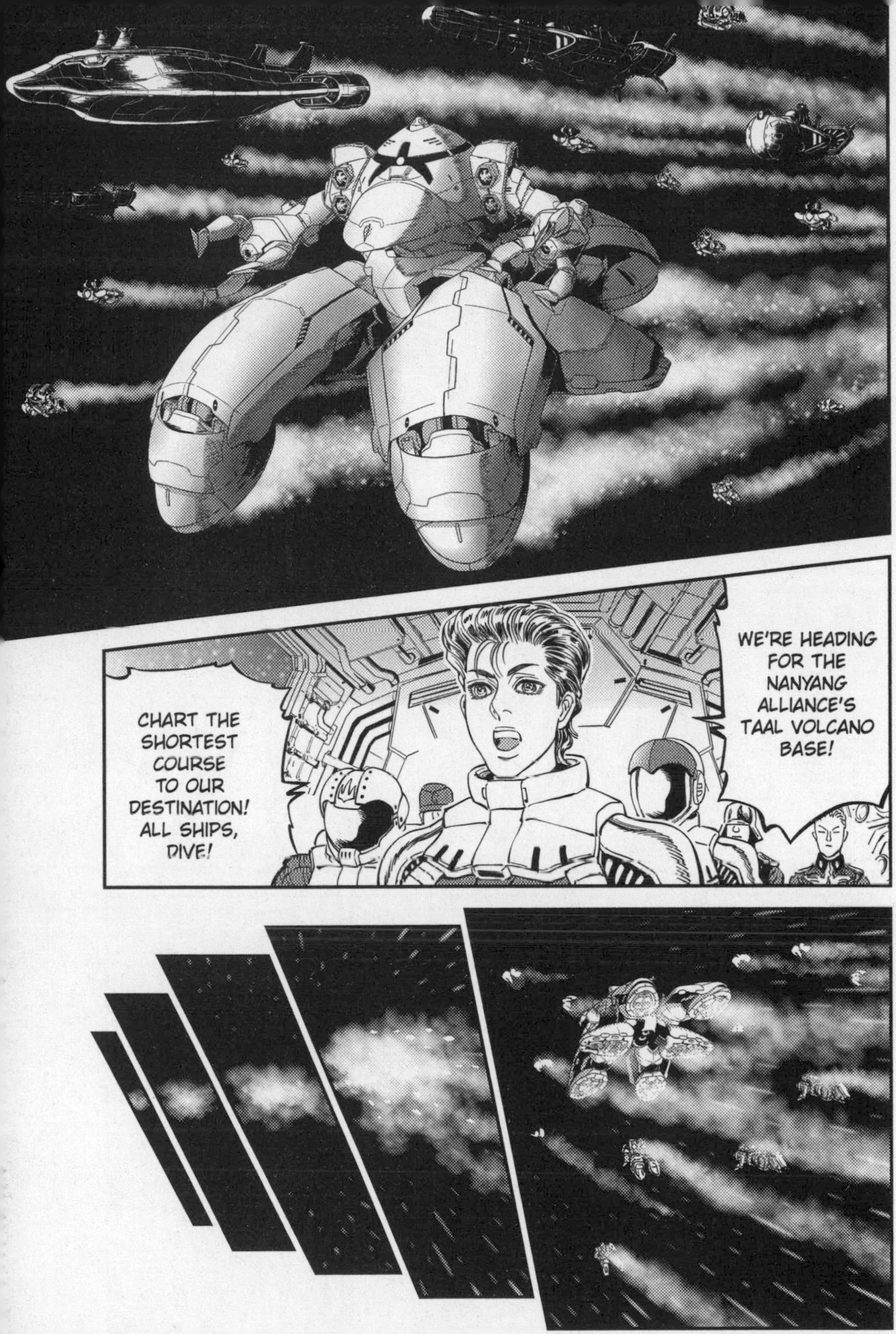
WE'RE HEADING FOR THE NANYANG ALLIANCE'S TAAL VOLCANO BASE!
CHART THE SHORTEST COURSE TO OUR DESTINATION! ALL SHIPS, DIVE!

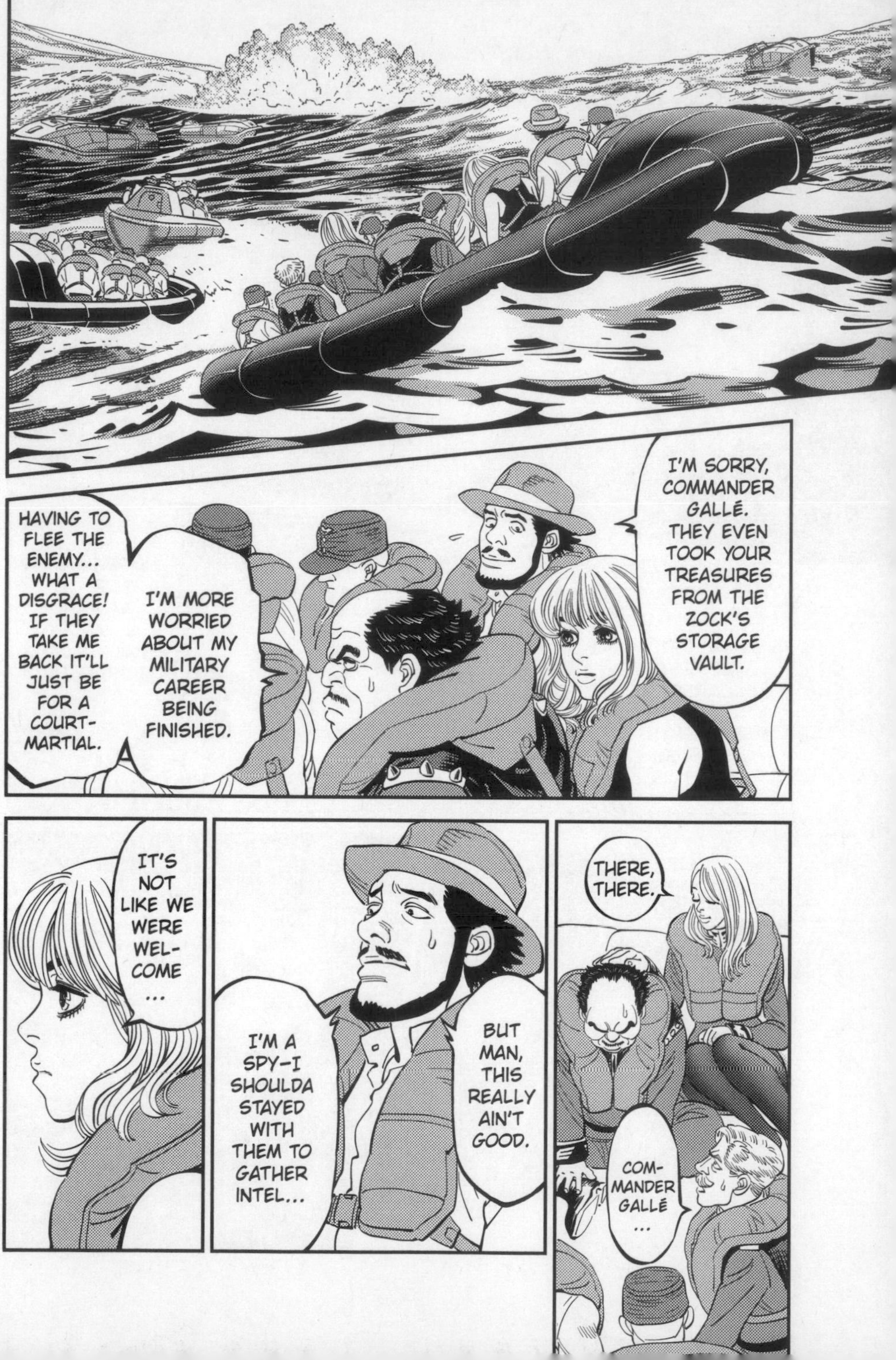

I'M SORRY, COMMANDER GALLÉ. THEY EVEN TOOK YOUR TREASURES FROM THE ZOCK'S STORAGE VAULT.
I'M MORE WORRIED ABOUT MY MILITARY CAREER BEING FINISHED.
HAVING TO FLEE THE ENEMY... WHAT A DISGRACE! IF THEY TAKE ME BACK IT'LL JUST BE FOR A COURT-MARTIAL.
THERE, THERE.
COM-MANDER GALLÉ...
BUT MAN, THIS REALLY AIN'T GOOD.
I'M A SPY—I SHOULDA STAYED WITH THEM TO GATHER INTEL...
IT'S NOT LIKE WE WERE WEL-COME...

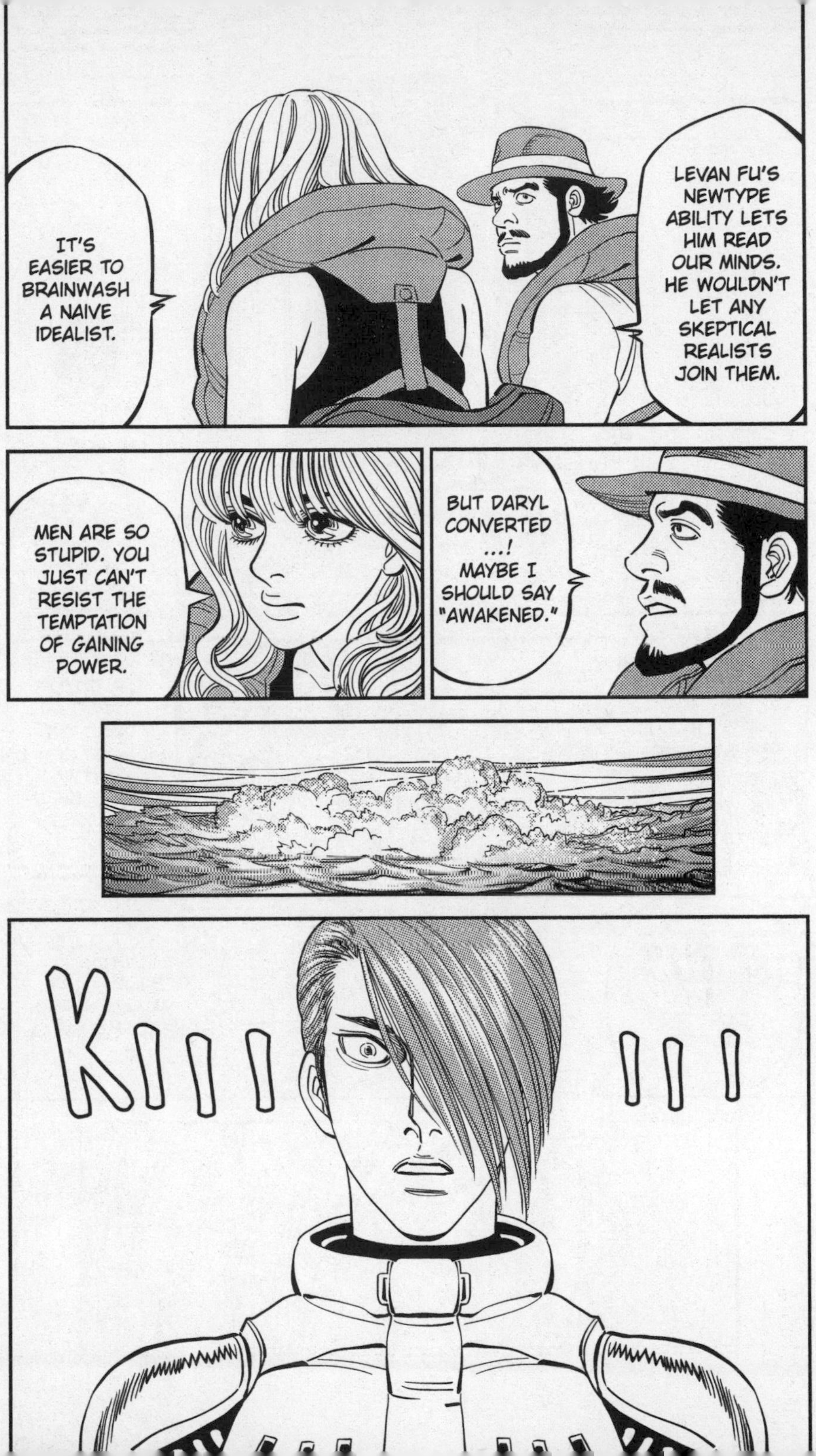
LEVAN FU'S NEWTYPE ABILITY LETS HIM READ OUR MINDS. HE WOULDN'T LET ANY SKEPTICAL REALISTS JOIN THEM.
IT'S EASIER TO BRAINWASH A NAIVE IDEALIST.
BUT DARYL CONVERTED ...! MAYBE I SHOULD SAY "AWAKENED."
MEN ARE SO STUPID. YOU JUST CAN'T RESIST THE TEMPTATION OF GAINING POWER.
KIIII IIII

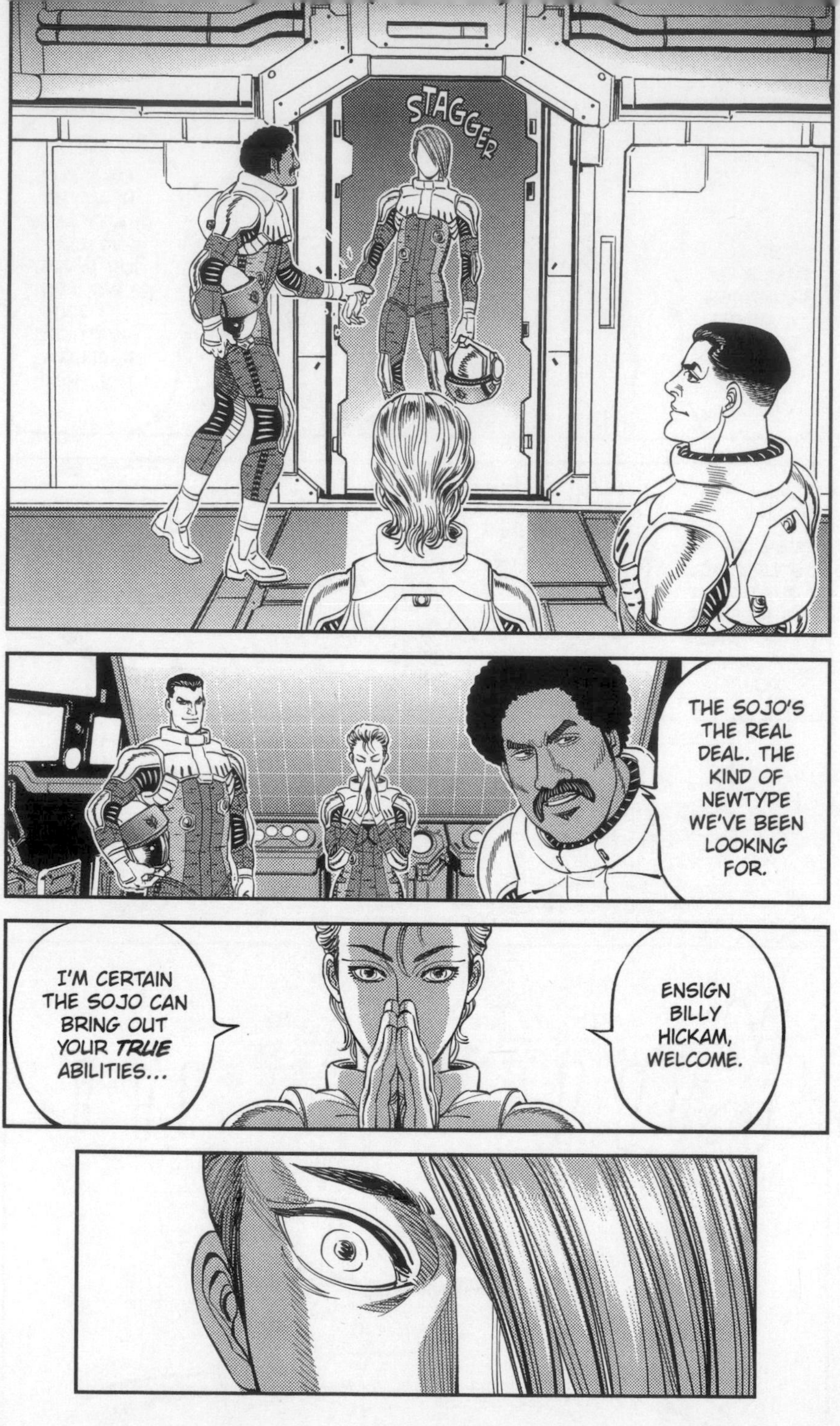
STAGGER
THE SOJO'S THE REAL DEAL. THE KIND OF NEWTYPE WE'VE BEEN LOOKING FOR.
ENSIGN BILLY HICKAM, WELCOME.
I'M CERTAIN THE SOJO CAN BRING OUT YOUR *TRUE* ABILITIES...

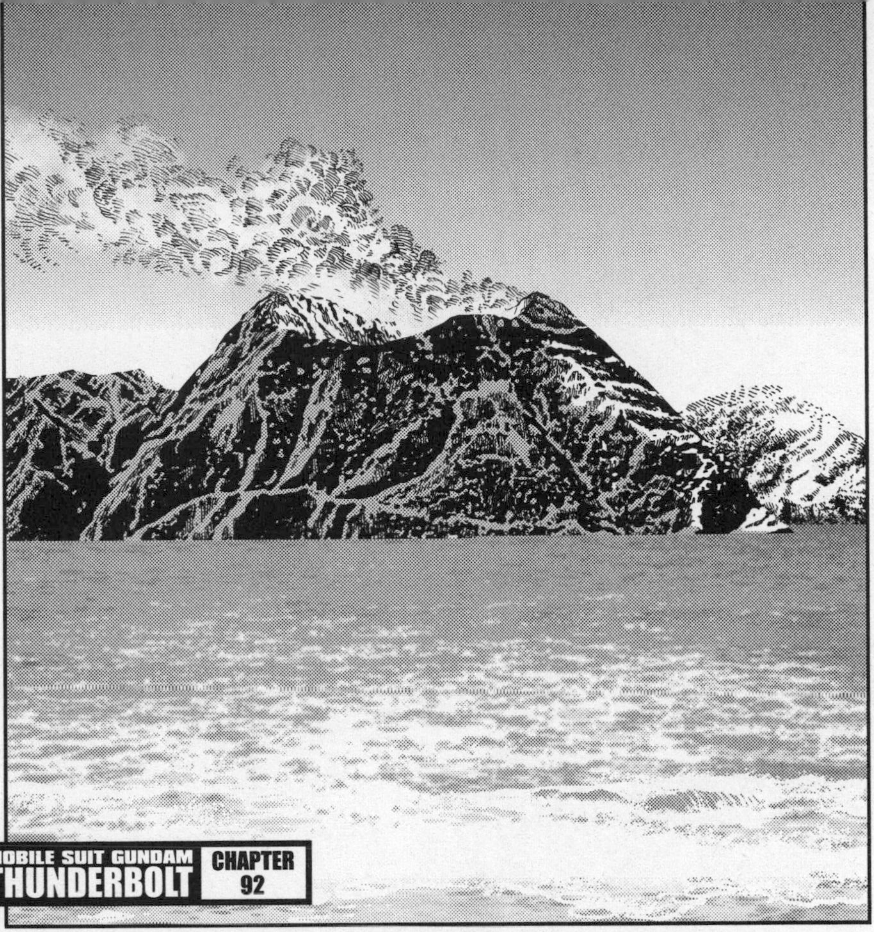
MOBILE SUIT GUNDAM
THUNDERBOLT
CHAPTER
92
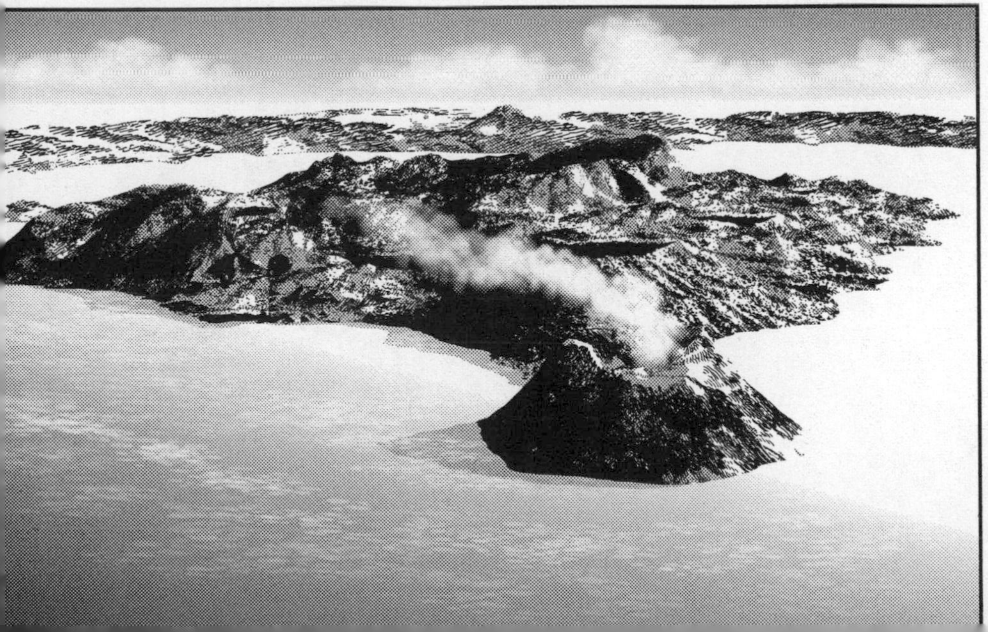

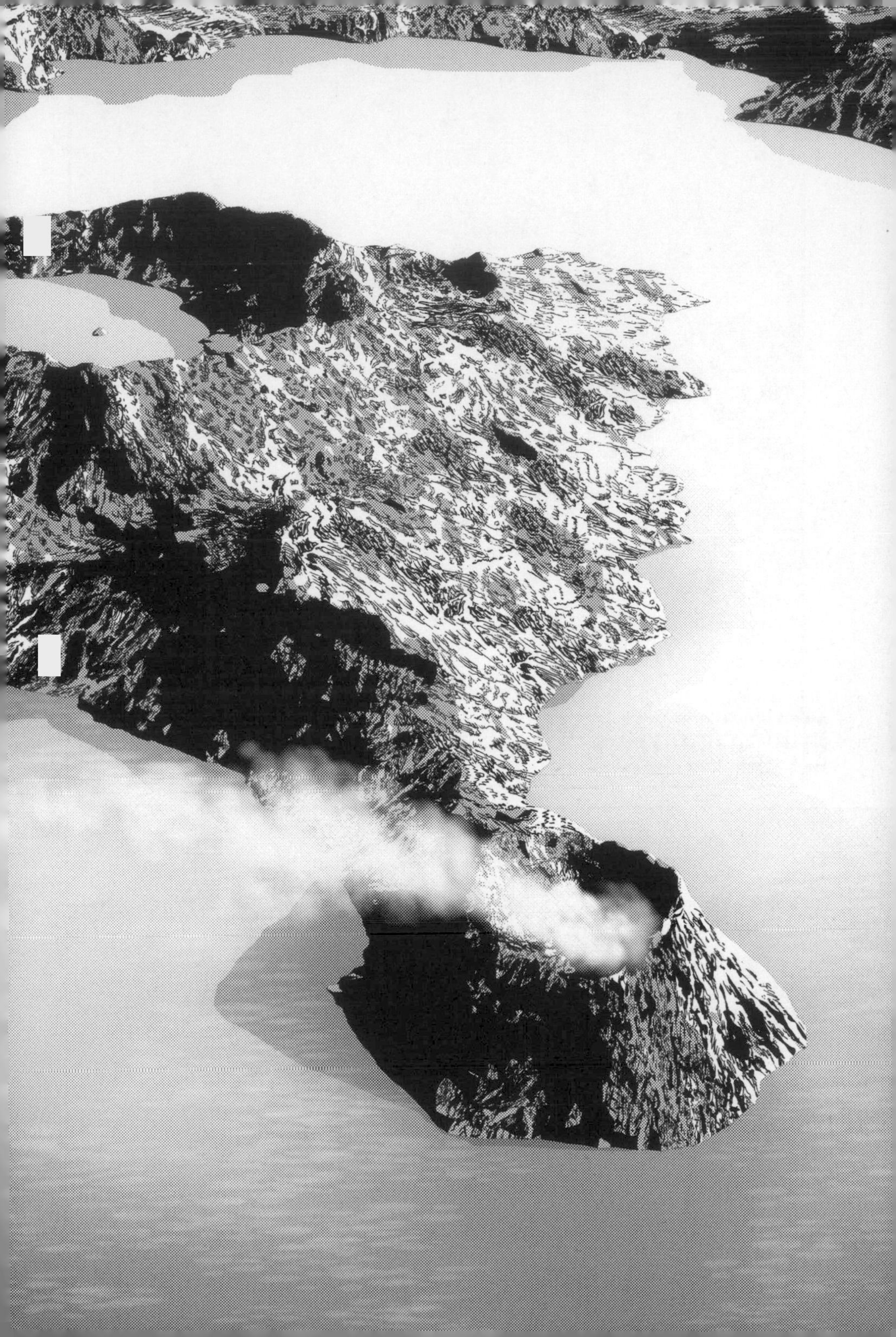

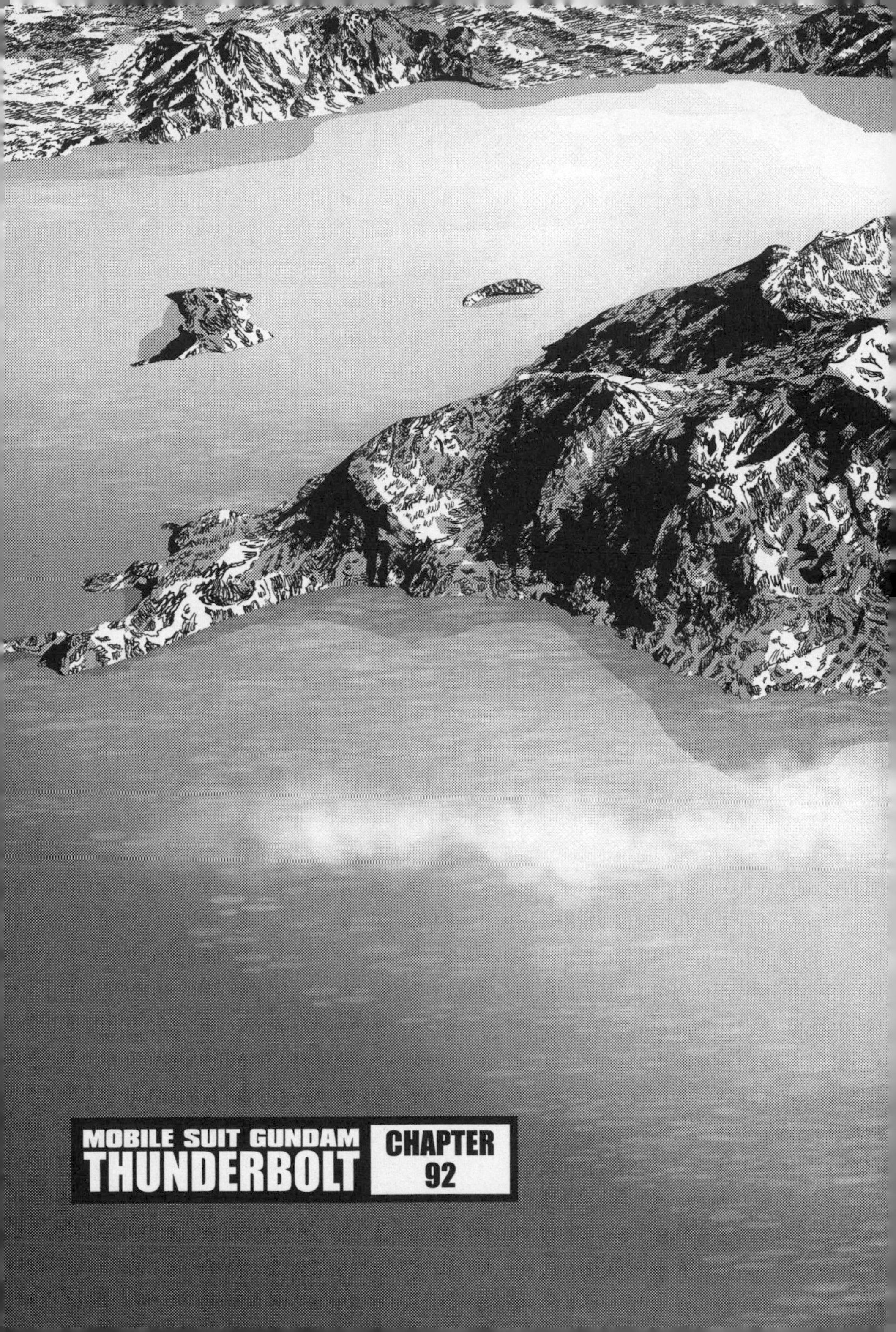
MOBILE SUIT GUNDAM
THUNDERBOLT
CHAPTER
92

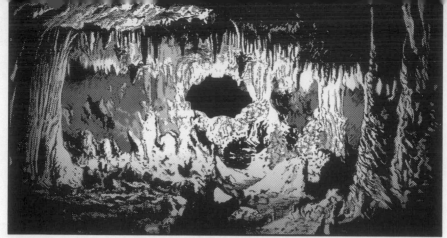

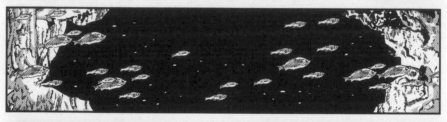

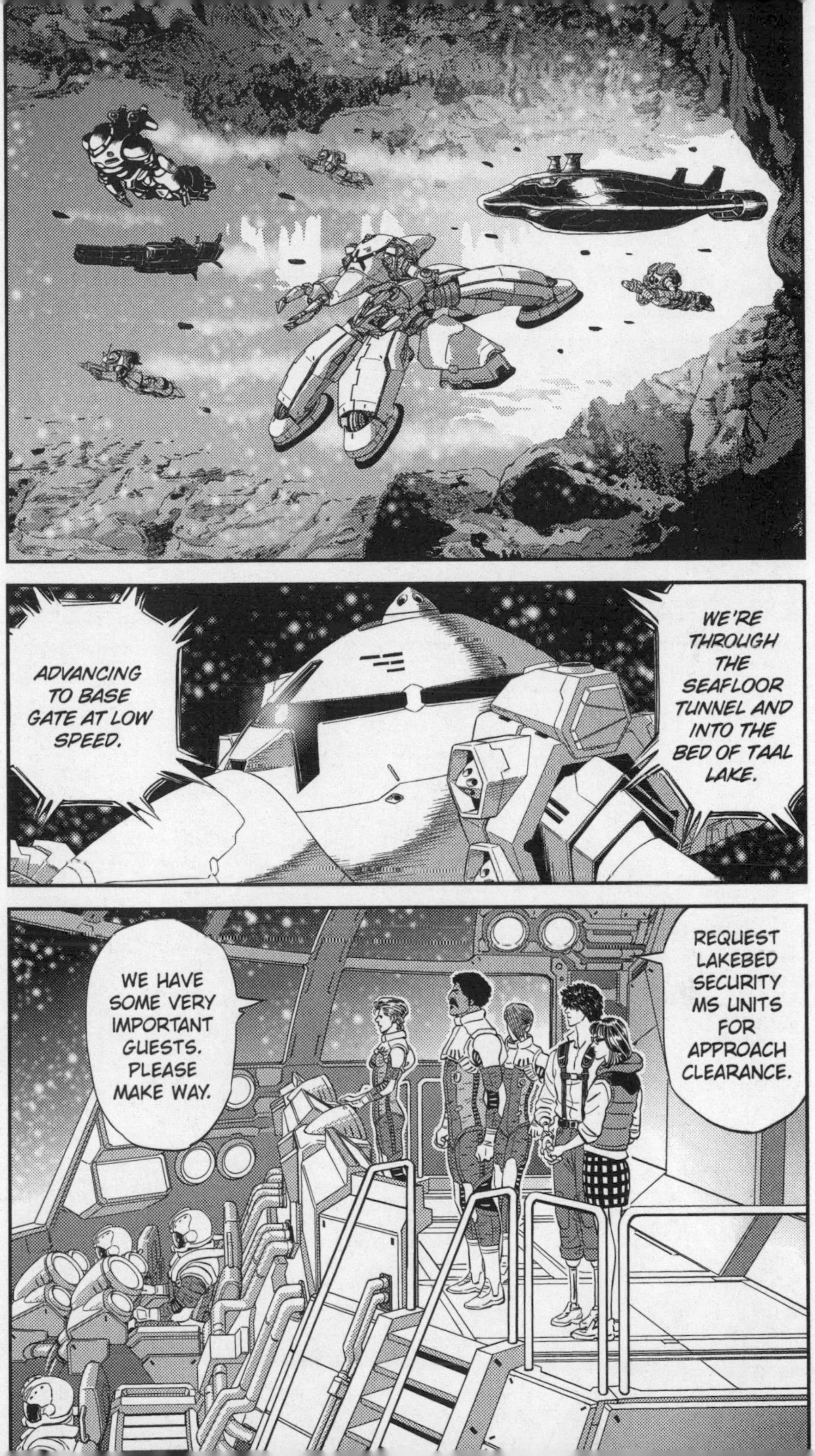
WE'RE THROUGH THE SEAFLOOR TUNNEL AND INTO THE BED OF TAAL LAKE.
ADVANCING TO BASE GATE AT LOW SPEED.
REQUEST LAKEBED SECURITY MS UNITS FOR APPROACH CLEARANCE.
WE HAVE SOME VERY IMPORTANT GUESTS. PLEASE MAKE WAY.

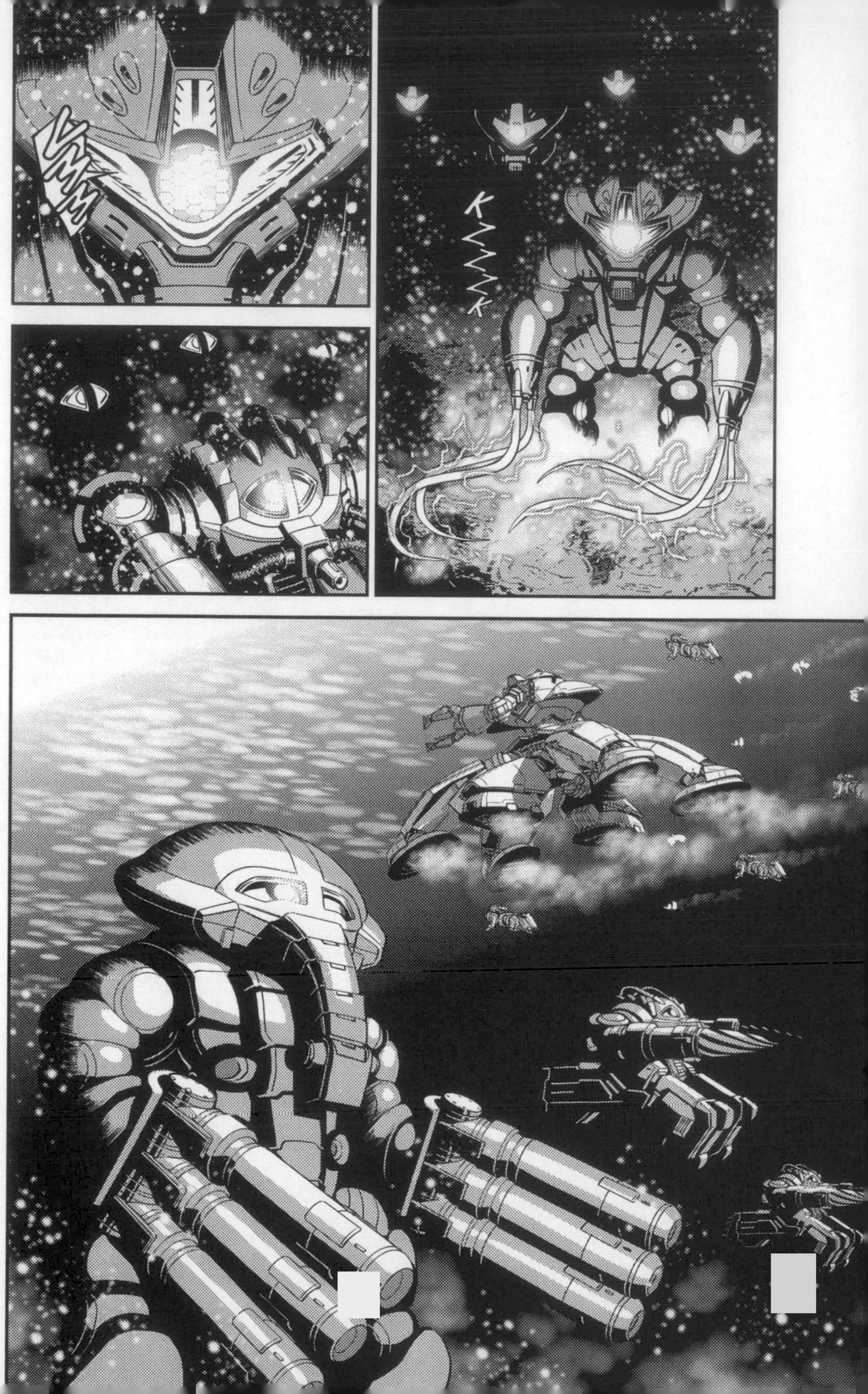
KZZZZK
VMMM

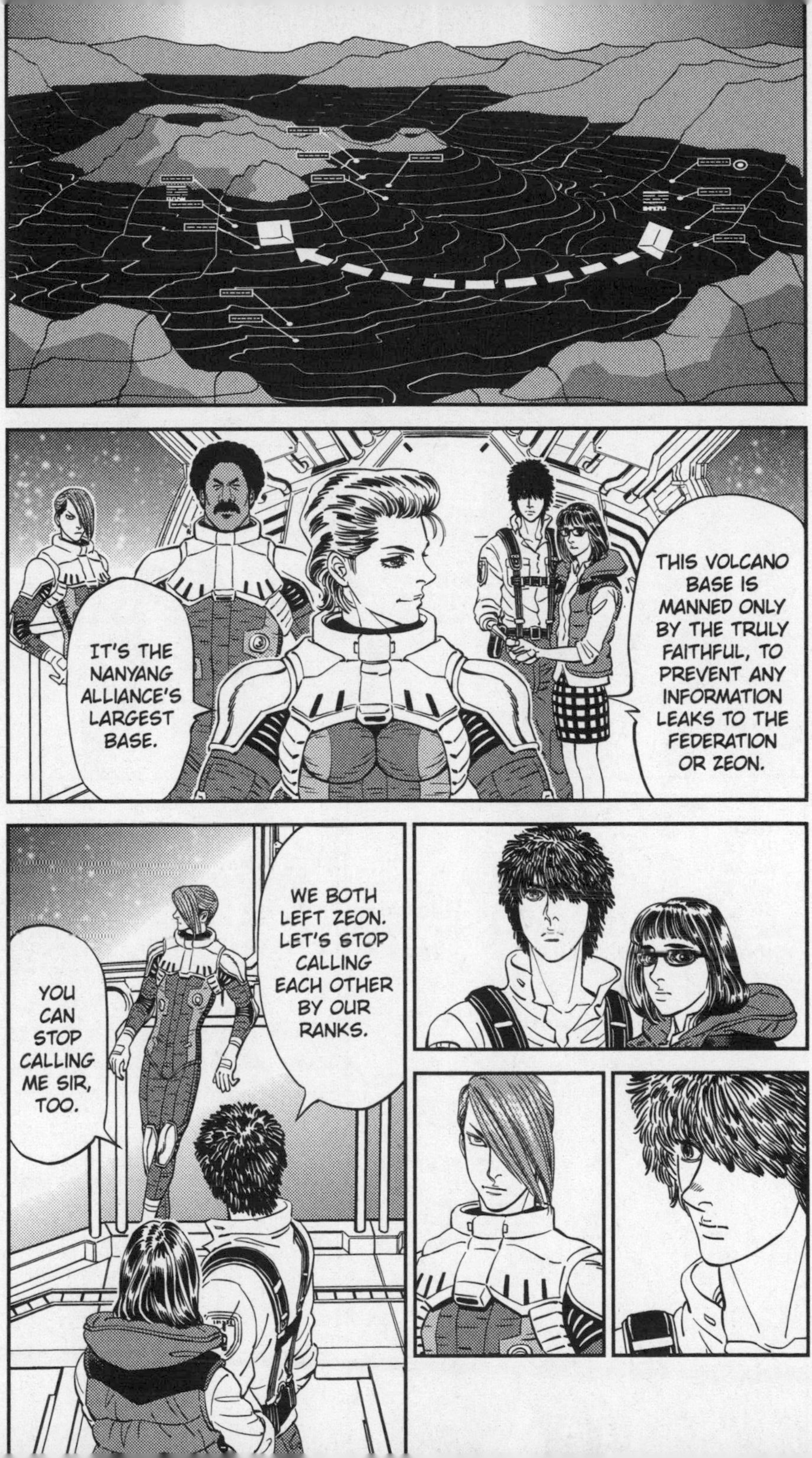
THIS VOLCANO BASE IS MANNED ONLY BY THE TRULY FAITHFUL, TO PREVENT ANY INFORMATION LEAKS TO THE FEDERATION OR ZEON.
IT'S THE NANYANG ALLIANCE'S LARGEST BASE.
WE BOTH LEFT ZEON. LET'S STOP CALLING EACH OTHER BY OUR RANKS.
YOU CAN STOP CALLING ME SIR, TOO.

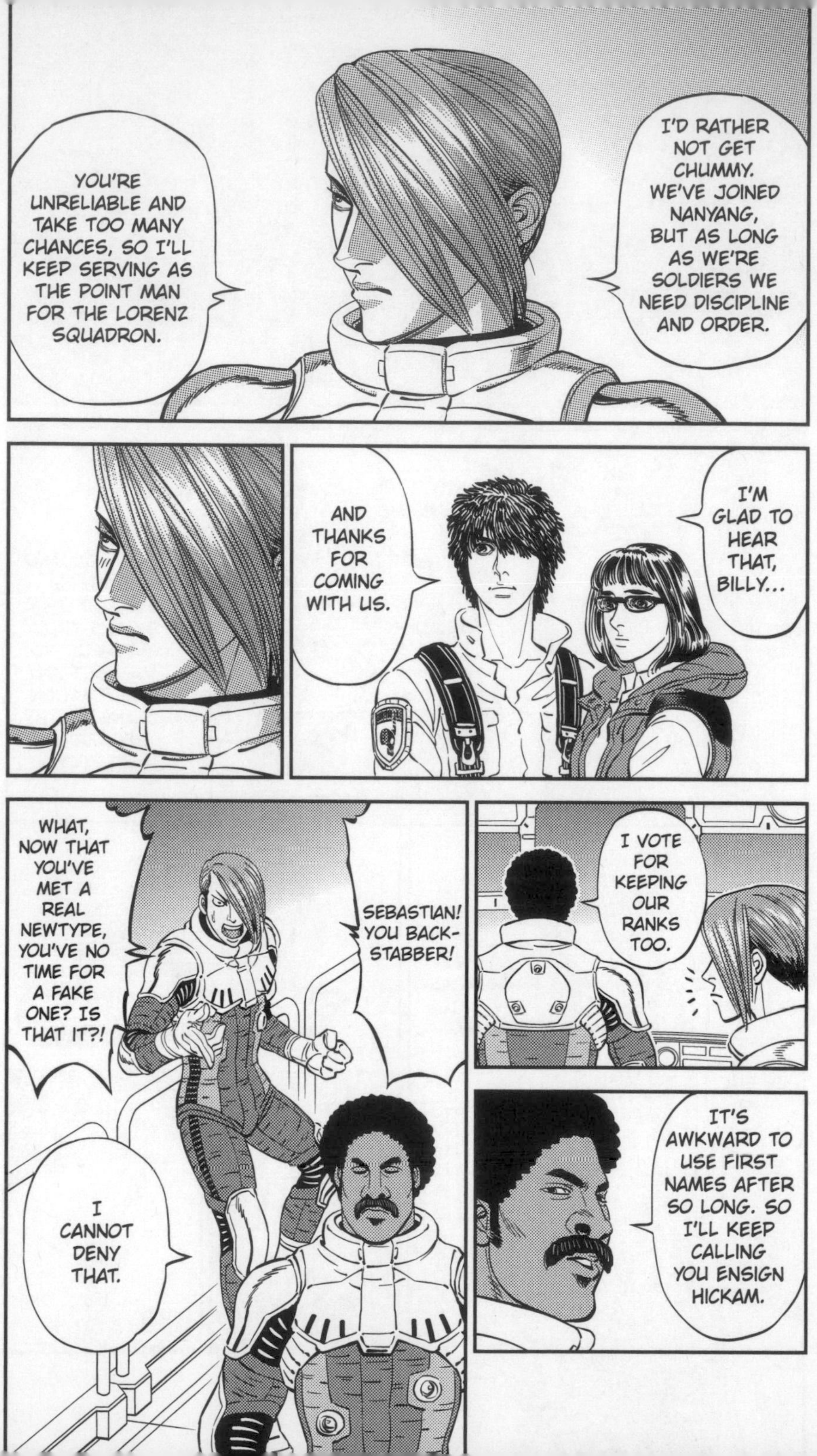
I'D RATHER NOT GET CHUMMY. WE'VE JOINED NANYANG, BUT AS LONG AS WE'RE SOLDIERS WE NEED DISCIPLINE AND ORDER.
YOU'RE UNRELIABLE AND TAKE TOO MANY CHANCES, SO I'LL KEEP SERVING AS THE POINT MAN FOR THE LORENZ SQUADRON.
I'M GLAD TO HEAR THAT, BILLY...
AND THANKS FOR COMING WITH US.
I VOTE FOR KEEPING OUR RANKS TOO.
IT'S AWKWARD TO USE FIRST NAMES AFTER SO LONG. SO I'LL KEEP CALLING YOU ENSIGN HICKAM.
SEBASTIAN! YOU BACK-STABBER!
WHAT, NOW THAT YOU'VE MET A REAL NEWTYPE, YOU'VE NO TIME FOR A FAKE ONE? IS THAT IT?!
I CANNOT DENY THAT.

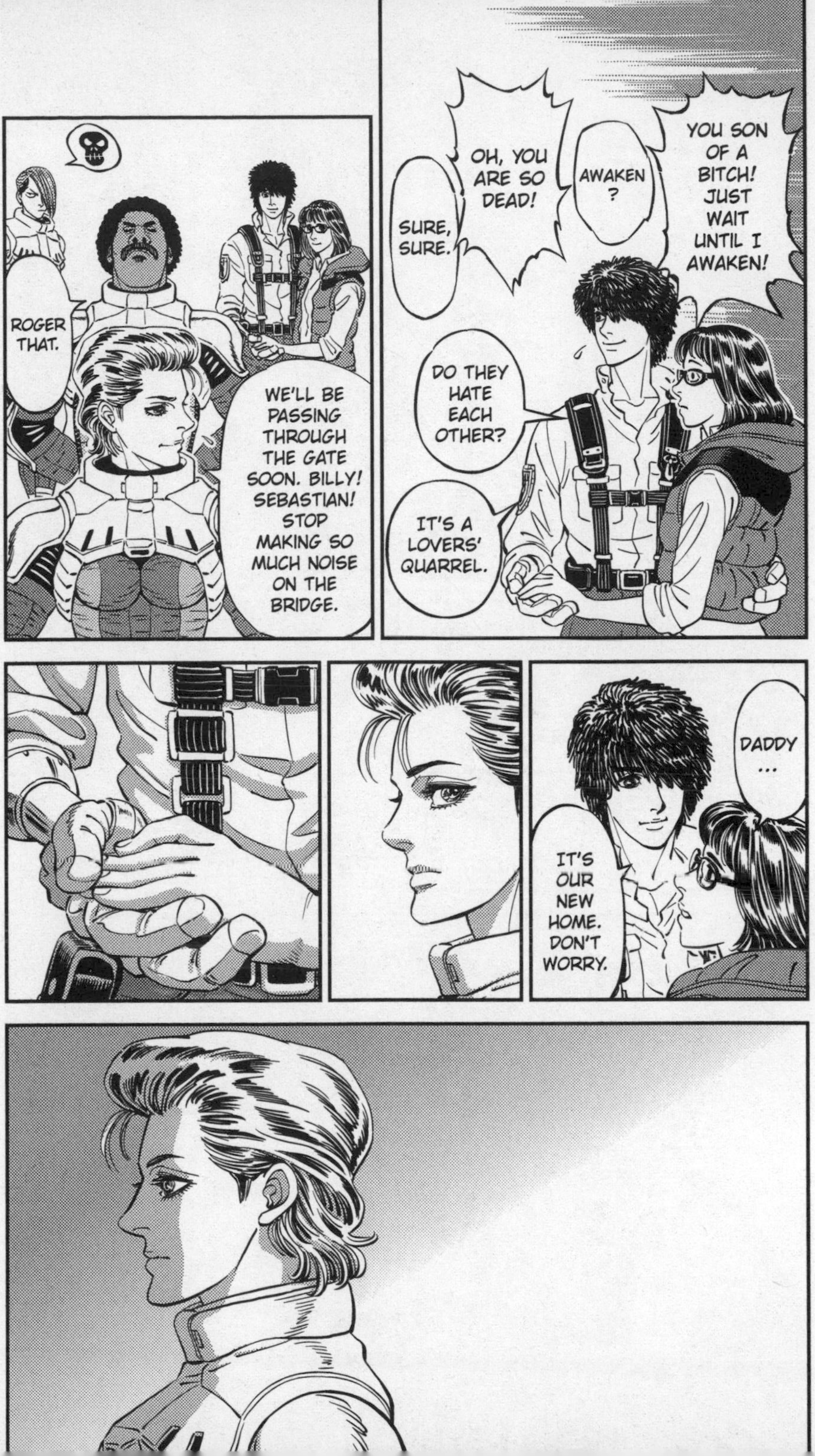
YOU SON OF A BITCH! JUST WAIT UNTIL I AWAKEN!
AWAKEN?
OH, YOU ARE SO DEAD!
SURE, SURE.
DO THEY HATE EACH OTHER?
IT'S A LOVERS' QUARREL.
WE'LL BE PASSING THROUGH THE GATE SOON. BILLY! SEBASTIAN! STOP MAKING SO MUCH NOISE ON THE BRIDGE.
ROGER THAT.
DADDY...
IT'S OUR NEW HOME. DON'T WORRY.

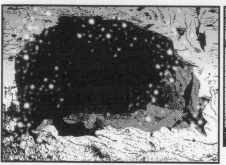

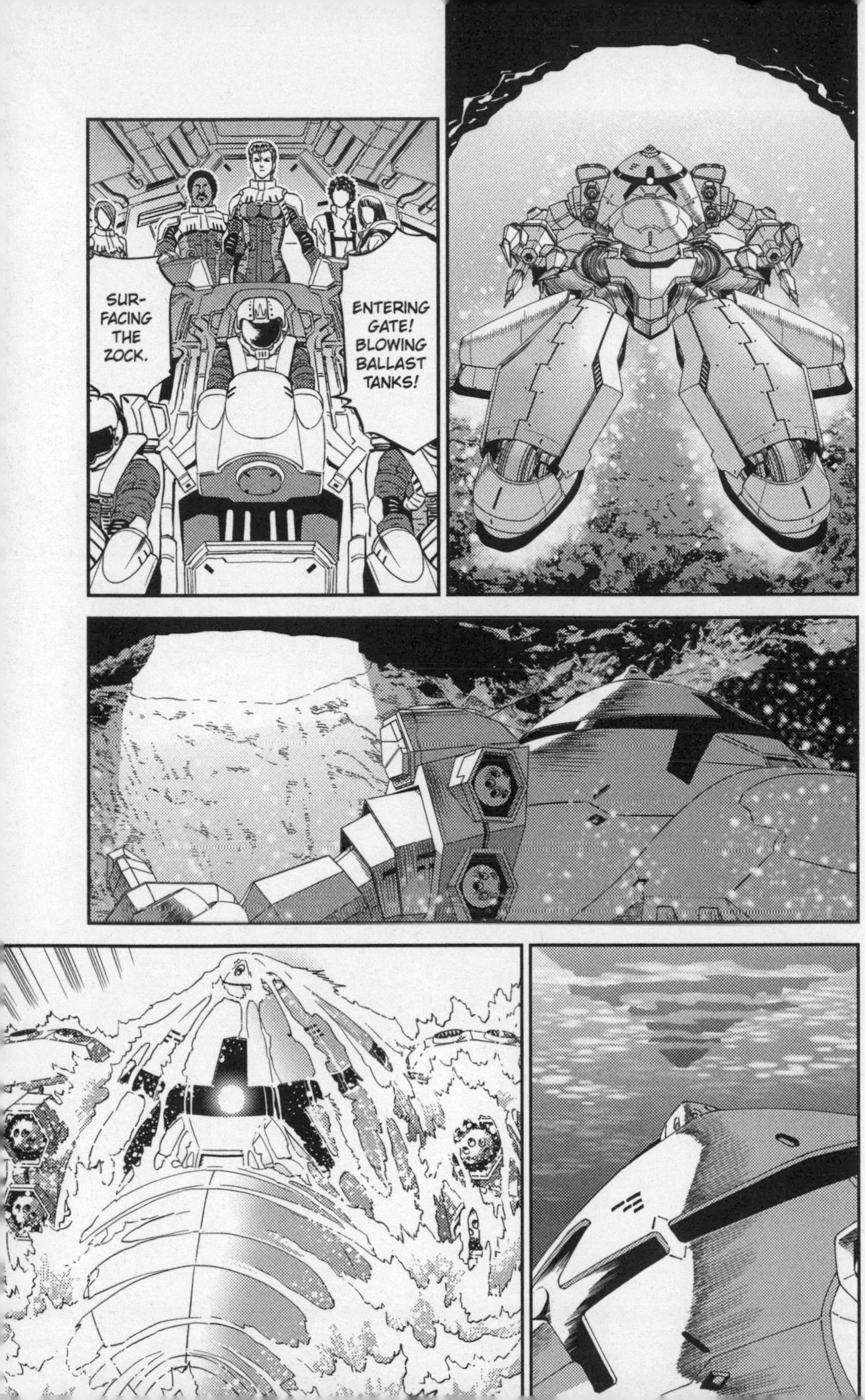
ENTERING GATE! BLOWING BALLAST TANKS!
SUR-FACING THE ZOCK.

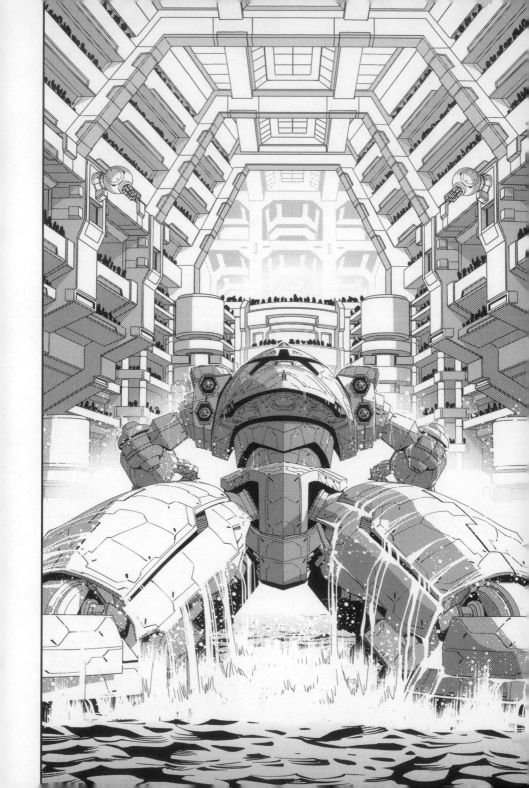

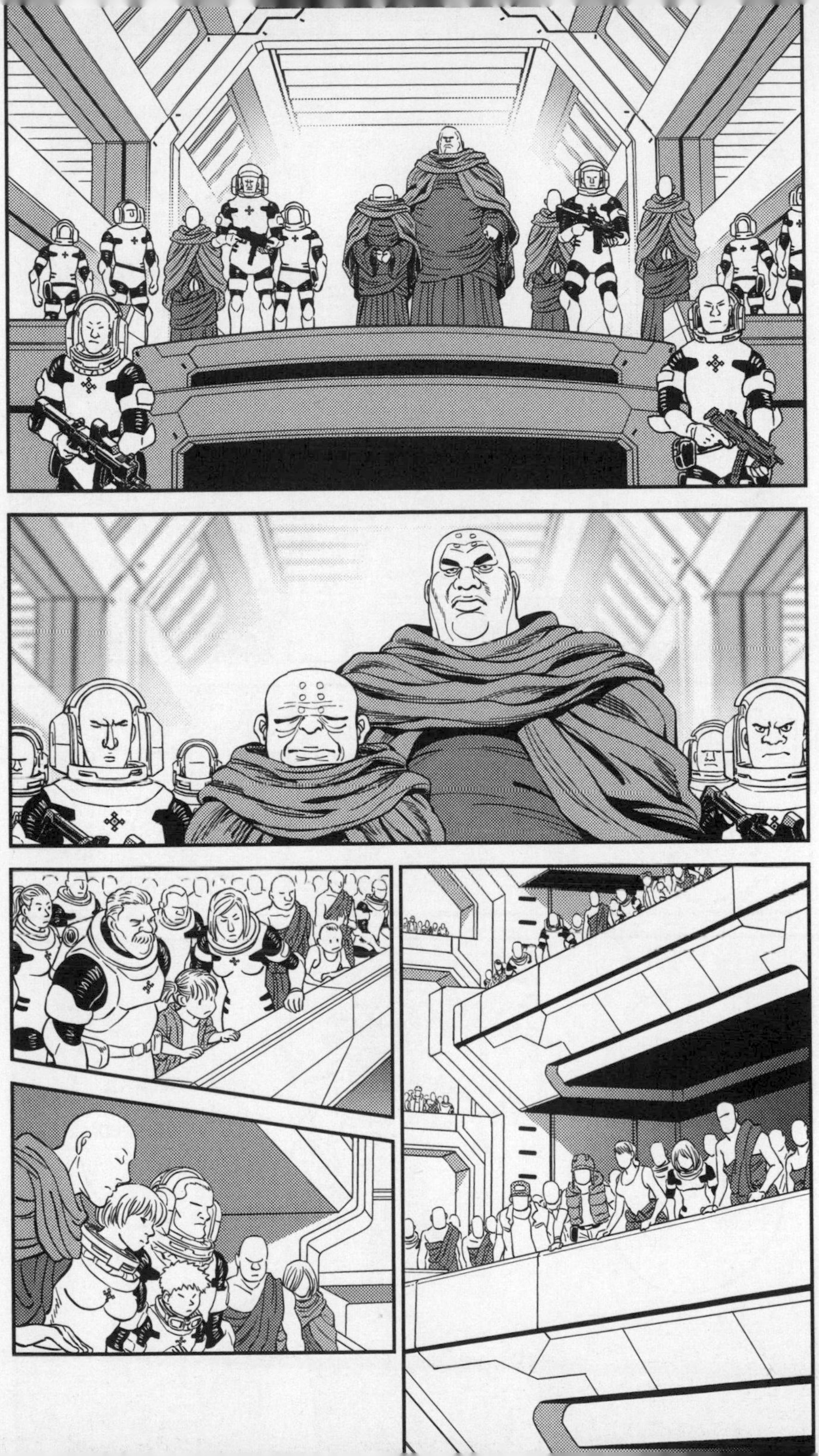

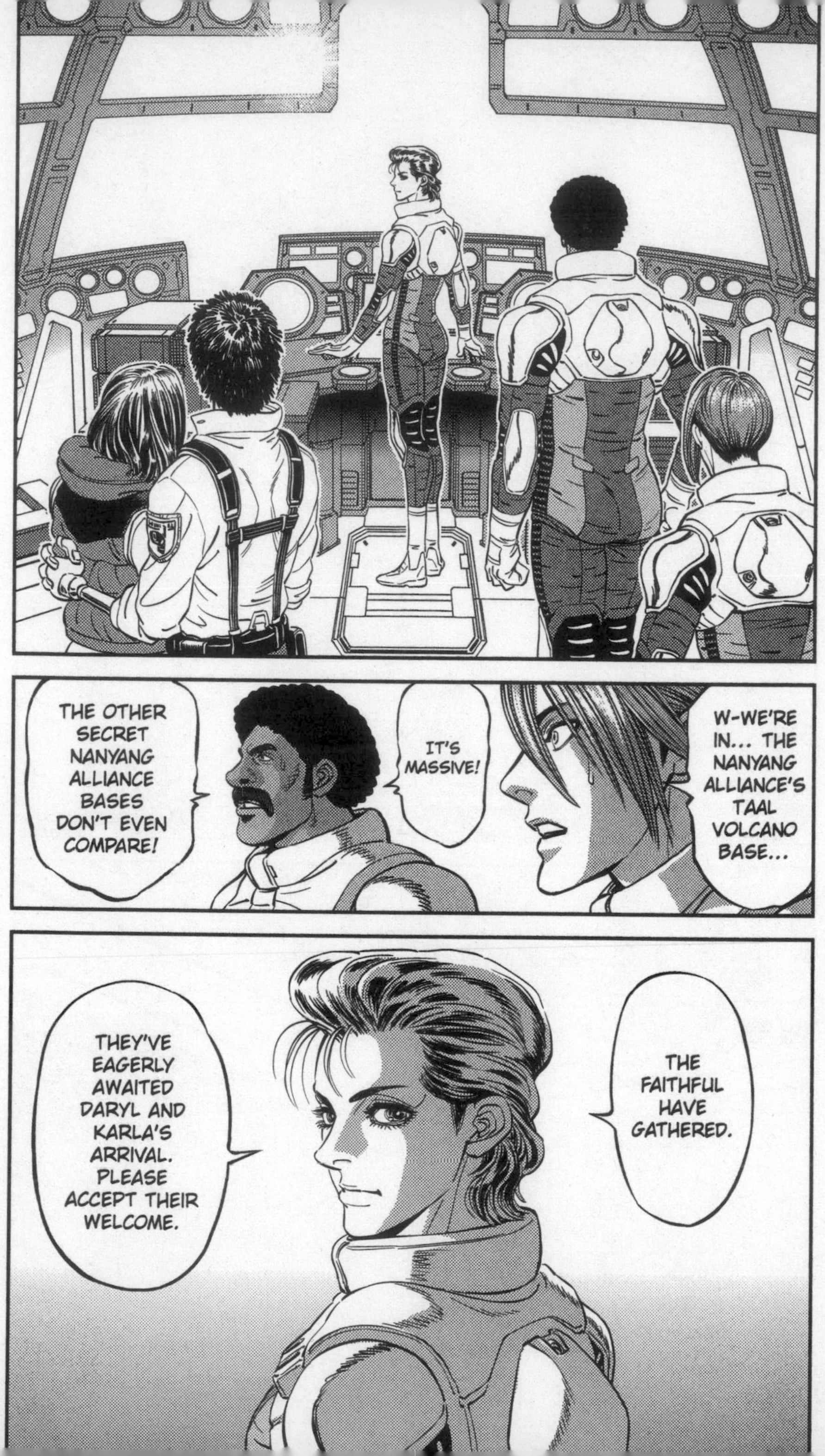
W-WE'RE IN... THE NANYANG ALLIANCE'S TAAL VOLCANO BASE...
IT'S MASSIVE!
THE OTHER SECRET NANYANG ALLIANCE BASES DON'T EVEN COMPARE!
THE FAITHFUL HAVE GATHERED.
THEY'VE EAGERLY AWAITED DARYL AND KARLA'S ARRIVAL. PLEASE ACCEPT THEIR WELCOME.

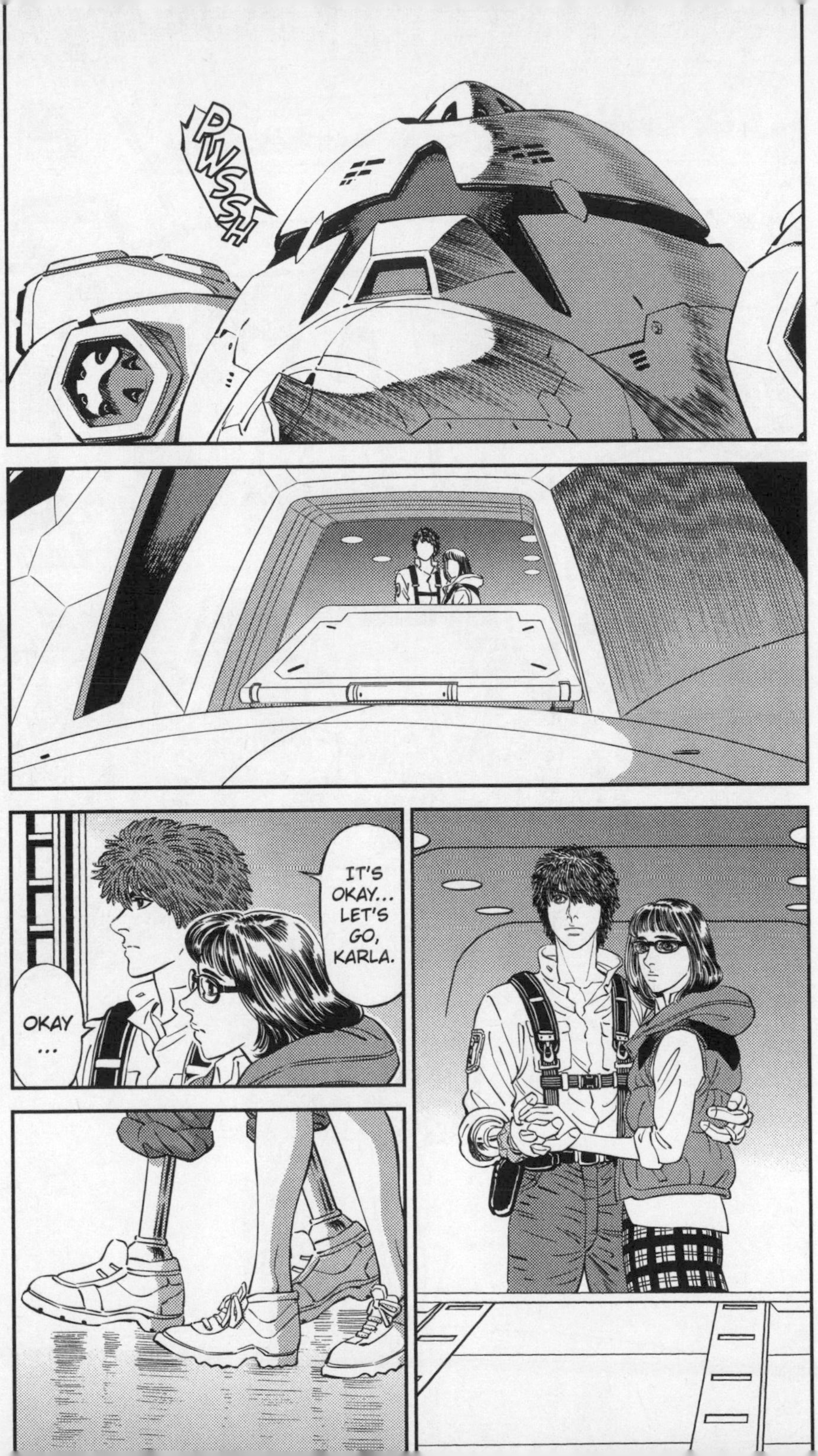
PWSSH
IT'S OKAY... LET'S GO, KARLA.
OKAY ...

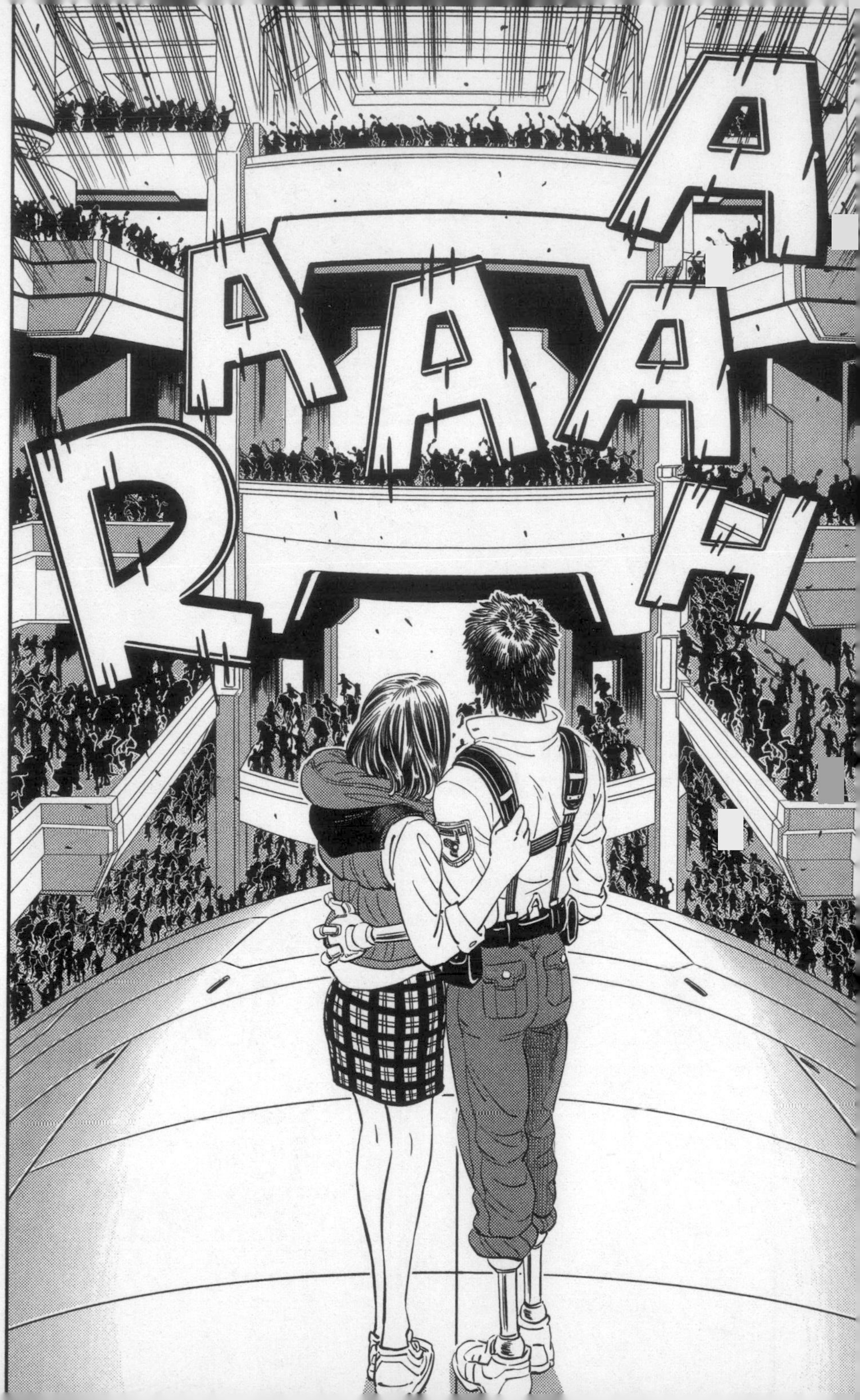
RAAAAH

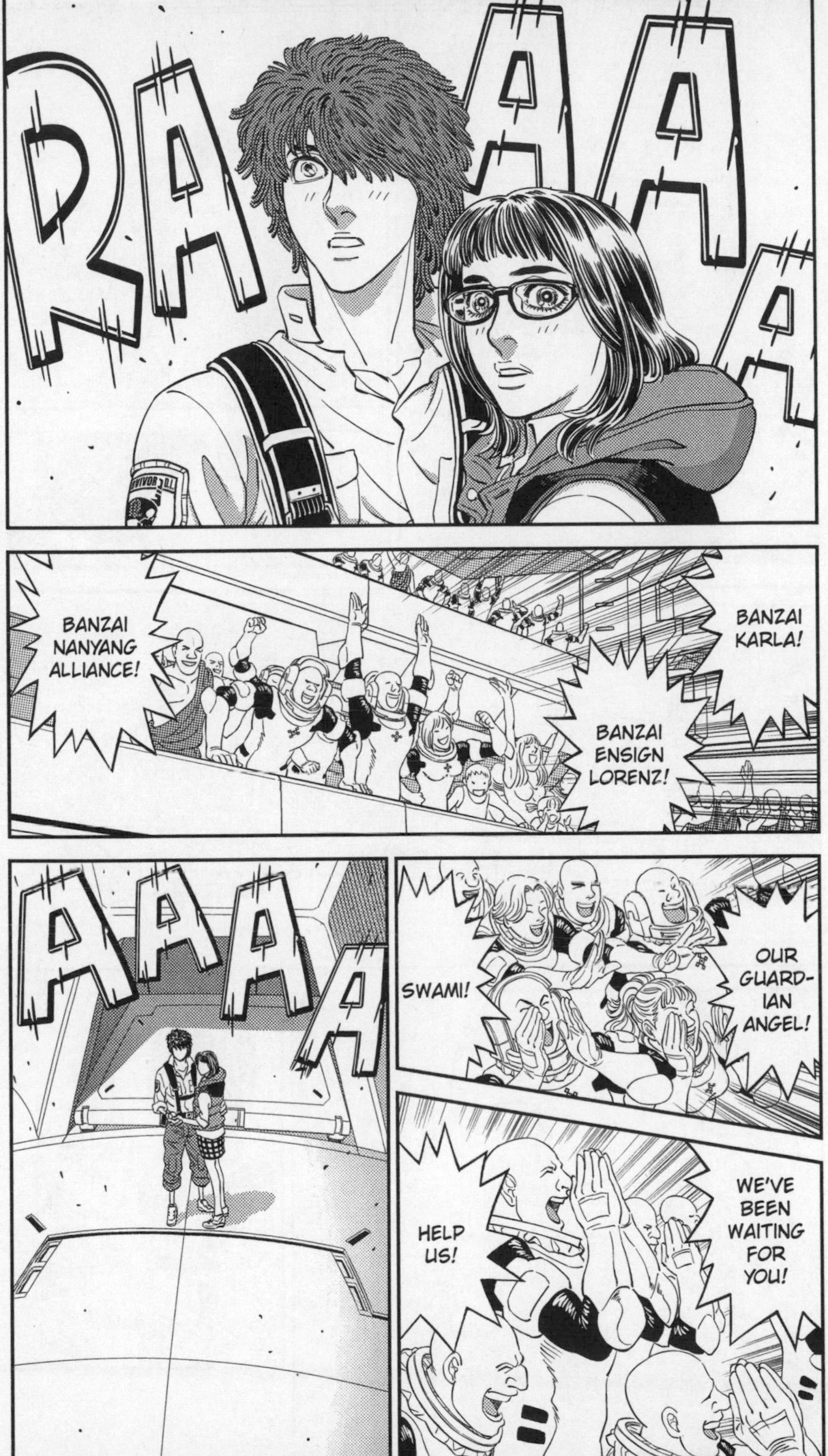
RAAAAAA
BANZAI KARLA!
BANZAI ENSIGN LORENZ!
BANZAI NANYANG ALLIANCE!
OUR GUARDIAN ANGEL!
SWAMI!
WE'VE BEEN WAITING FOR YOU!
HELP US!
AAAAA

YEAH
...

WOW, DADDY. THEY REALLY *ARE* GLAD TO SEE US.

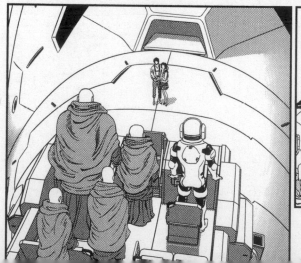

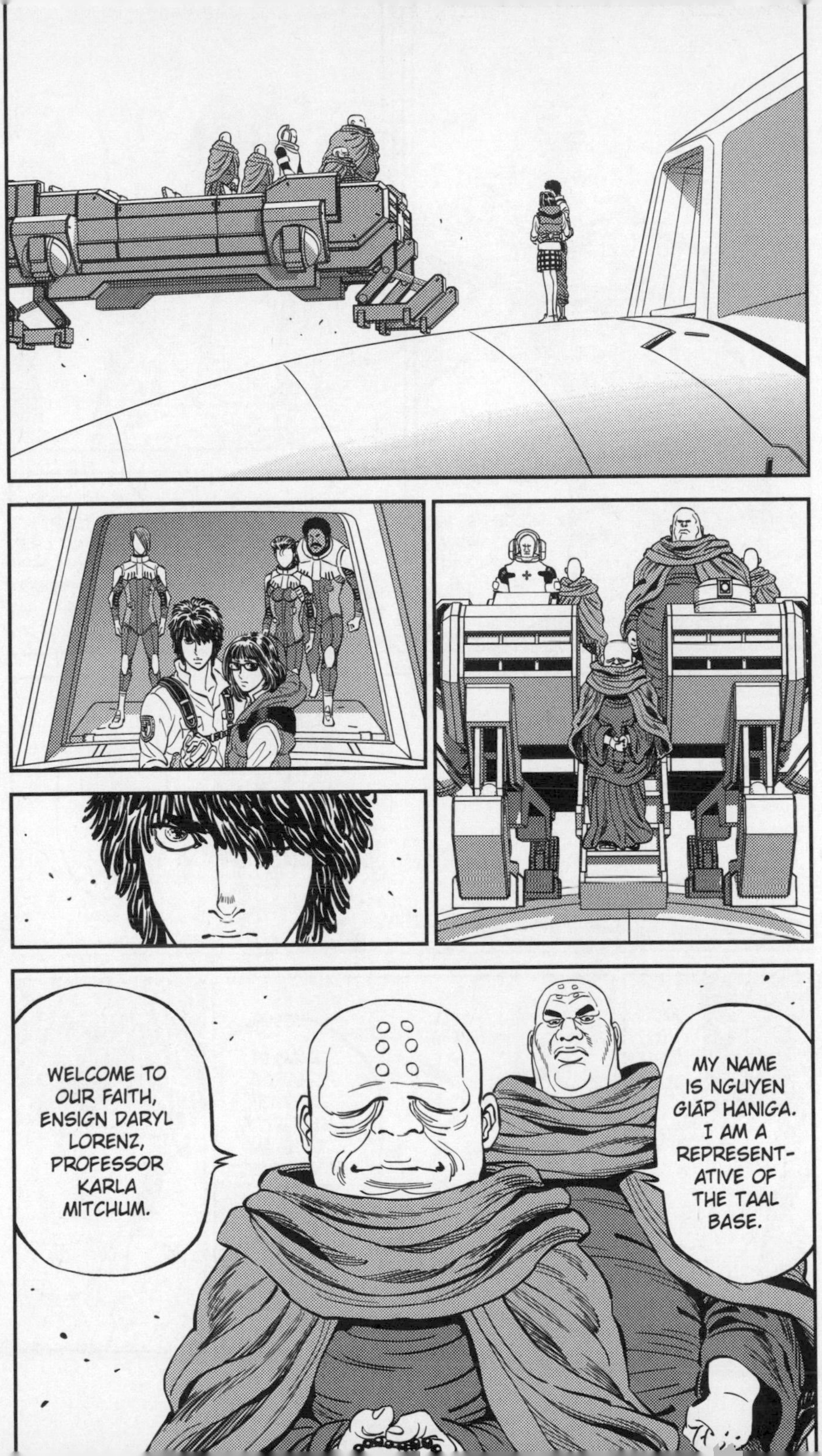
MY NAME IS NGUYEN GIÁP HANIGA. I AM A REPRESENTATIVE OF THE TAAL BASE.
WELCOME TO OUR FAITH, ENSIGN DARYL LORENZ, PROFESSOR KARLA MITCHUM.

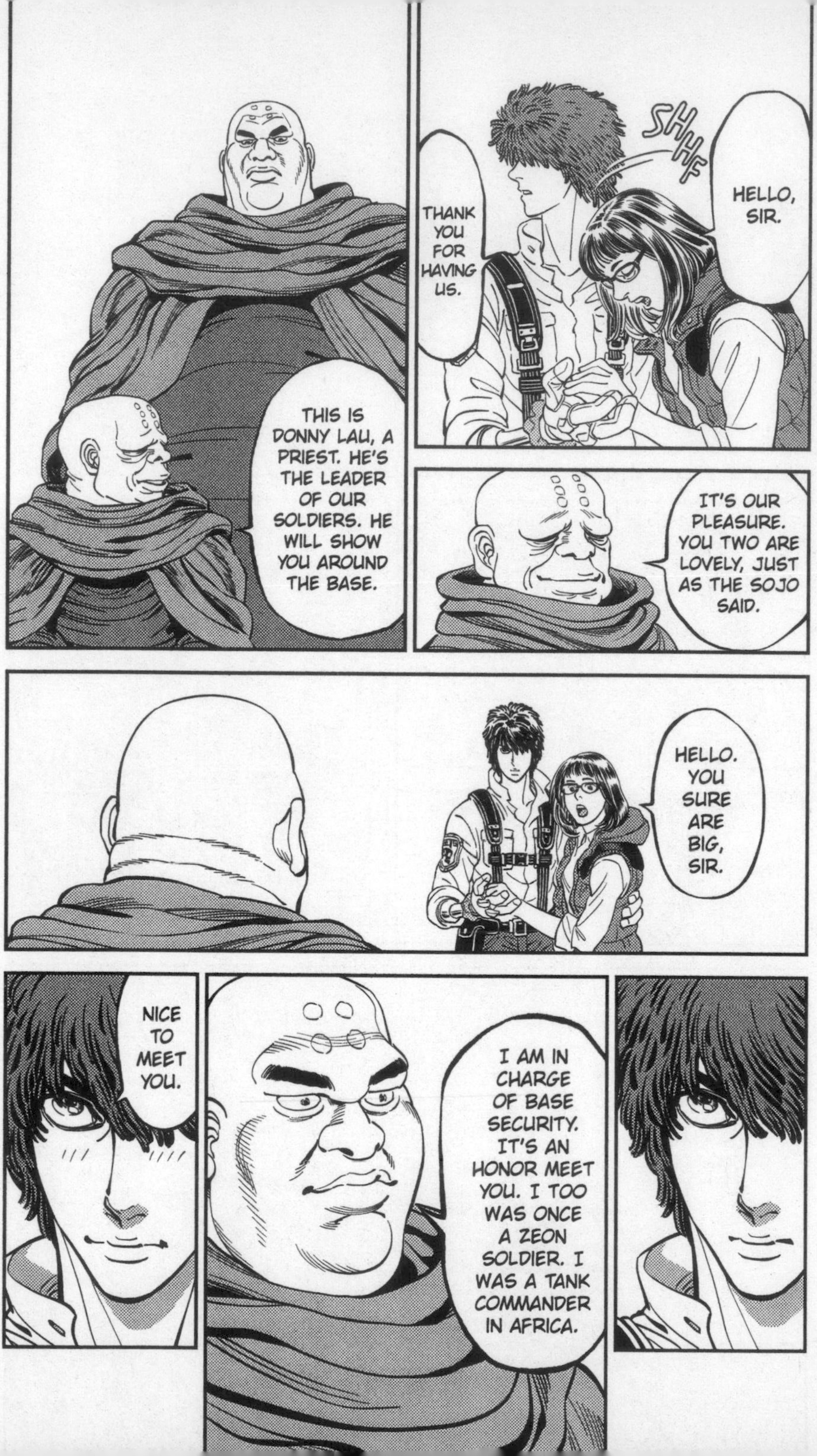
SHHF
HELLO, SIR.
THANK YOU FOR HAVING US.
IT'S OUR PLEASURE. YOU TWO ARE LOVELY, JUST AS THE SOJO SAID.
THIS IS DONNY LAU, A PRIEST. HE'S THE LEADER OF OUR SOLDIERS. HE WILL SHOW YOU AROUND THE BASE.
HELLO. YOU SURE ARE BIG, SIR.
I AM IN CHARGE OF BASE SECURITY. IT'S AN HONOR MEET YOU. I TOO WAS ONCE A ZEON SOLDIER. I WAS A TANK COMMANDER IN AFRICA.
NICE TO MEET YOU.

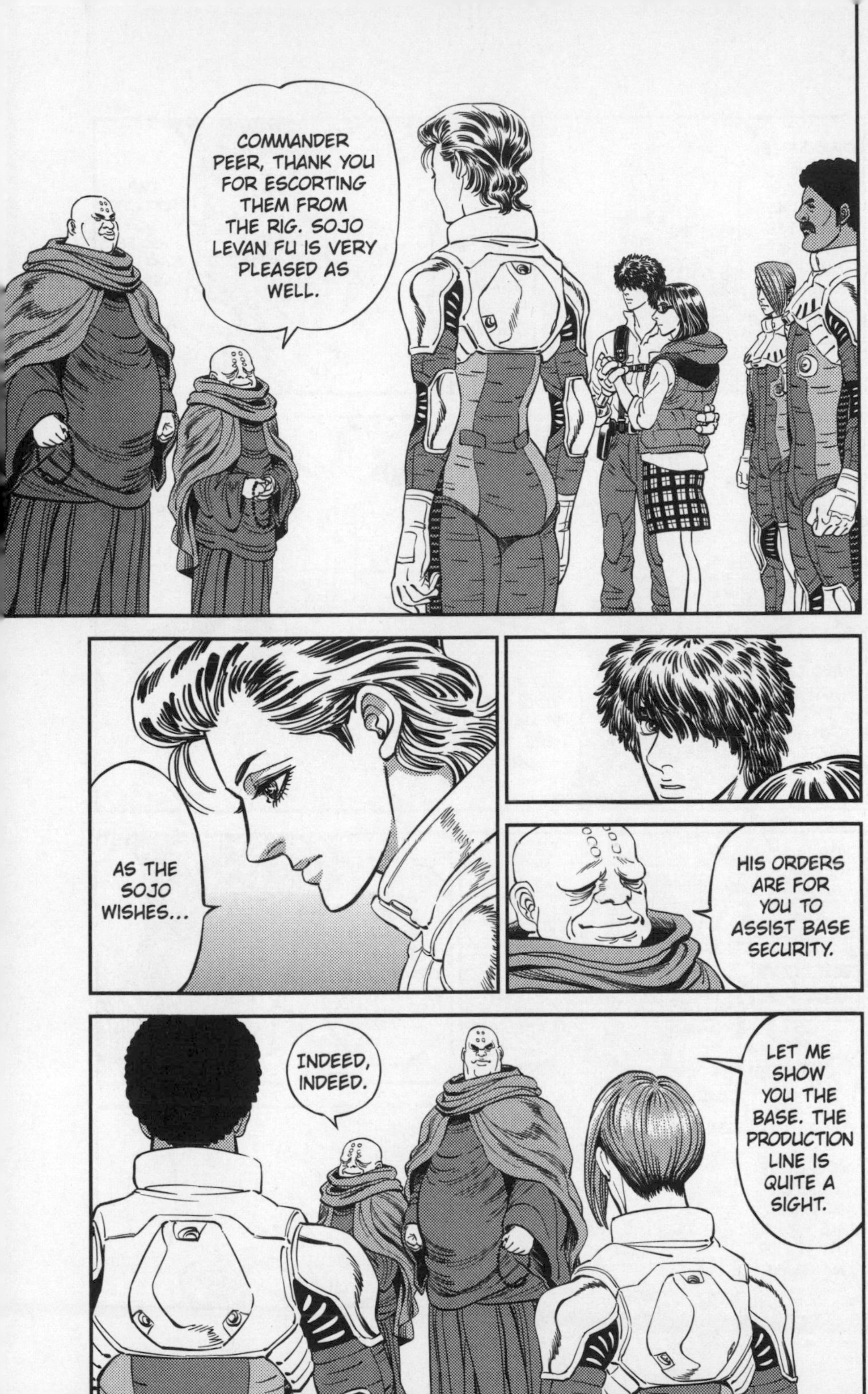
COMMANDER PEER, THANK YOU FOR ESCORTING THEM FROM THE RIG. SOJO LEVAN FU IS VERY PLEASED AS WELL.
HIS ORDERS ARE FOR YOU TO ASSIST BASE SECURITY.
AS THE SOJO WISHES...
LET ME SHOW YOU THE BASE. THE PRODUCTION LINE IS QUITE A SIGHT.
INDEED, INDEED.

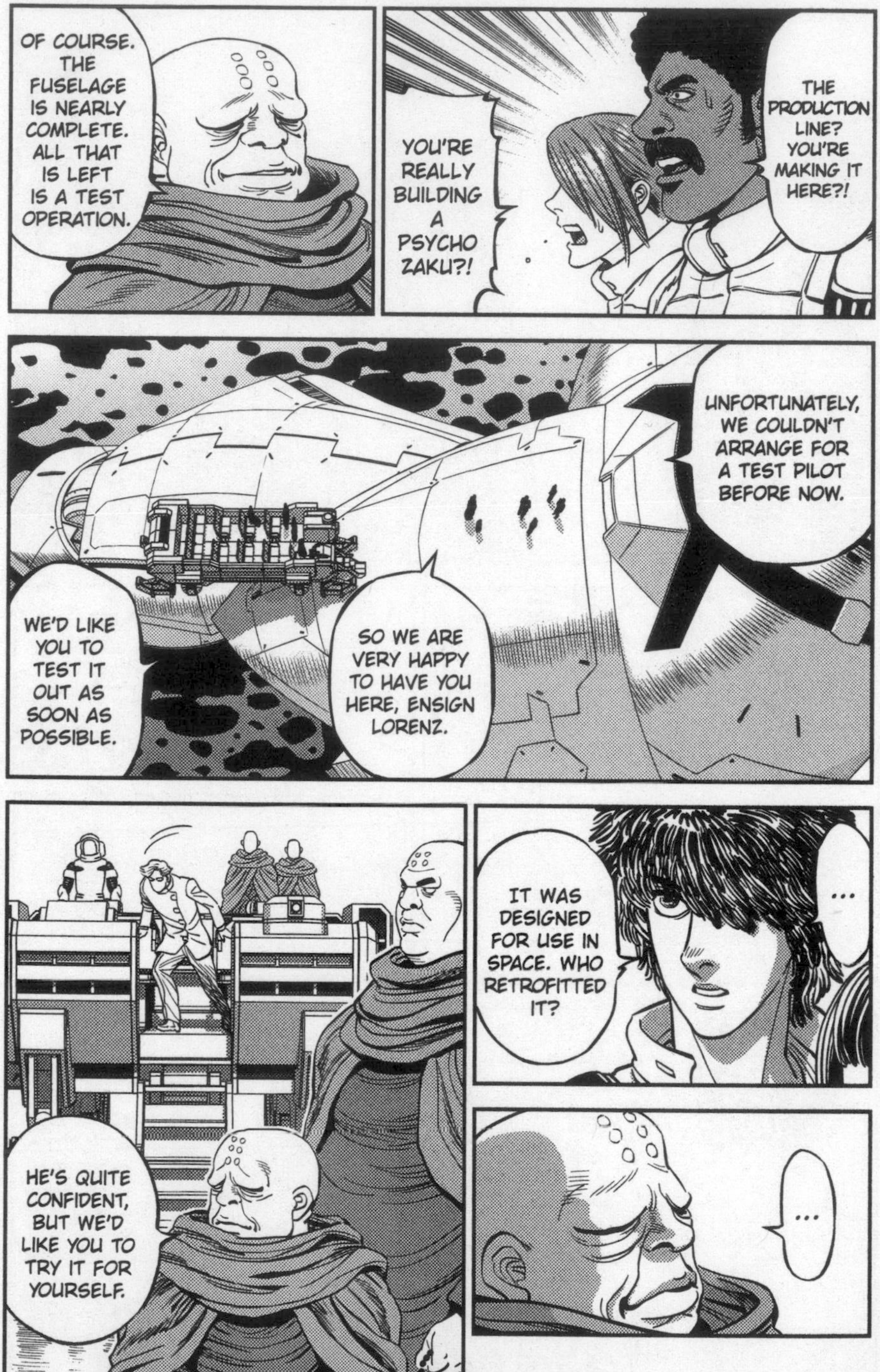
THE PRODUCTION LINE? YOU'RE MAKING IT HERE?!
YOU'RE REALLY BUILDING A PSYCHO ZAKU?!
OF COURSE. THE FUSELAGE IS NEARLY COMPLETE. ALL THAT IS LEFT IS A TEST OPERATION.
UNFORTUNATELY, WE COULDN'T ARRANGE FOR A TEST PILOT BEFORE NOW.
SO WE ARE VERY HAPPY TO HAVE YOU HERE, ENSIGN LORENZ.
WE'D LIKE YOU TO TEST IT OUT AS SOON AS POSSIBLE.
...
IT WAS DESIGNED FOR USE IN SPACE. WHO RETROFITTED IT?
...
HE'S QUITE CONFIDENT, BUT WE'D LIKE YOU TO TRY IT FOR YOURSELF.

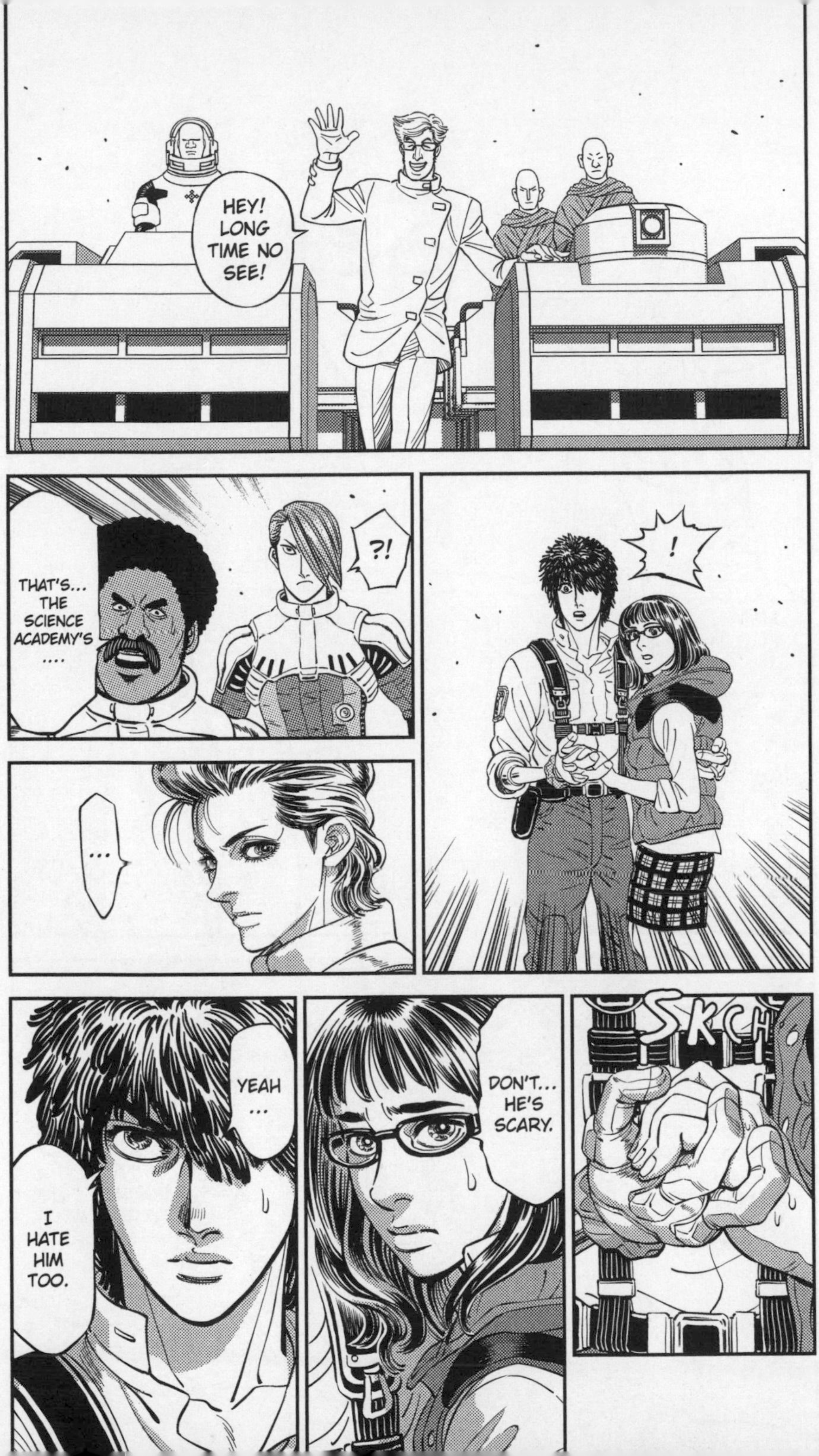
HEY! LONG TIME NO SEE!
!
?!
THAT'S... THE SCIENCE ACADEMY'S ....
...
SKCH
DON'T... HE'S SCARY.
YEAH ...
I HATE HIM TOO.

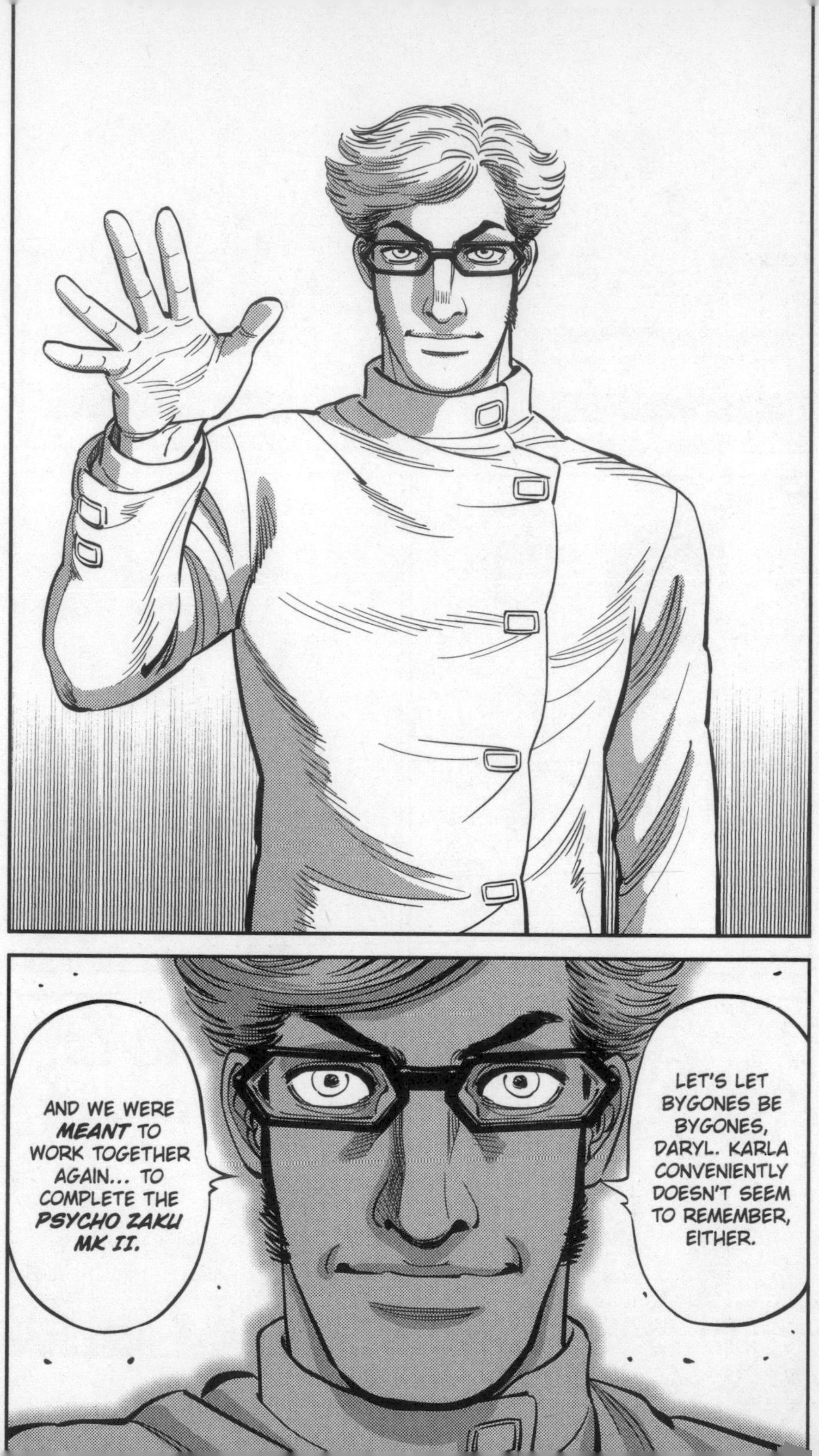
LET'S LET BYGONES BE BYGONES, DARYL. KARLA CONVENIENTLY DOESN'T SEEM TO REMEMBER, EITHER.
AND WE WERE *MEANT* TO WORK TOGETHER AGAIN... TO COMPLETE THE *PSYCHO ZAKU MK II.*

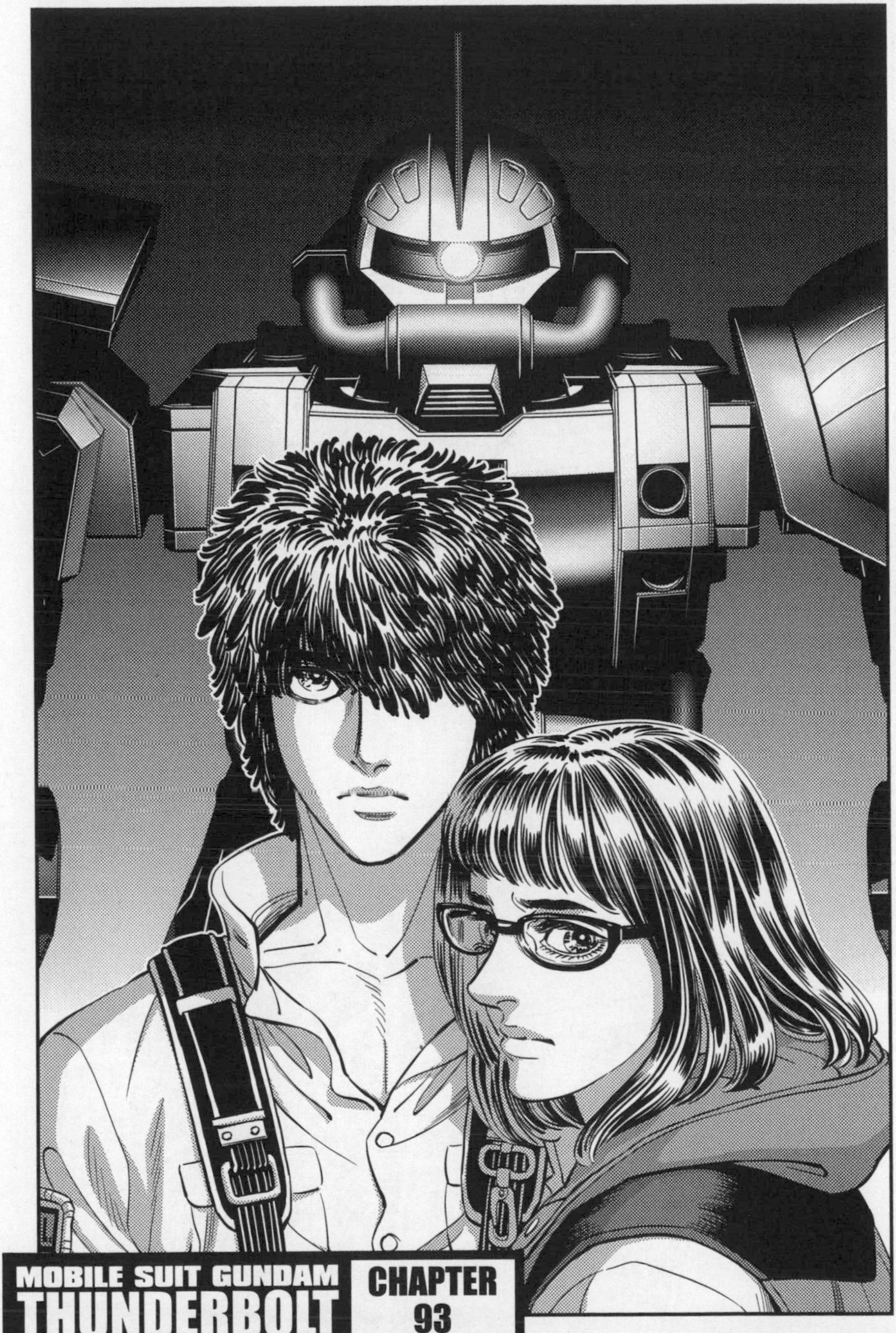
MOBILE SUIT GUNDAM
THUNDERBOLT
CHAPTER
93

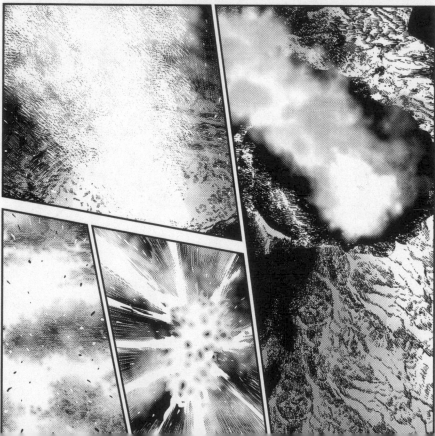

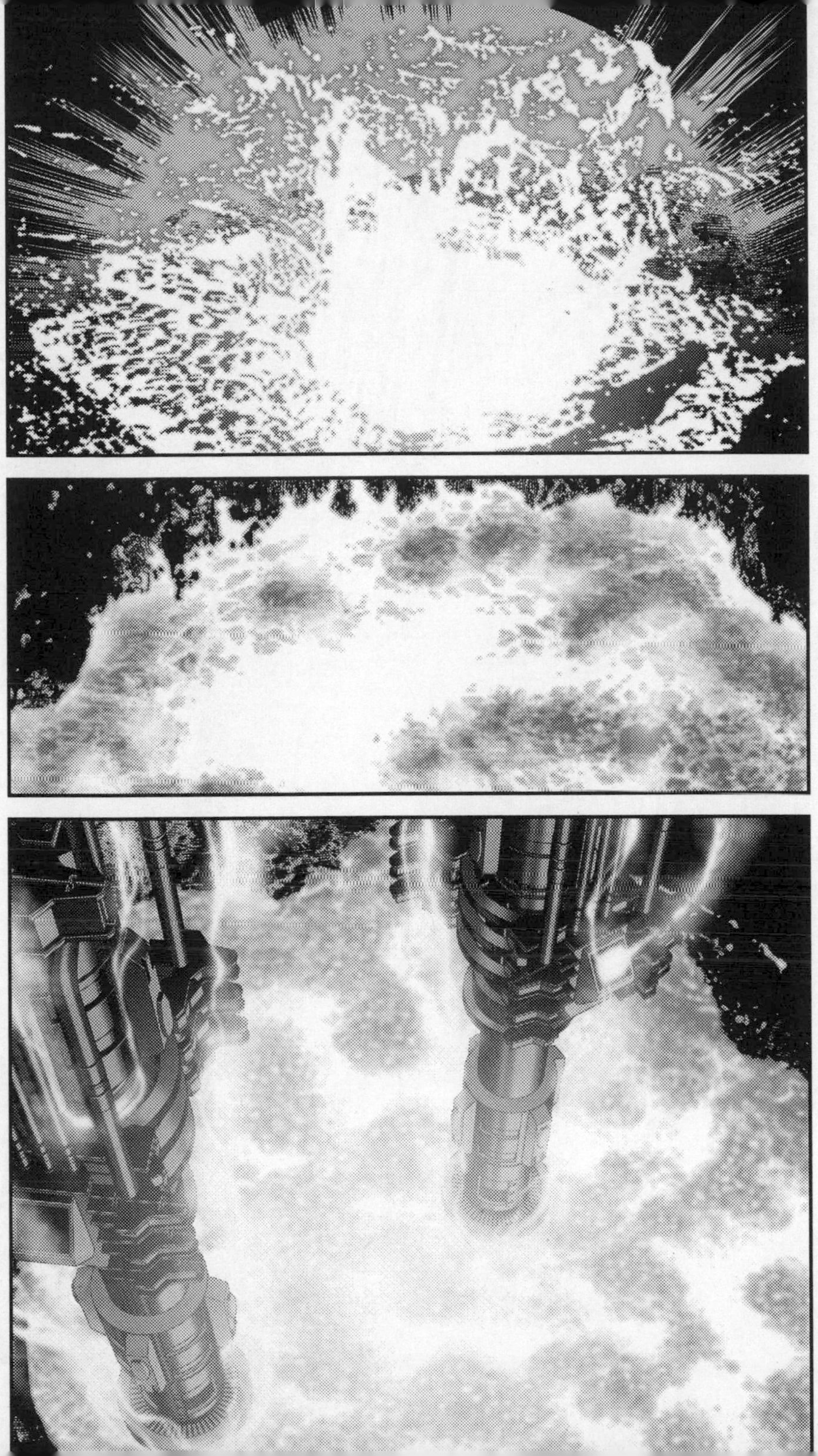

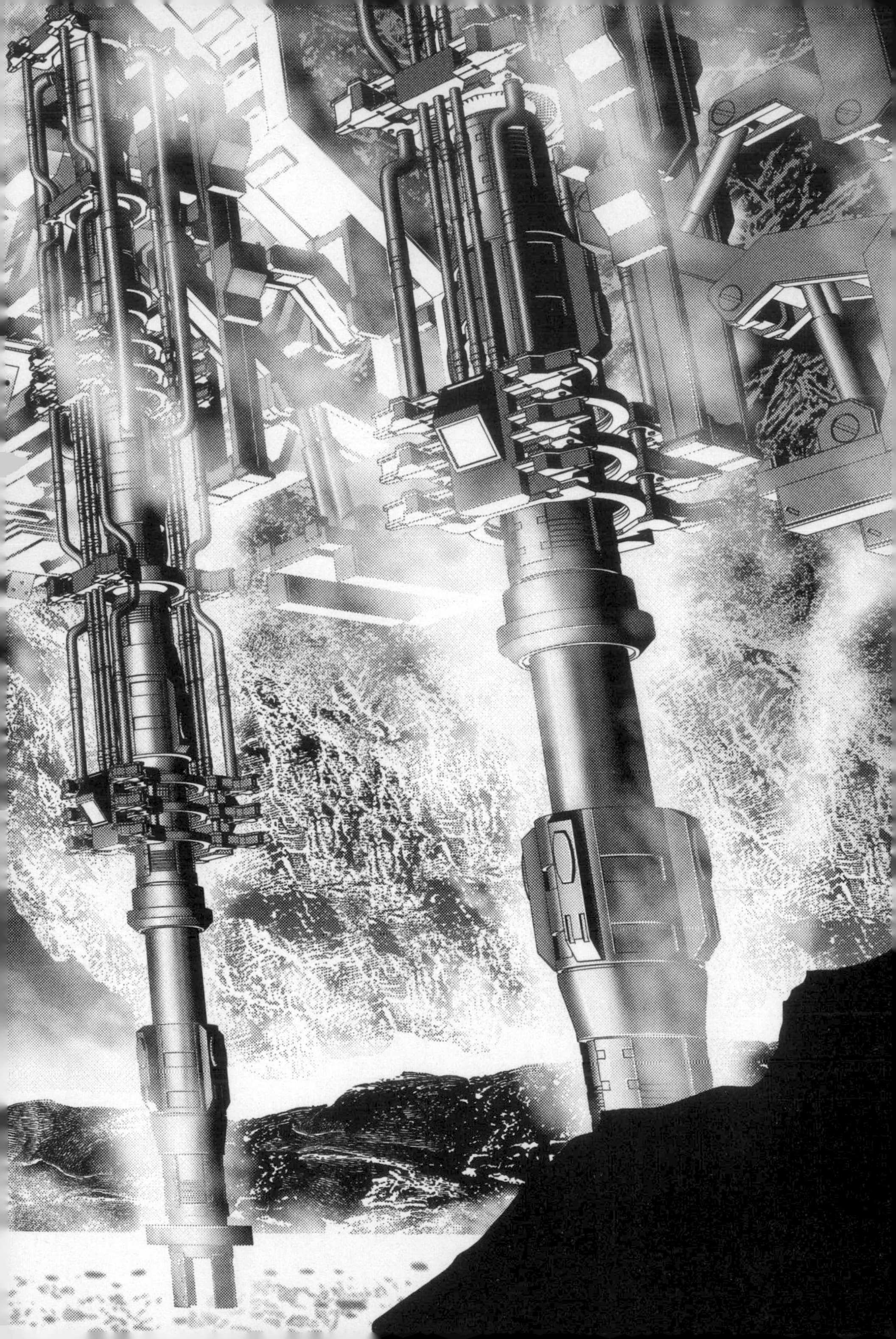

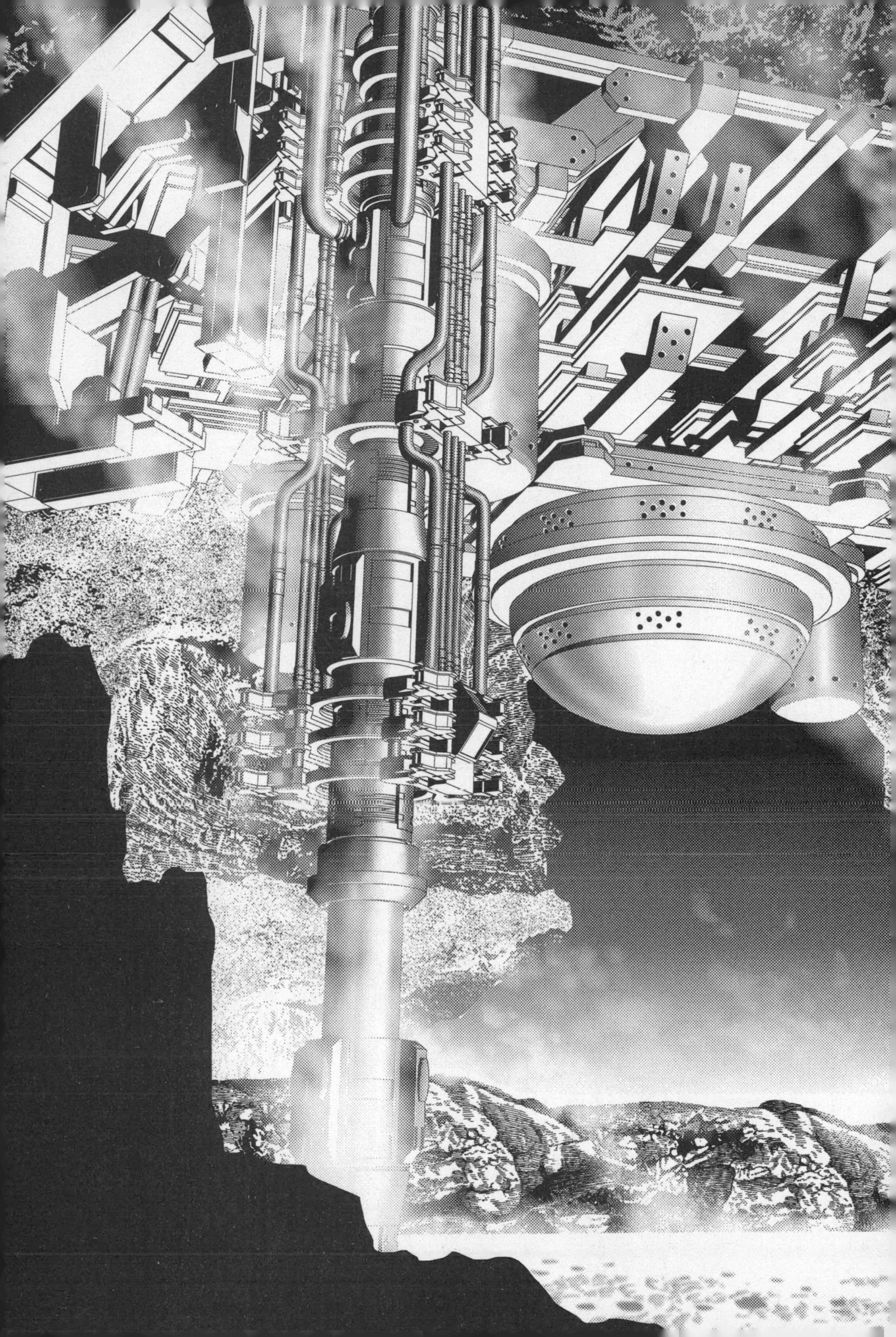

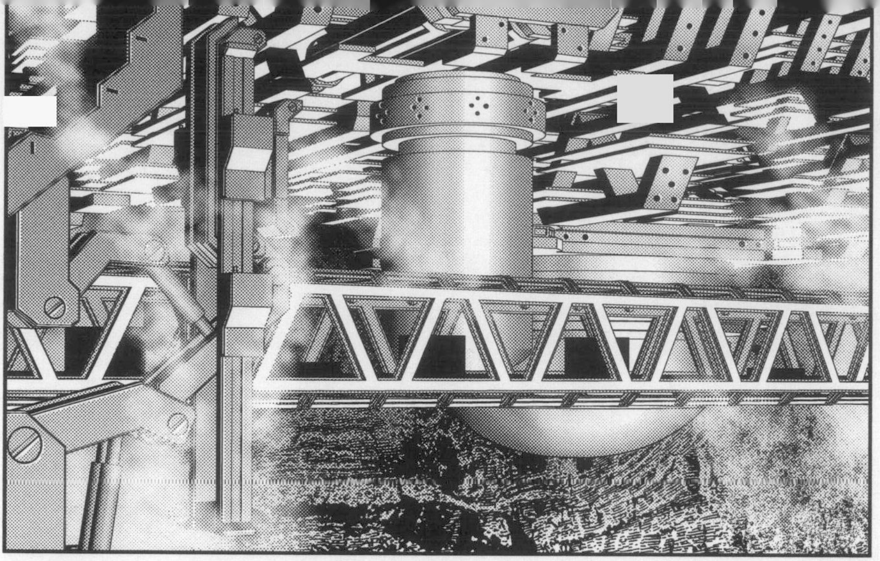
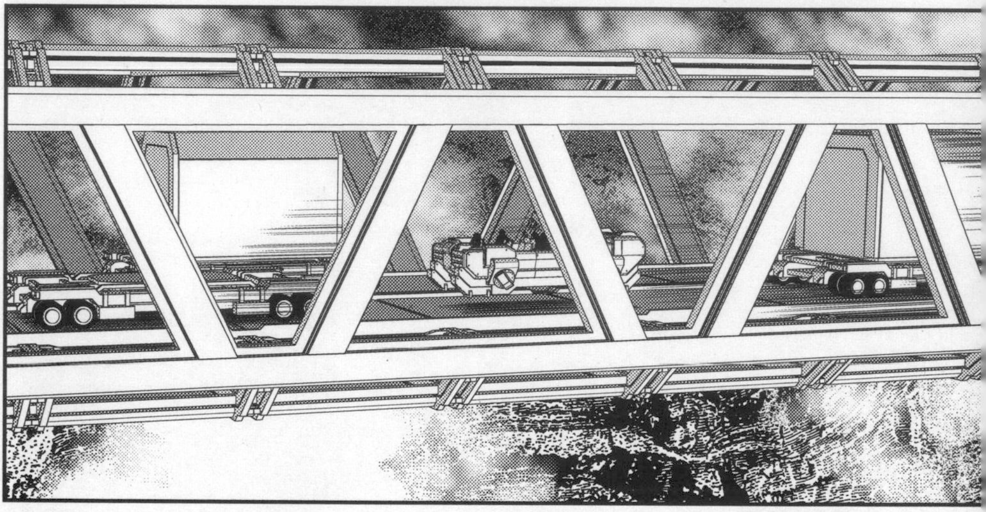
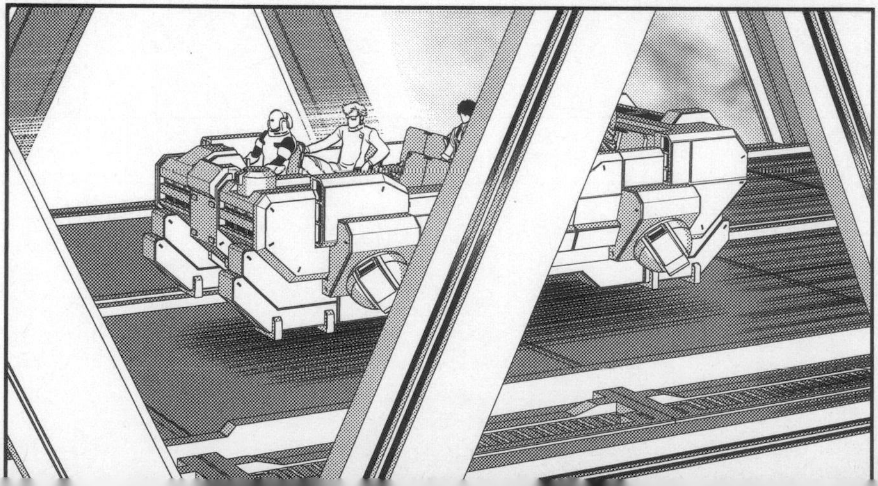

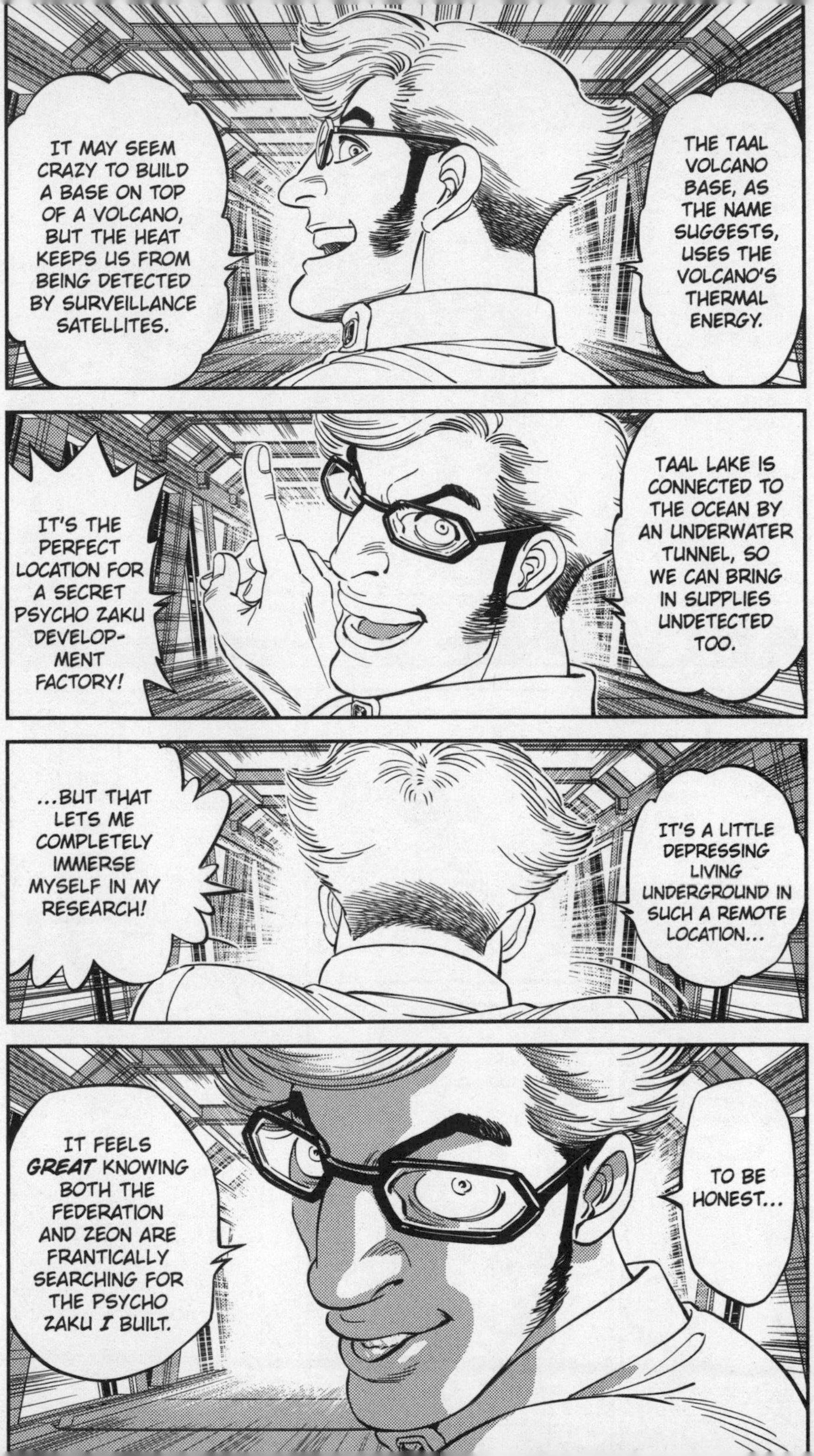
THE TAAL VOLCANO BASE, AS THE NAME SUGGESTS, USES THE VOLCANO'S THERMAL ENERGY.
IT MAY SEEM CRAZY TO BUILD A BASE ON TOP OF A VOLCANO, BUT THE HEAT KEEPS US FROM BEING DETECTED BY SURVEILLANCE SATELLITES.
TAAL LAKE IS CONNECTED TO THE OCEAN BY AN UNDERWATER TUNNEL, SO WE CAN BRING IN SUPPLIES UNDETECTED TOO.
IT'S THE PERFECT LOCATION FOR A SECRET PSYCHO ZAKU DEVELOPMENT FACTORY!
IT'S A LITTLE DEPRESSING LIVING UNDERGROUND IN SUCH A REMOTE LOCATION...
...BUT THAT LETS ME COMPLETELY IMMERSE MYSELF IN MY RESEARCH!
TO BE HONEST...
IT FEELS ***GREAT*** KNOWING BOTH THE FEDERATION AND ZEON ARE FRANTICALLY SEARCHING FOR THE PSYCHO ZAKU ***I*** BUILT.

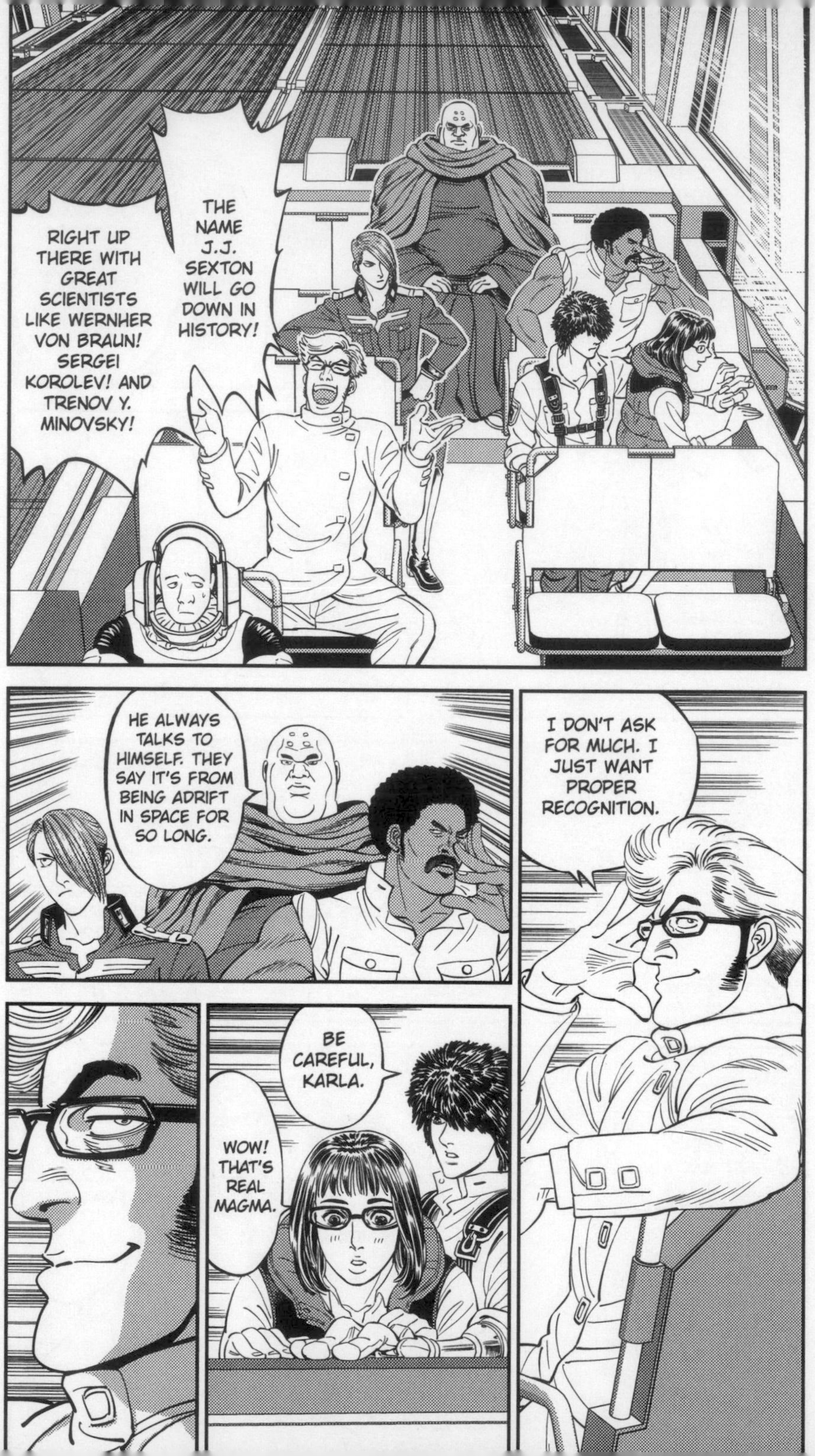
THE NAME J.J. SEXTON WILL GO DOWN IN HISTORY!
RIGHT UP THERE WITH GREAT SCIENTISTS LIKE WERNHER VON BRAUN! SERGEI KOROLEV! AND TRENOV Y. MINOVSKY!
I DON'T ASK FOR MUCH. I JUST WANT PROPER RECOGNITION.
HE ALWAYS TALKS TO HIMSELF. THEY SAY IT'S FROM BEING ADRIFT IN SPACE FOR SO LONG.
BE CAREFUL, KARLA.
WOW! THAT'S REAL MAGMA.

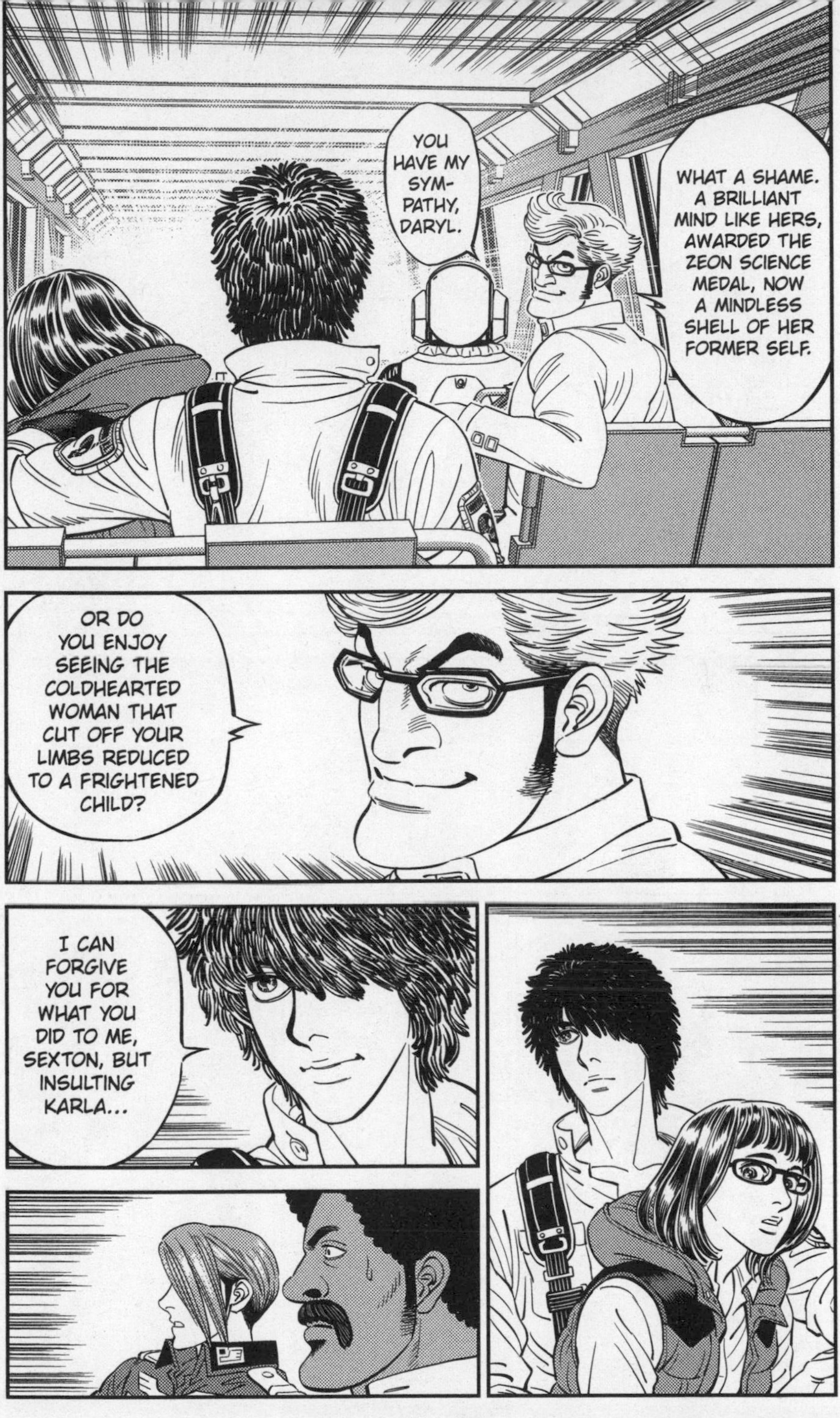
WHAT A SHAME. A BRILLIANT MIND LIKE HERS, AWARDED THE ZEON SCIENCE MEDAL, NOW A MINDLESS SHELL OF HER FORMER SELF.
YOU HAVE MY SYMPATHY, DARYL.
OR DO YOU ENJOY SEEING THE COLDHEARTED WOMAN THAT CUT OFF YOUR LIMBS REDUCED TO A FRIGHTENED CHILD?
I CAN FORGIVE YOU FOR WHAT YOU DID TO ME, SEXTON, BUT INSULTING KARLA...

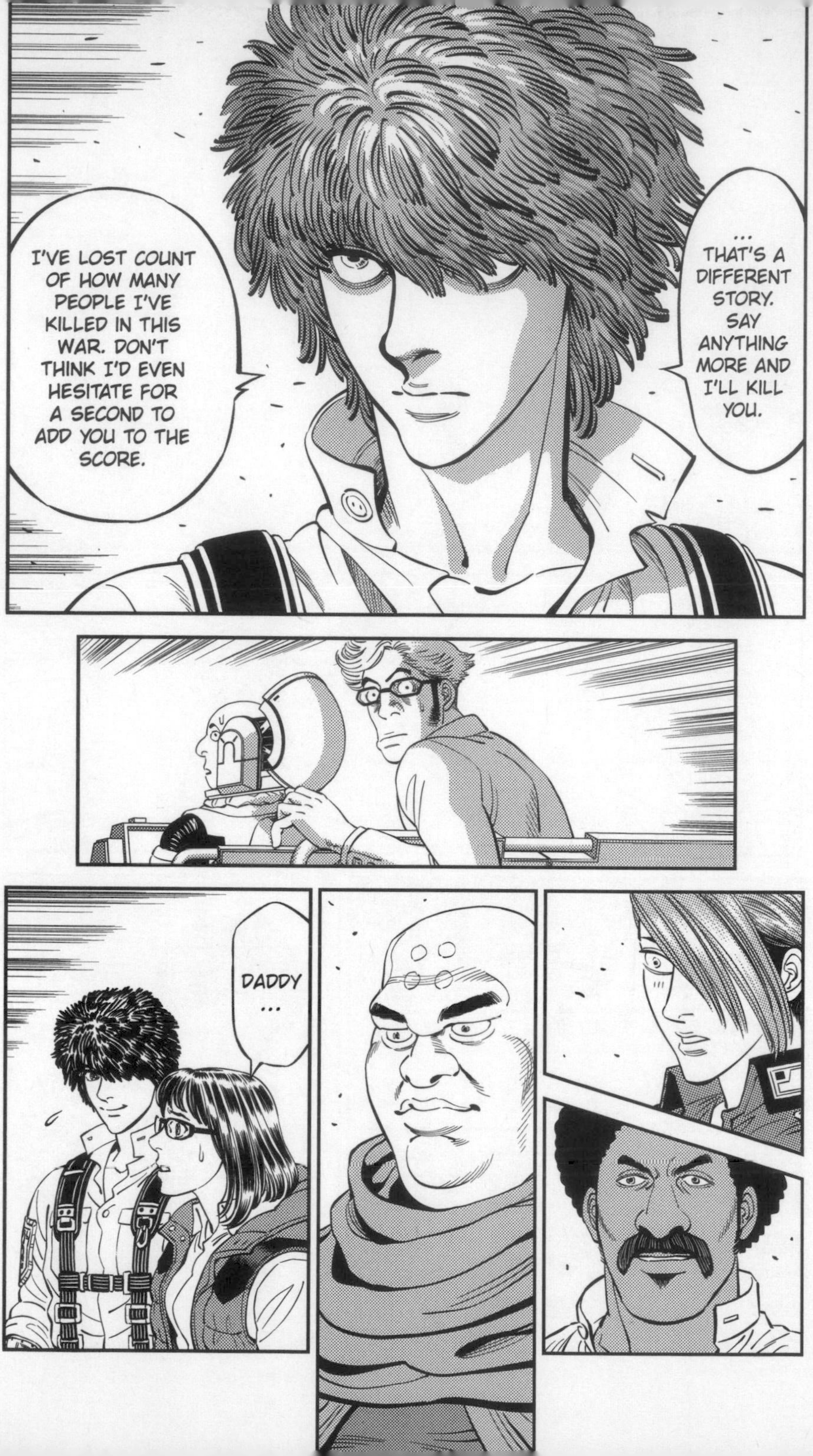
... THAT'S A DIFFERENT STORY. SAY ANYTHING MORE AND I'LL KILL YOU.
I'VE LOST COUNT OF HOW MANY PEOPLE I'VE KILLED IN THIS WAR. DON'T THINK I'D EVEN HESITATE FOR A SECOND TO ADD YOU TO THE SCORE.
DADDY ...

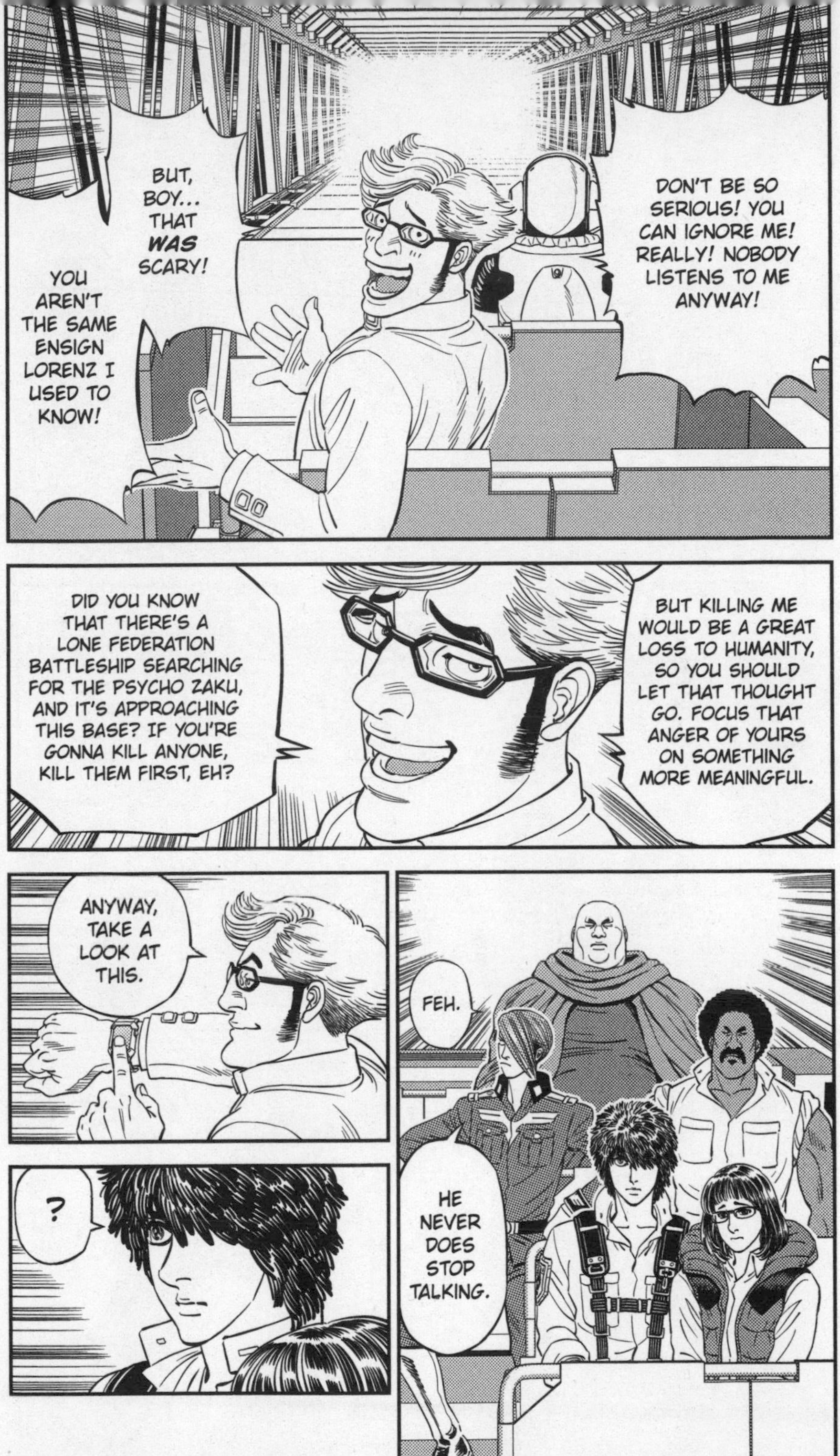
DON'T BE SO SERIOUS! YOU CAN IGNORE ME! REALLY! NOBODY LISTENS TO ME ANYWAY!
BUT, BOY... THAT WAS SCARY!
YOU AREN'T THE SAME ENSIGN LORENZ I USED TO KNOW!
BUT KILLING ME WOULD BE A GREAT LOSS TO HUMANITY, SO YOU SHOULD LET THAT THOUGHT GO. FOCUS THAT ANGER OF YOURS ON SOMETHING MORE MEANINGFUL.
DID YOU KNOW THAT THERE'S A LONE FEDERATION BATTLESHIP SEARCHING FOR THE PSYCHO ZAKU, AND IT'S APPROACHING THIS BASE? IF YOU'RE GONNA KILL ANYONE, KILL THEM FIRST, EH?
FEH.
HE NEVER DOES STOP TALKING.
ANYWAY, TAKE A LOOK AT THIS.
?

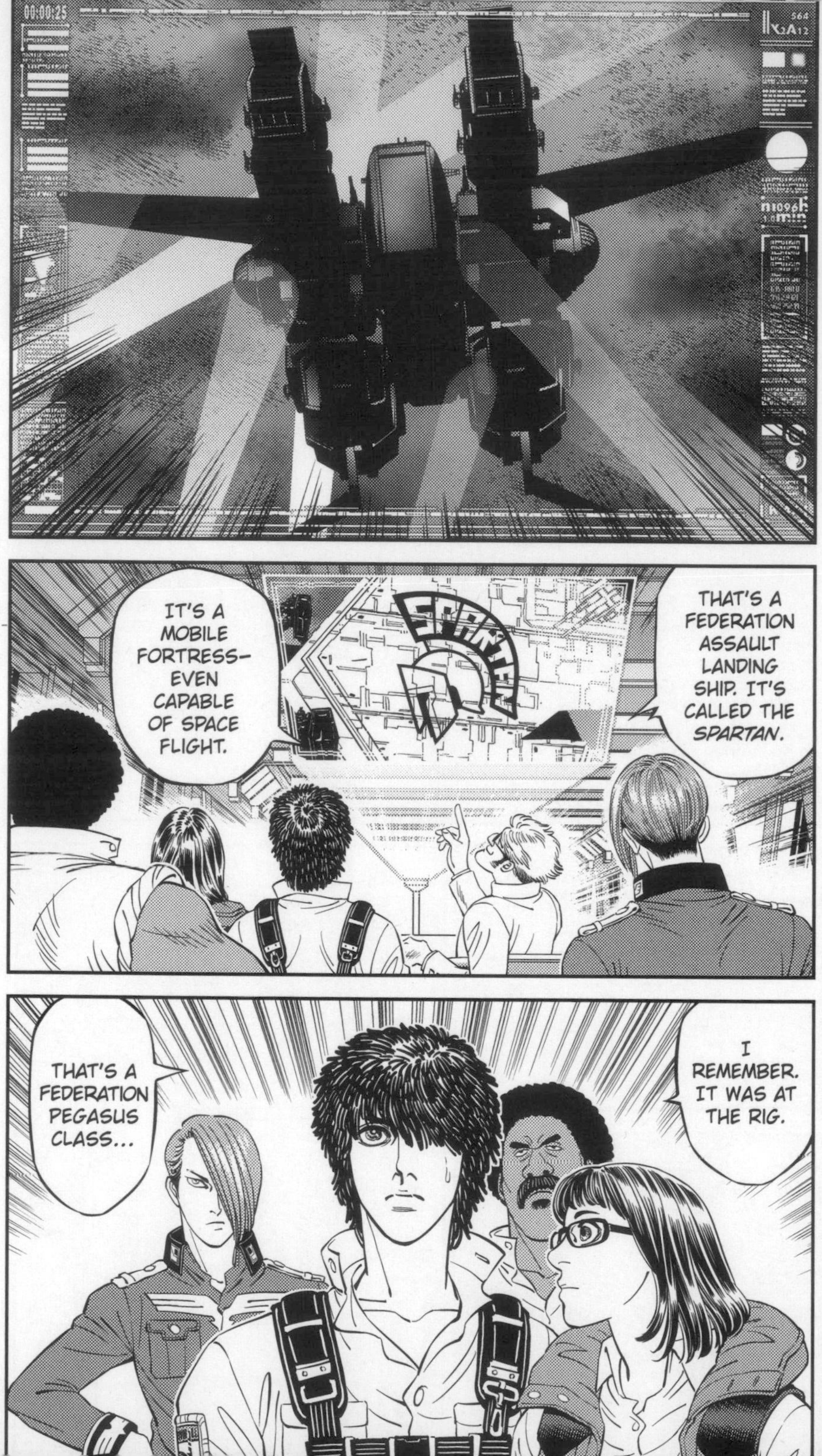
00:00:25
THAT'S A FEDERATION ASSAULT LANDING SHIP. IT'S CALLED THE *SPARTAN*.
IT'S A MOBILE FORTRESS—EVEN CAPABLE OF SPACE FLIGHT.
I REMEMBER. IT WAS AT THE RIG.
THAT'S A FEDERATION PEGASUS CLASS...

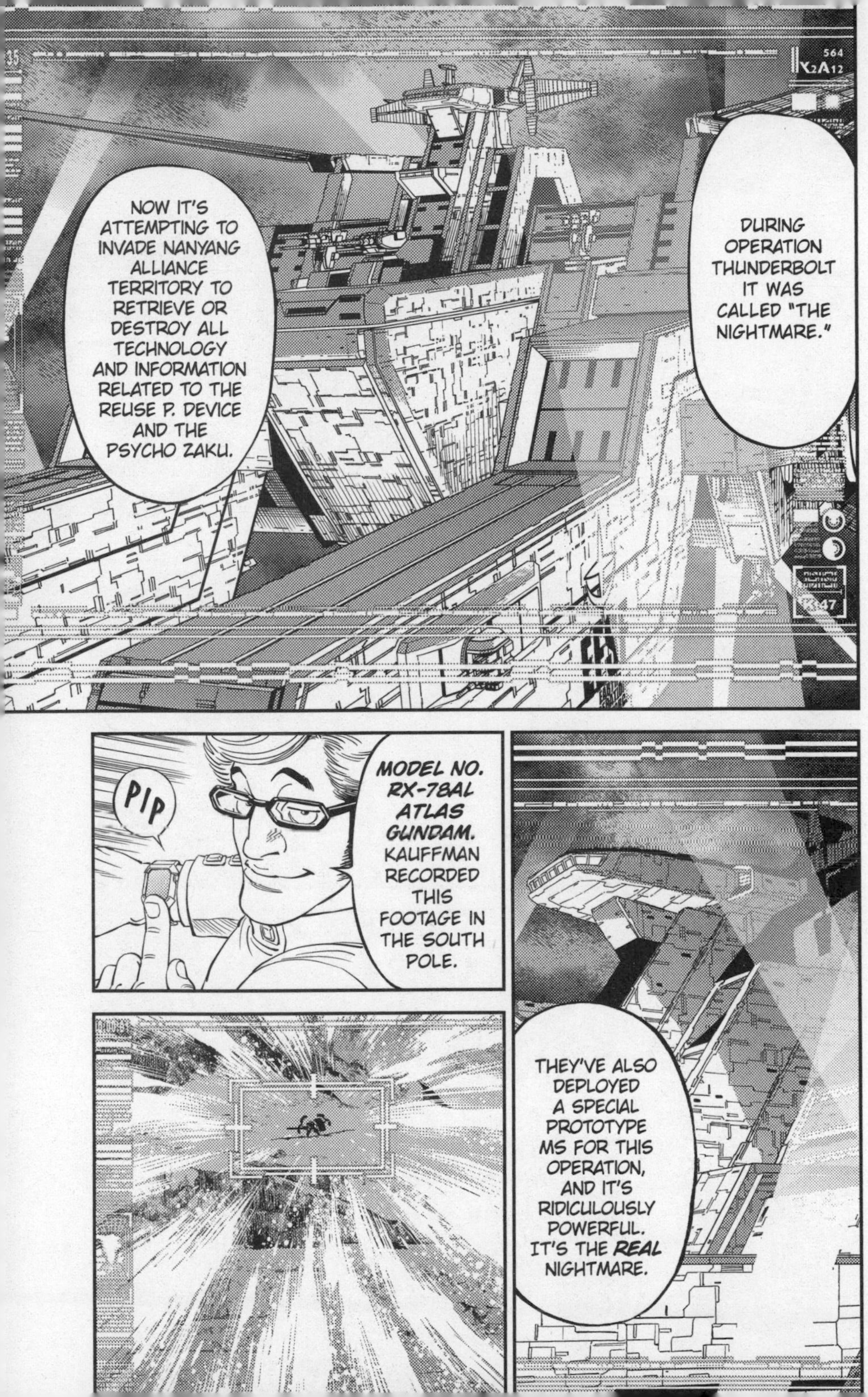

DURING OPERATION THUNDERBOLT IT WAS CALLED "THE NIGHTMARE."
NOW IT'S ATTEMPTING TO INVADE NANYANG ALLIANCE TERRITORY TO RETRIEVE OR DESTROY ALL TECHNOLOGY AND INFORMATION RELATED TO THE REUSE P. DEVICE AND THE PSYCHO ZAKU.
THEY'VE ALSO DEPLOYED A SPECIAL PROTOTYPE MS FOR THIS OPERATION, AND IT'S RIDICULOUSLY POWERFUL. IT'S THE REAL NIGHTMARE.
MODEL NO. RX-78AL ATLAS GUNDAM. KAUFFMAN RECORDED THIS FOOTAGE IN THE SOUTH POLE.
PIP

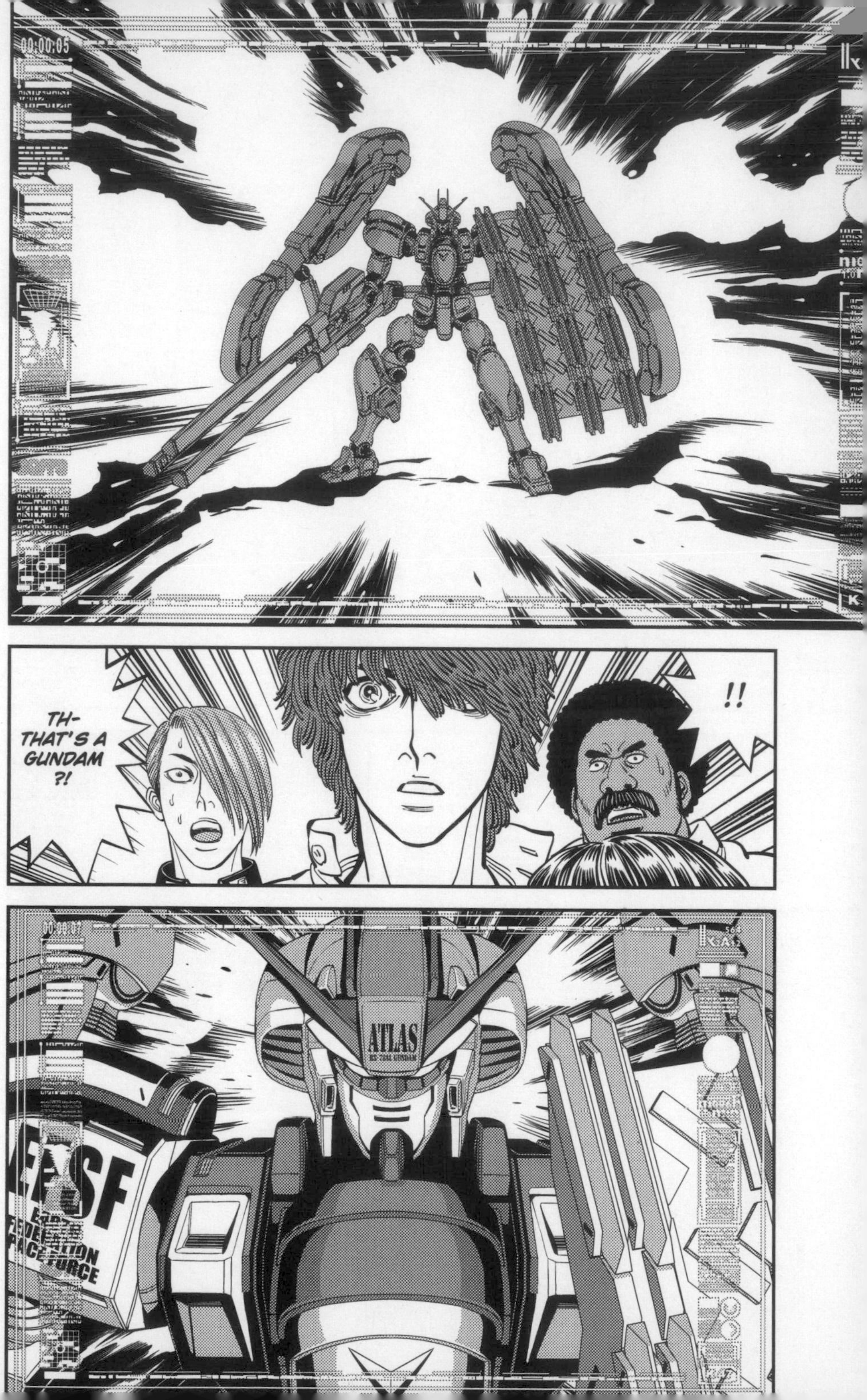
!!
TH- THAT'S A GUNDAM ?!
ATLAS

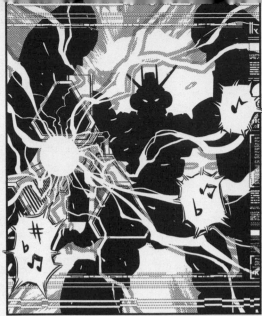

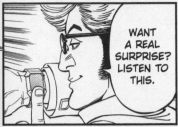

WANT A REAL SURPRISE? LISTEN TO THIS.
JAZZ AND A GUNDAM...
SUITS YOU PERFECTLY, IO FLEMING.

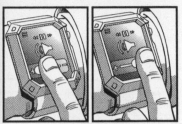

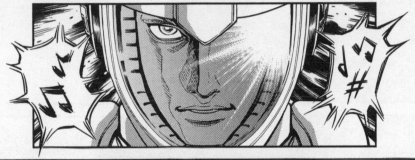

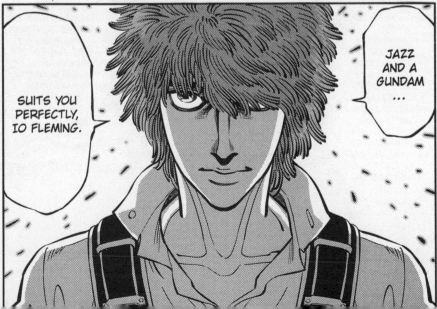

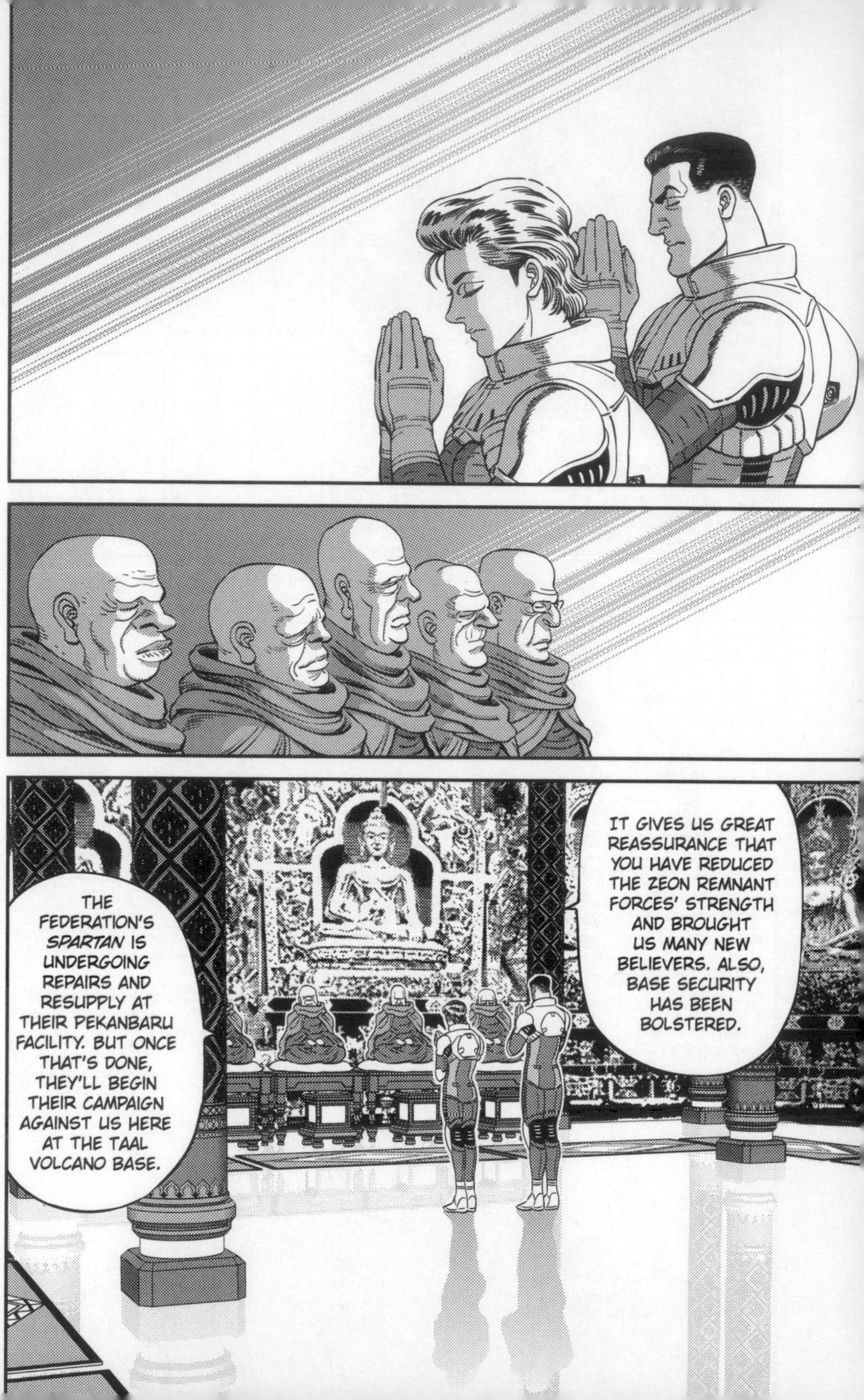
IT GIVES US GREAT REASSURANCE THAT YOU HAVE REDUCED THE ZEON REMNANT FORCES' STRENGTH AND BROUGHT US MANY NEW BELIEVERS. ALSO, BASE SECURITY HAS BEEN BOLSTERED.
THE FEDERATION'S *SPARTAN* IS UNDERGOING REPAIRS AND RESUPPLY AT THEIR PEKANBARU FACILITY. BUT ONCE THAT'S DONE, THEY'LL BEGIN THEIR CAMPAIGN AGAINST US HERE AT THE TAAL VOLCANO BASE.

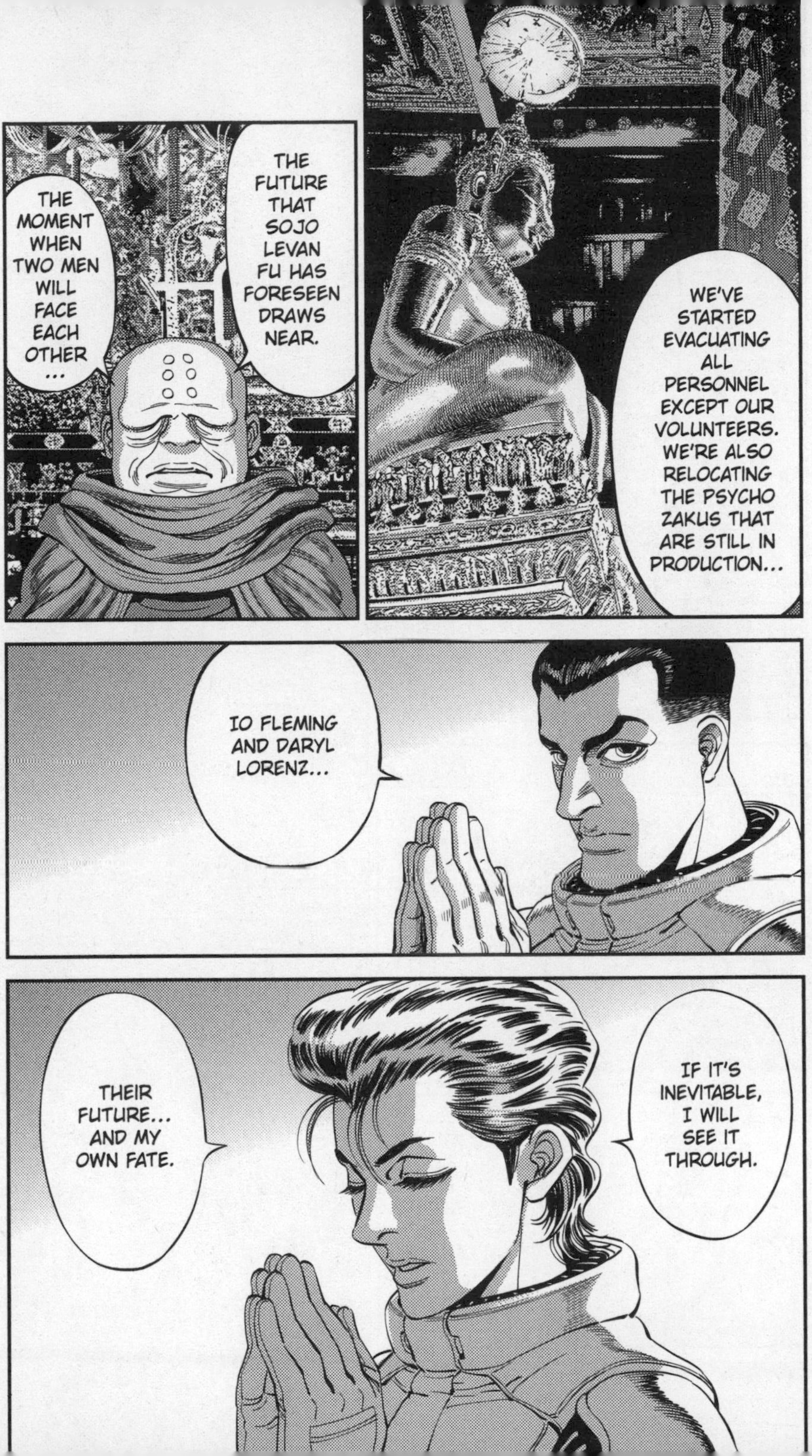
WE'VE STARTED EVACUATING ALL PERSONNEL EXCEPT OUR VOLUNTEERS. WE'RE ALSO RELOCATING THE PSYCHO ZAKUS THAT ARE STILL IN PRODUCTION...
THE FUTURE THAT SOJO LEVAN FU HAS FORESEEN DRAWS NEAR.
THE MOMENT WHEN TWO MEN WILL FACE EACH OTHER ...
IO FLEMING AND DARYL LORENZ...
IF IT'S INEVITABLE, I WILL SEE IT THROUGH.
THEIR FUTURE... AND MY OWN FATE.

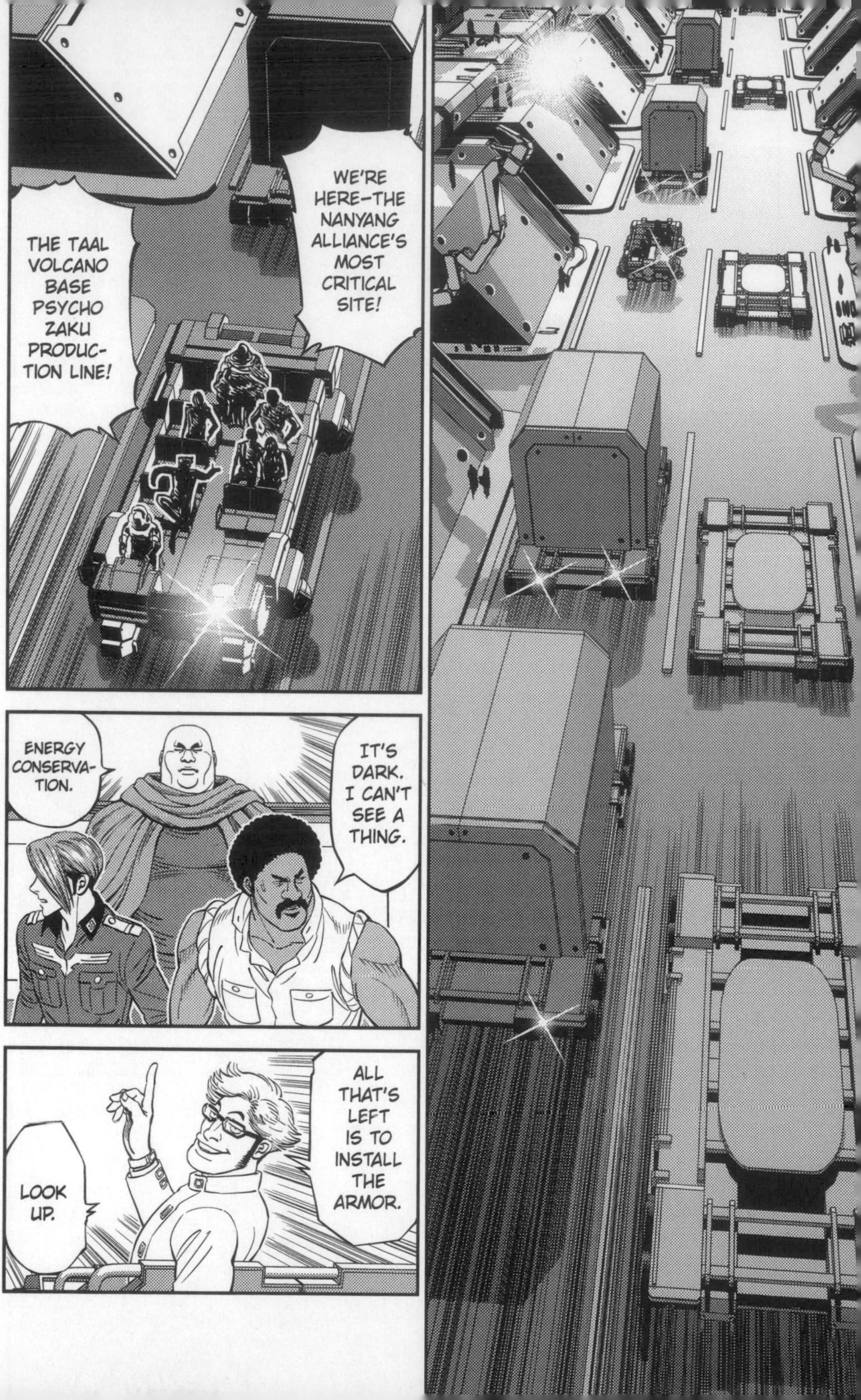
WE'RE HERE—THE NANYANG ALLIANCE'S MOST CRITICAL SITE!
THE TAAL VOLCANO BASE PSYCHO ZAKU PRODUCTION LINE!
IT'S DARK. I CAN'T SEE A THING.
ENERGY CONSERVATION.
ALL THAT'S LEFT IS TO INSTALL THE ARMOR.
LOOK UP.

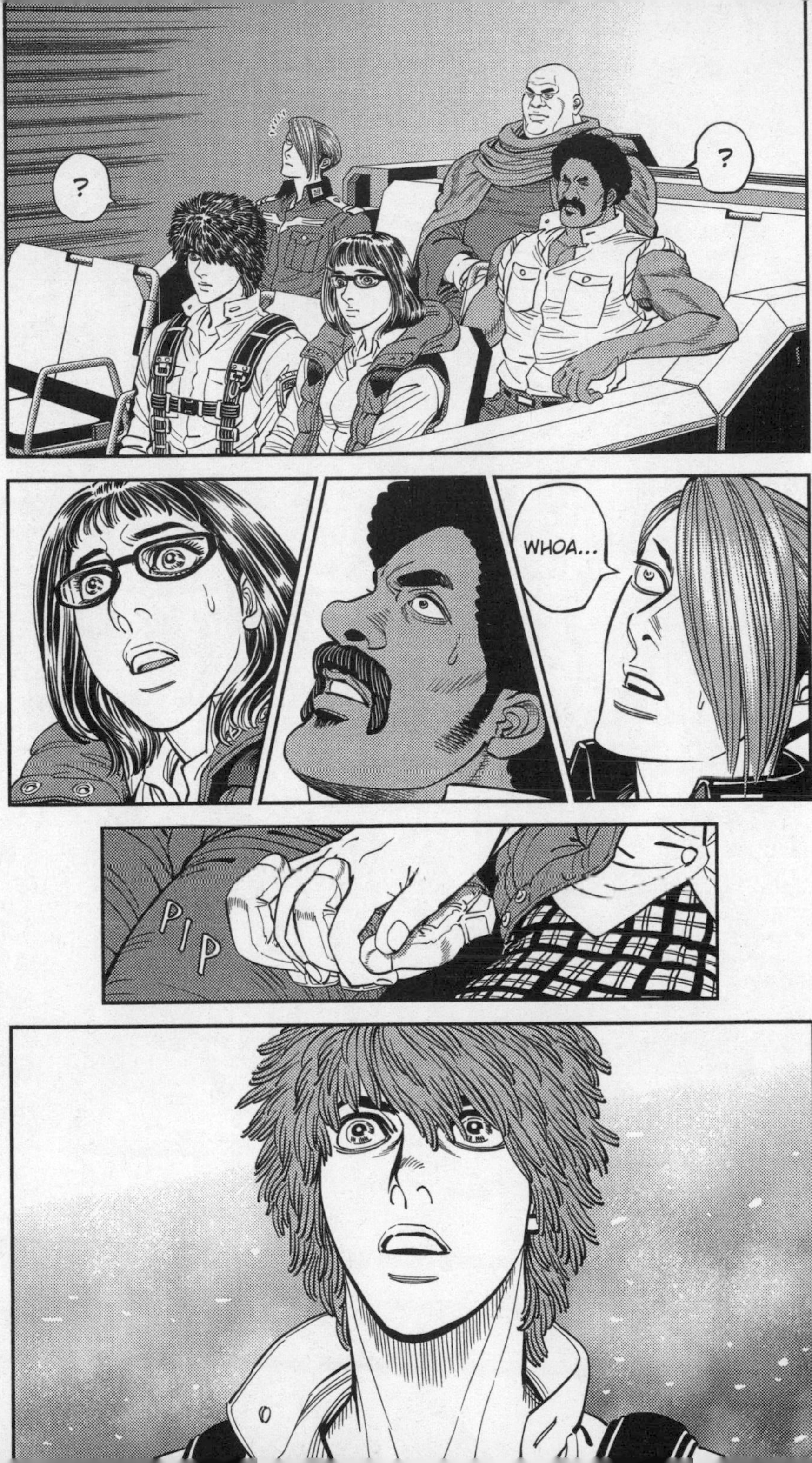
?
?
WHOA...
PIP

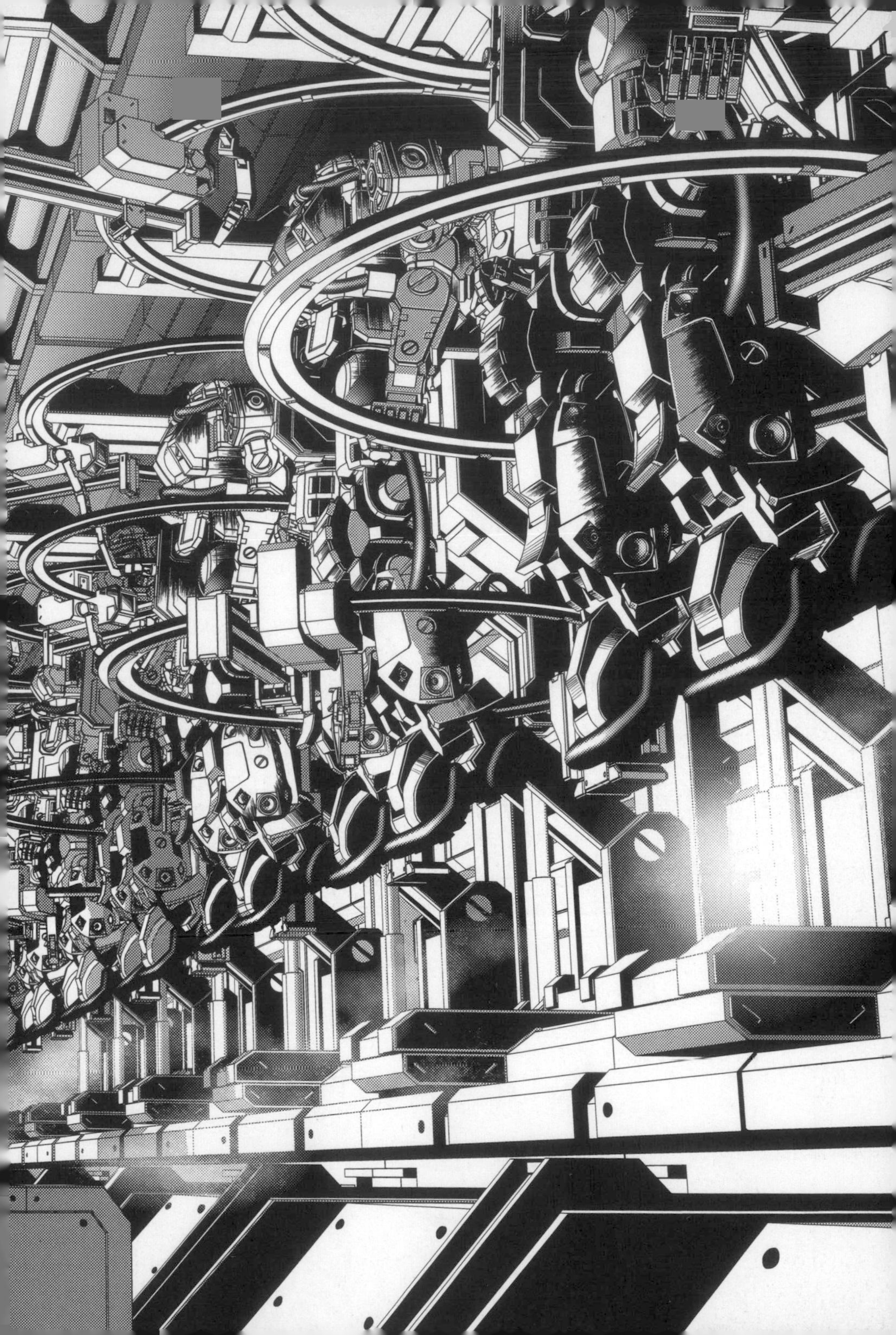

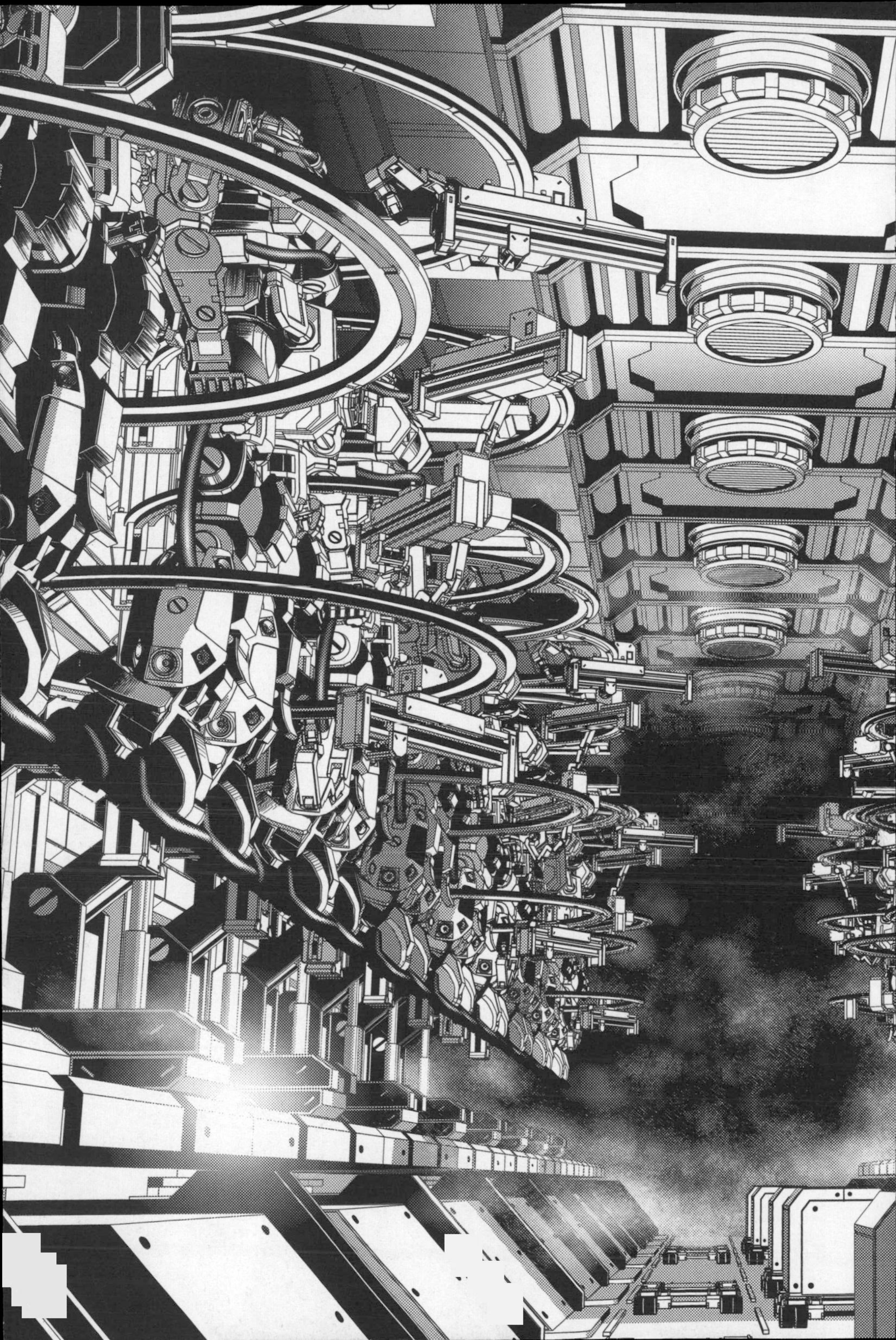

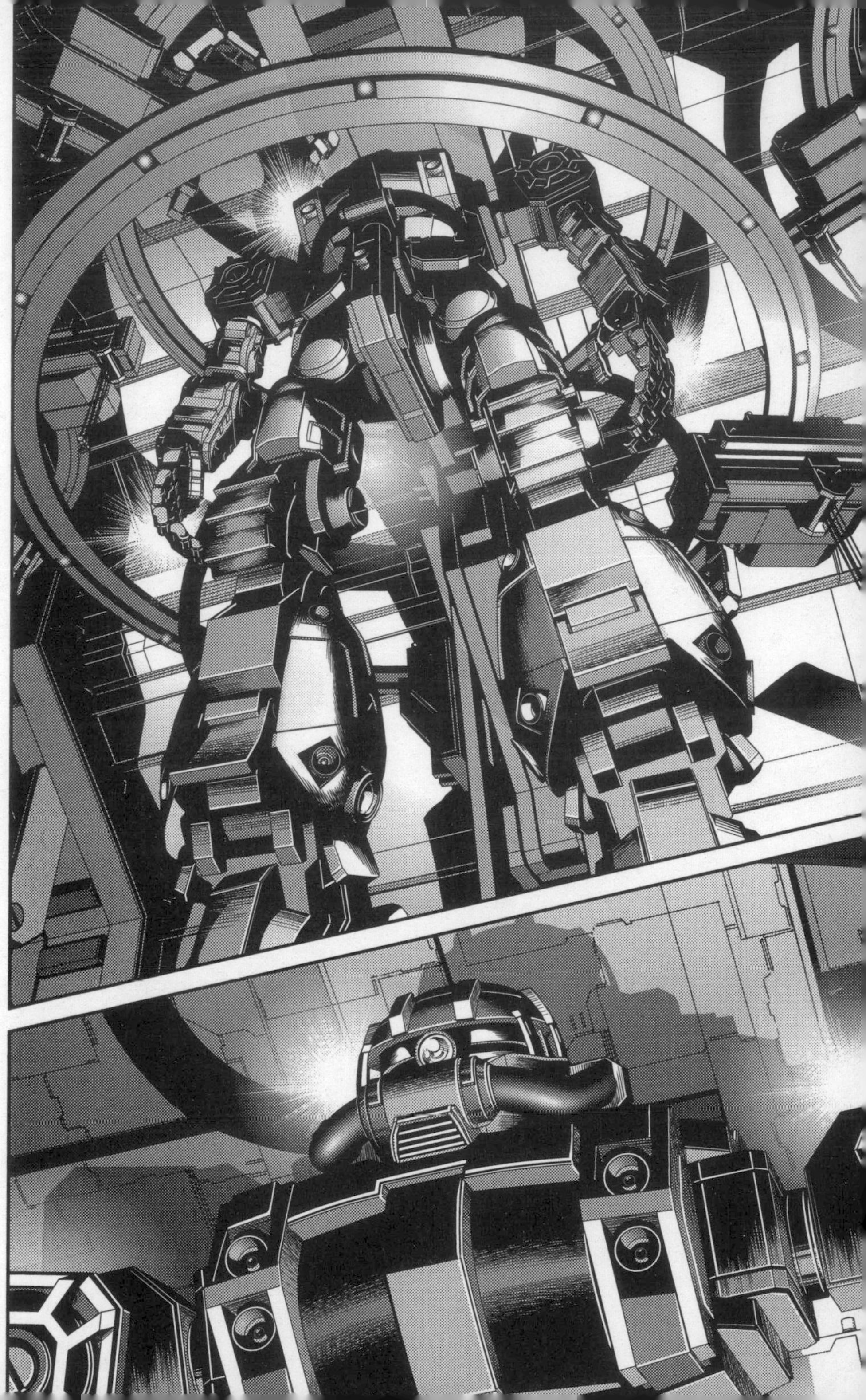

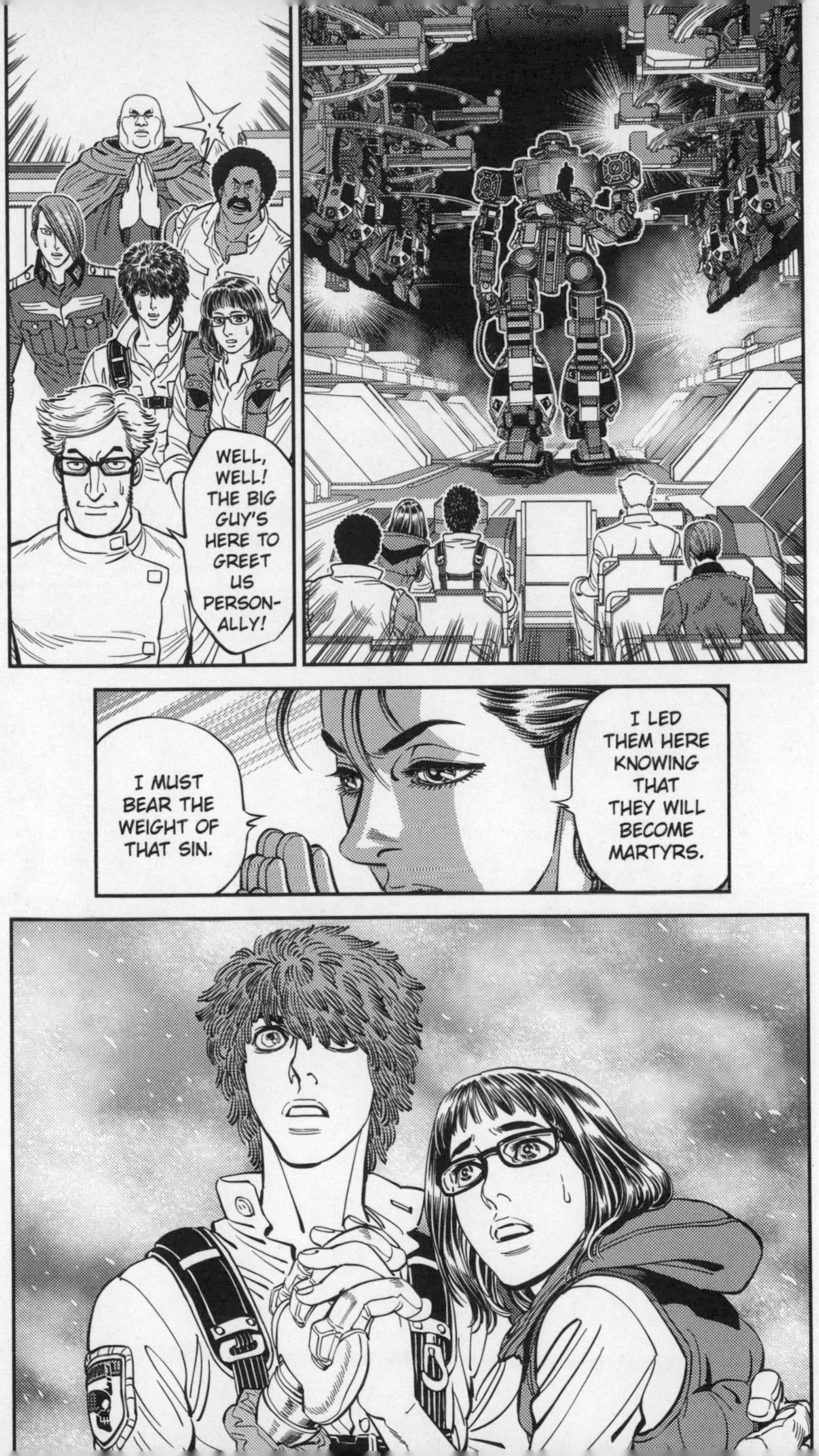
WELL, WELL! THE BIG GUY'S HERE TO GREET US PERSON-ALLY!
I LED THEM HERE KNOWING THAT THEY WILL BECOME MARTYRS.
I MUST BEAR THE WEIGHT OF THAT SIN.

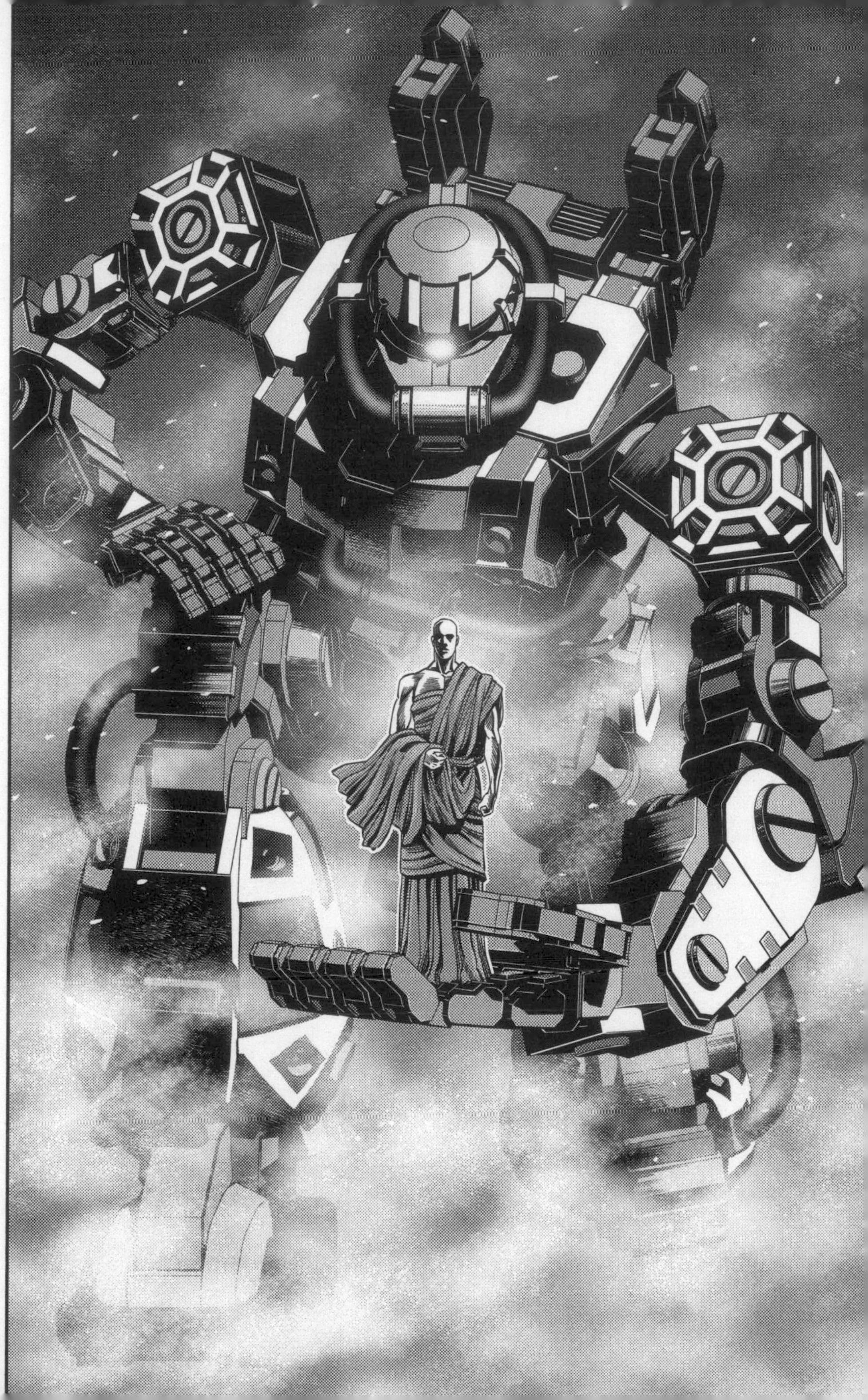

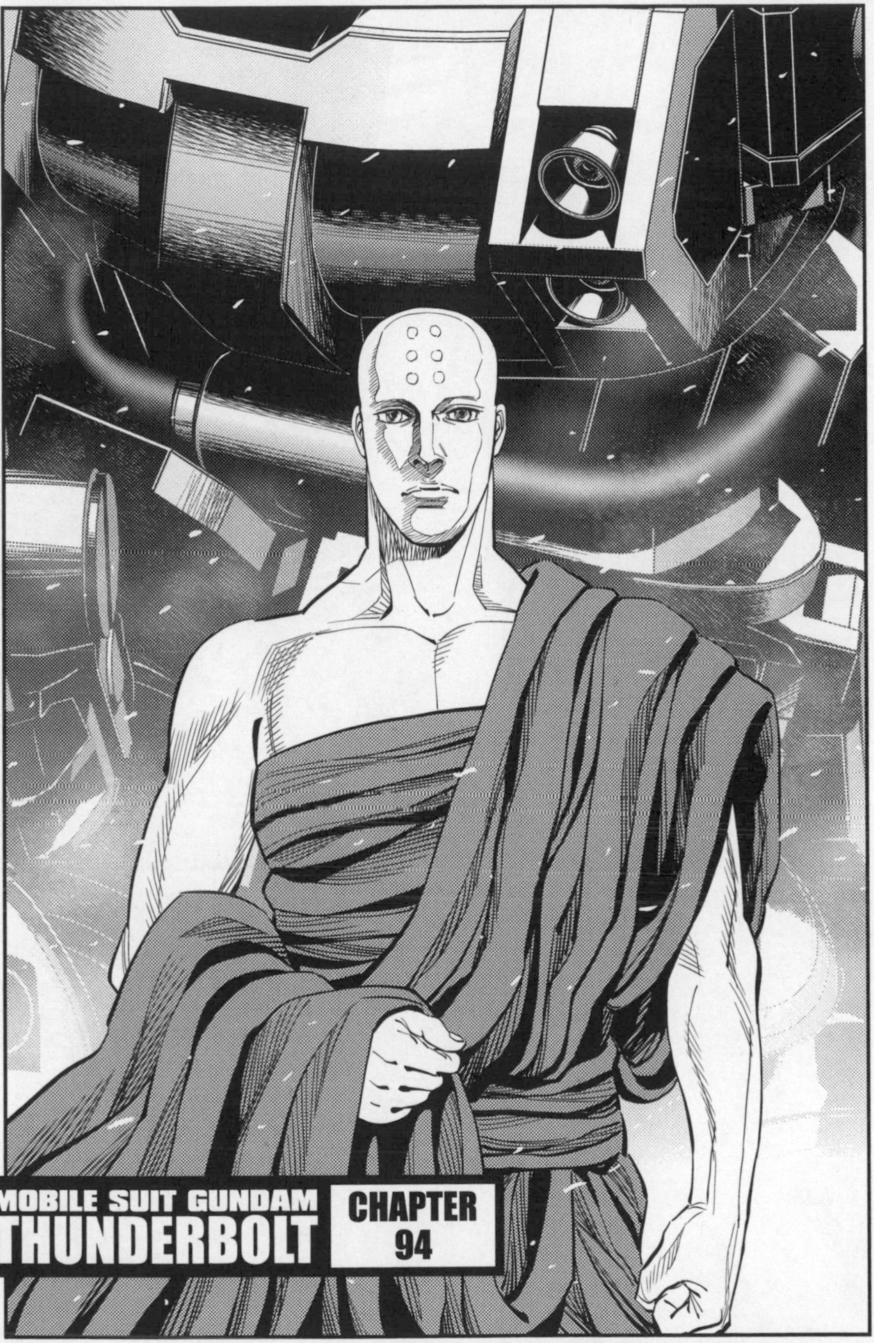
MOBILE SUIT GUNDAM
THUNDERBOLT
CHAPTER
94

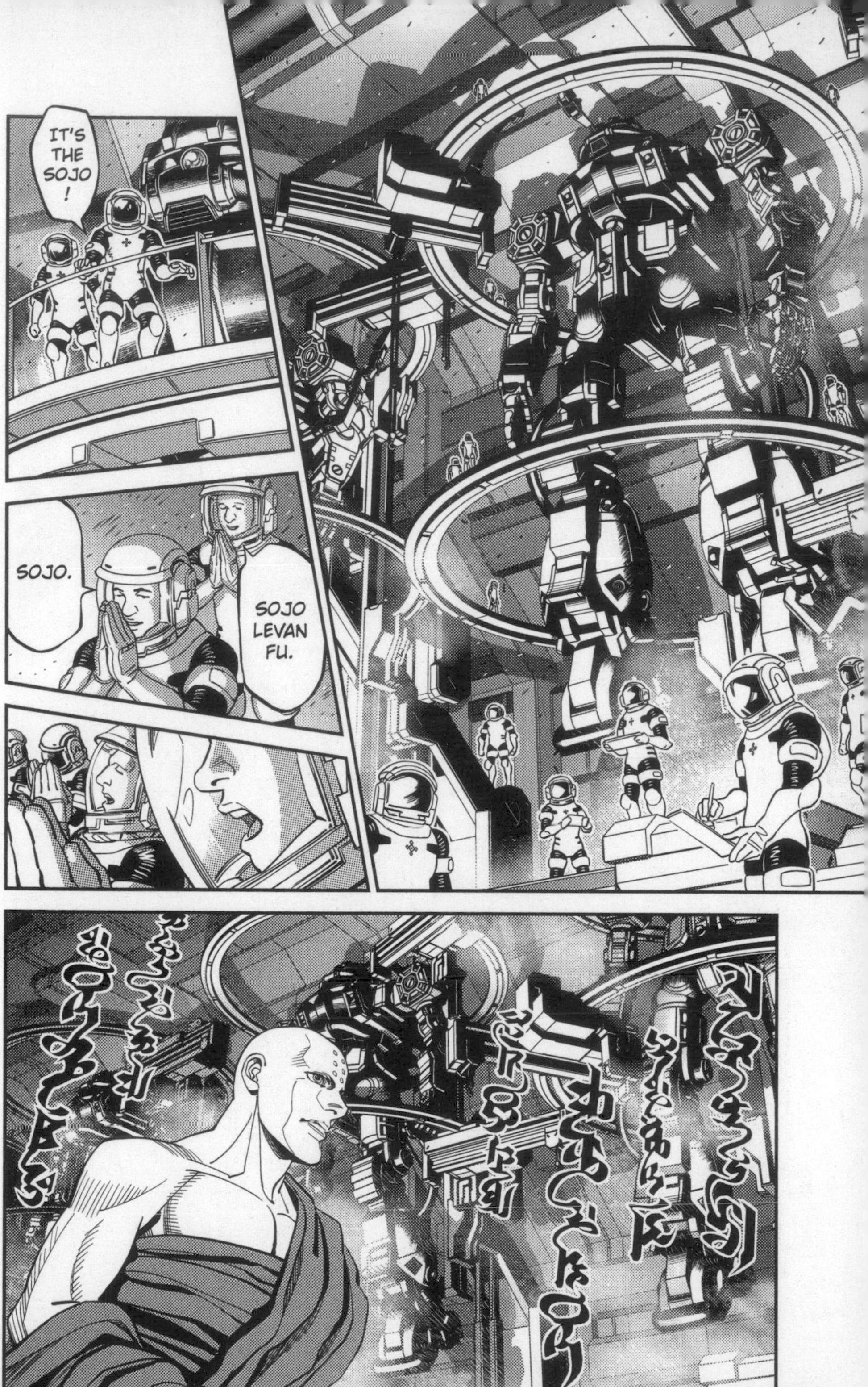
IT'S THE SOJO!
SOJO LEVAN FU.
SOJO.

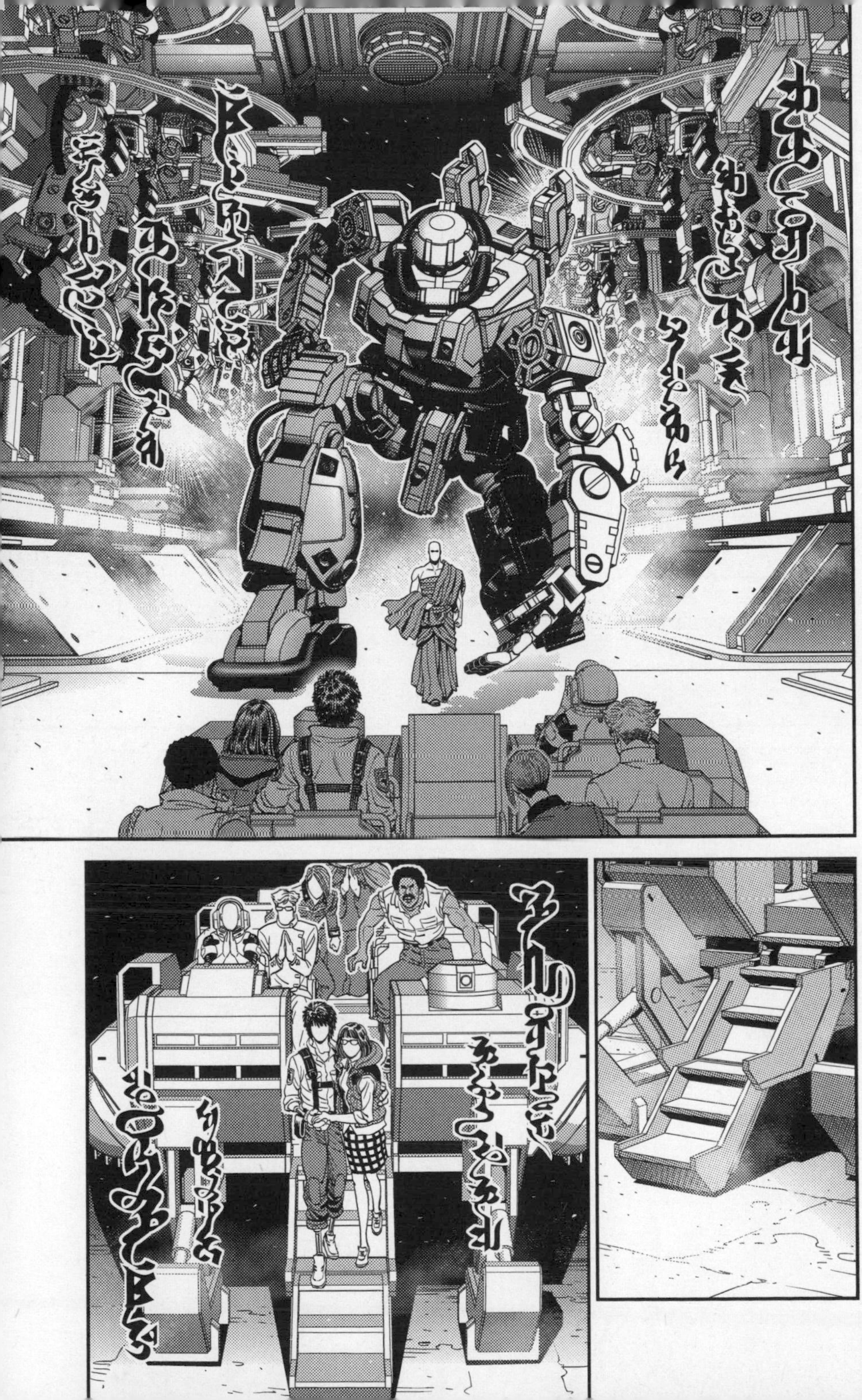

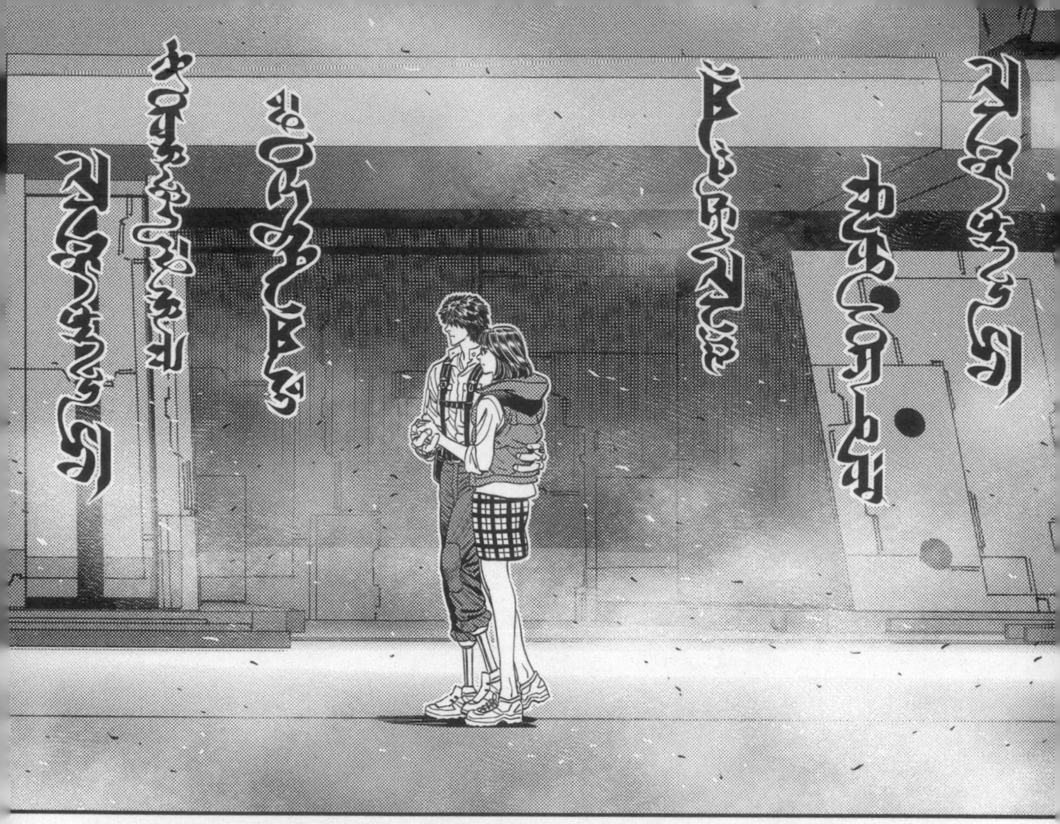

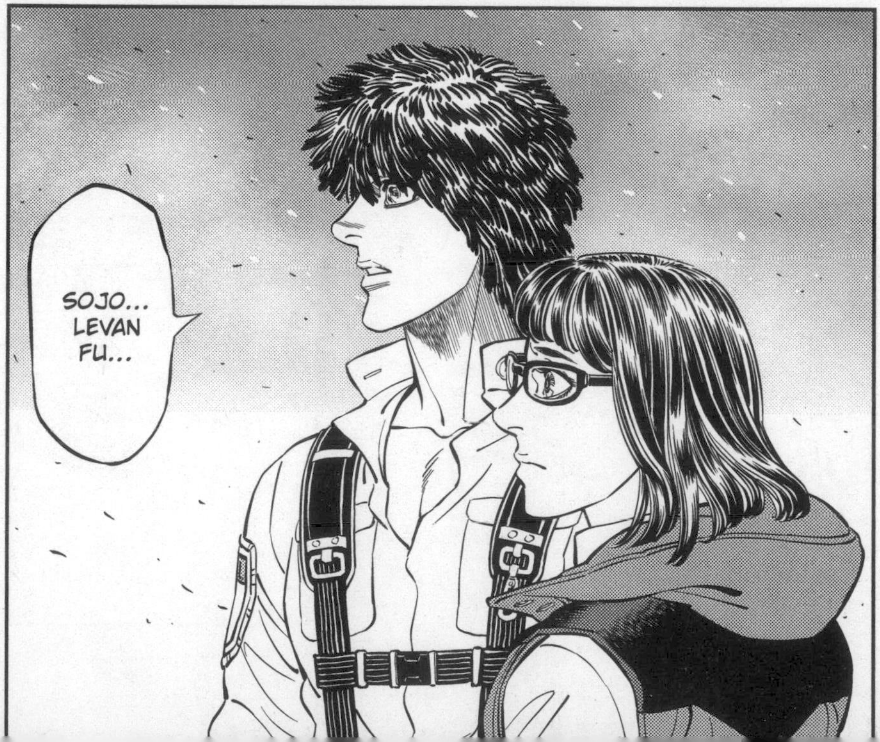
SOJO... LEVAN FU...

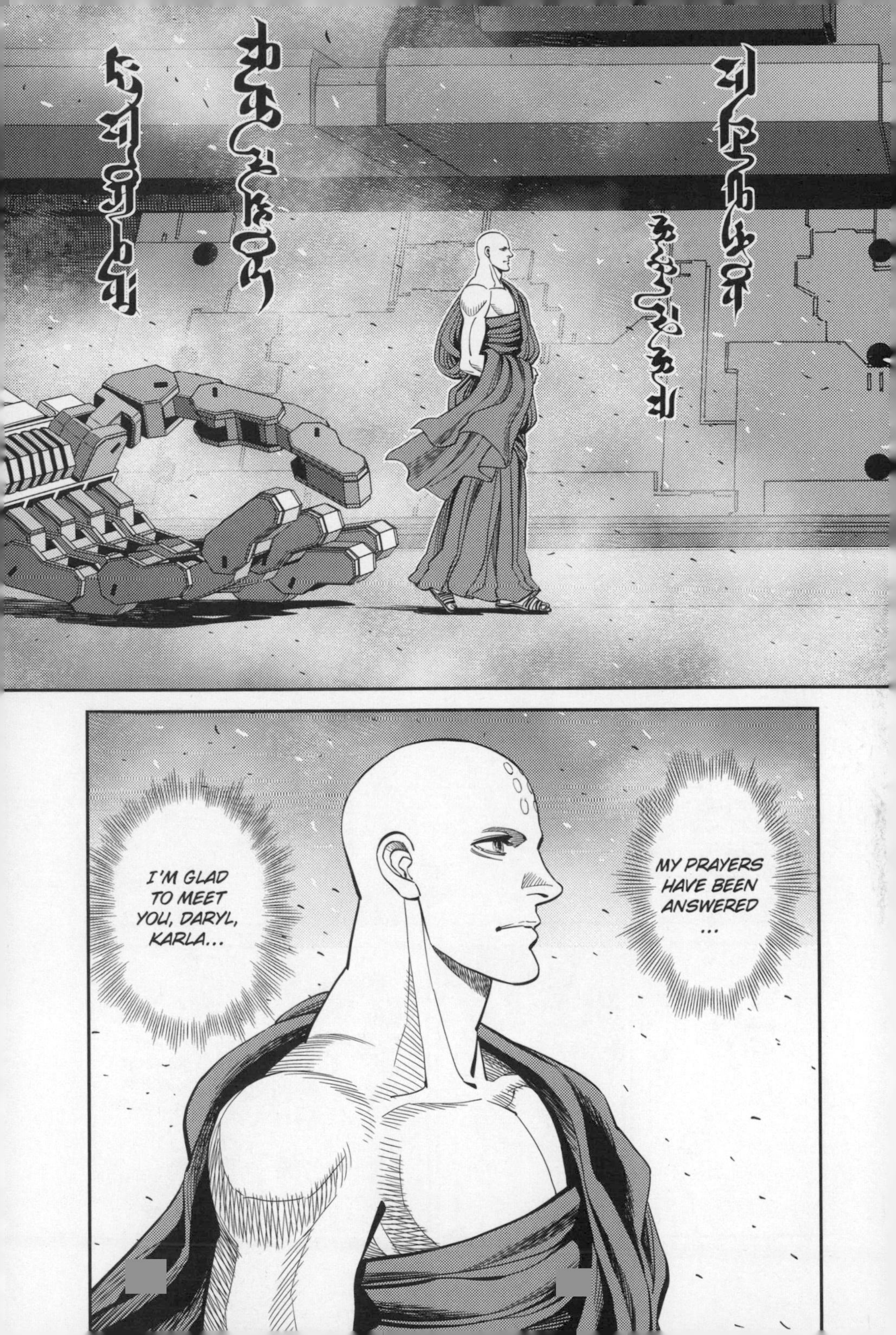
MY PRAYERS HAVE BEEN ANSWERED ...
I'M GLAD TO MEET YOU, DARYL, KARLA...

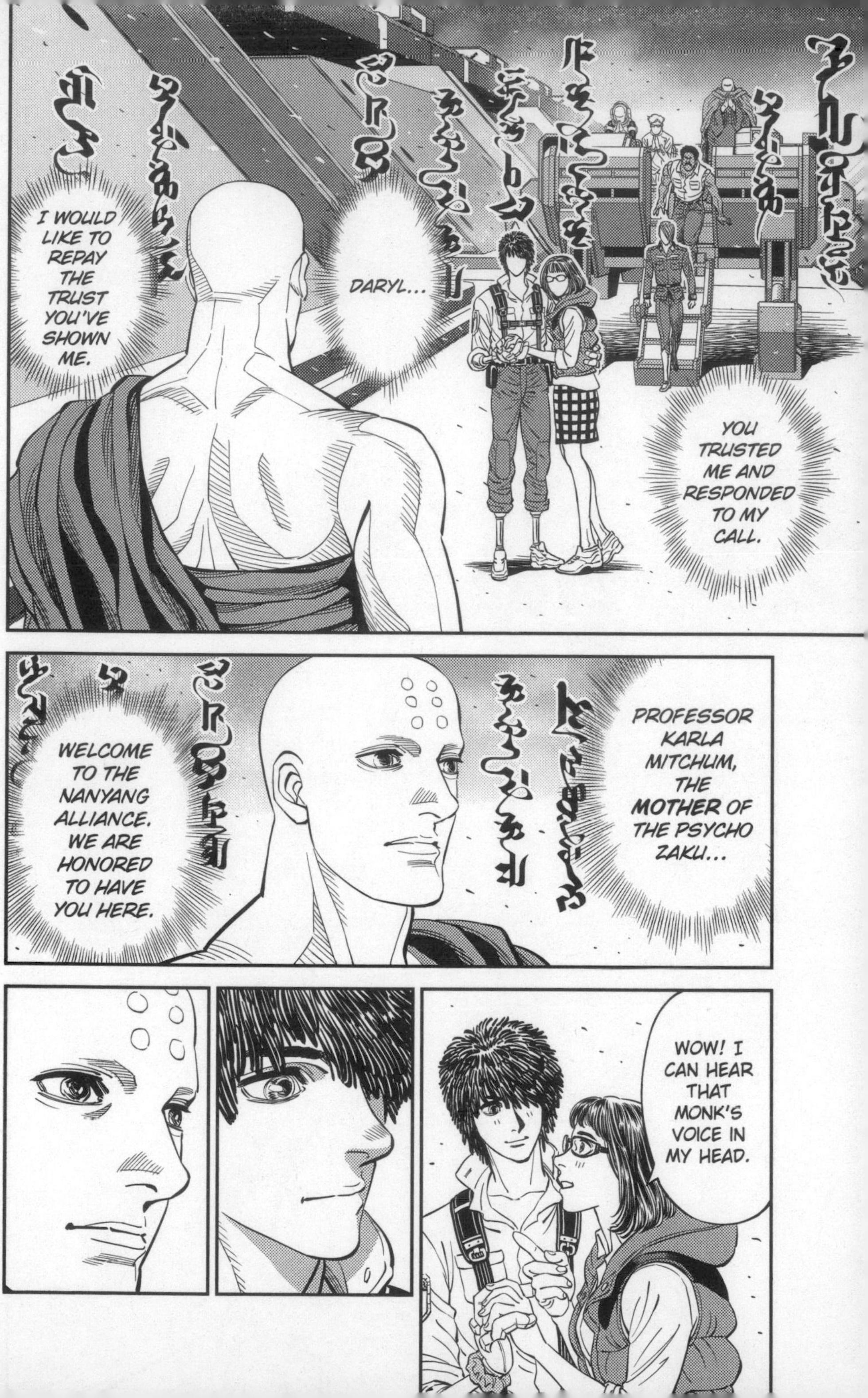
YOU TRUSTED ME AND RESPONDED TO MY CALL.
DARYL...
I WOULD LIKE TO REPAY THE TRUST YOU'VE SHOWN ME.
PROFESSOR KARLA MITCHUM, THE **MOTHER** OF THE PSYCHO ZAKU...
WELCOME TO THE NANYANG ALLIANCE. WE ARE HONORED TO HAVE YOU HERE.
WOW! I CAN HEAR THAT MONK'S VOICE IN MY HEAD.

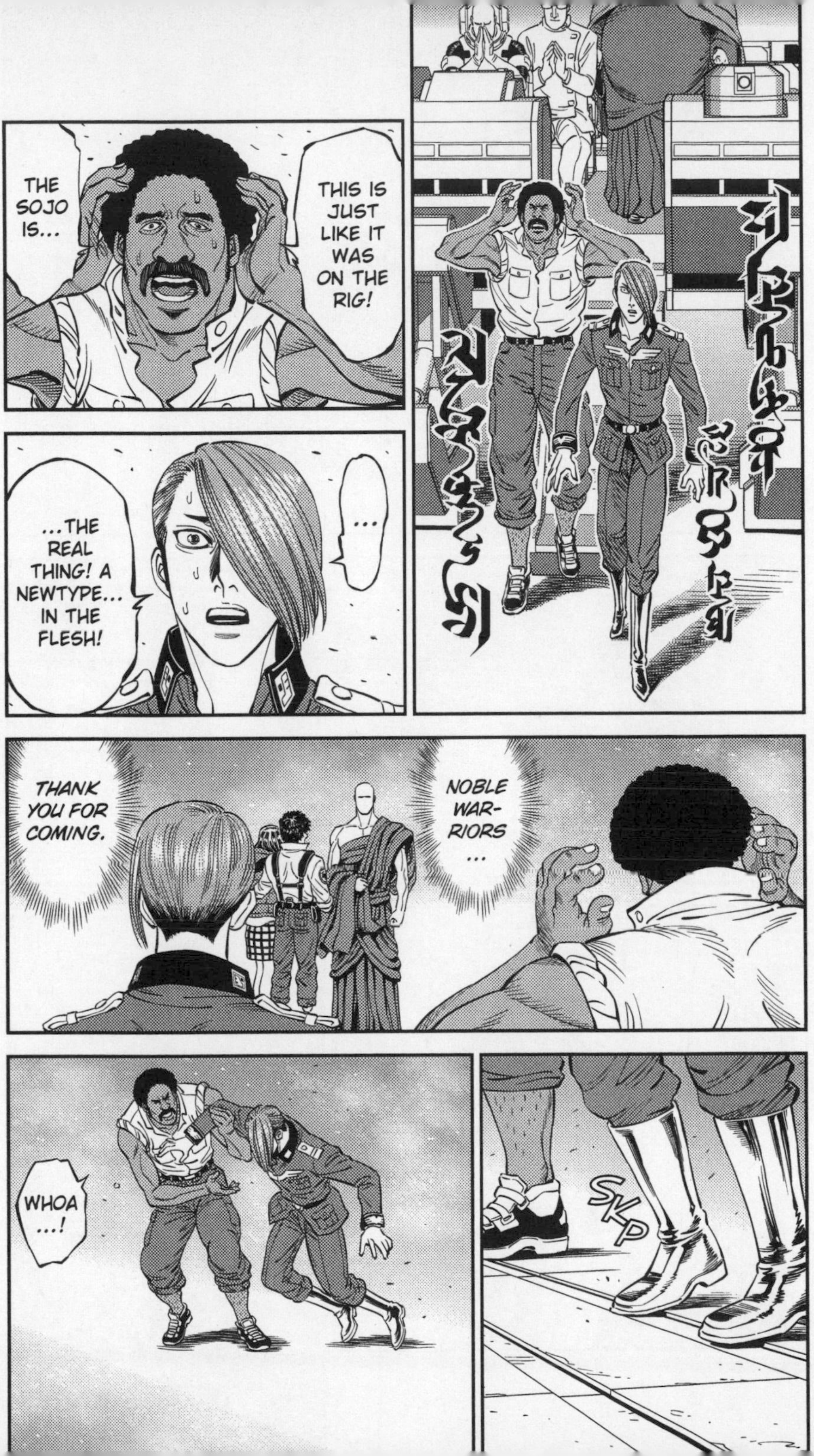
THIS IS JUST LIKE IT WAS ON THE RIG!
THE SOJO IS...
...
...THE REAL THING! A NEWTYPE... IN THE FLESH!
NOBLE WAR-RIORS ...
THANK YOU FOR COMING.
SKP
WHOA ...!

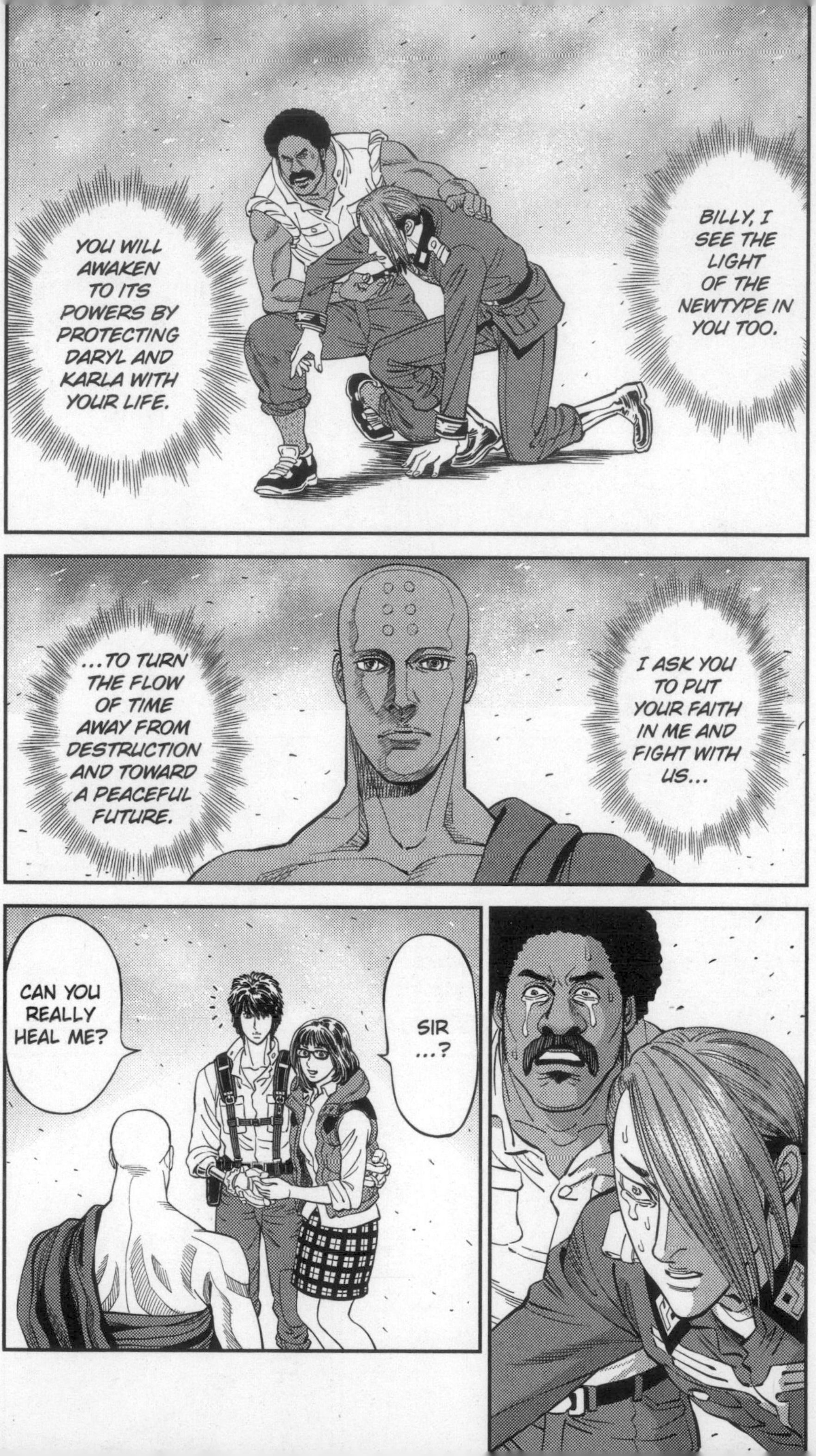
BILLY, I SEE THE LIGHT OF THE NEWTYPE IN YOU TOO.
YOU WILL AWAKEN TO ITS POWERS BY PROTECTING DARYL AND KARLA WITH YOUR LIFE.
I ASK YOU TO PUT YOUR FAITH IN ME AND FIGHT WITH US...
...TO TURN THE FLOW OF TIME AWAY FROM DESTRUCTION AND TOWARD A PEACEFUL FUTURE.
SIR ...?
CAN YOU REALLY HEAL ME?

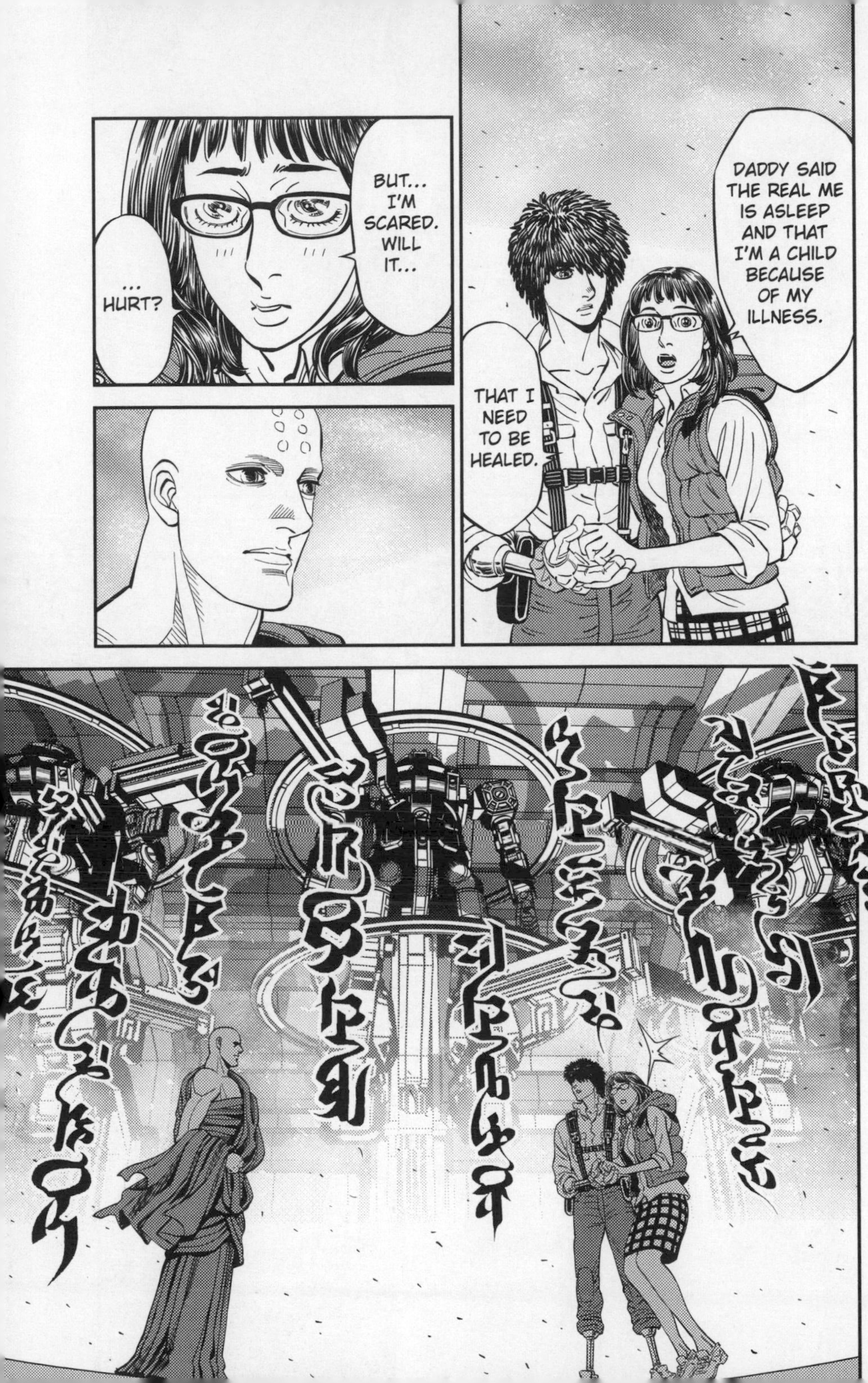
DADDY SAID THE REAL ME IS ASLEEP AND THAT I'M A CHILD BECAUSE OF MY ILLNESS.
THAT I NEED TO BE HEALED.
BUT... I'M SCARED. WILL IT...
... HURT?

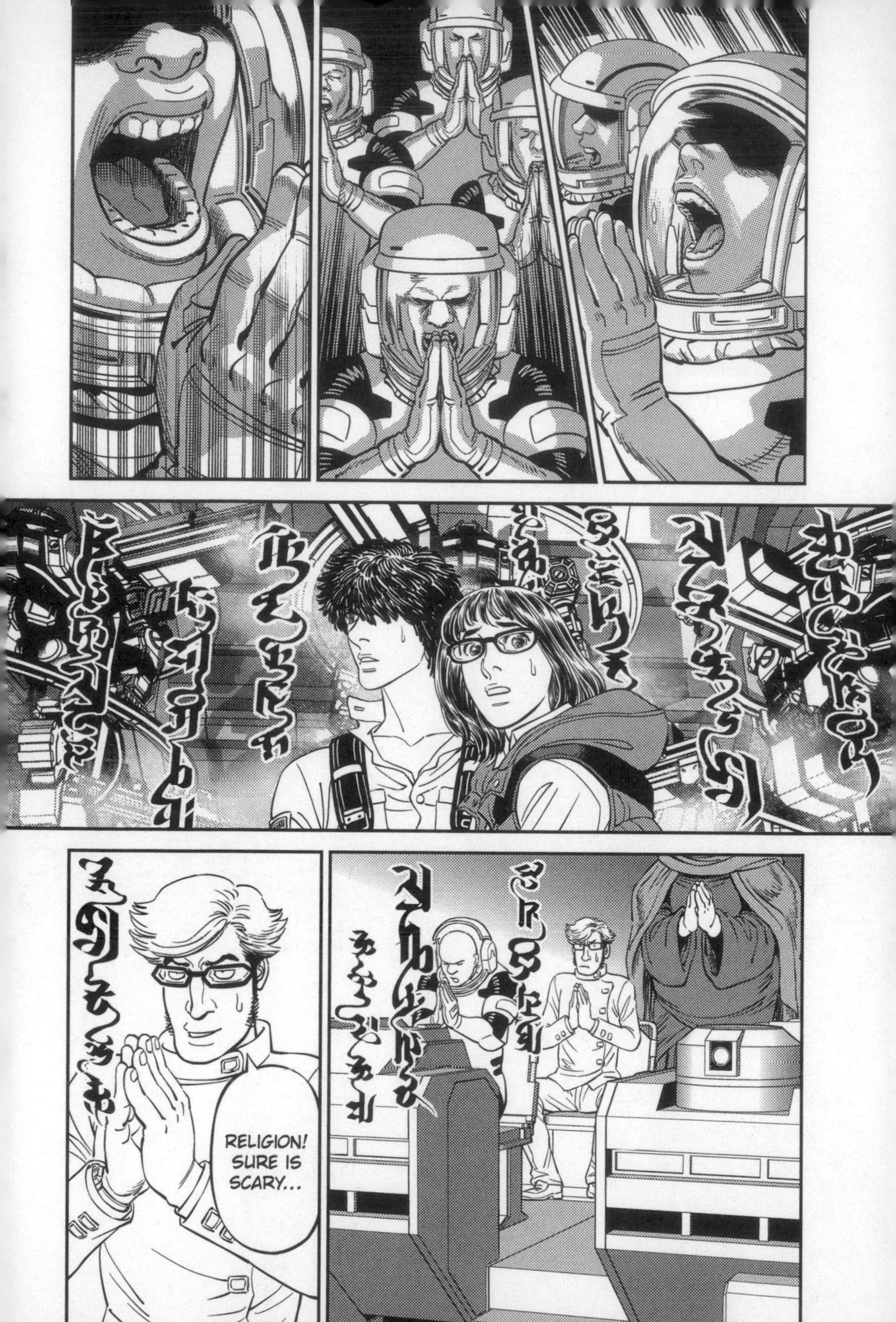
RELIGION! SURE IS SCARY...

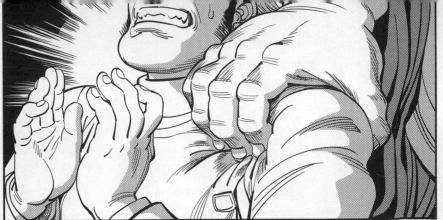

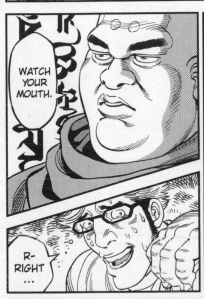

WATCH YOUR MOUTH.
R-RIGHT ...
PROFESSOR MITCHUM, WE ARE ALL WAITING FOR YOU TO AWAKEN FROM YOUR SLUMBER...
...BECAUSE YOUR MIND AND YOUR CREATION HAVE THE POWER TO CHANGE THE WORLD.

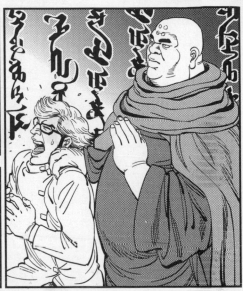

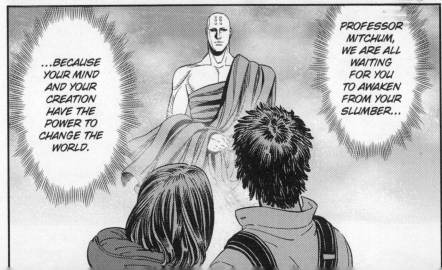

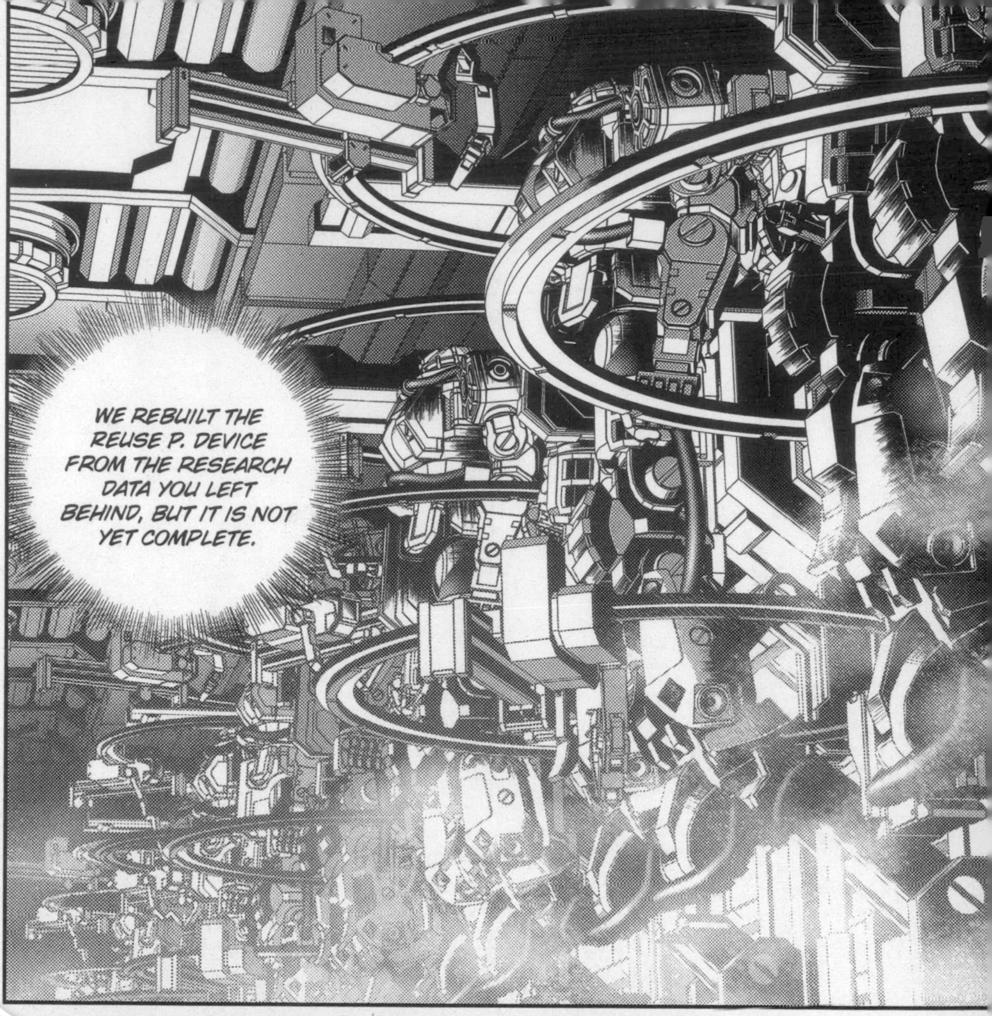
WE REBUILT THE REUSE P. DEVICE FROM THE RESEARCH DATA YOU LEFT BEHIND, BUT IT IS NOT YET COMPLETE.
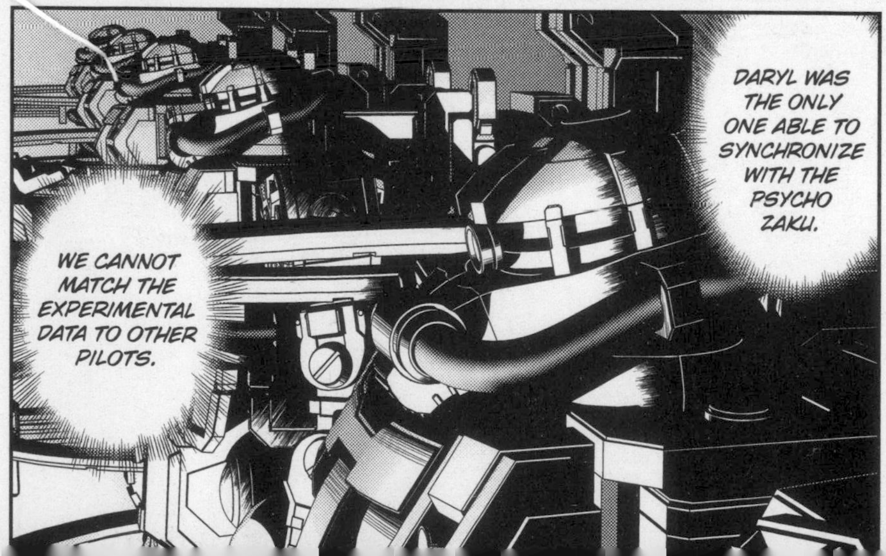
DARYL WAS THE ONLY ONE ABLE TO SYNCHRONIZE WITH THE PSYCHO ZAKU.
WE CANNOT MATCH THE EXPERIMENTAL DATA TO OTHER PILOTS.

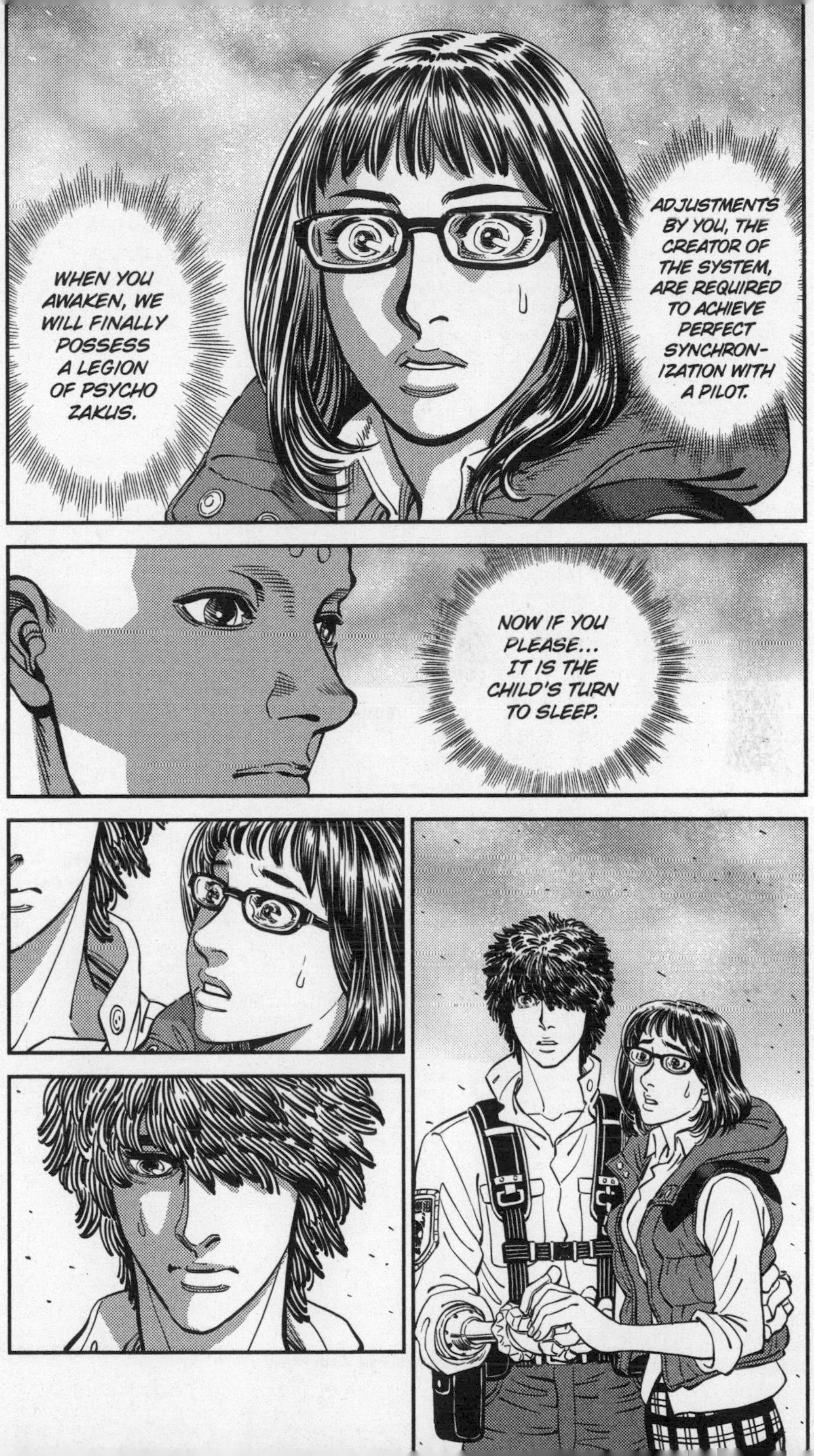
ADJUSTMENTS BY YOU, THE CREATOR OF THE SYSTEM, ARE REQUIRED TO ACHIEVE PERFECT SYNCHRON-IZATION WITH A PILOT.
WHEN YOU AWAKEN, WE WILL FINALLY POSSESS A LEGION OF PSYCHO ZAKUS.
NOW IF YOU PLEASE... IT IS THE CHILD'S TURN TO SLEEP.

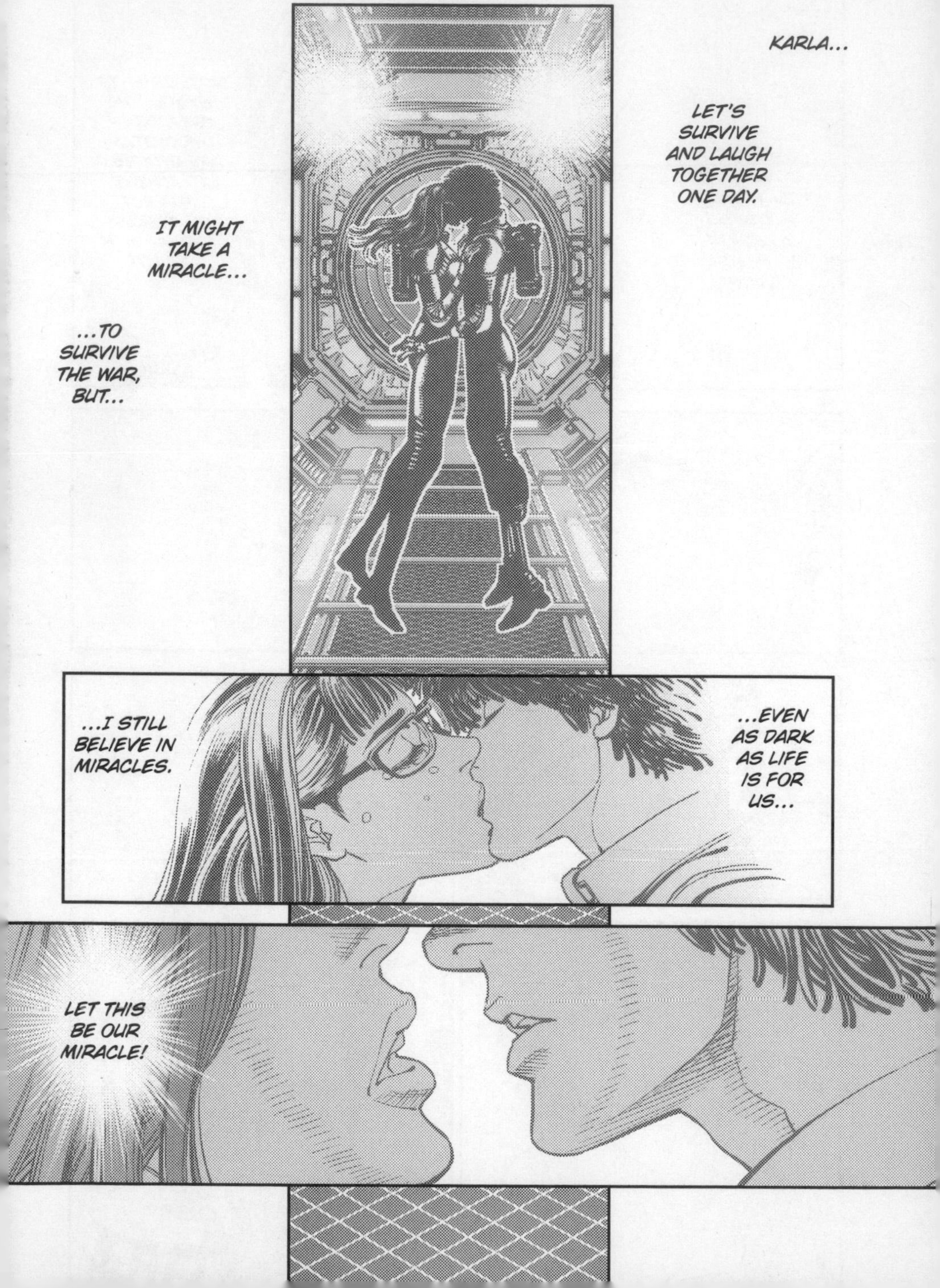
KARLA...
LET'S SURVIVE AND LAUGH TOGETHER ONE DAY.
IT MIGHT TAKE A MIRACLE...
...TO SURVIVE THE WAR, BUT...
...EVEN AS DARK AS LIFE IS FOR US...
...I STILL BELIEVE IN MIRACLES.
LET THIS BE OUR MIRACLE!

I'M SORRY, KARLA...

DADDY ...?

...SEE YOU AGAIN.

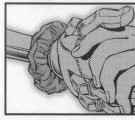

I WANT TO...

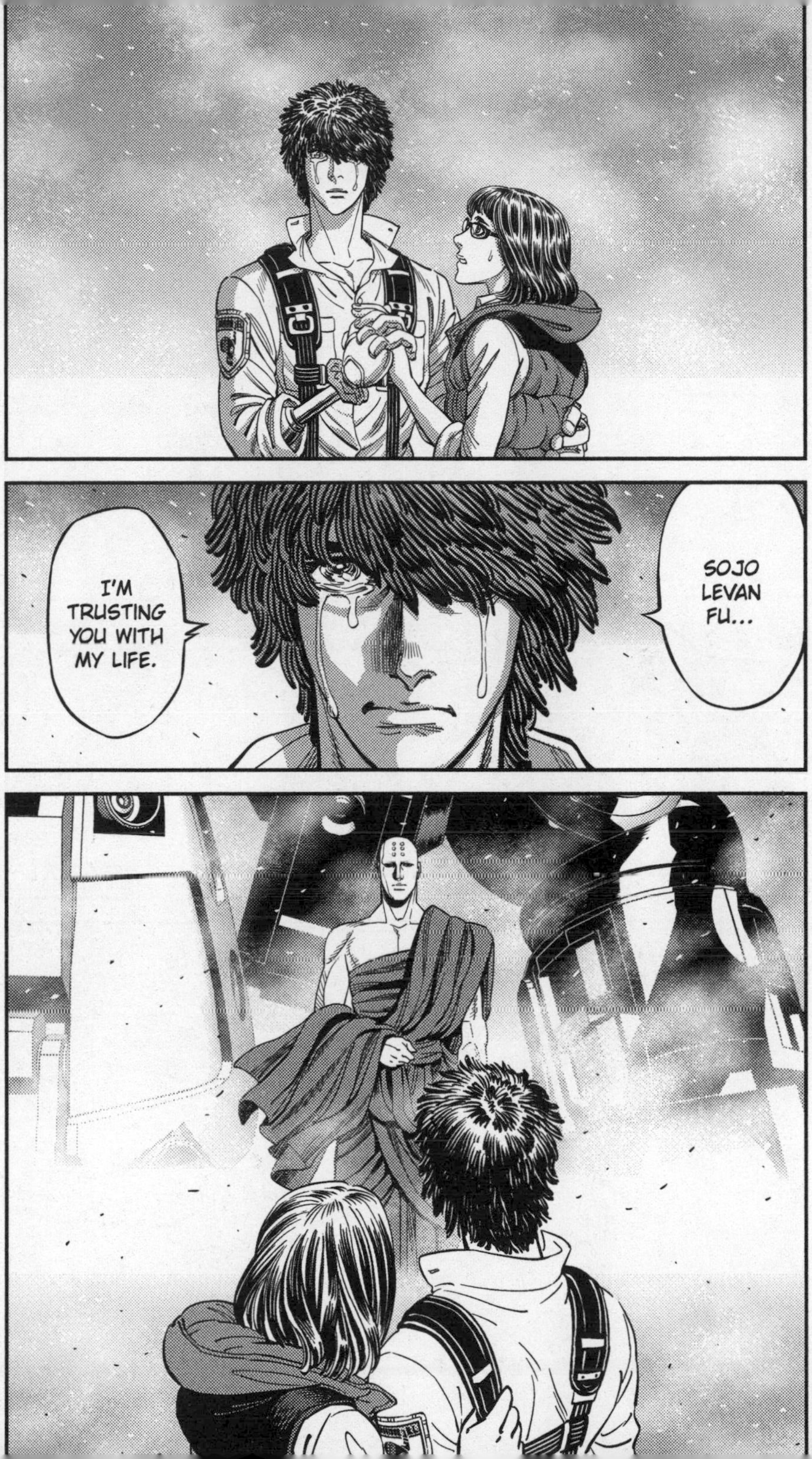
SOJO LEVAN FU...
I'M TRUSTING YOU WITH MY LIFE.

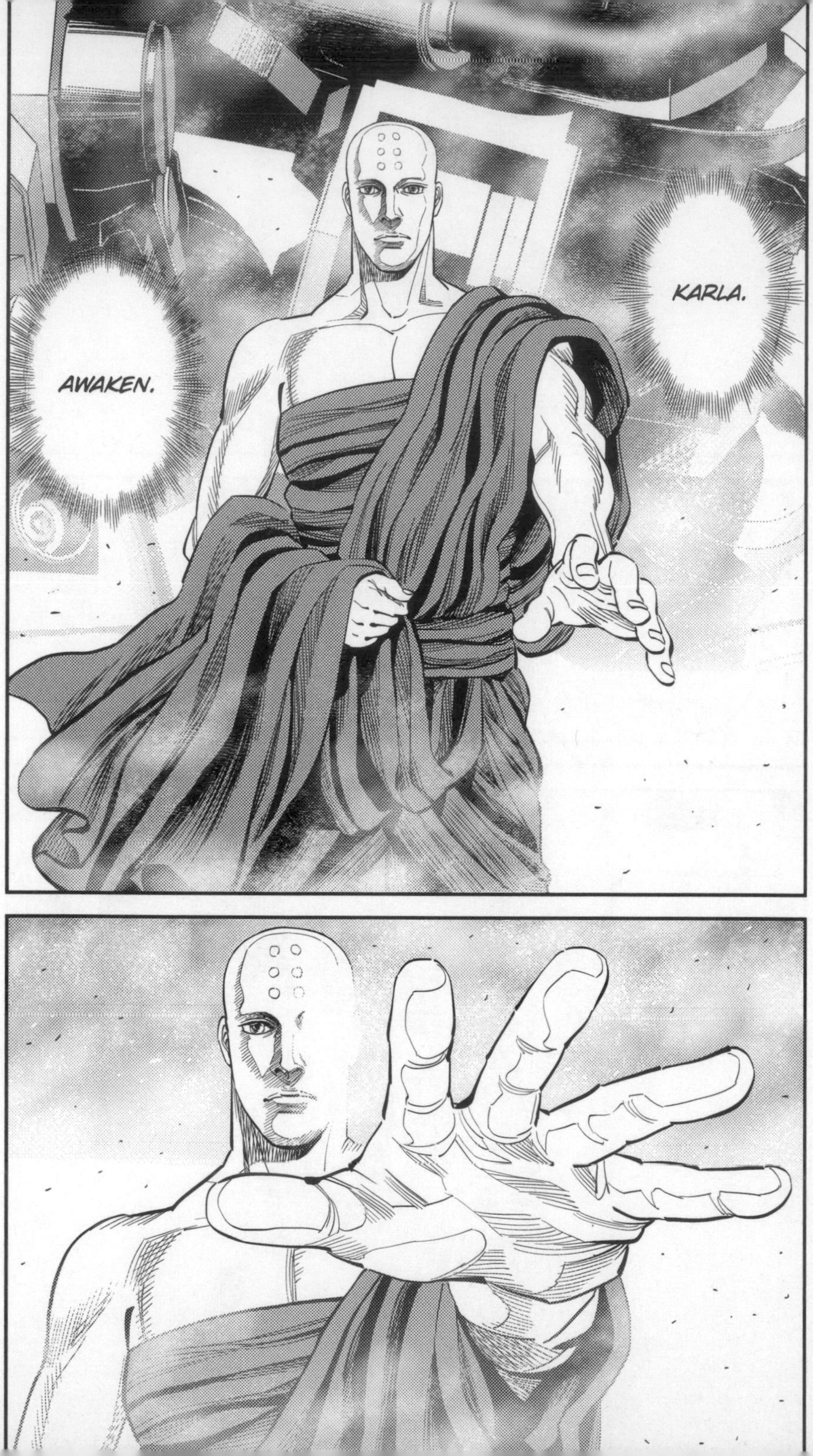
KARLA.
AWAKEN.

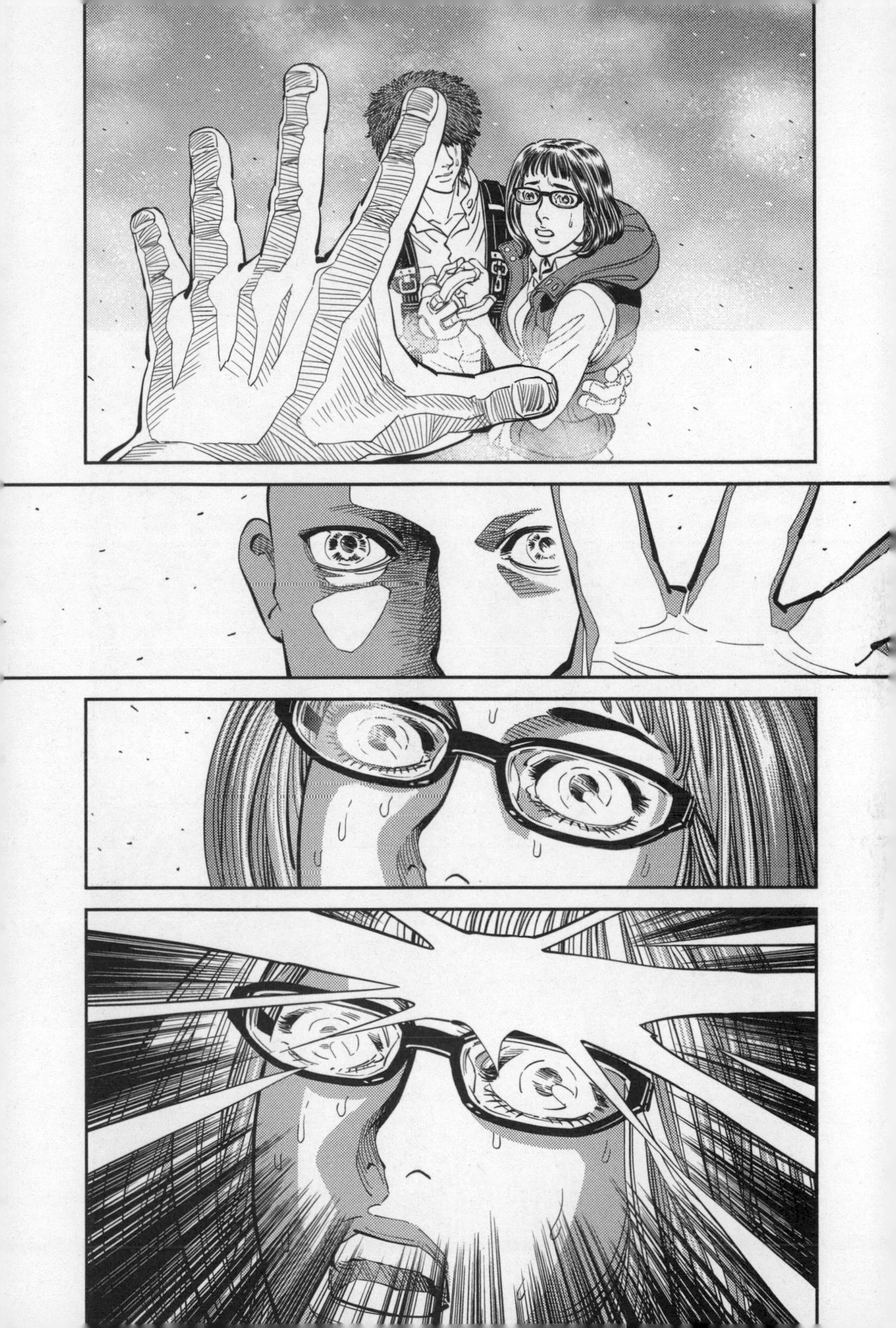

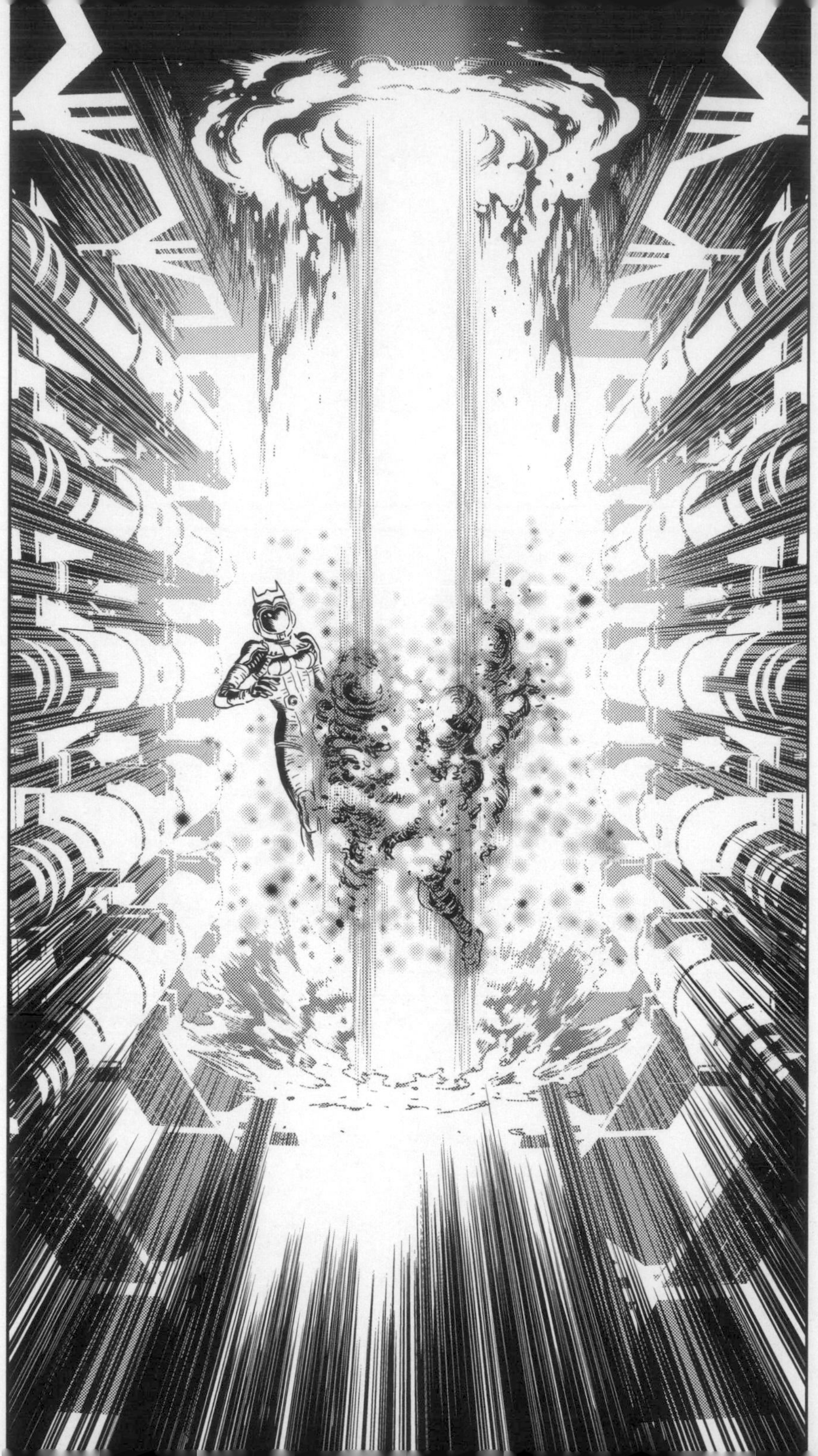

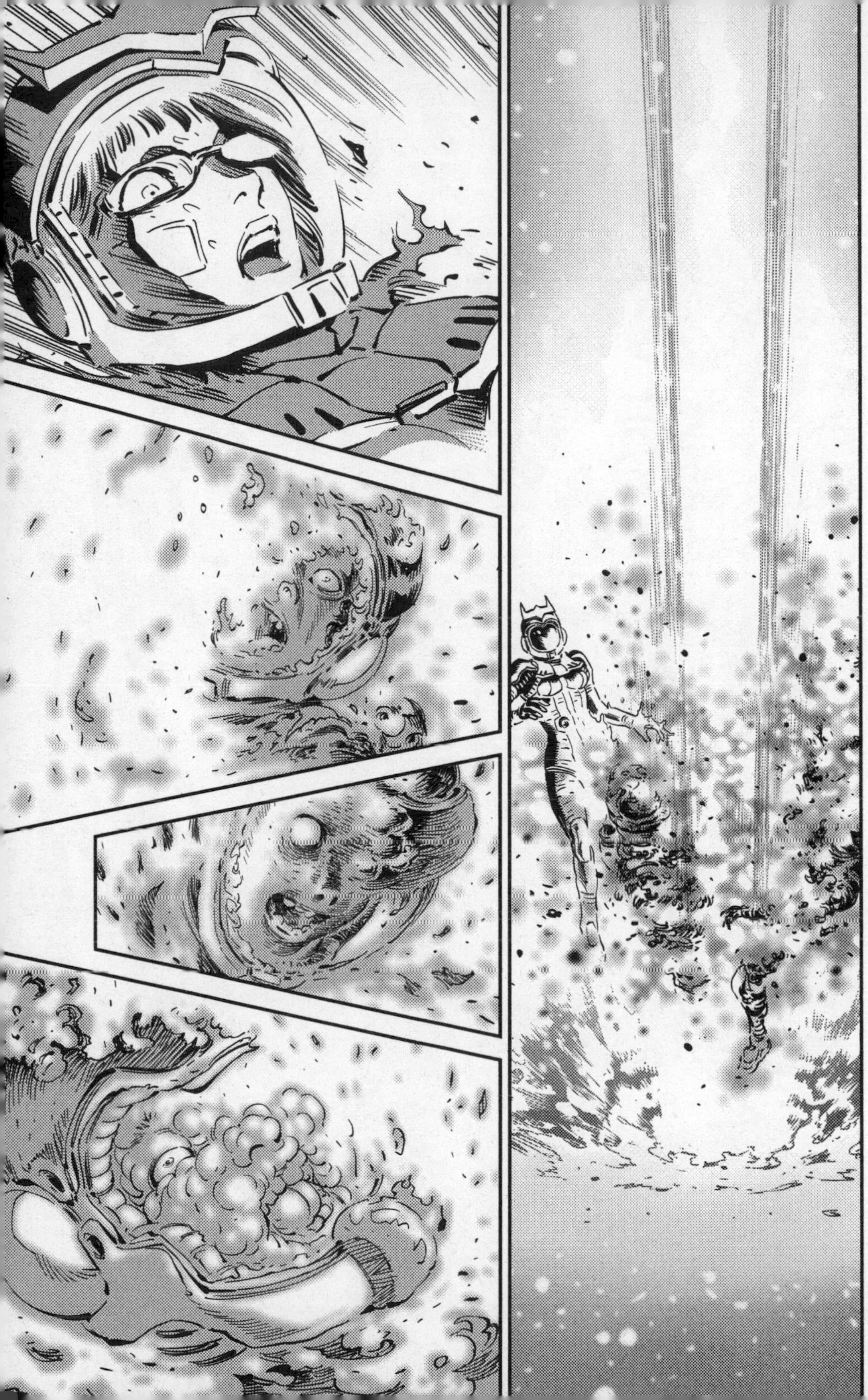

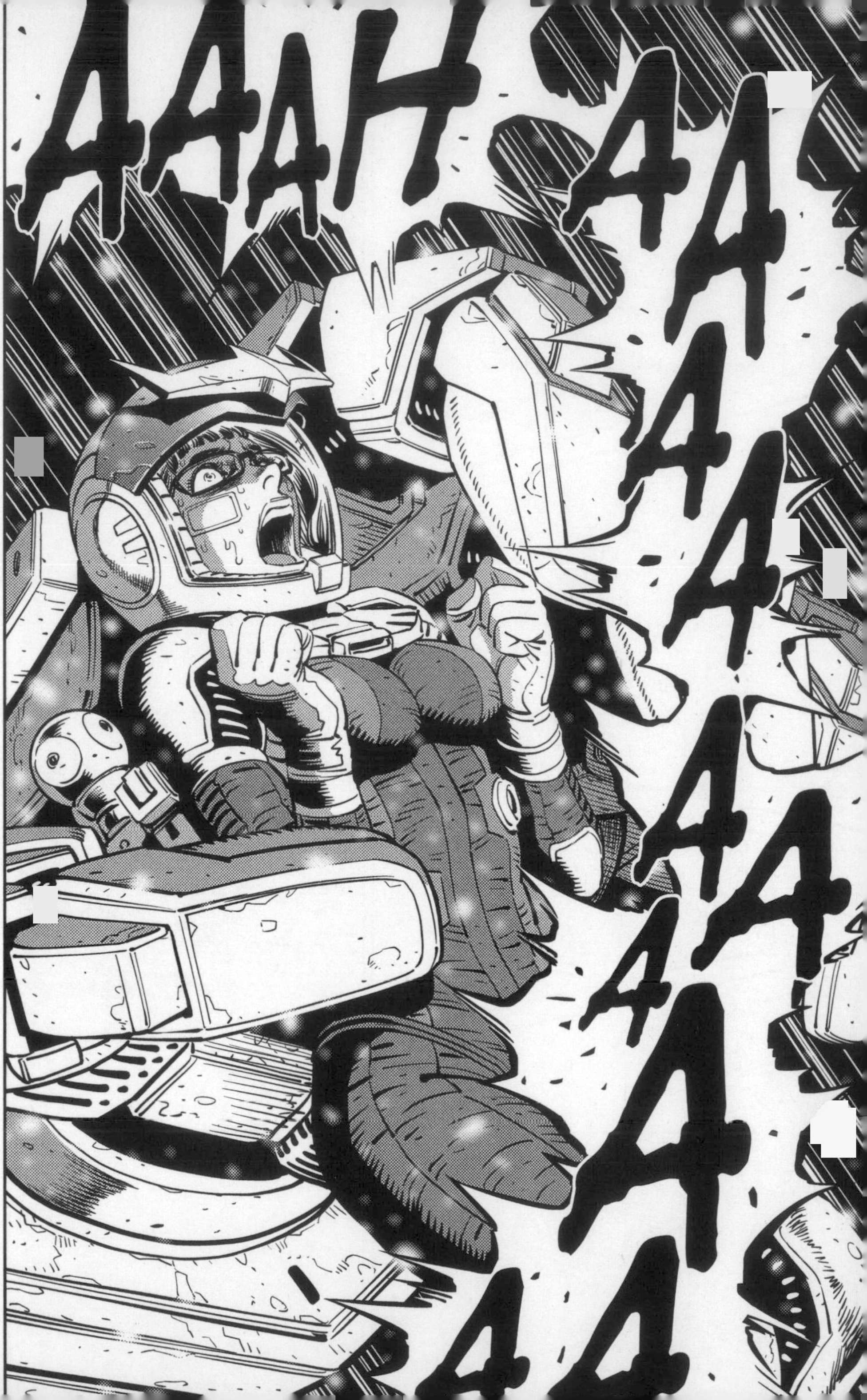
AAAH
AAAAAAAAAAAAAA

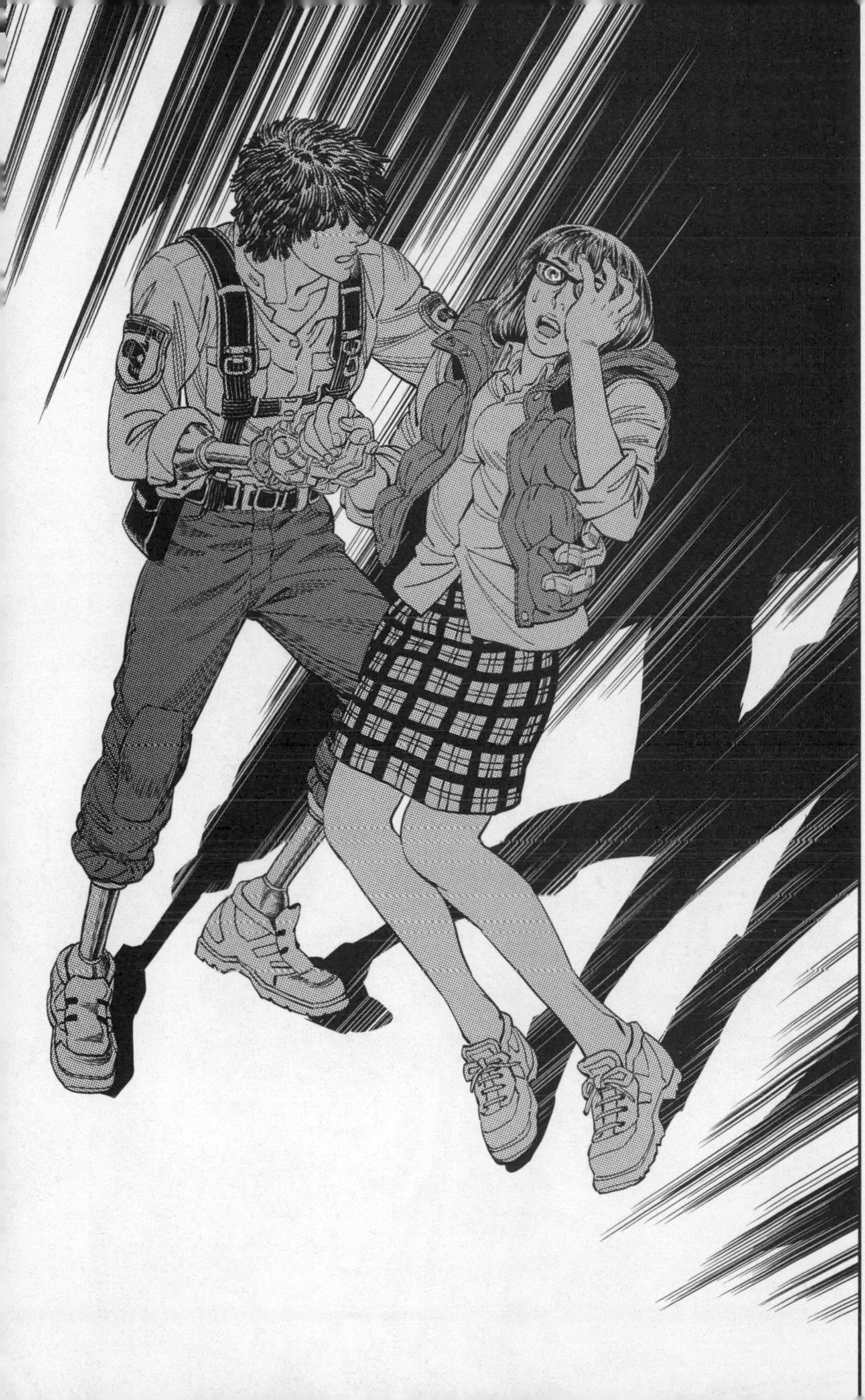

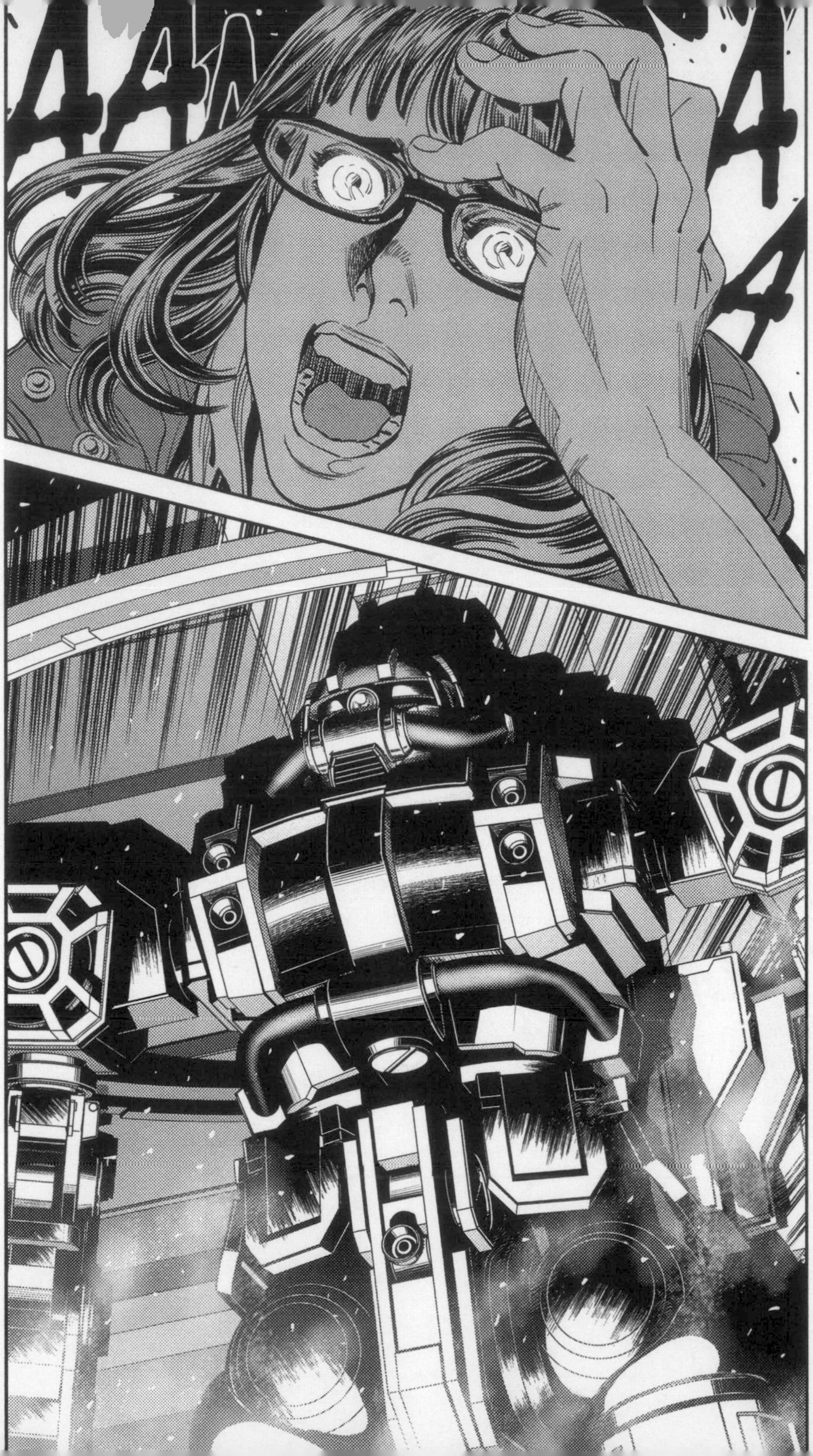
AAAAAA

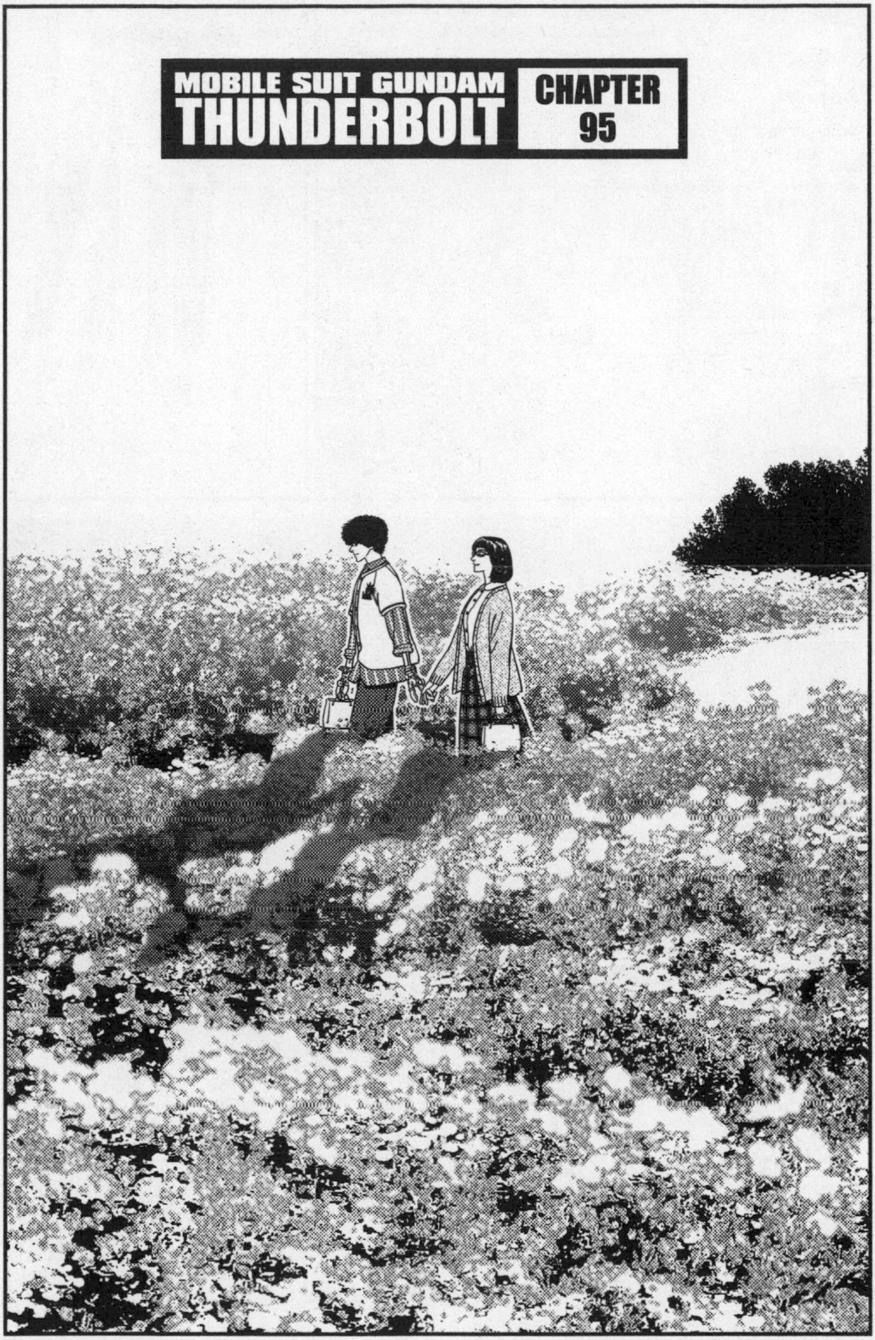
MOBILE SUIT GUNDAM
THUNDERBOLT
CHAPTER
95

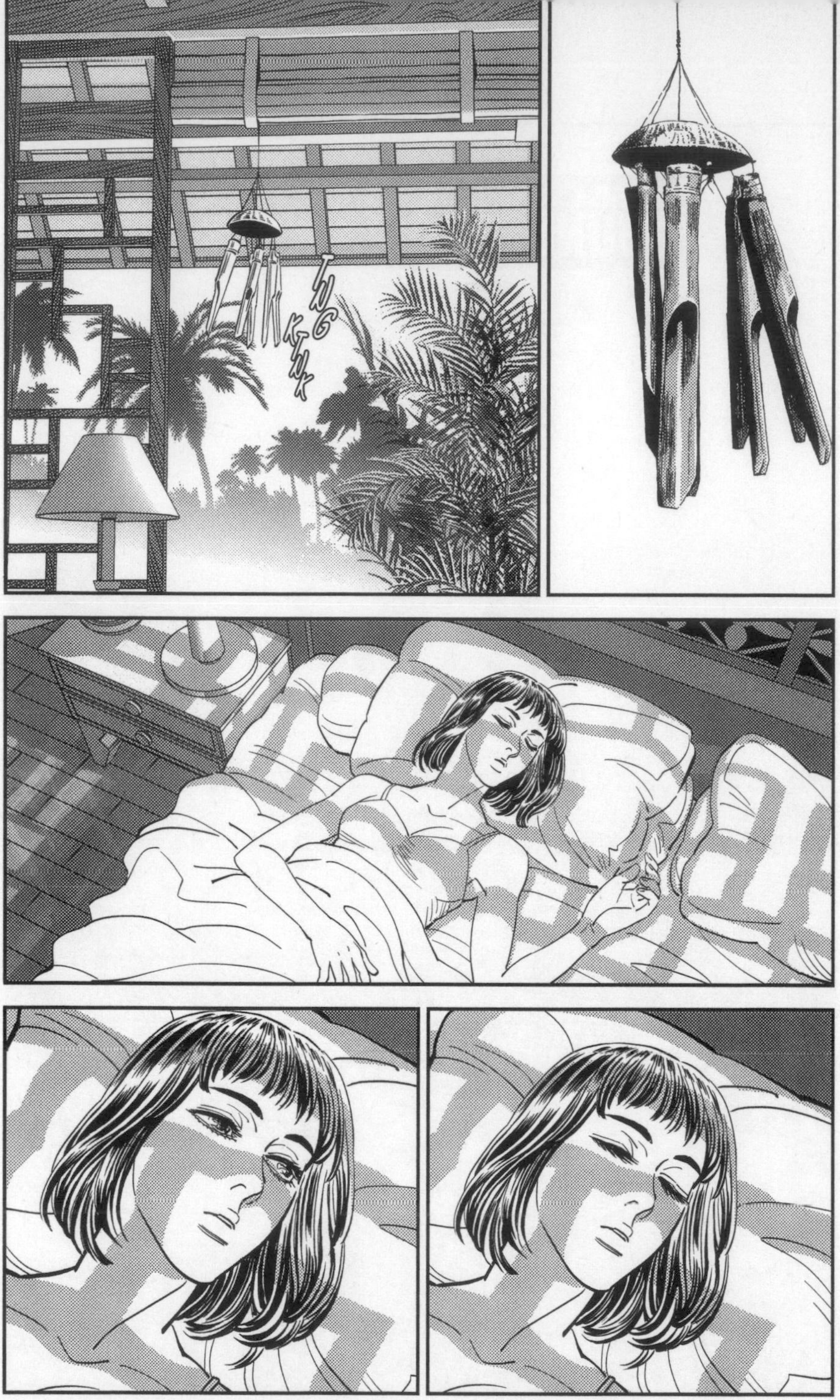
TING
KTINK

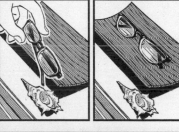

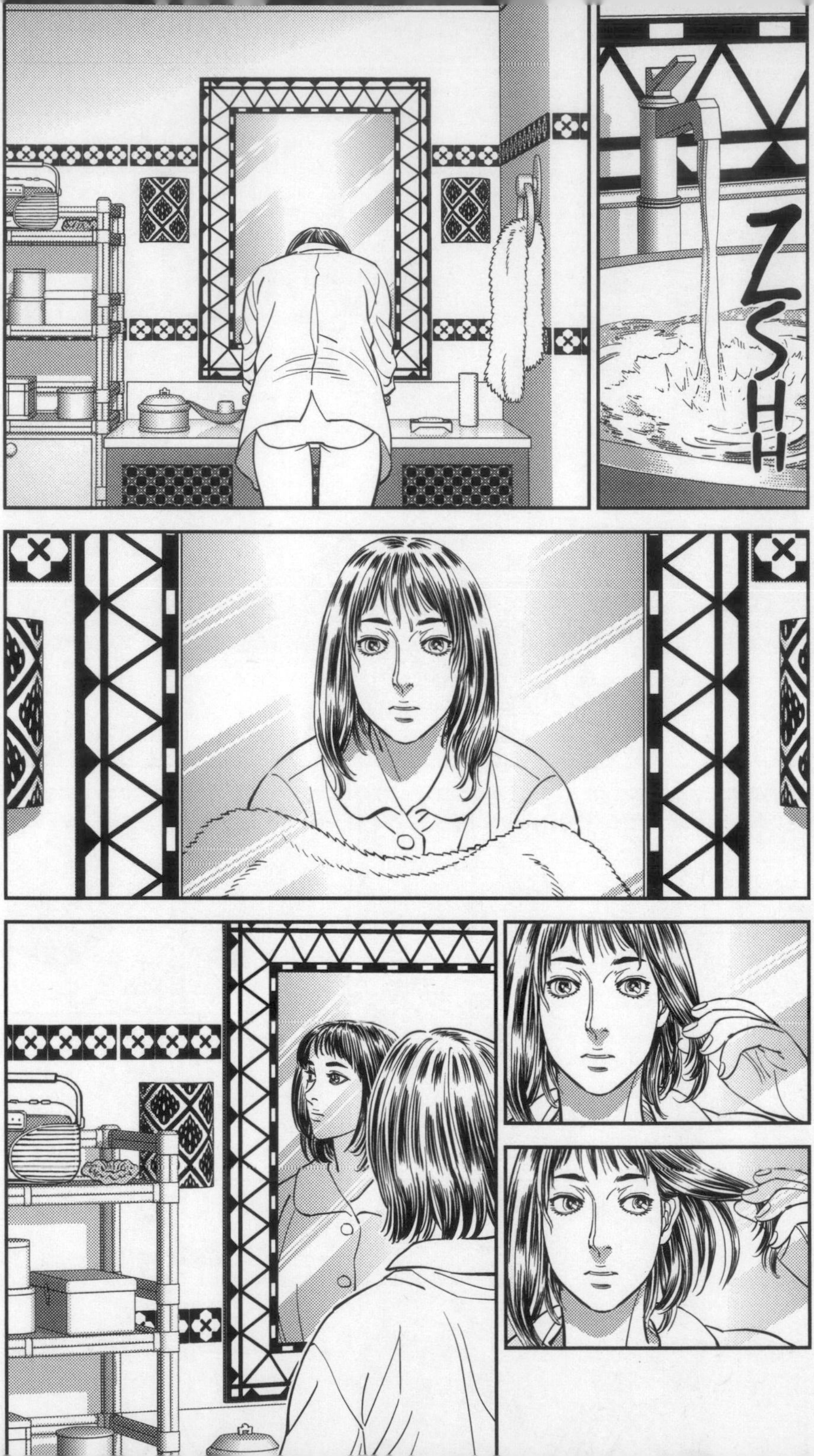
ZSHH

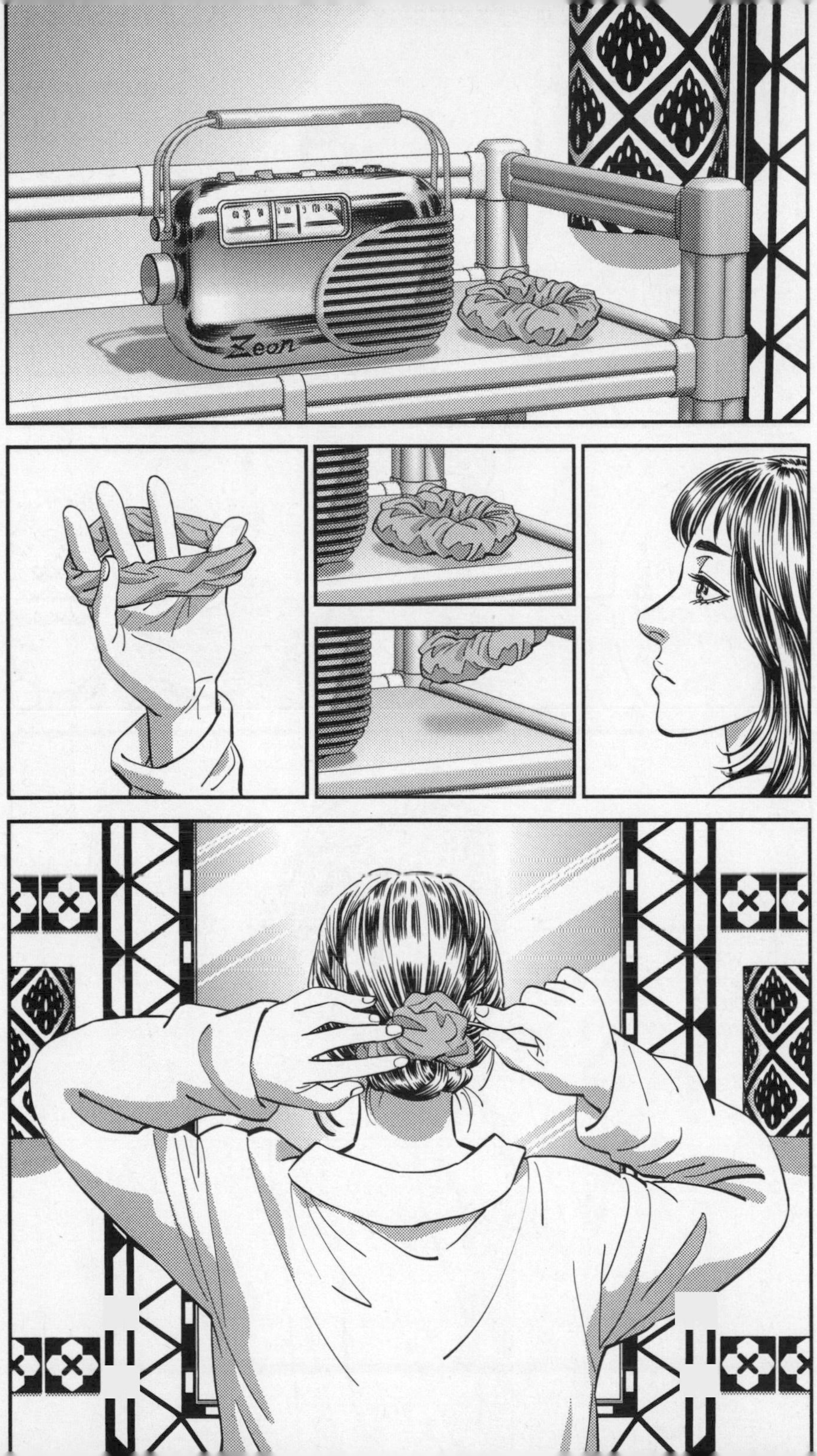
Zeon

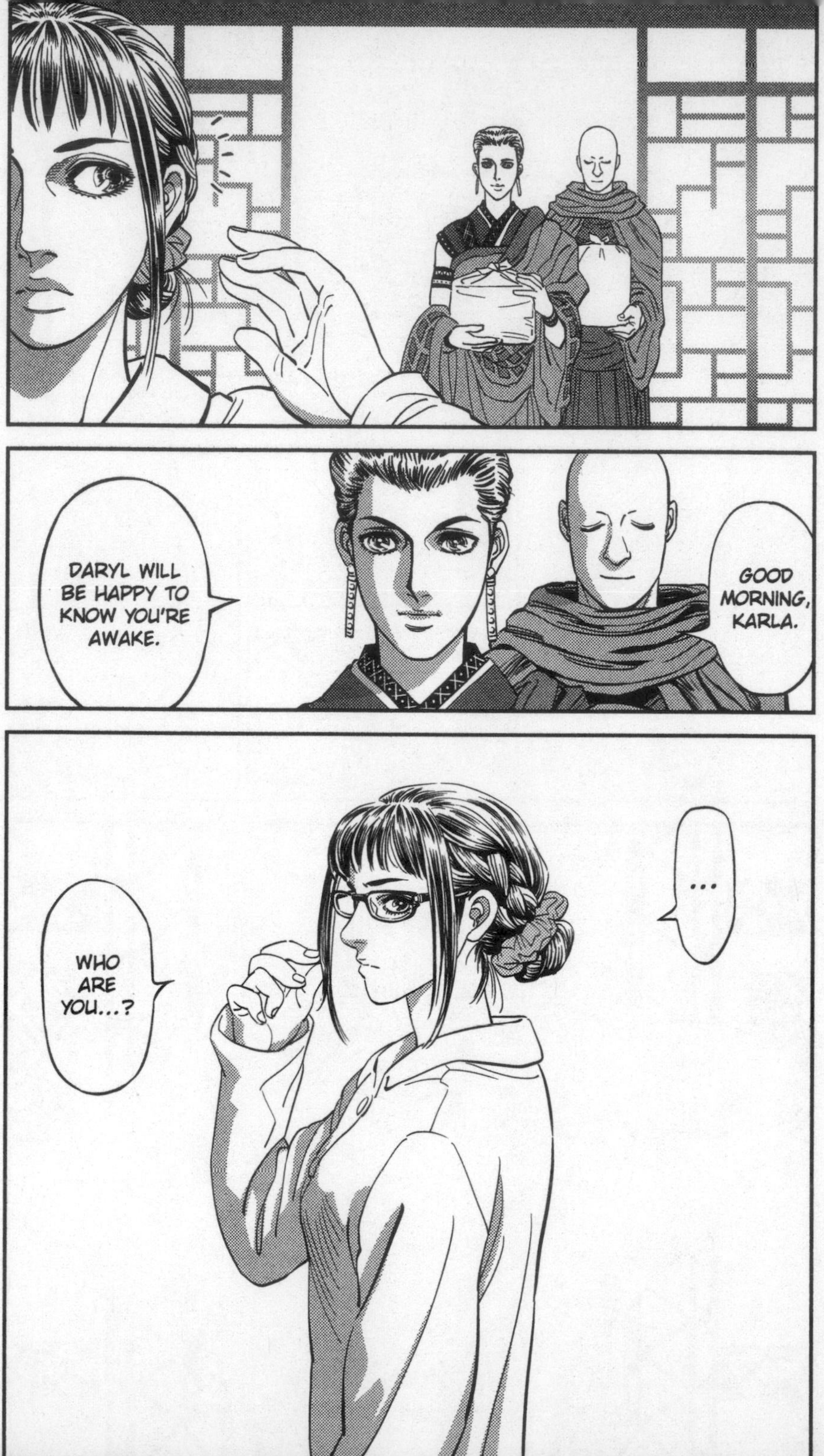
GOOD MORNING, KARLA.
DARYL WILL BE HAPPY TO KNOW YOU'RE AWAKE.
...
WHO ARE YOU...?

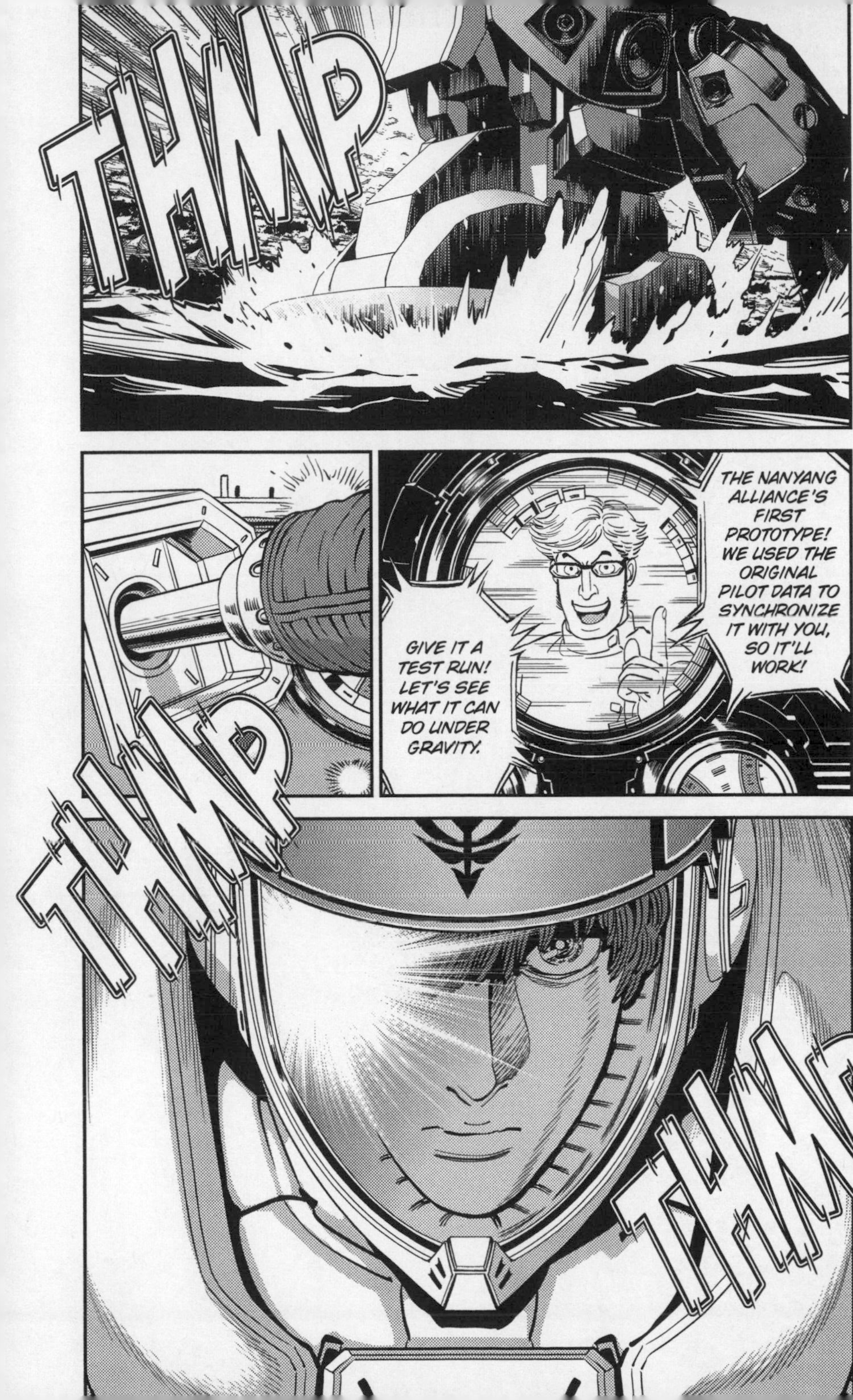
THMP
THE NANYANG ALLIANCE'S FIRST PROTOTYPE! WE USED THE ORIGINAL PILOT DATA TO SYNCHRONIZE IT WITH YOU, SO IT'LL WORK!
GIVE IT A TEST RUN! LET'S SEE WHAT IT CAN DO UNDER GRAVITY.
THMP
THMP

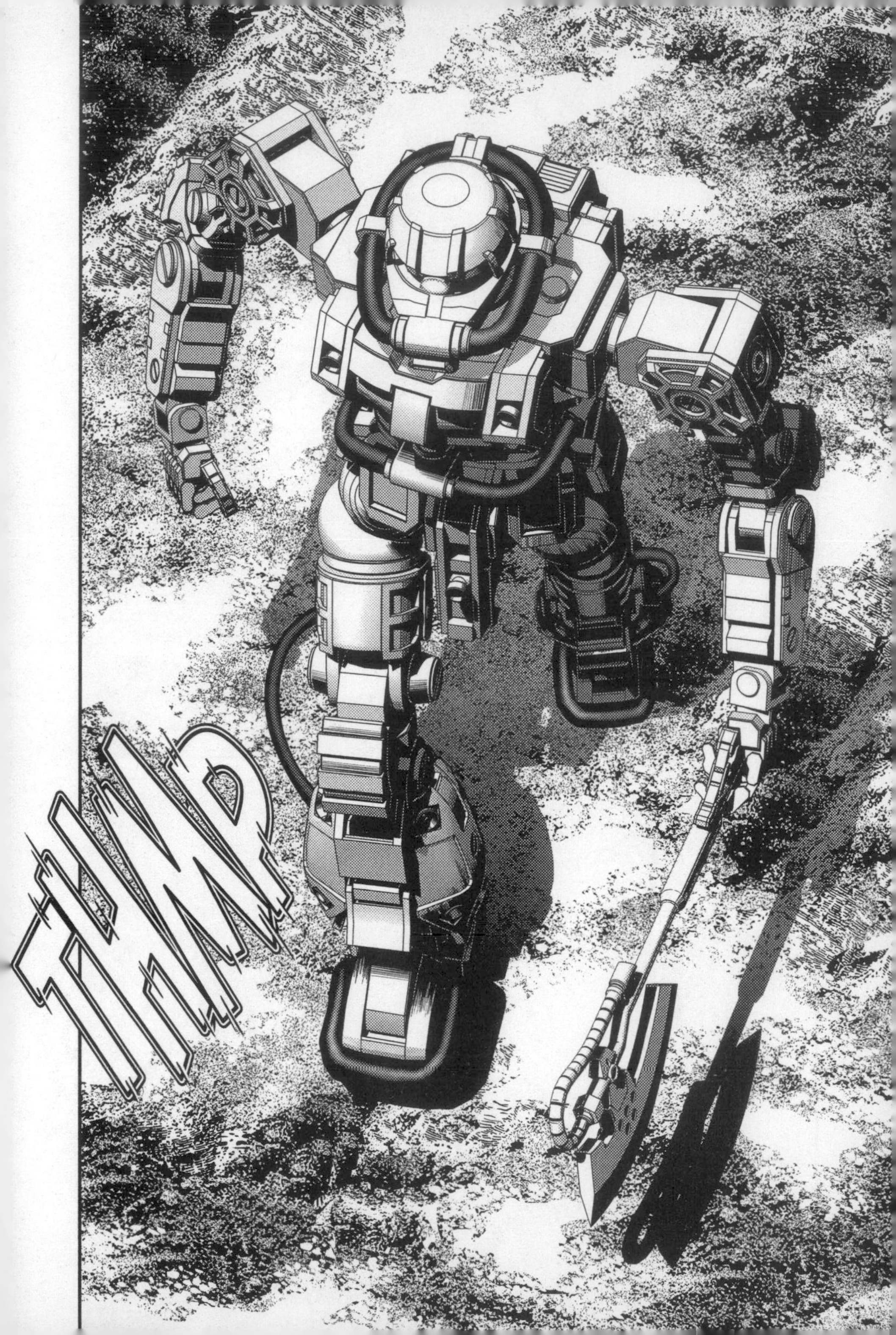
THMP

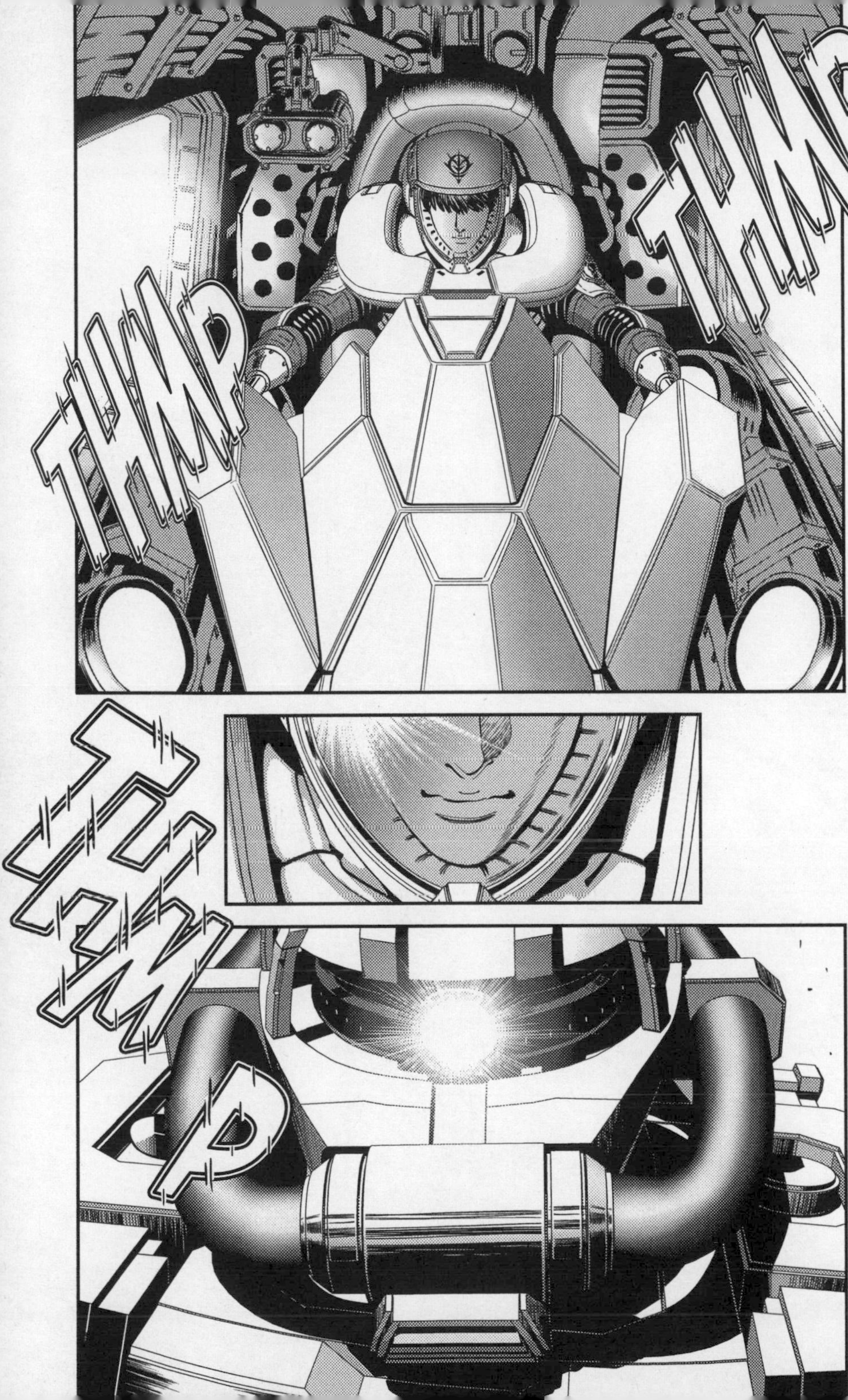
THMP
THMP
THUMP

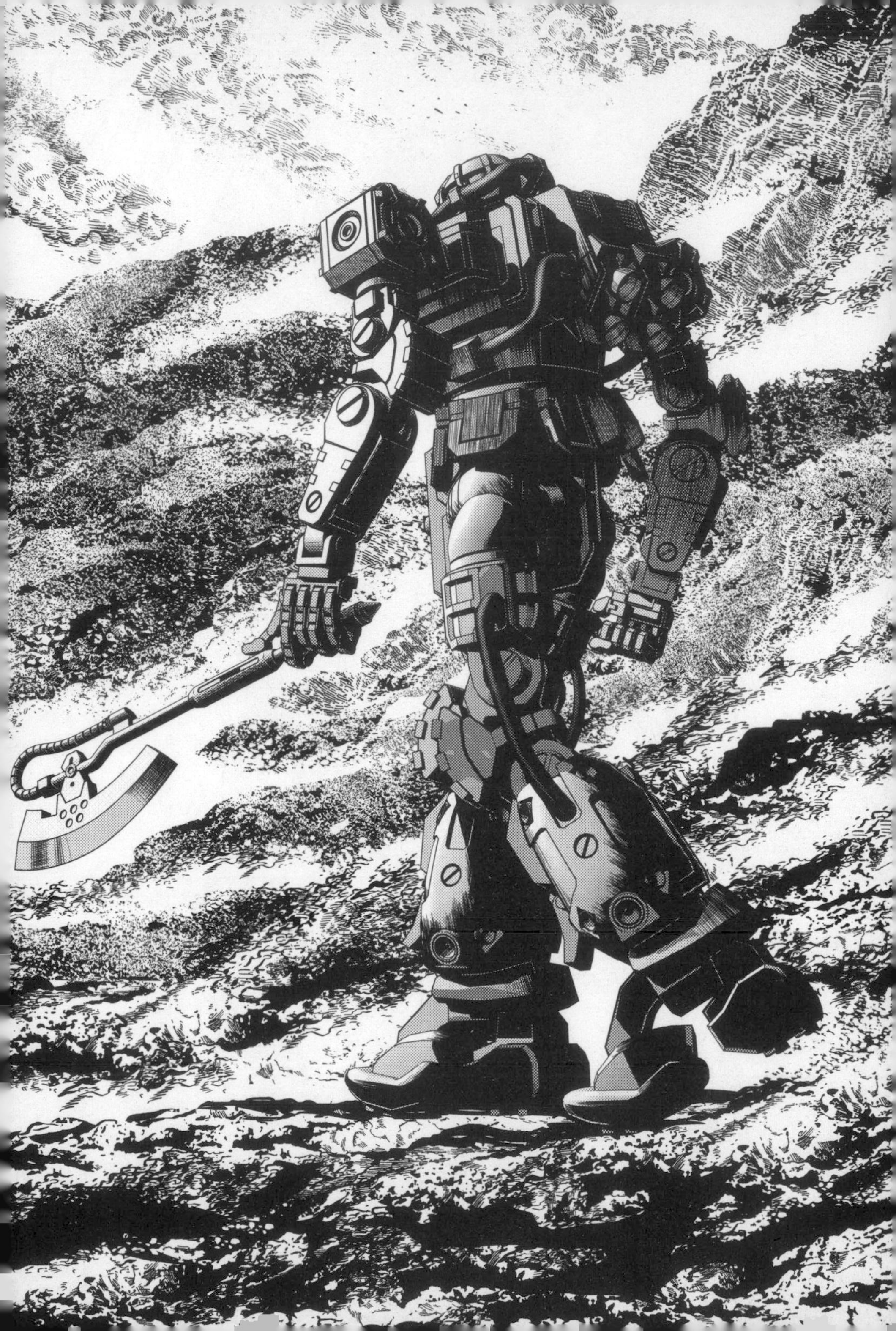

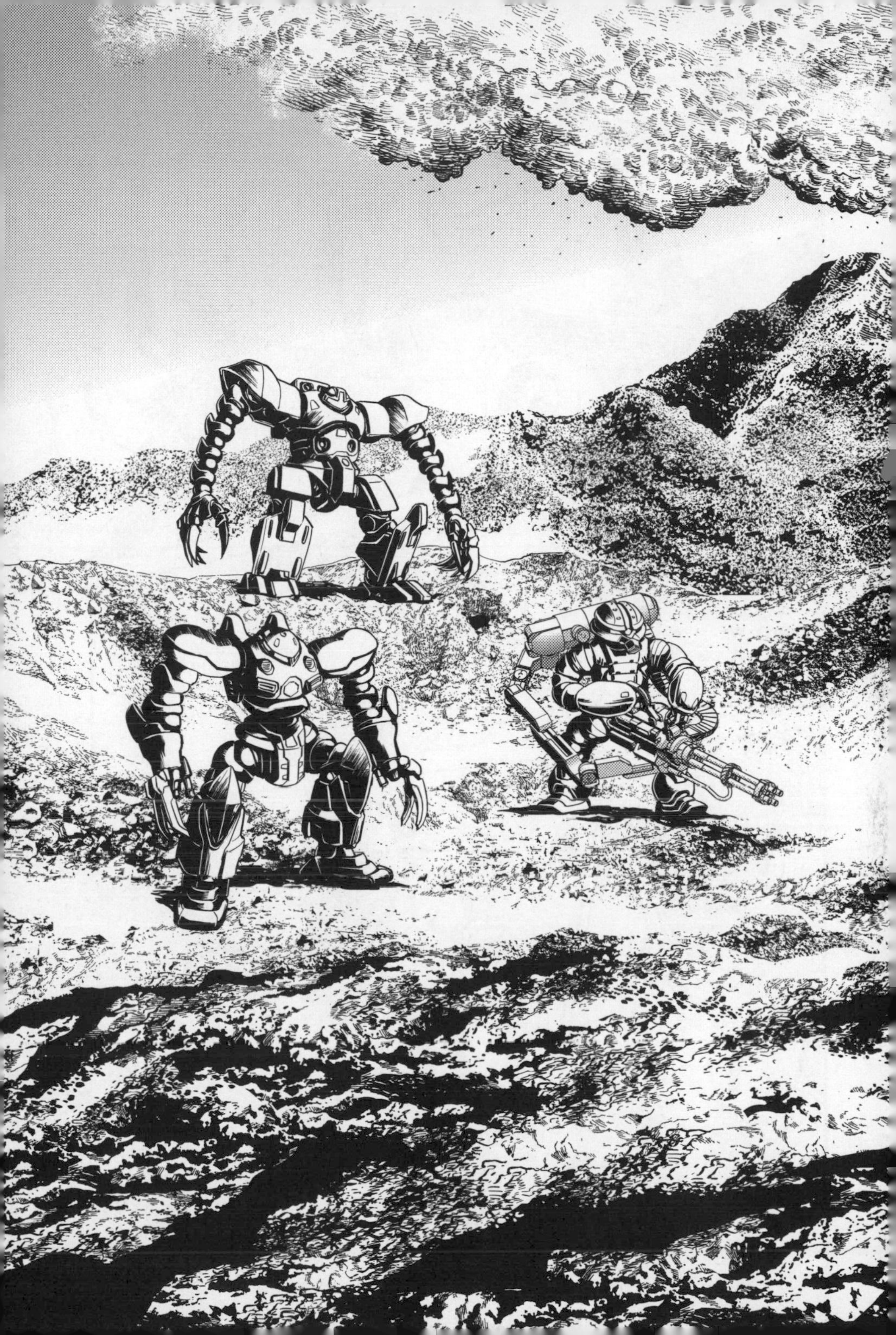

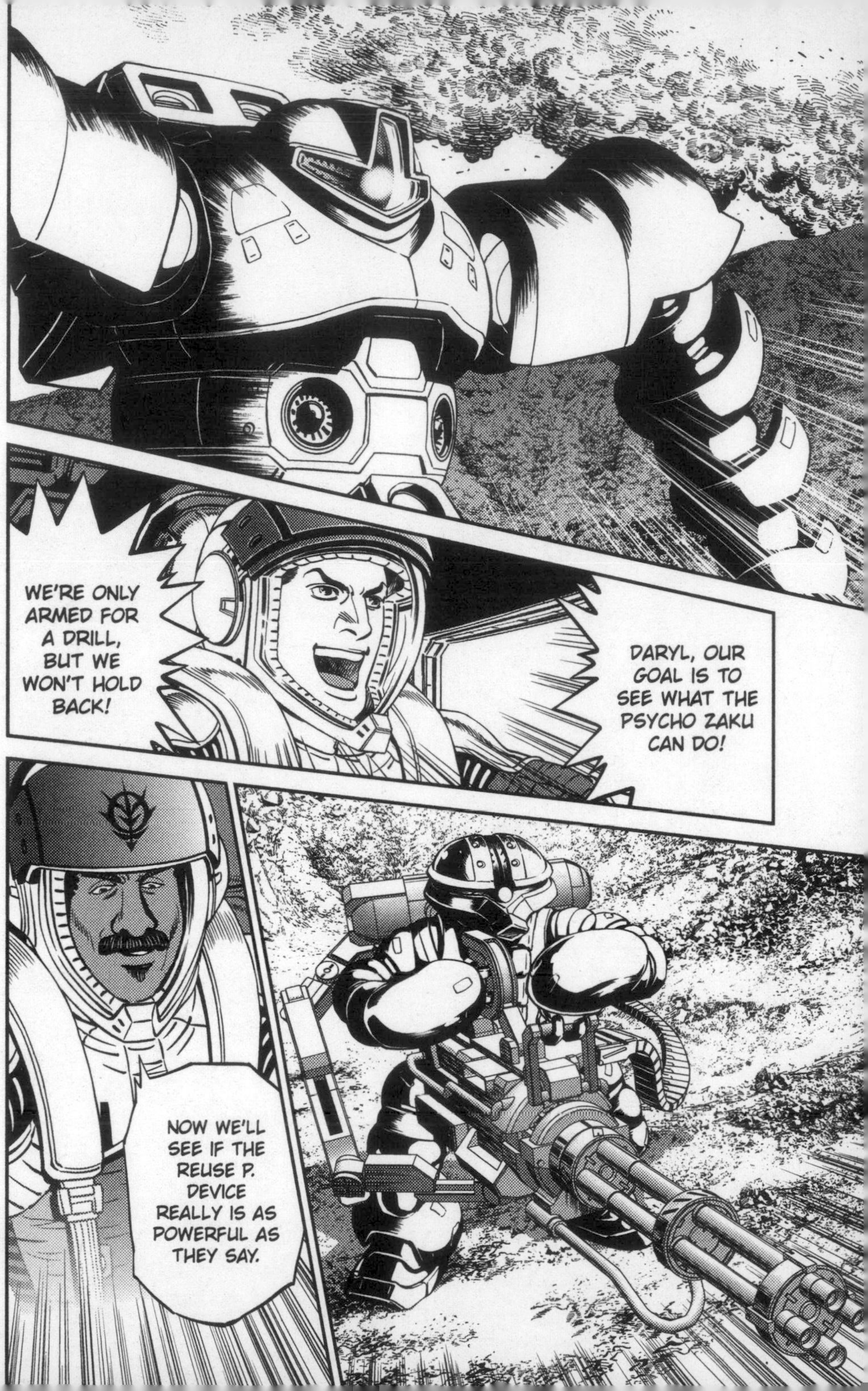
DARYL, OUR GOAL IS TO SEE WHAT THE PSYCHO ZAKU CAN DO!
WE'RE ONLY ARMED FOR A DRILL, BUT WE WON'T HOLD BACK!
NOW WE'LL SEE IF THE REUSE P. DEVICE REALLY IS AS POWERFUL AS THEY SAY.

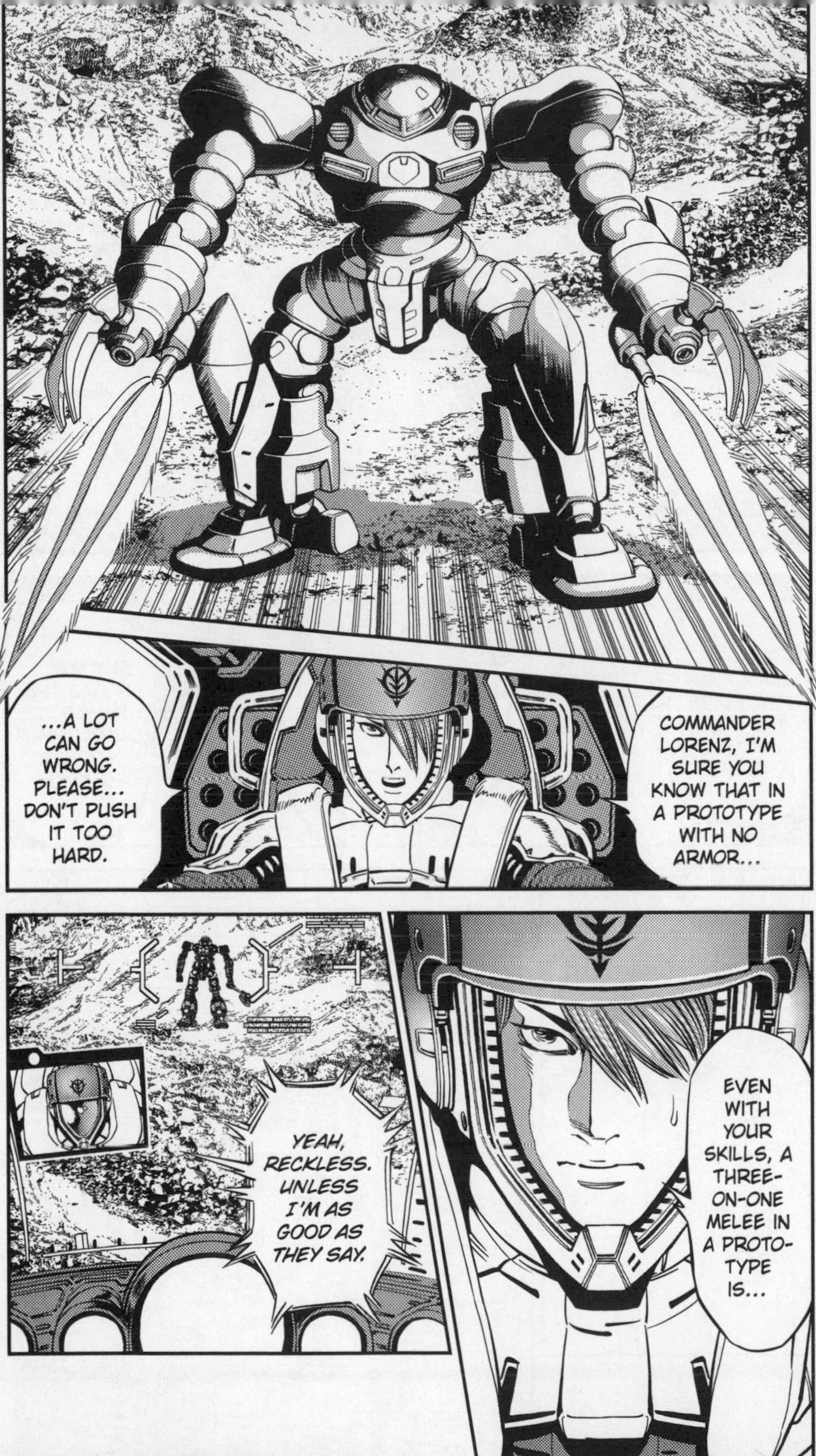
COMMANDER LORENZ, I'M SURE YOU KNOW THAT IN A PROTOTYPE WITH NO ARMOR...
...A LOT CAN GO WRONG. PLEASE... DON'T PUSH IT TOO HARD.
EVEN WITH YOUR SKILLS, A THREE-ON-ONE MELEE IN A PROTOTYPE IS...
YEAH, RECKLESS. UNLESS I'M AS GOOD AS THEY SAY.

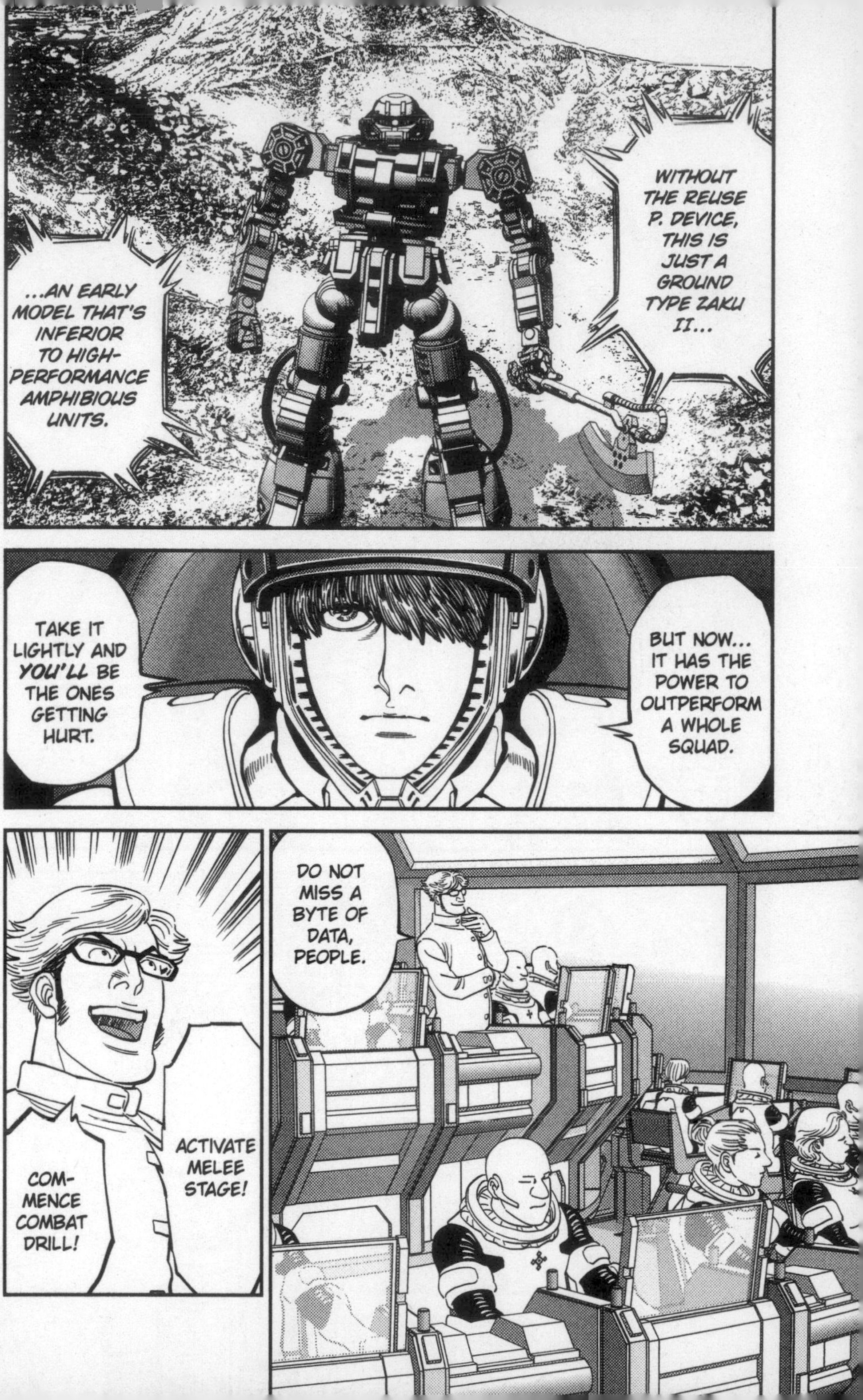
WITHOUT THE REUSE P. DEVICE, THIS IS JUST A GROUND TYPE ZAKU II...
...AN EARLY MODEL THAT'S INFERIOR TO HIGH-PERFORMANCE AMPHIBIOUS UNITS.
BUT NOW... IT HAS THE POWER TO OUTPERFORM A WHOLE SQUAD.
TAKE IT LIGHTLY AND *YOU'LL* BE THE ONES GETTING HURT.
DO NOT MISS A BYTE OF DATA, PEOPLE.
ACTIVATE MELEE STAGE!
COM-MENCE COMBAT DRILL!

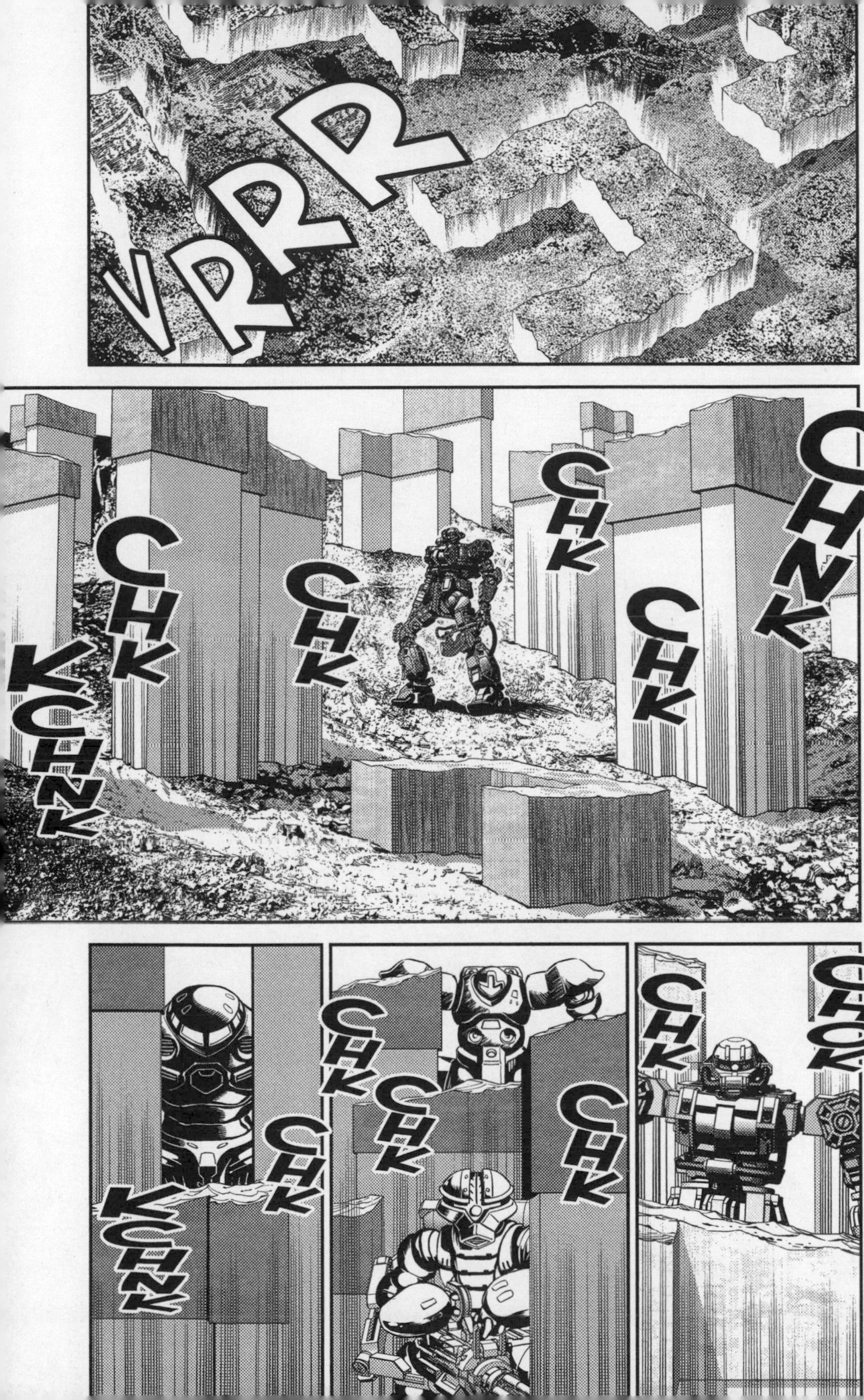
VRRP
CHNK
CHK
CHK
CHK
CHK
KCHNK
CHOK
CHK
CHK
CHK
CHK
CHK
KCHNK

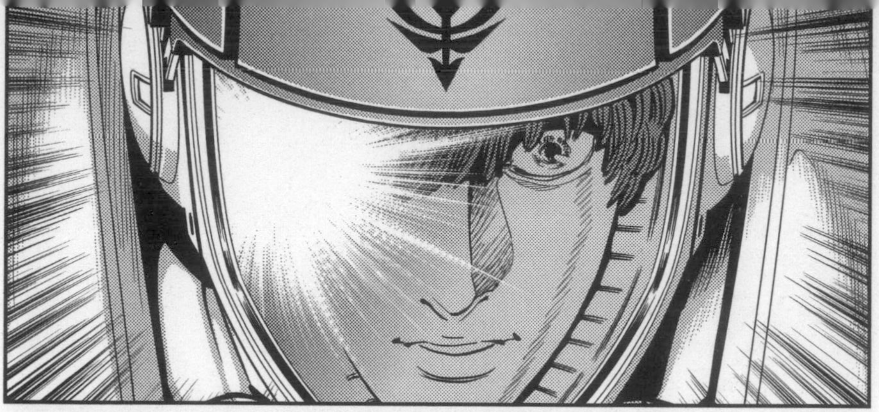
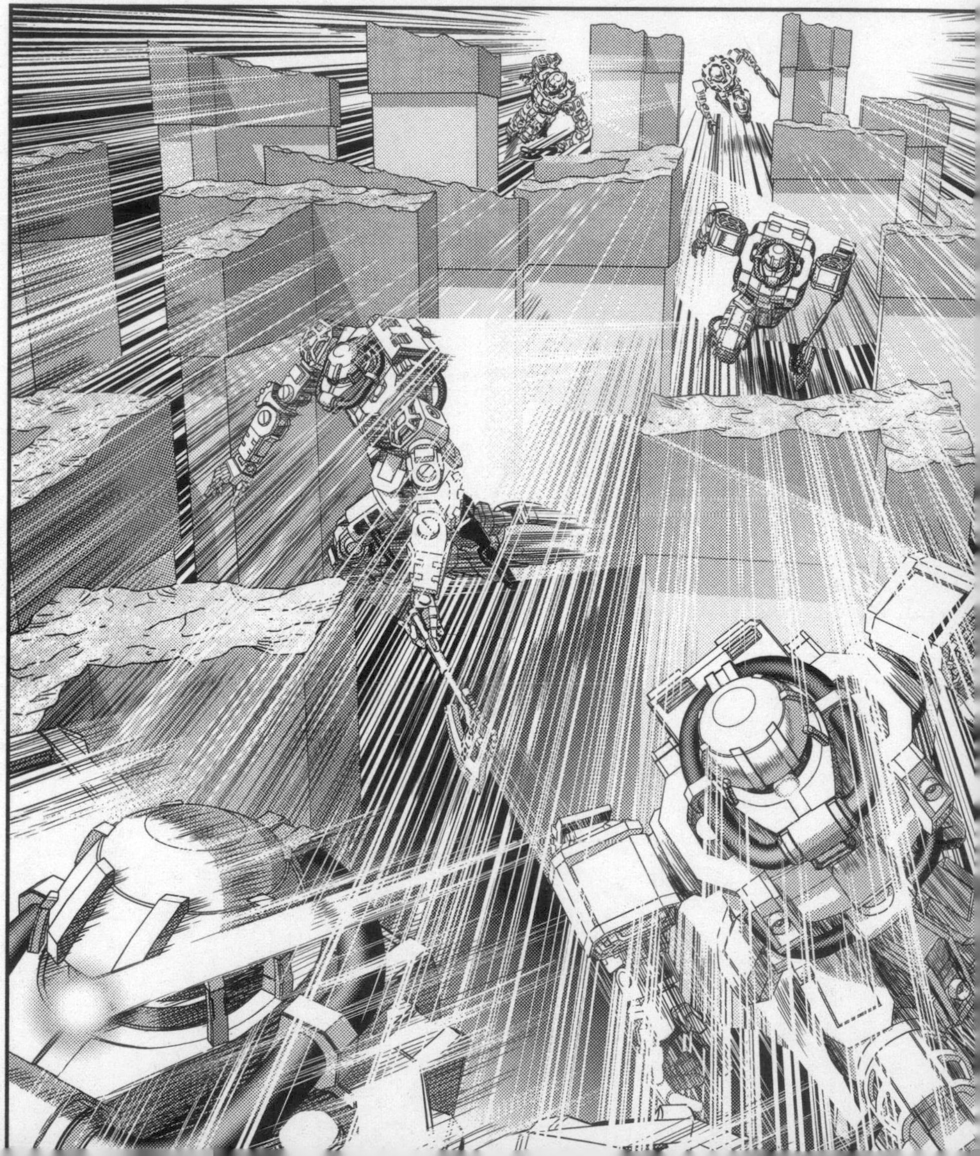

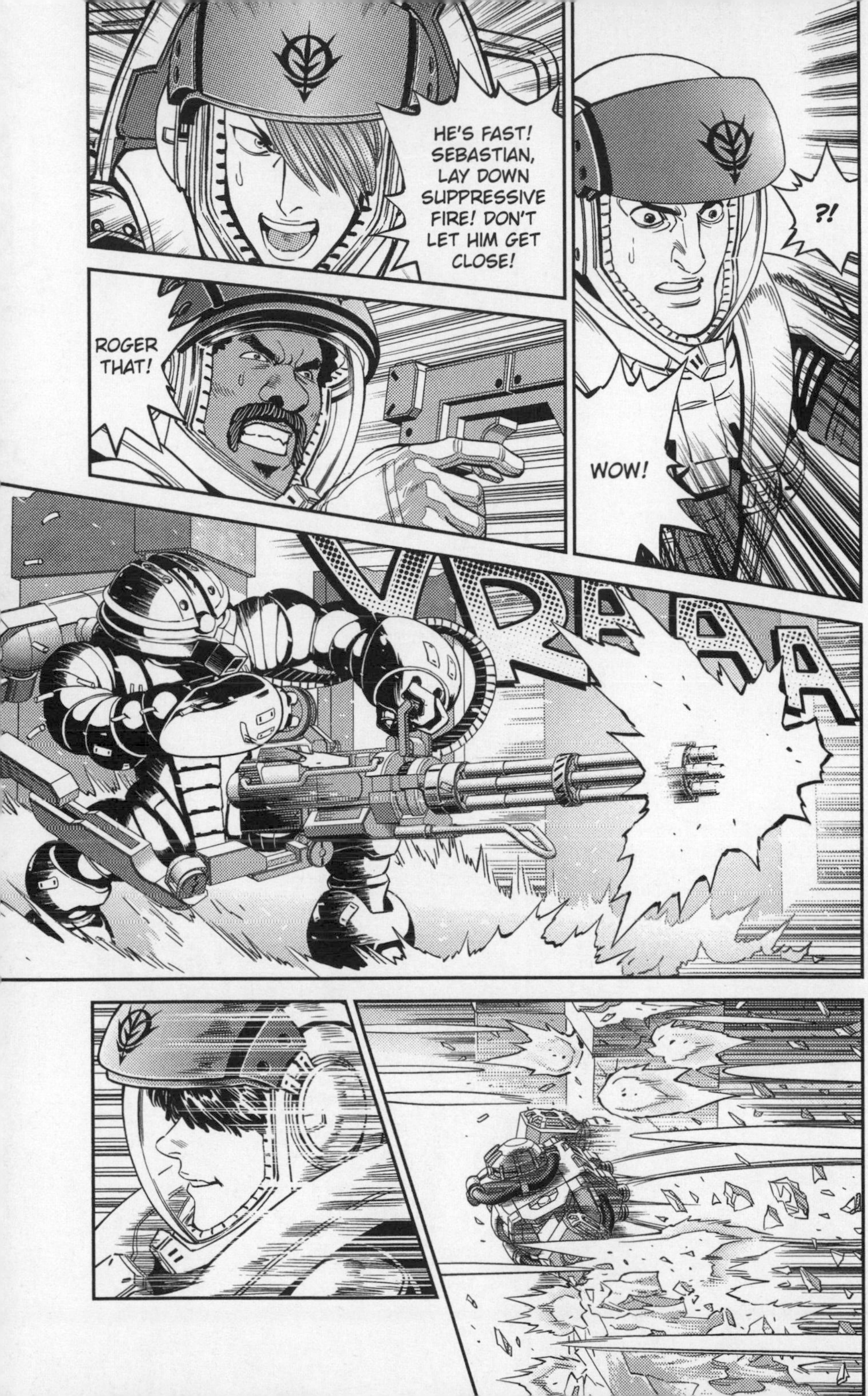
?!
WOW!
HE'S FAST! SEBASTIAN, LAY DOWN SUPPRESSIVE FIRE! DON'T LET HIM GET CLOSE!
ROGER THAT!
VRAAA

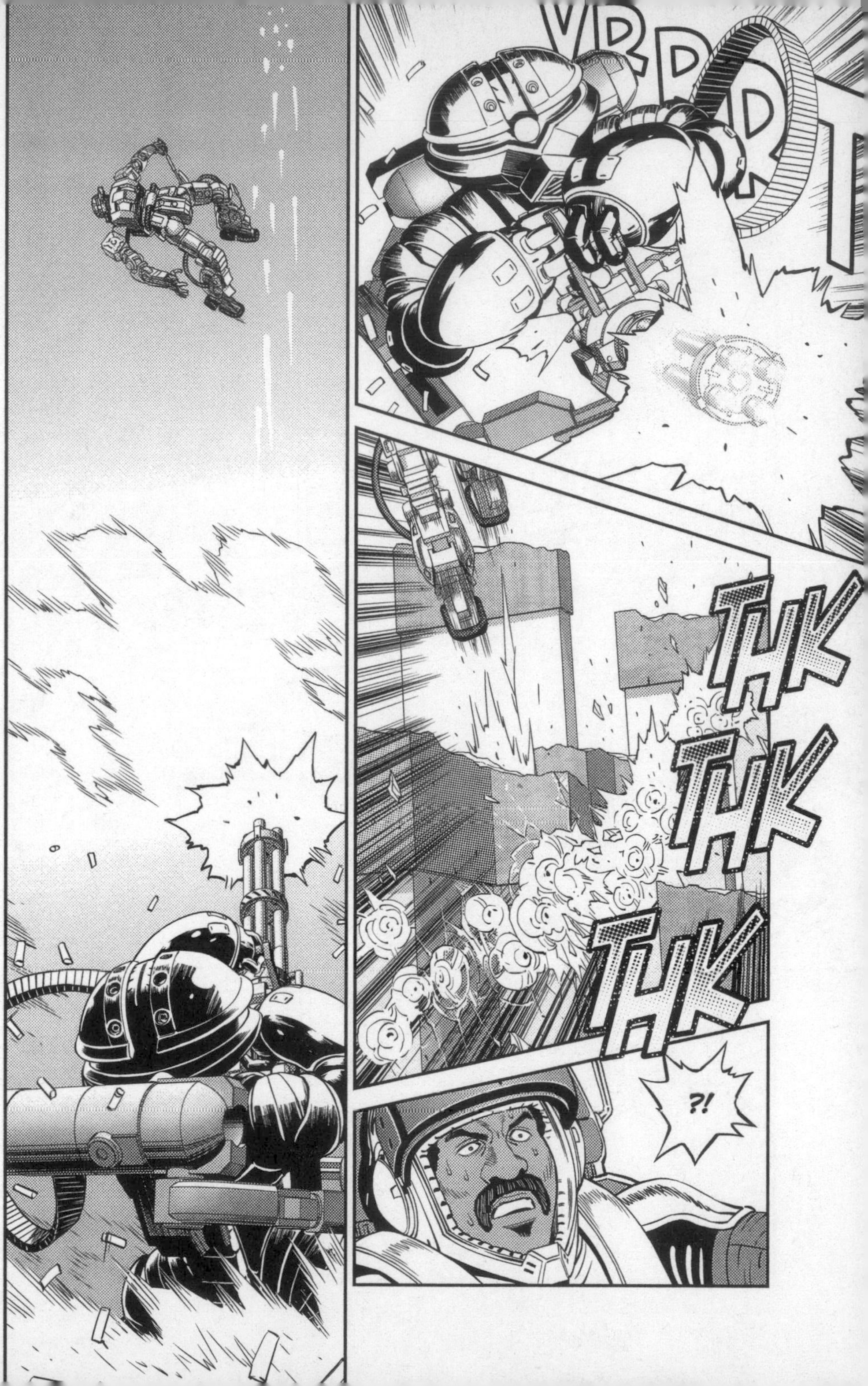
VRRRT
THK
THK
THK
?!

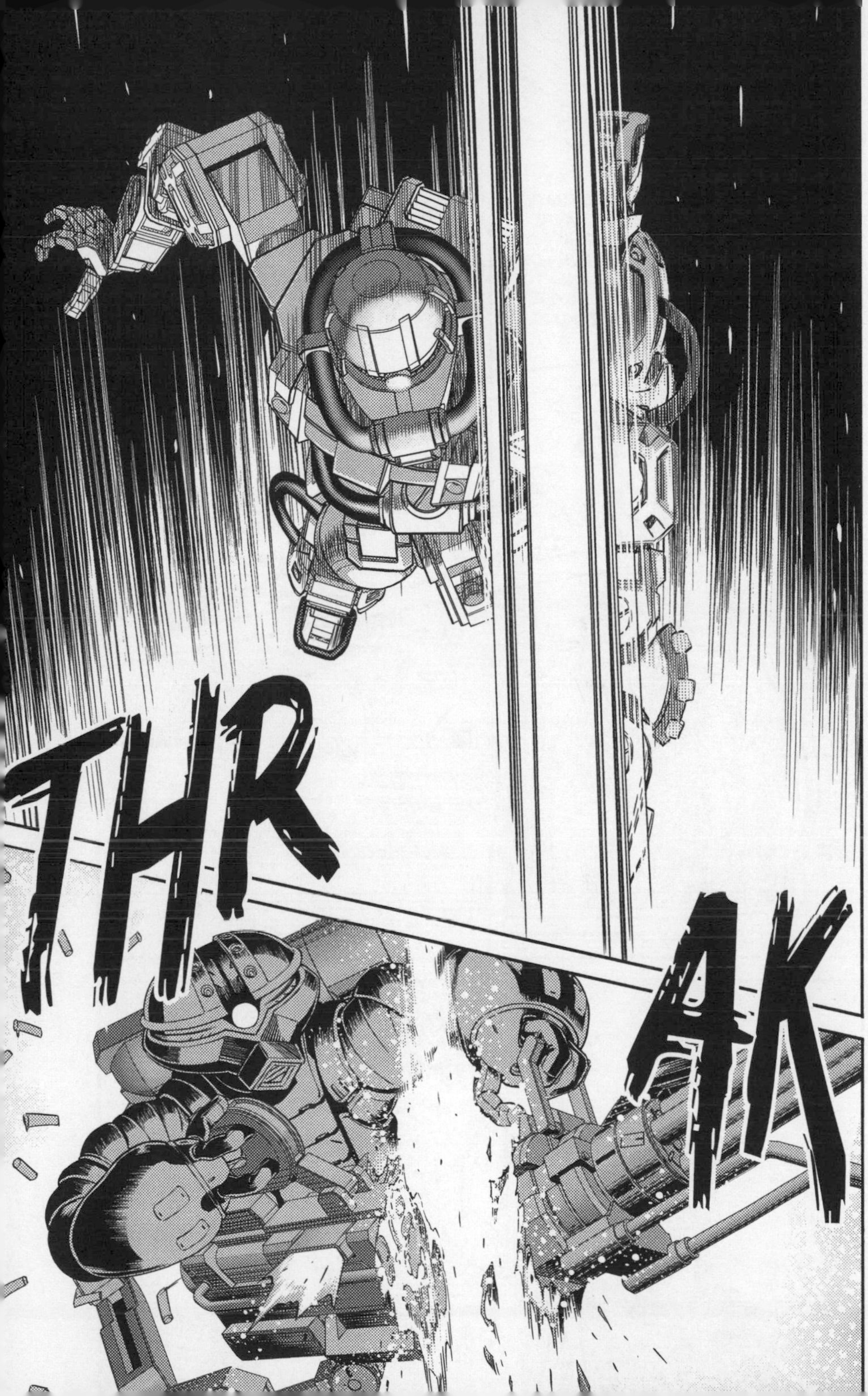
THRAK

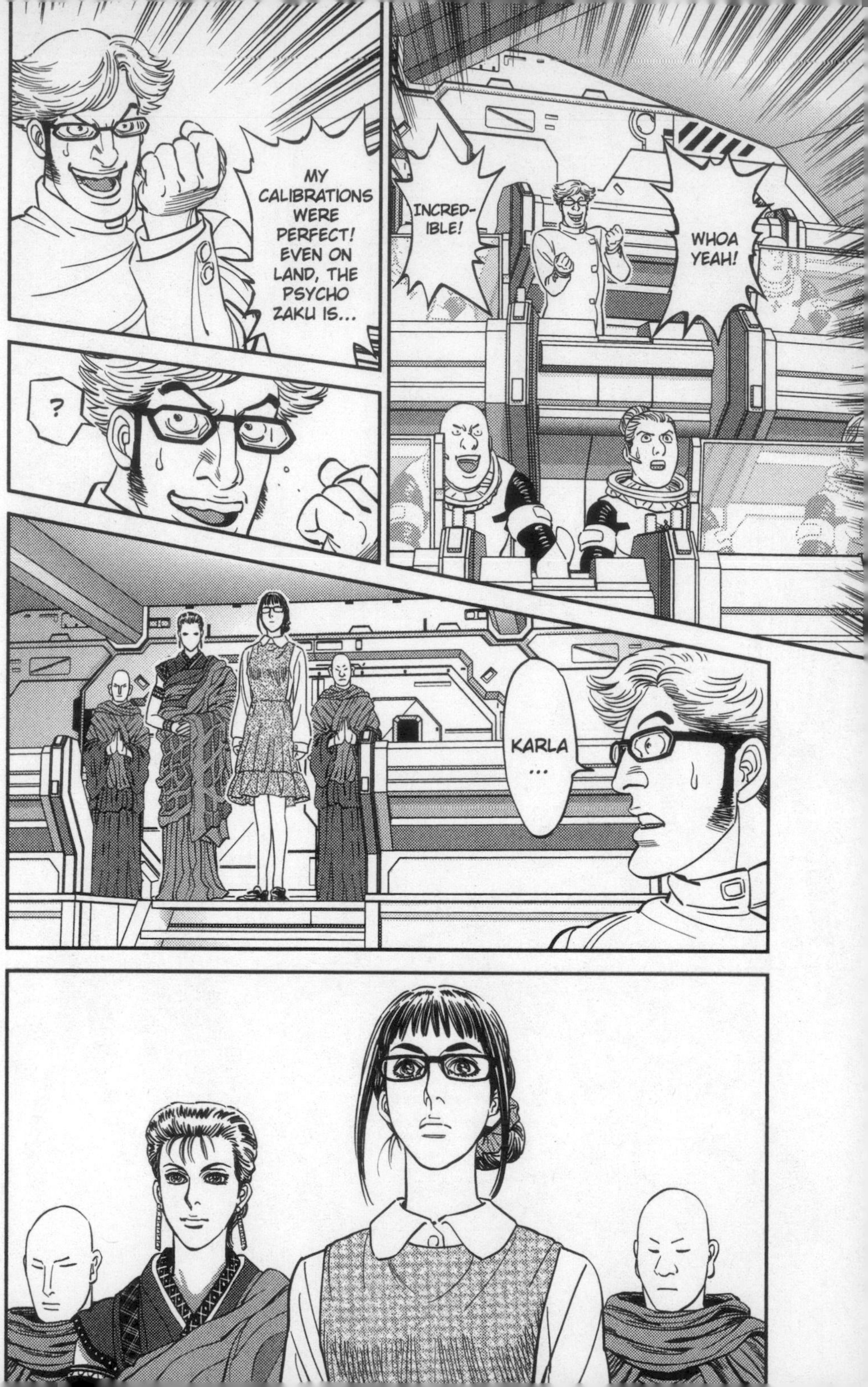
WHOA YEAH!
INCRED-IBLE!
MY CALIBRATIONS WERE PERFECT! EVEN ON LAND, THE PSYCHO ZAKU IS...
?
KARLA ...

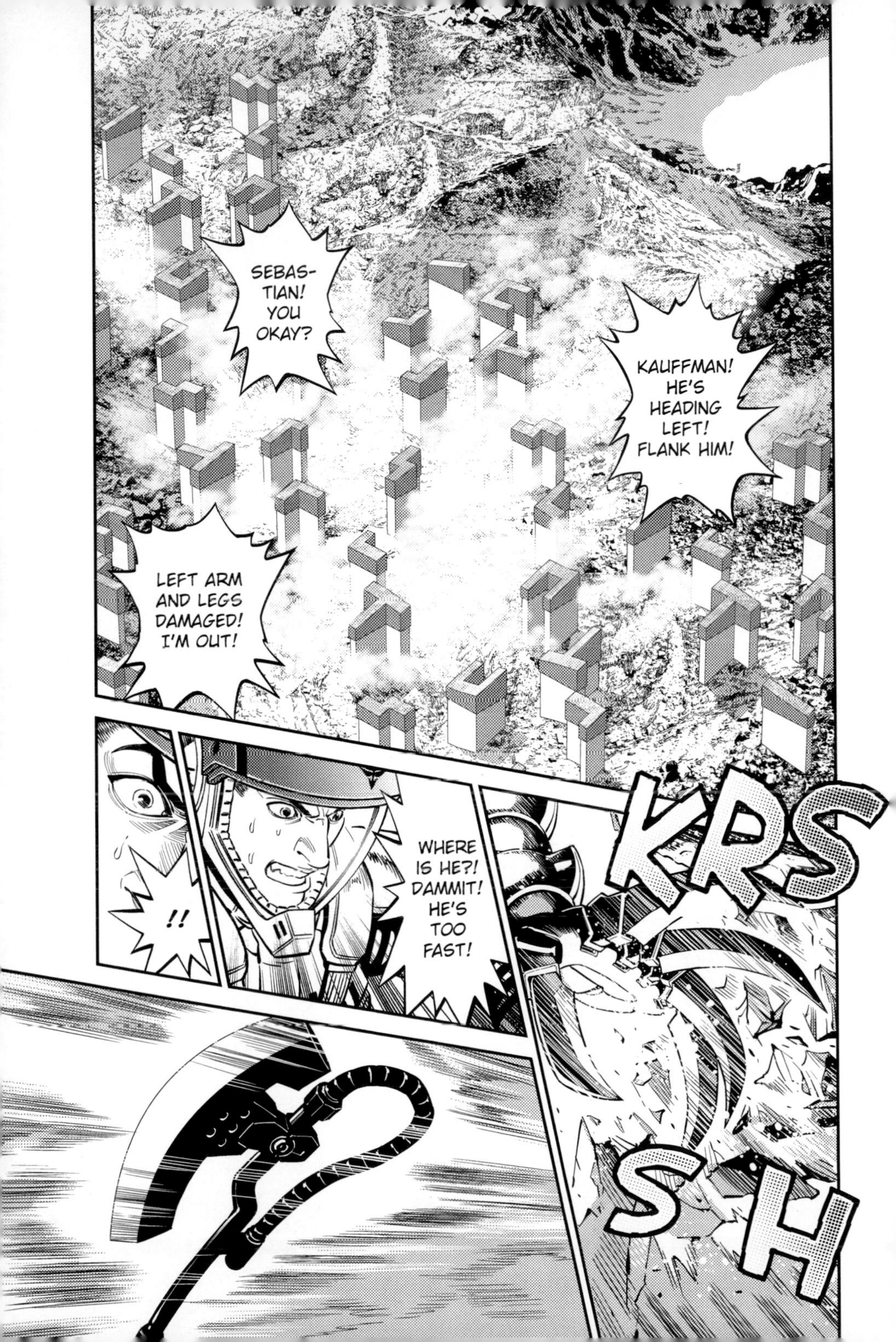
SEBAS-TIAN! YOU OKAY?
LEFT ARM AND LEGS DAMAGED! I'M OUT!
KAUFFMAN! HE'S HEADING LEFT! FLANK HIM!
KRS
WHERE IS HE?! DAMMIT! HE'S TOO FAST!
!!
SH

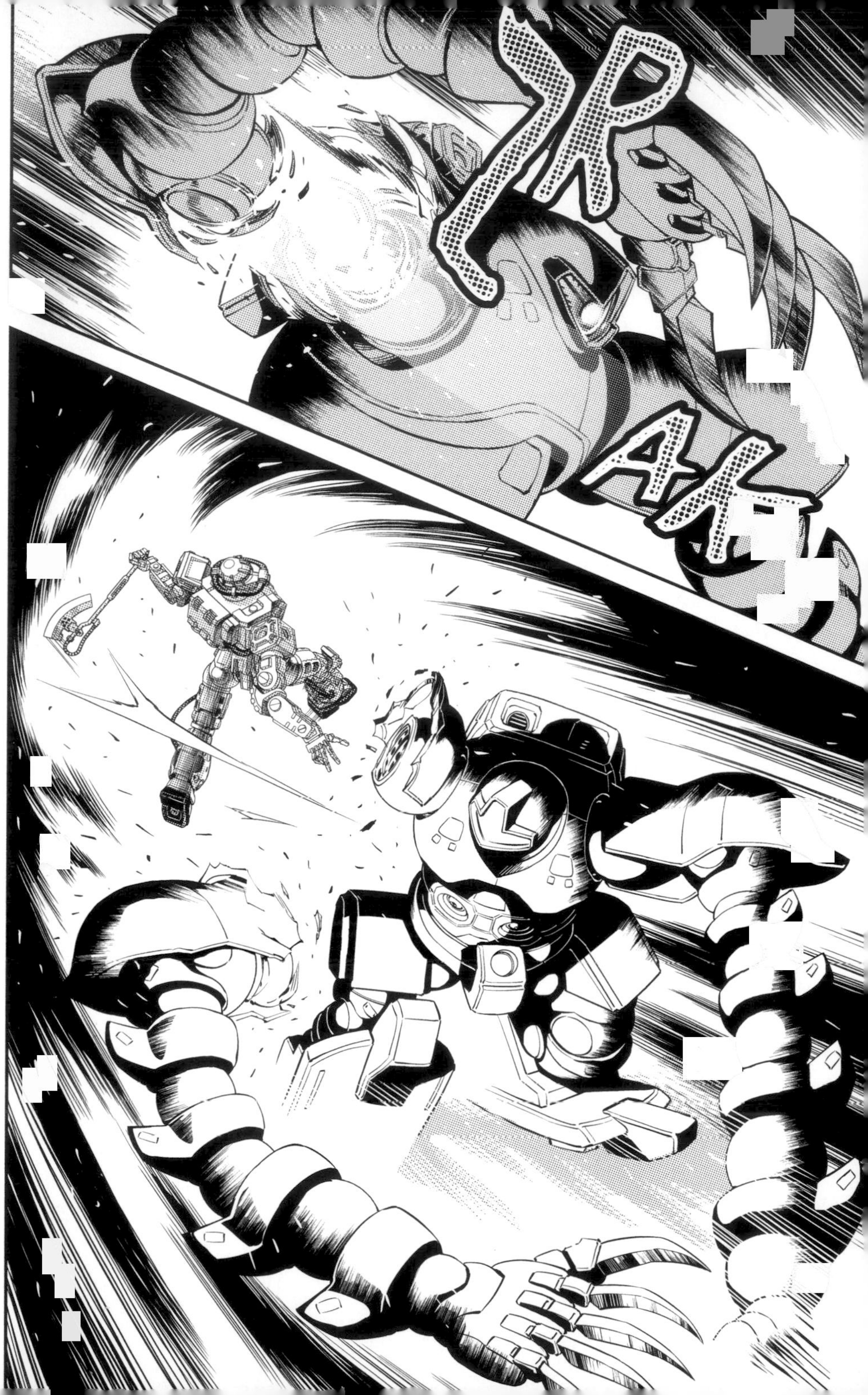
KRAK

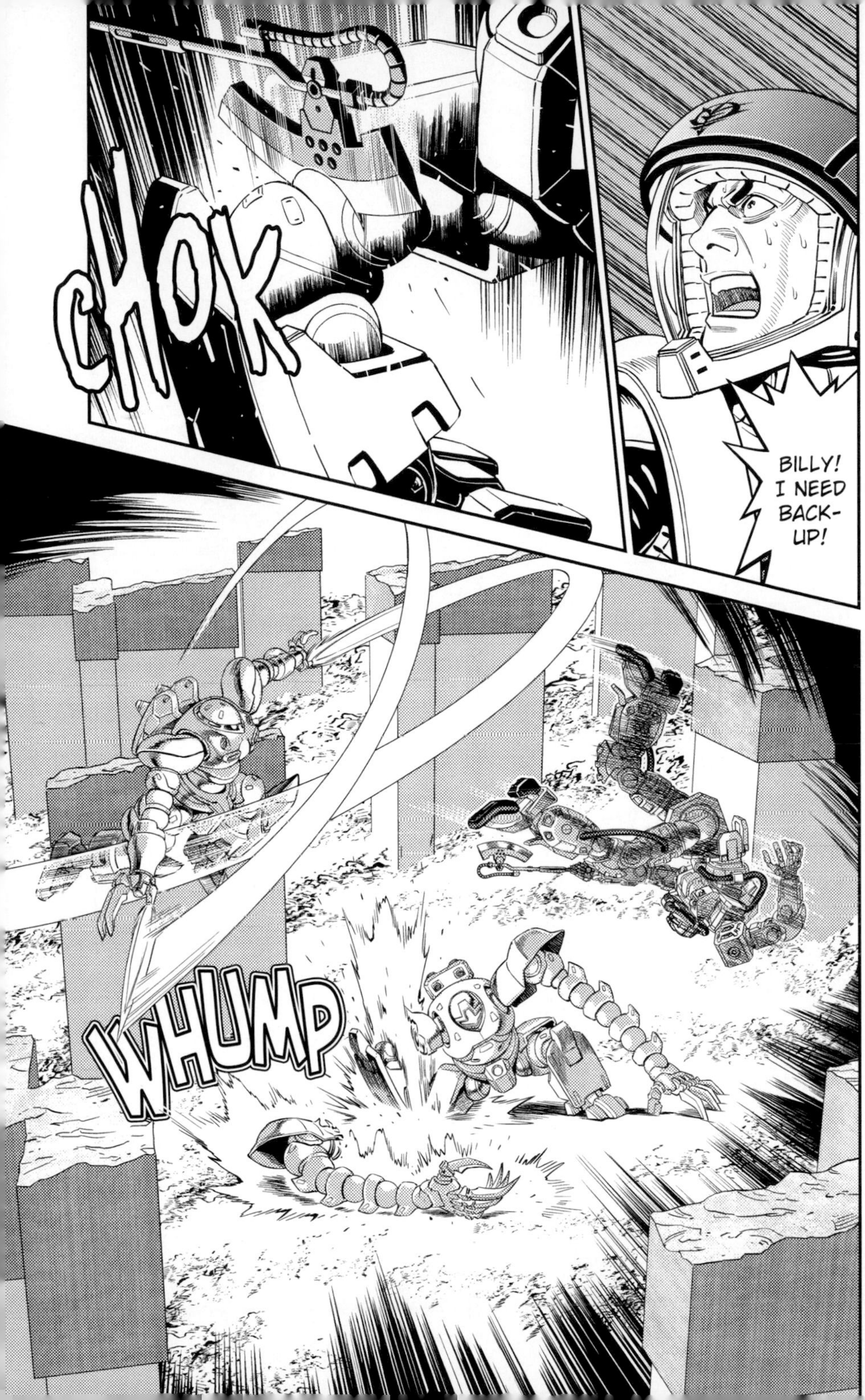
BILLY! I NEED BACK-UP!
CHOK
WHUMP

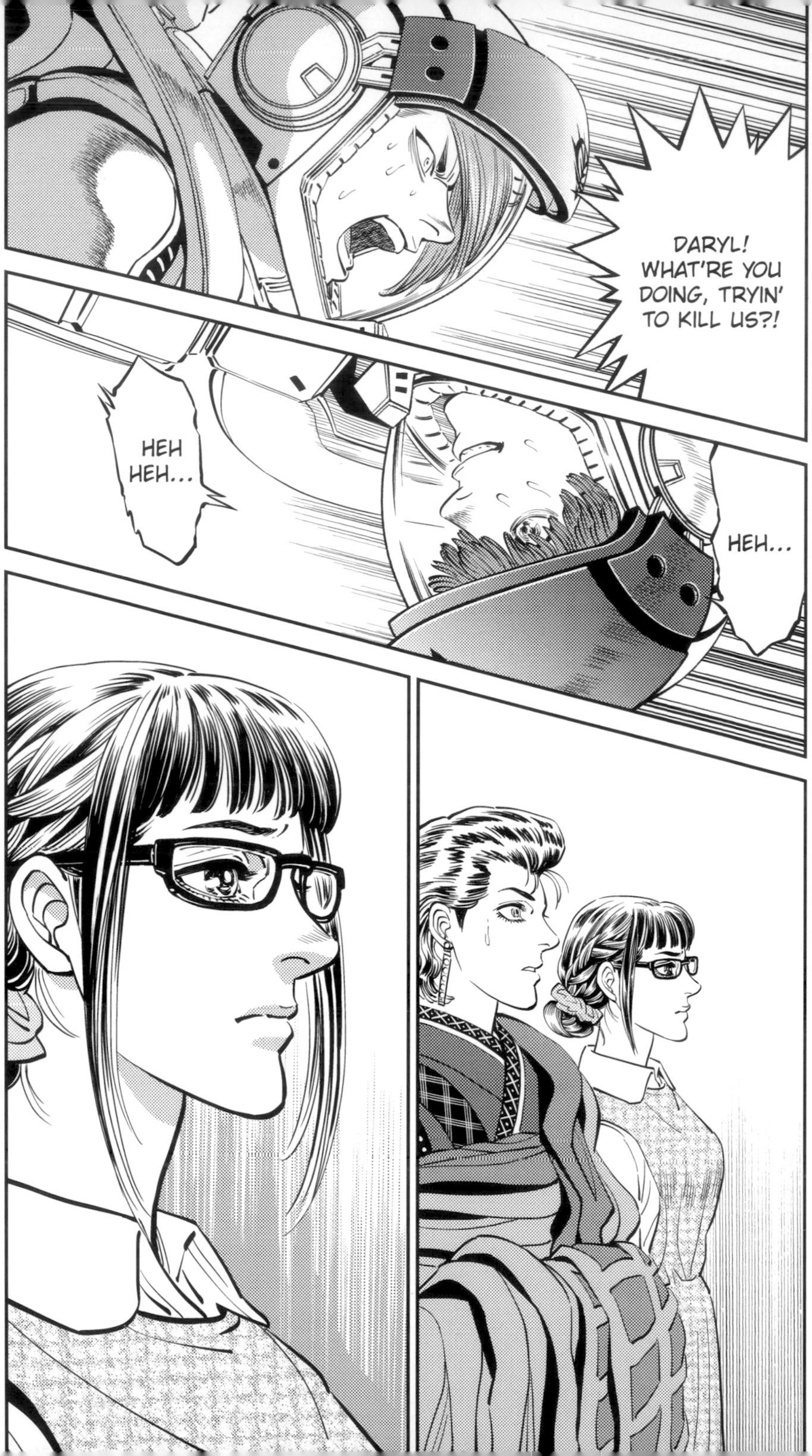
DARYL! WHAT'RE YOU DOING, TRYIN' TO KILL US?!
HEH...
HEH HEH...

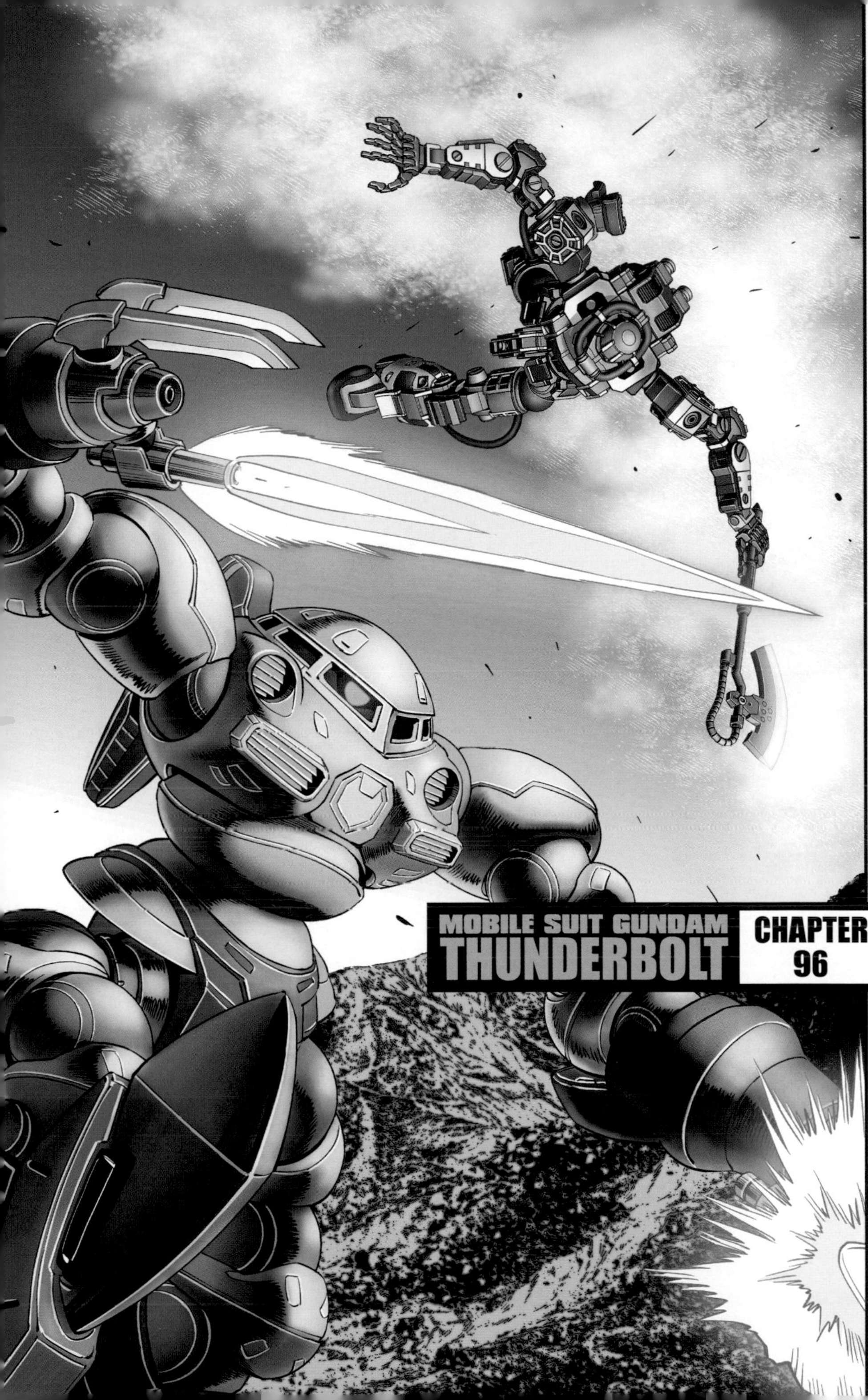
MOBILE SUIT GUNDAM
THUNDERBOLT
CHAPTER
96

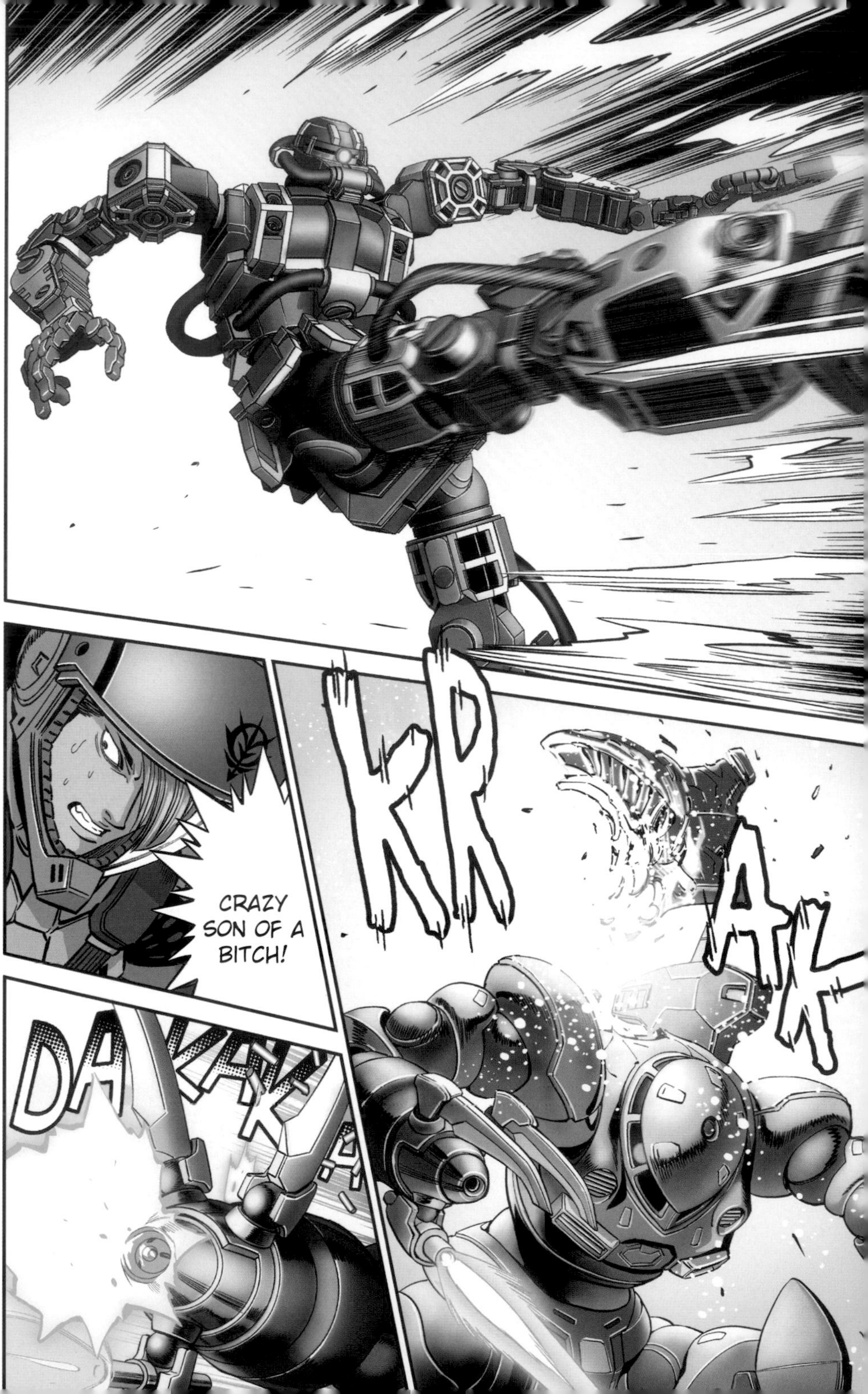
KRRAK
CRAZY SON OF A BITCH!
DAKAKA

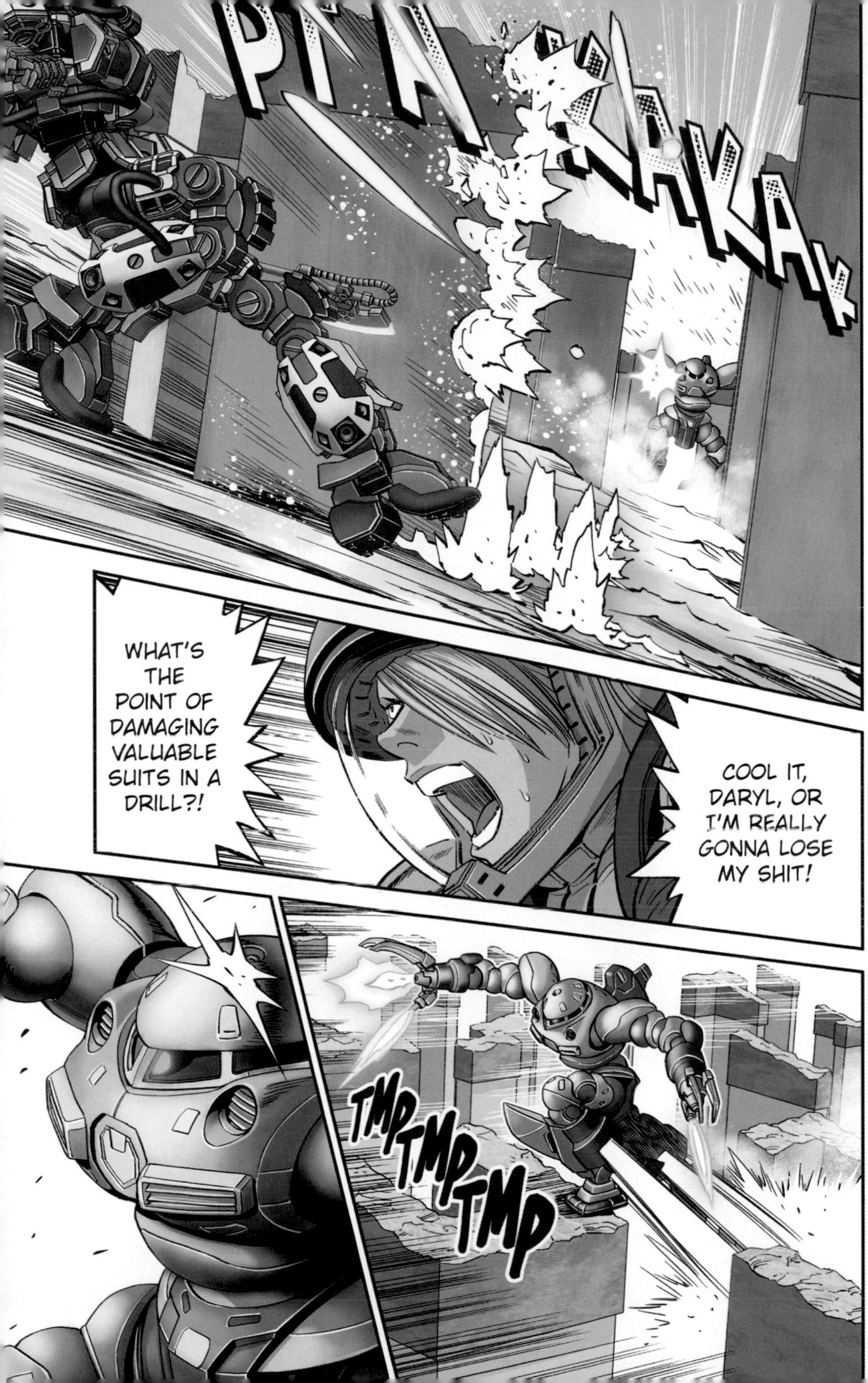
PTAKAKA
COOL IT, DARYL, OR I'M REALLY GONNA LOSE MY SHIT!
WHAT'S THE POINT OF DAMAGING VALUABLE SUITS IN A DRILL?!
TMP TMP TMP TMP

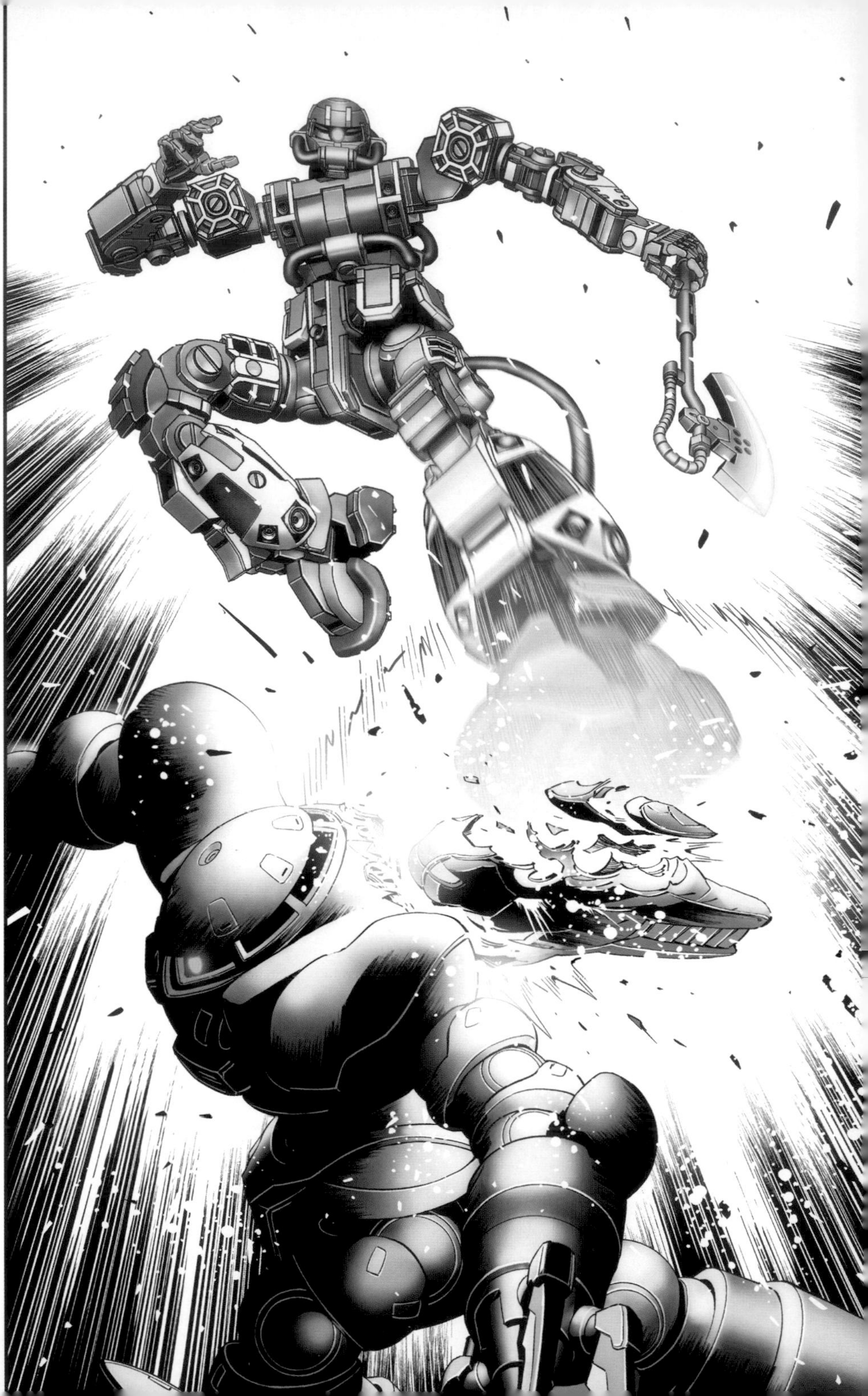

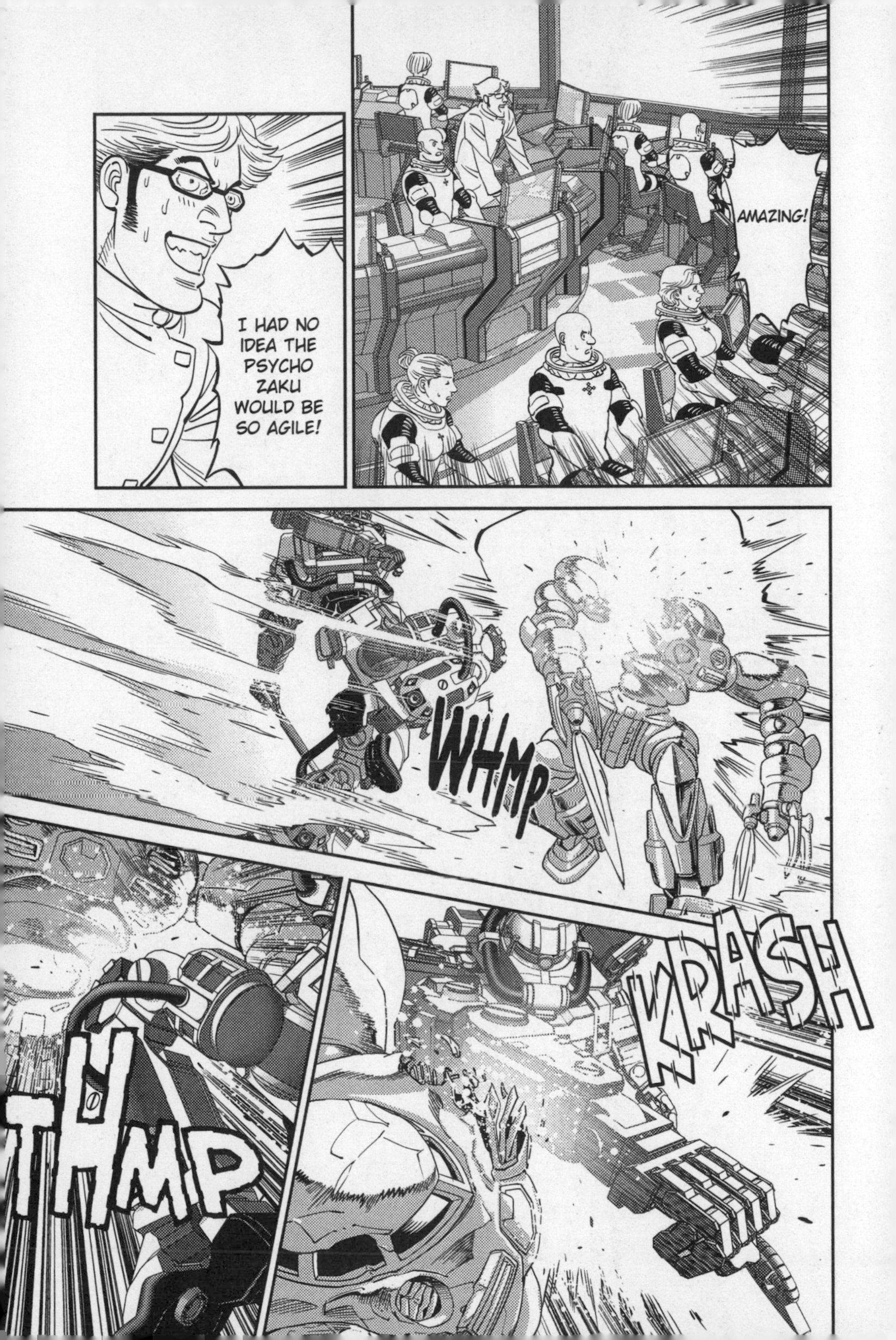
AMAZING!
I HAD NO IDEA THE PSYCHO ZAKU WOULD BE SO AGILE!
WHMP
KRASH
THMP

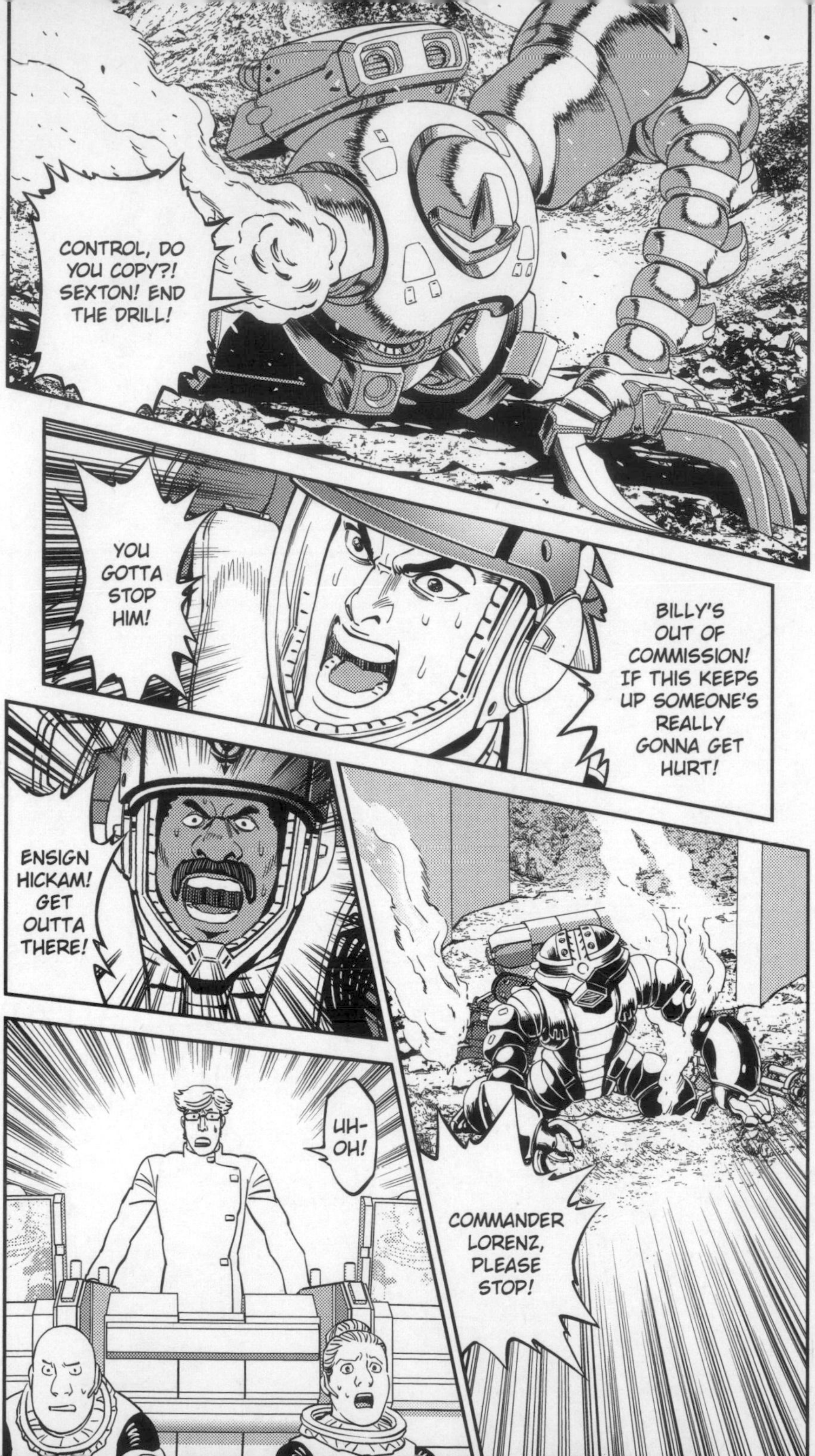
CONTROL, DO YOU COPY?! SEXTON! END THE DRILL!
BILLY'S OUT OF COMMISSION! IF THIS KEEPS UP SOMEONE'S REALLY GONNA GET HURT!
YOU GOTTA STOP HIM!
COMMANDER LORENZ, PLEASE STOP!
ENSIGN HICKAM! GET OUTTA THERE!
UH-OH!

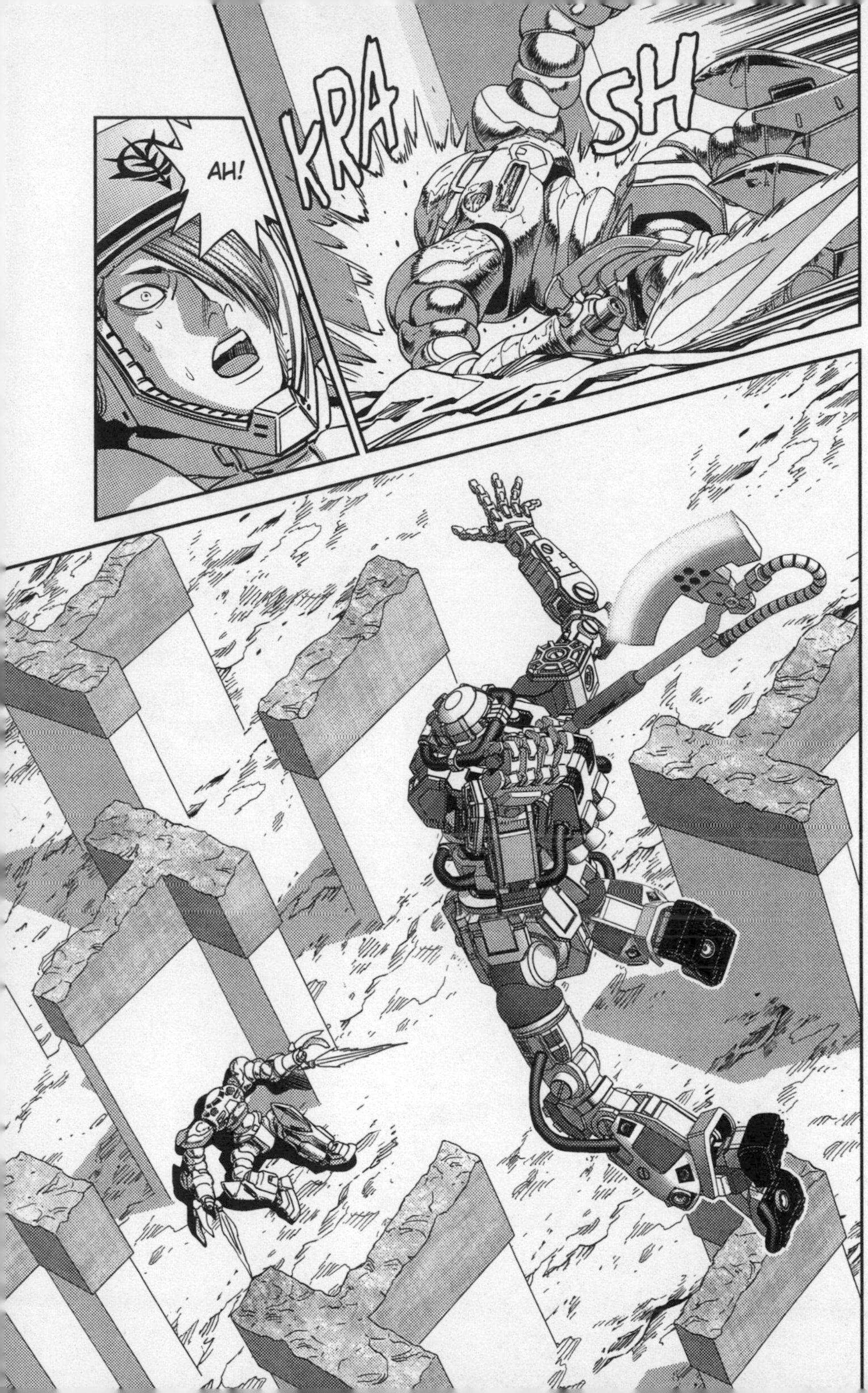
KRASH
AH!

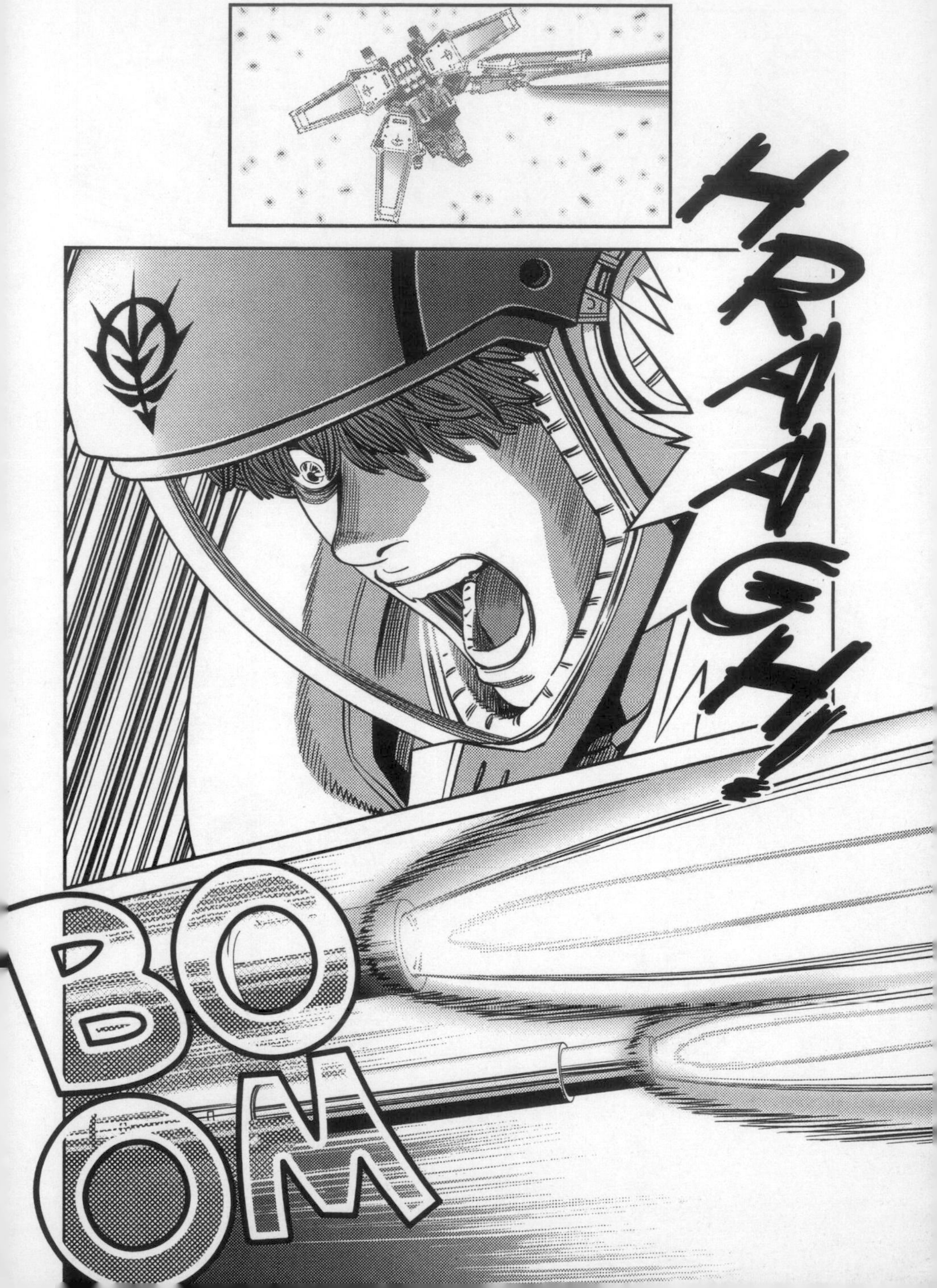
HRAAAGH!!
BOOM

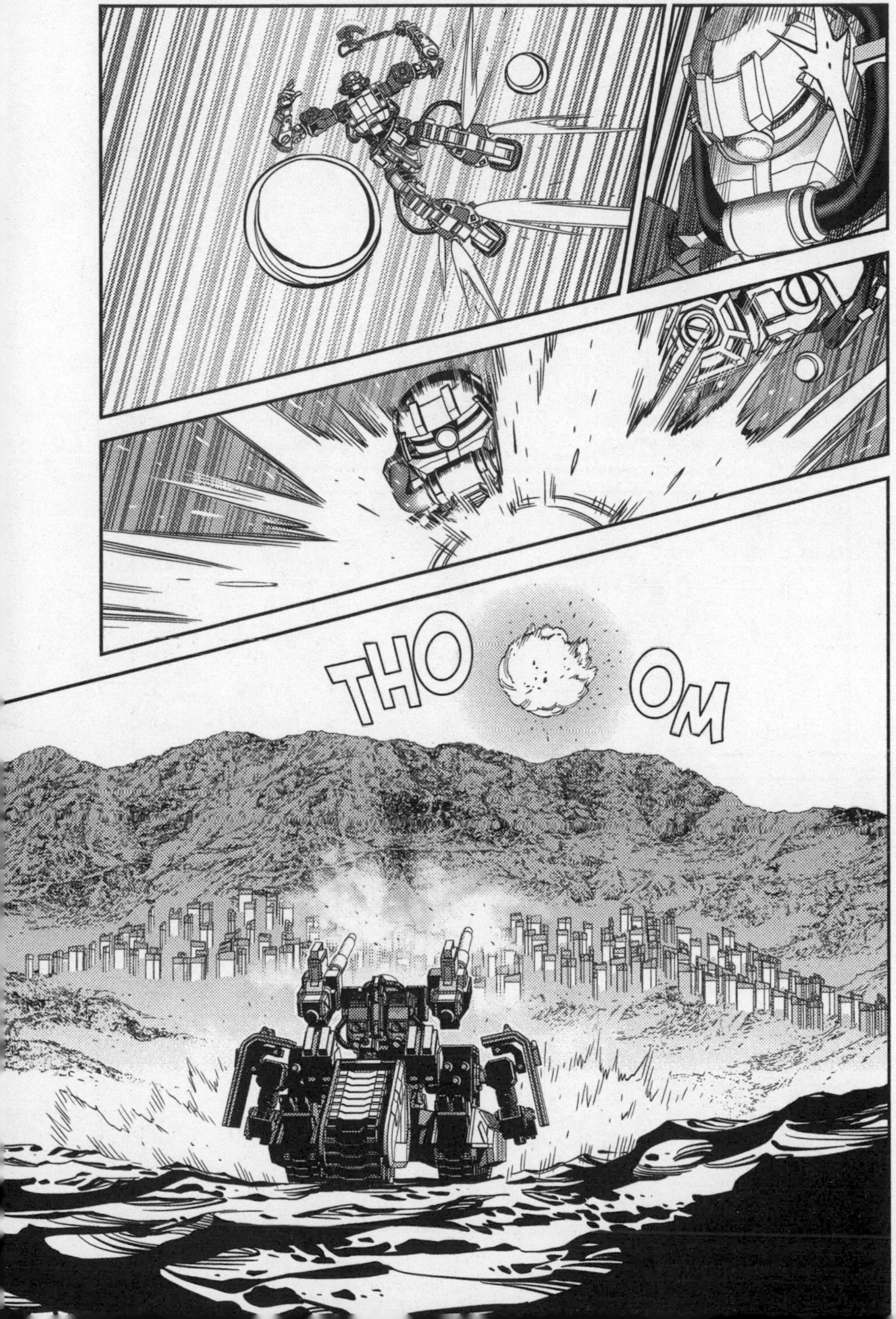
THO OM

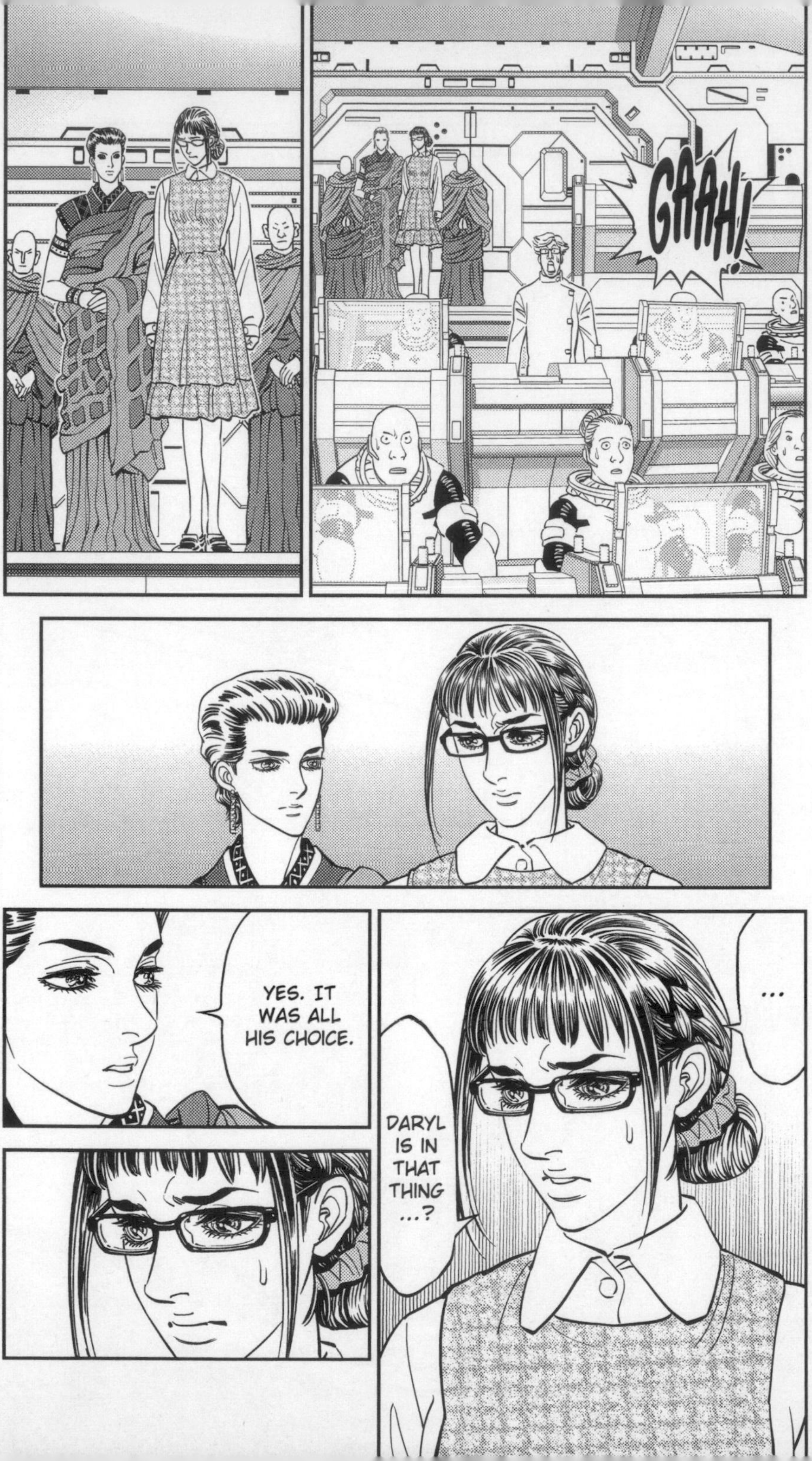
GAAH!
...
DARYL IS IN THAT THING ...?
YES. IT WAS ALL HIS CHOICE.

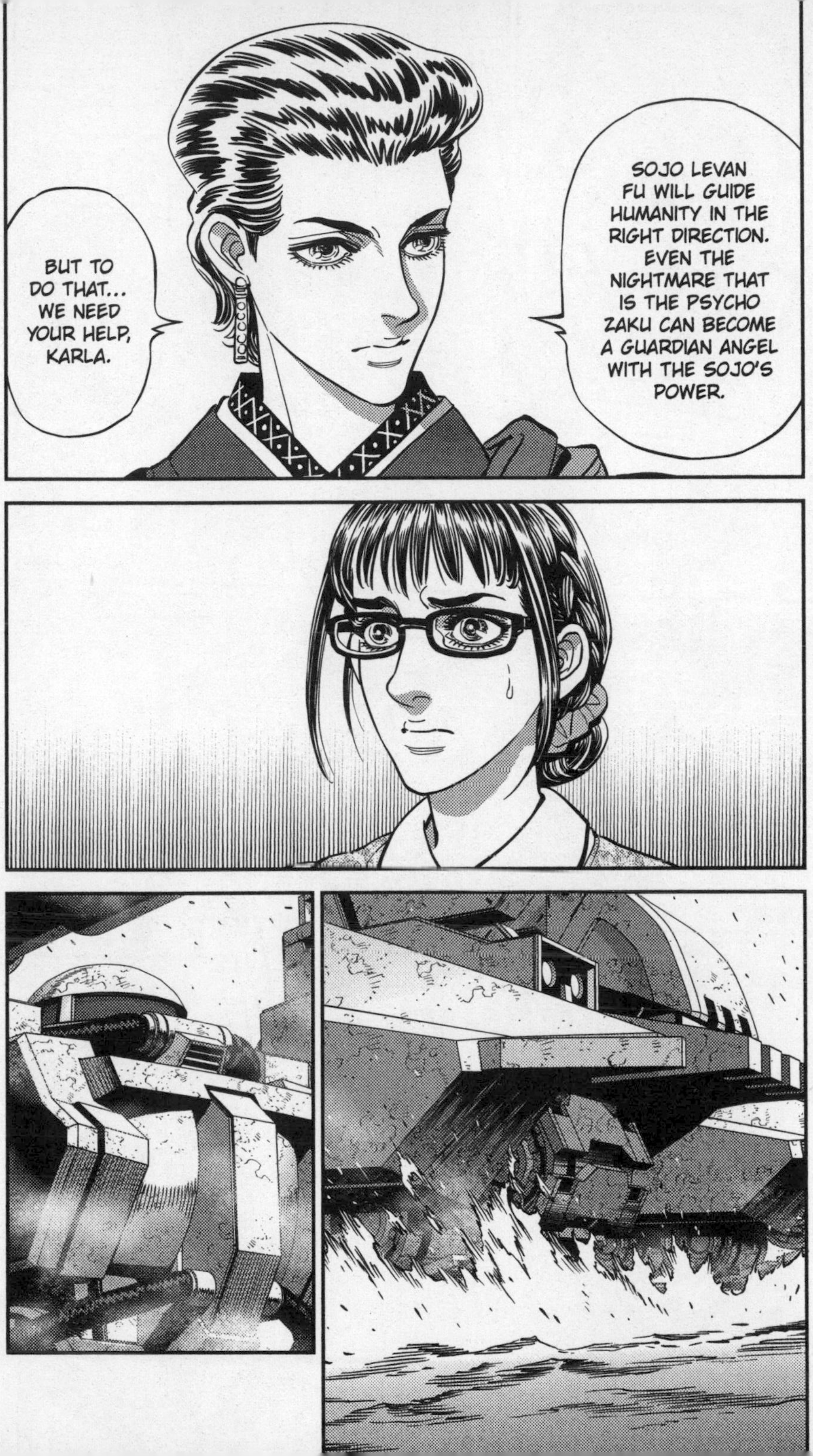
SOJO LEVAN FU WILL GUIDE HUMANITY IN THE RIGHT DIRECTION. EVEN THE NIGHTMARE THAT IS THE PSYCHO ZAKU CAN BECOME A GUARDIAN ANGEL WITH THE SOJO'S POWER.
BUT TO DO THAT... WE NEED YOUR HELP, KARLA.

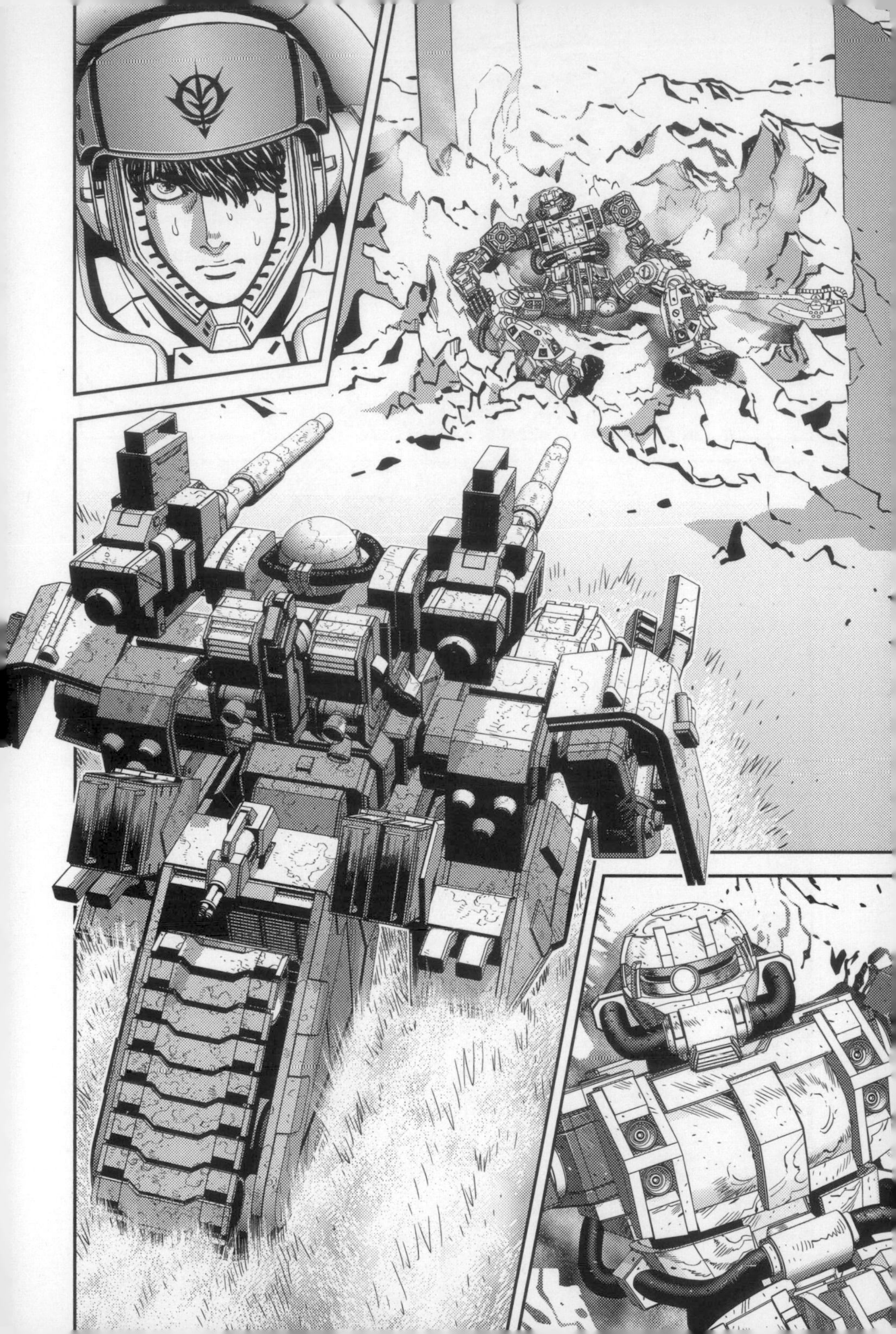

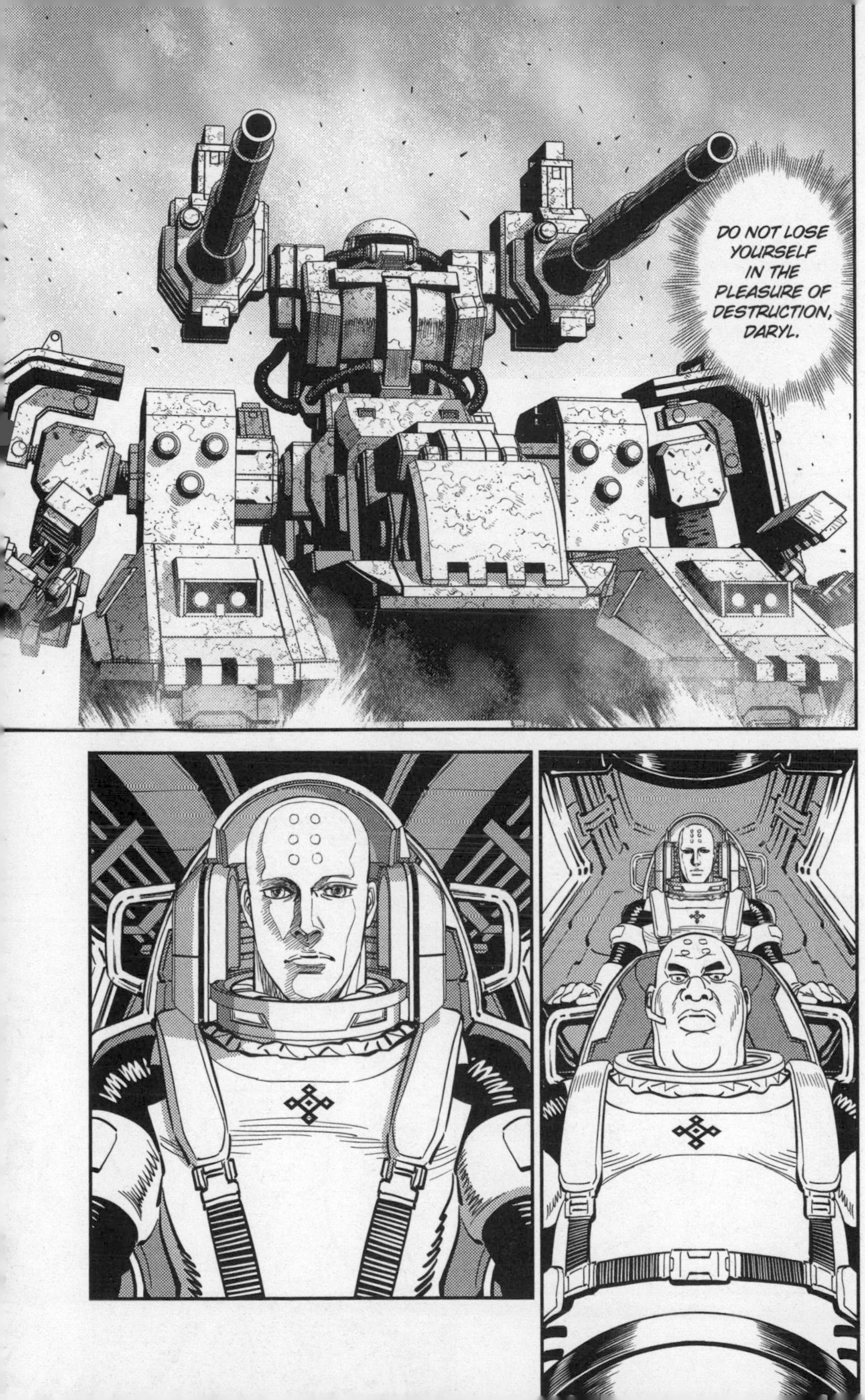
DO NOT LOSE YOURSELF IN THE PLEASURE OF DESTRUCTION, DARYL.

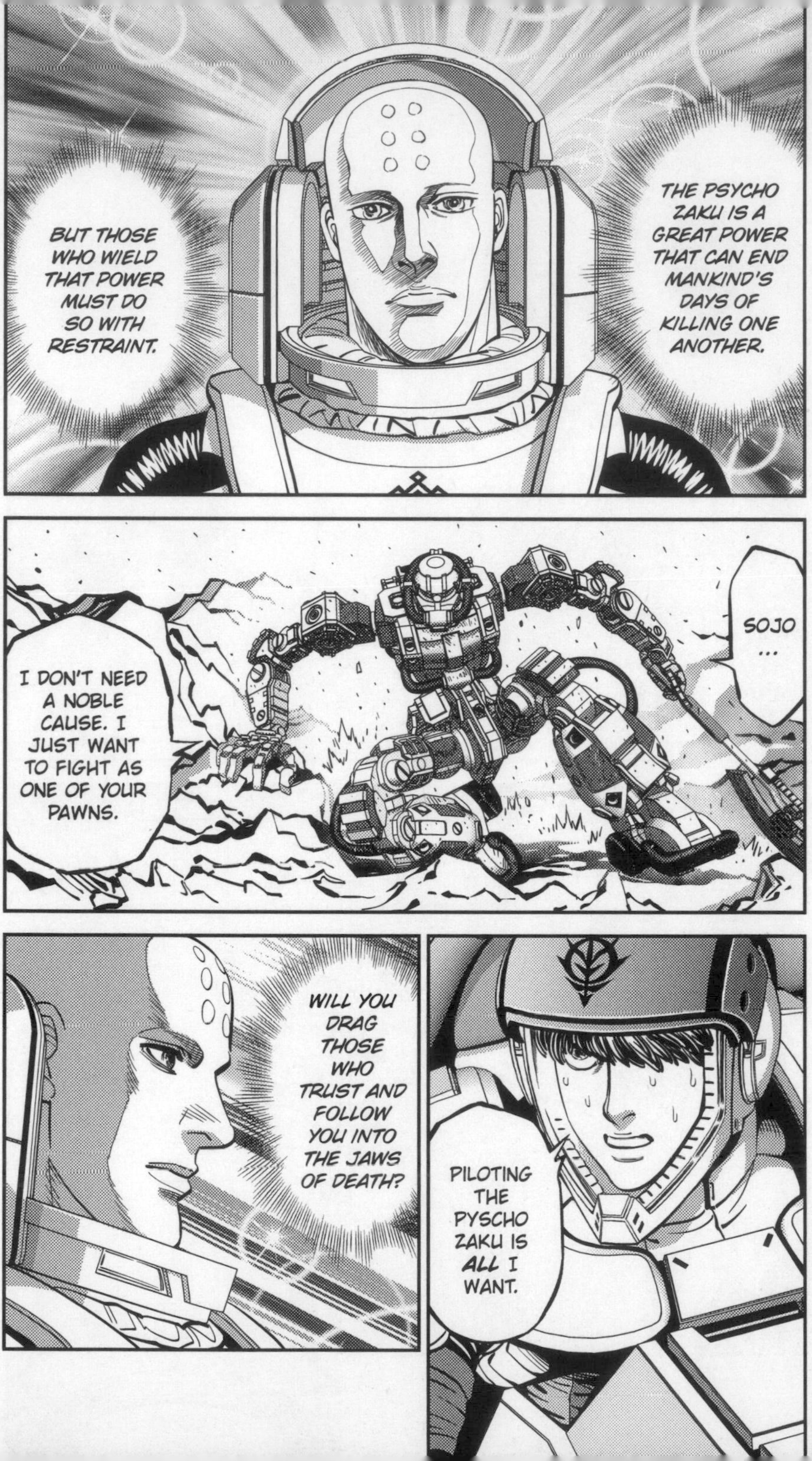
THE PSYCHO ZAKU IS A GREAT POWER THAT CAN END MANKIND'S DAYS OF KILLING ONE ANOTHER.
BUT THOSE WHO WIELD THAT POWER MUST DO SO WITH RESTRAINT.
SOJO ...
I DON'T NEED A NOBLE CAUSE. I JUST WANT TO FIGHT AS ONE OF YOUR PAWNS.
PILOTING THE PYSCHO ZAKU IS *ALL* I WANT.
WILL YOU DRAG THOSE WHO TRUST AND FOLLOW YOU INTO THE JAWS OF DEATH?

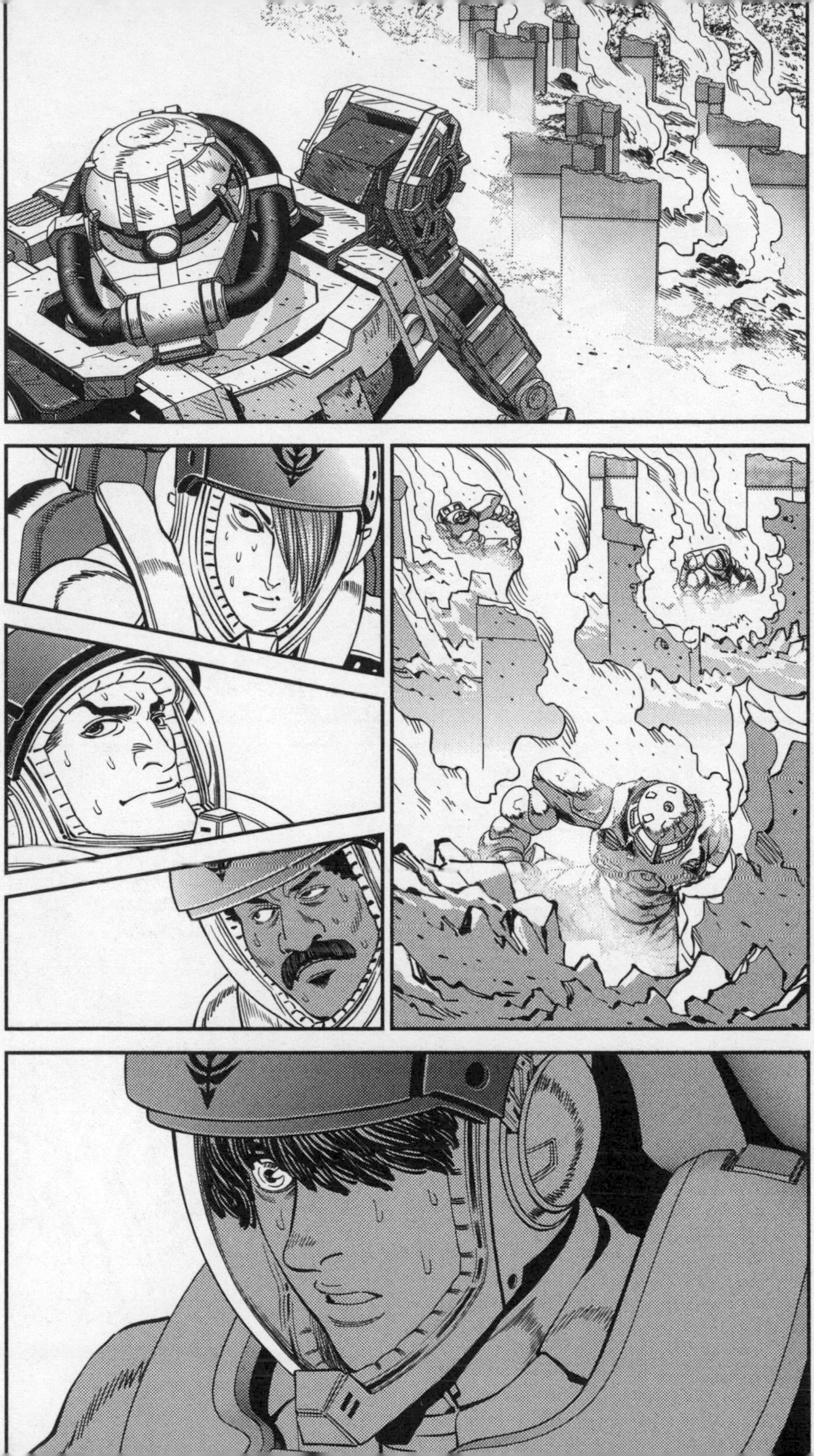

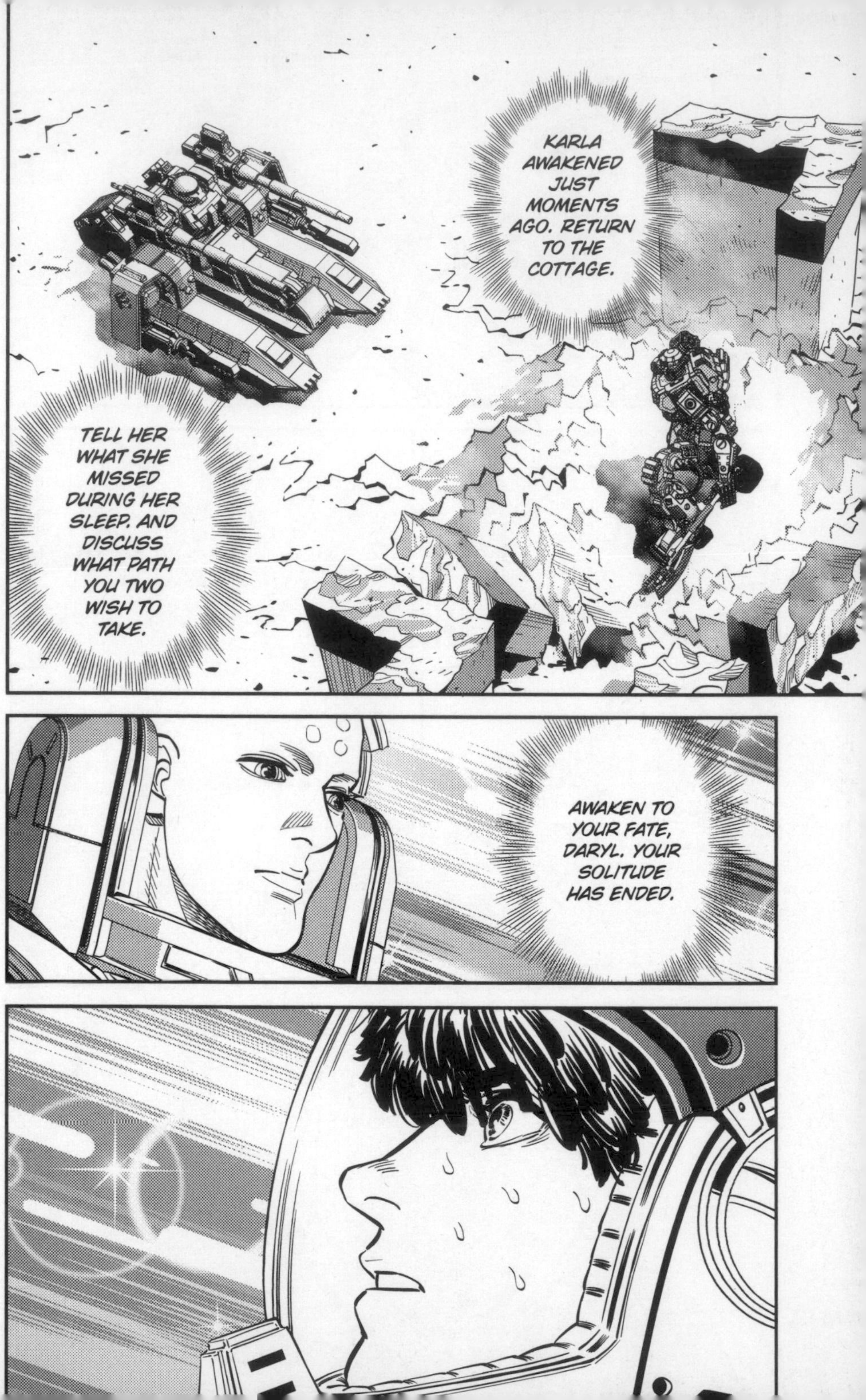
KARLA AWAKENED JUST MOMENTS AGO. RETURN TO THE COTTAGE.
TELL HER WHAT SHE MISSED DURING HER SLEEP. AND DISCUSS WHAT PATH YOU TWO WISH TO TAKE.
AWAKEN TO YOUR FATE, DARYL. YOUR SOLITUDE HAS ENDED.

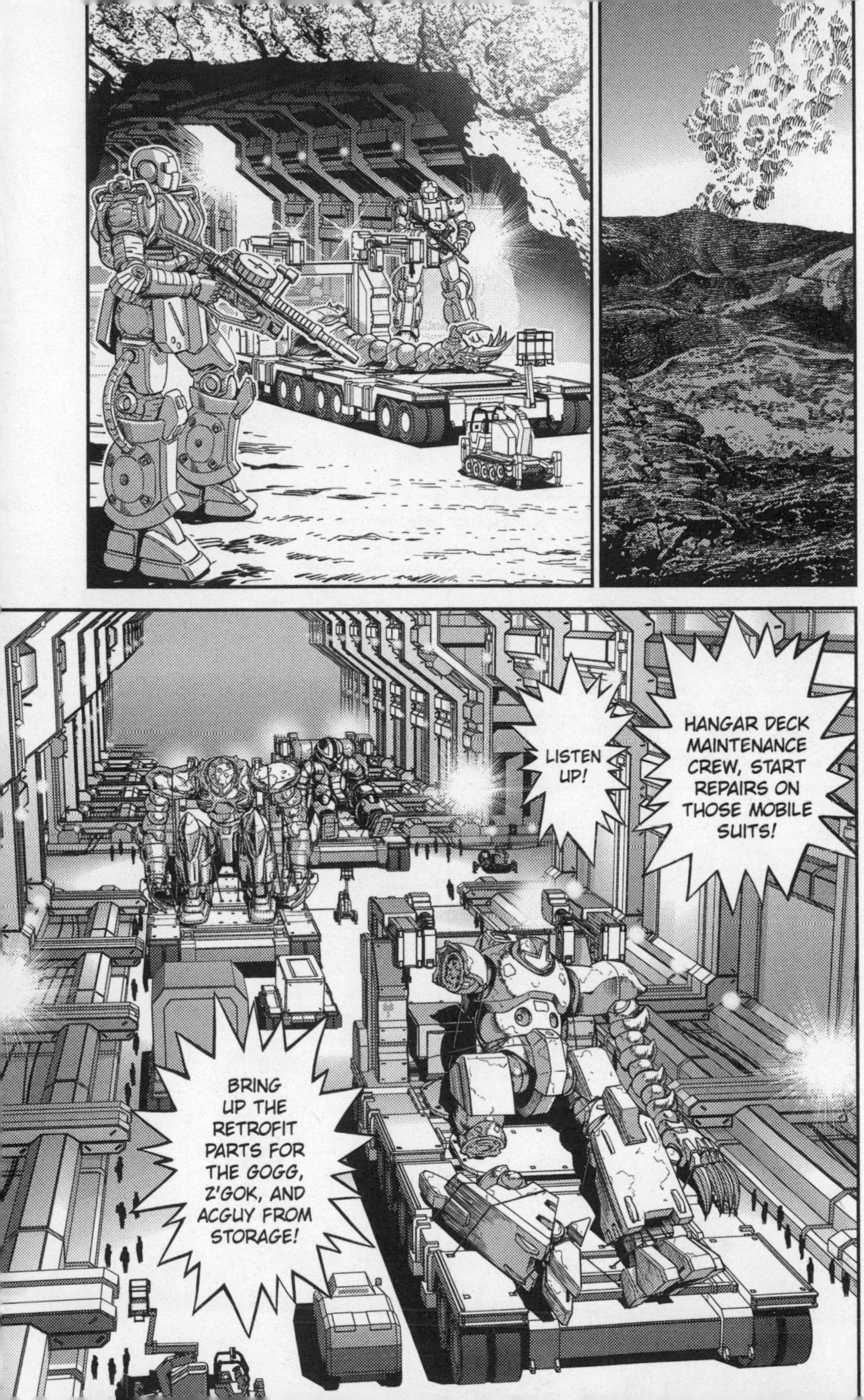
LISTEN UP!
HANGAR DECK MAINTENANCE CREW, START REPAIRS ON THOSE MOBILE SUITS!
BRING UP THE RETROFIT PARTS FOR THE GOGG, Z'GOK, AND ACGUY FROM STORAGE!

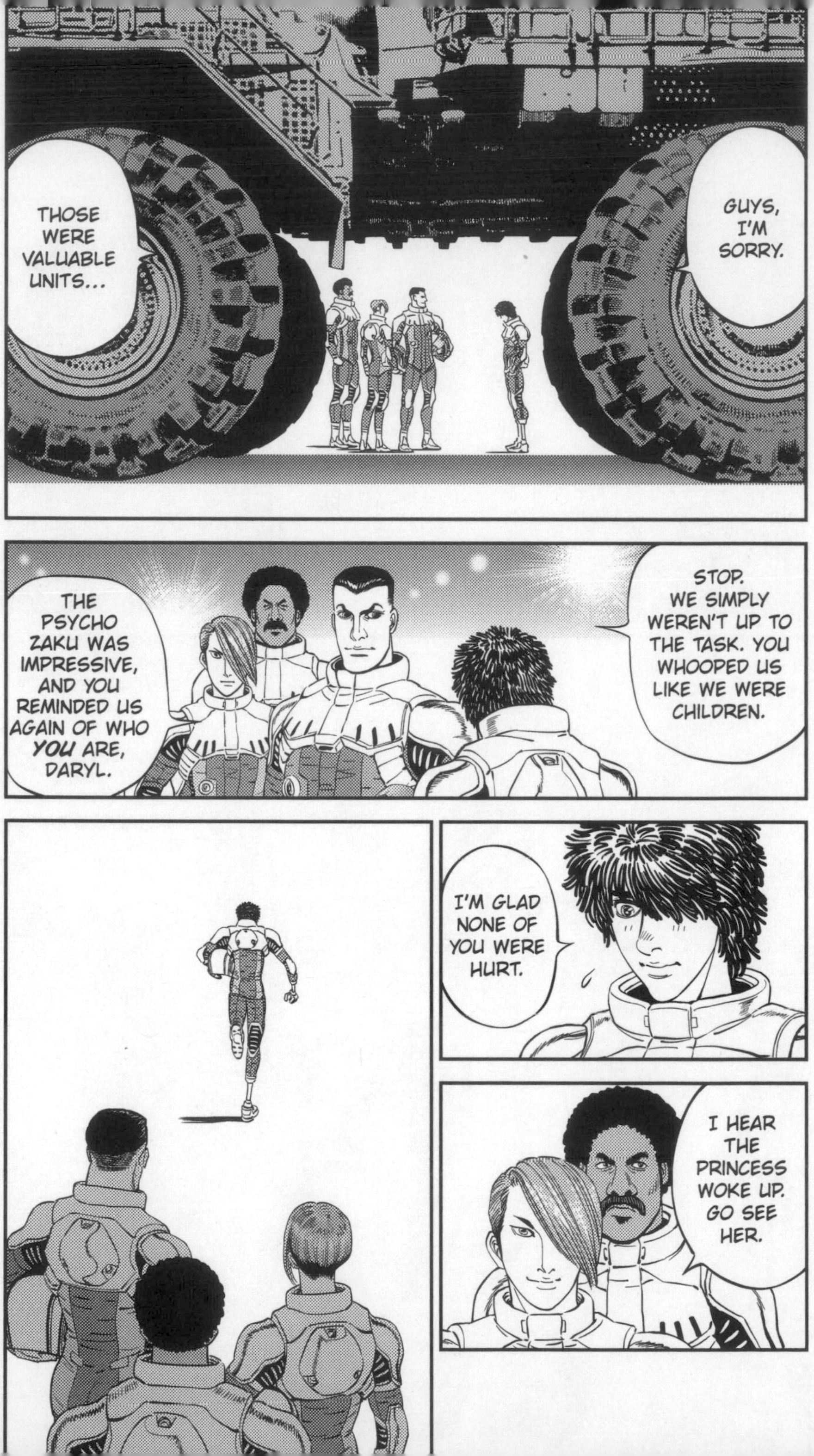
GUYS, I'M SORRY.
THOSE WERE VALUABLE UNITS...
STOP. WE SIMPLY WEREN'T UP TO THE TASK. YOU WHOOPED US LIKE WE WERE CHILDREN.
THE PSYCHO ZAKU WAS IMPRESSIVE, AND YOU REMINDED US AGAIN OF WHO *YOU* ARE, DARYL.
I'M GLAD NONE OF YOU WERE HURT.
I HEAR THE PRINCESS WOKE UP. GO SEE HER.

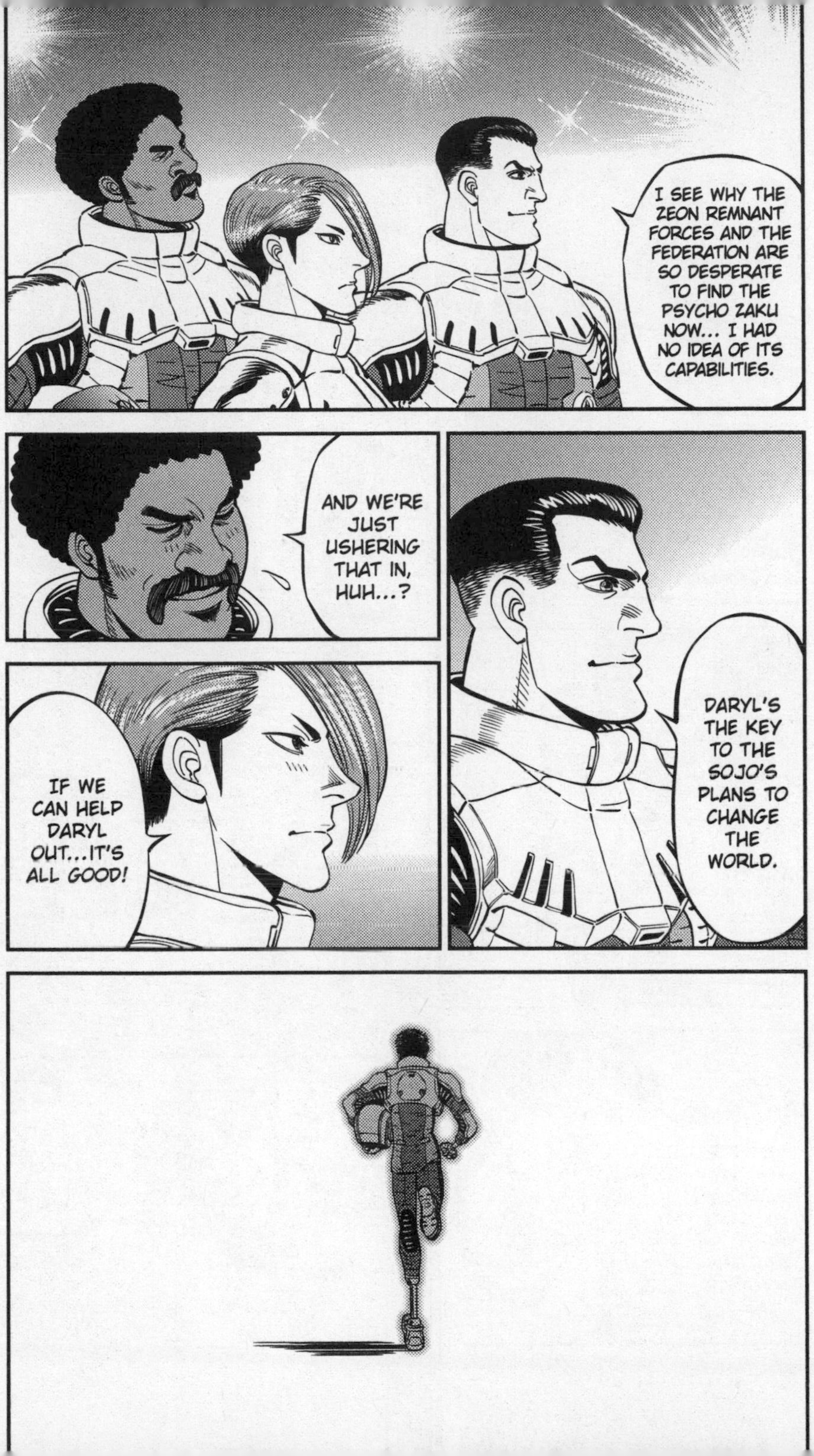
I SEE WHY THE ZEON REMNANT FORCES AND THE FEDERATION ARE SO DESPERATE TO FIND THE PSYCHO ZAKU NOW... I HAD NO IDEA OF ITS CAPABILITIES.
DARYL'S THE KEY TO THE SOJO'S PLANS TO CHANGE THE WORLD.
AND WE'RE JUST USHERING THAT IN, HUH...?
IF WE CAN HELP DARYL OUT...IT'S ALL GOOD!

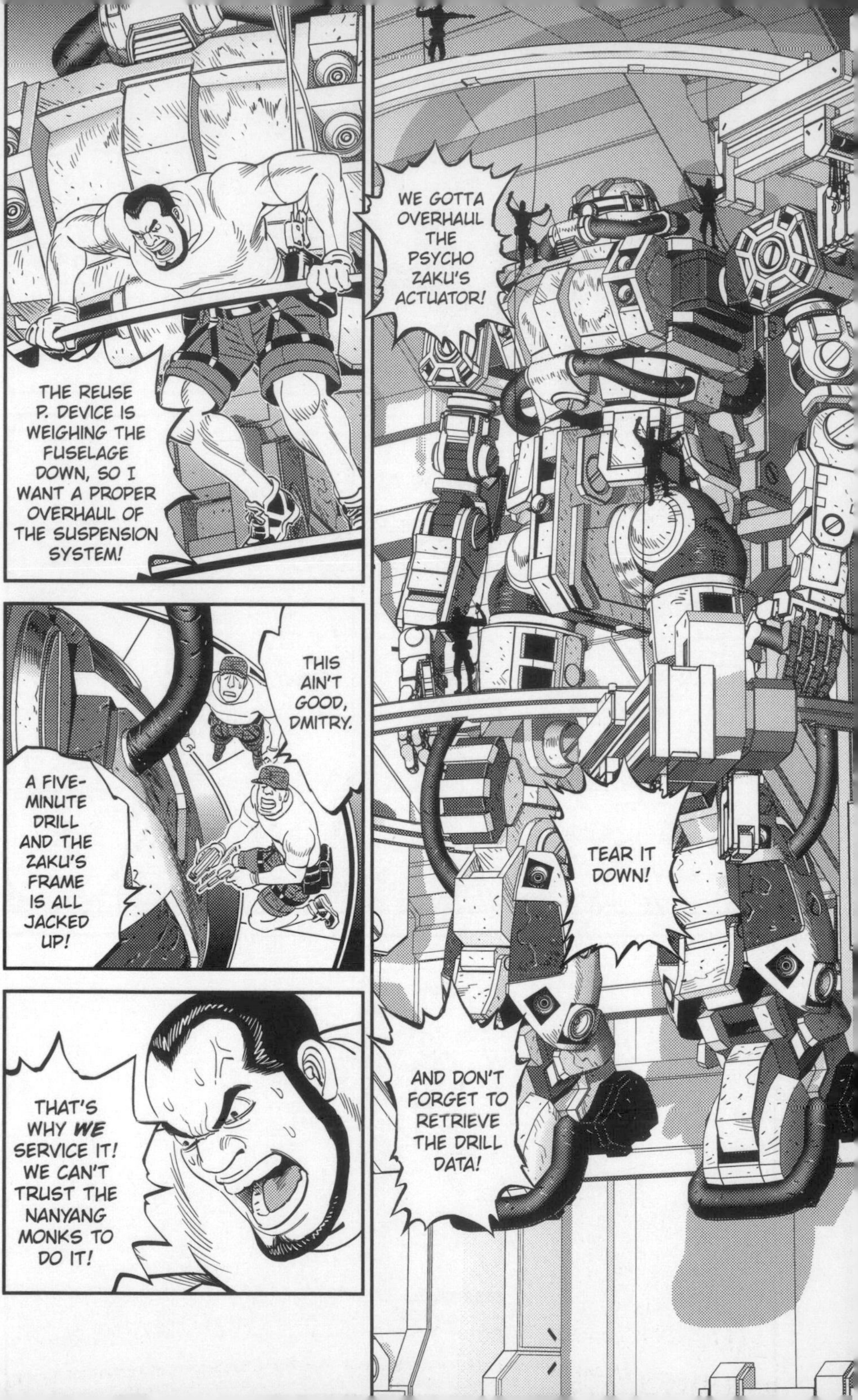
WE GOTTA OVERHAUL THE PSYCHO ZAKU'S ACTUATOR!
TEAR IT DOWN!
AND DON'T FORGET TO RETRIEVE THE DRILL DATA!
THE REUSE P. DEVICE IS WEIGHING THE FUSELAGE DOWN, SO I WANT A PROPER OVERHAUL OF THE SUSPENSION SYSTEM!
THIS AIN'T GOOD, DMITRY.
A FIVE-MINUTE DRILL AND THE ZAKU'S FRAME IS ALL JACKED UP!
THAT'S WHY *WE* SERVICE IT! WE CAN'T TRUST THE NANYANG MONKS TO DO IT!

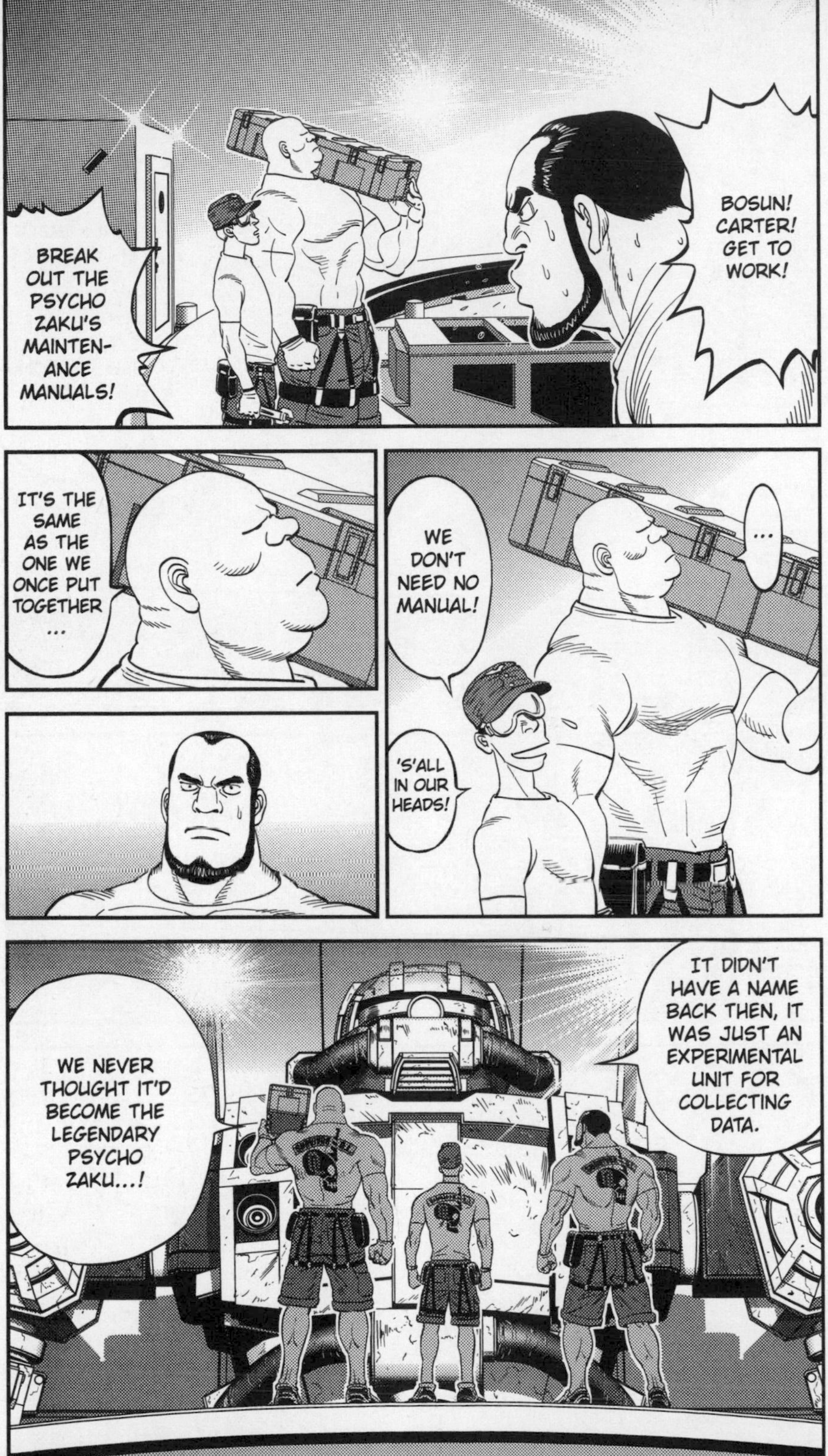
BOSUN! CARTER! GET TO WORK!
BREAK OUT THE PSYCHO ZAKU'S MAINTEN-ANCE MANUALS!
...
WE DON'T NEED NO MANUAL!
'S'ALL IN OUR HEADS!
IT'S THE SAME AS THE ONE WE ONCE PUT TOGETHER ...
IT DIDN'T HAVE A NAME BACK THEN, IT WAS JUST AN EXPERIMENTAL UNIT FOR COLLECTING DATA.
WE NEVER THOUGHT IT'D BECOME THE LEGENDARY PSYCHO ZAKU...!

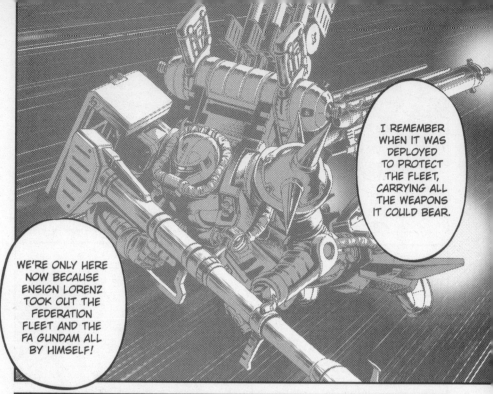

I REMEMBER WHEN IT WAS DEPLOYED TO PROTECT THE FLEET, CARRYING ALL THE WEAPONS IT COULD BEAR.

WE'RE ONLY HERE NOW BECAUSE ENSIGN LORENZ TOOK OUT THE FEDERATION FLEET AND THE FA GUNDAM ALL BY HIMSELF!

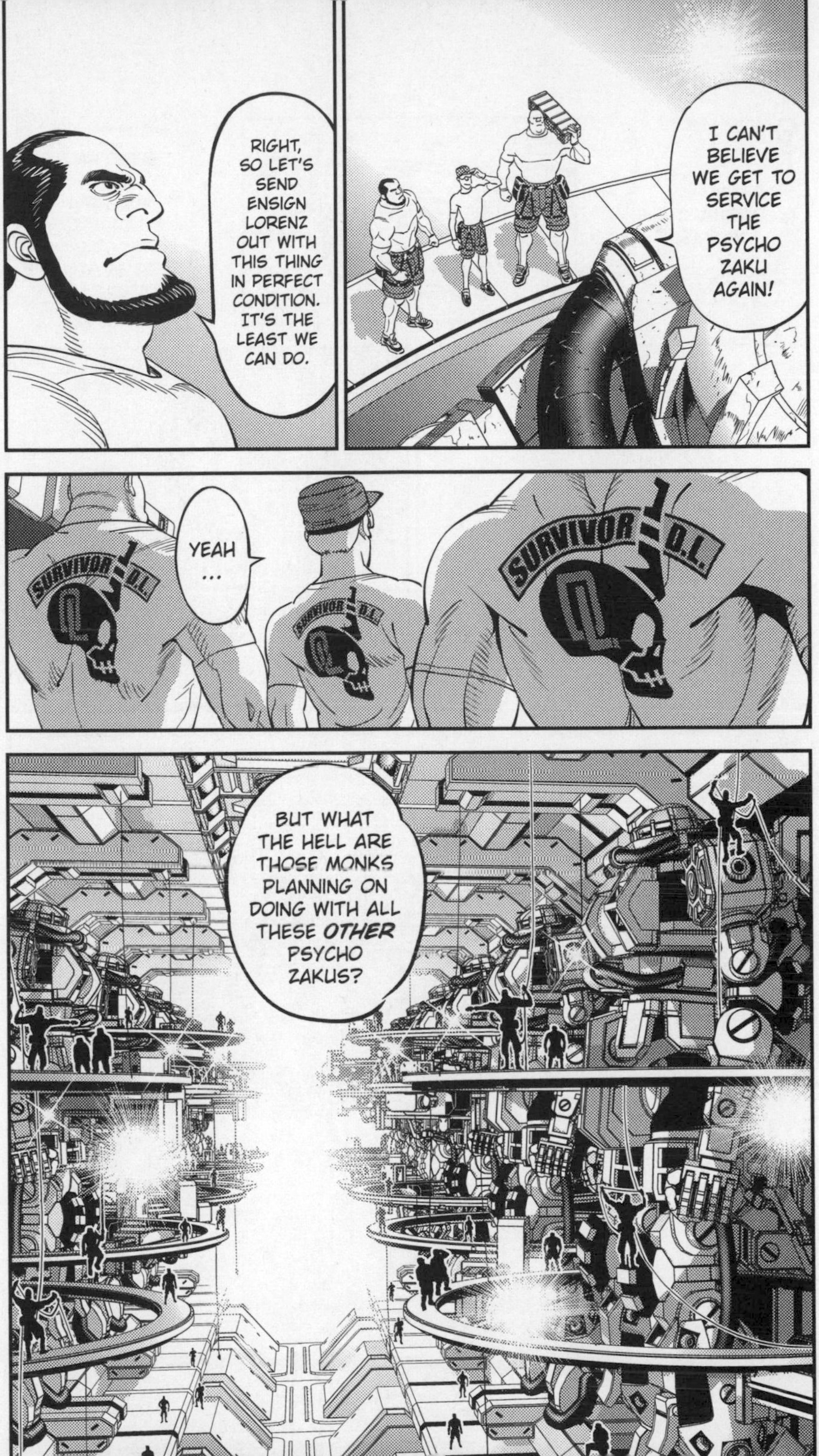
I CAN'T BELIEVE WE GET TO SERVICE THE PSYCHO ZAKU AGAIN!
RIGHT, SO LET'S SEND ENSIGN LORENZ OUT WITH THIS THING IN PERFECT CONDITION. IT'S THE LEAST WE CAN DO.
SURVIVOR O.L.
YEAH ...
BUT WHAT THE HELL ARE THOSE MONKS PLANNING ON DOING WITH ALL THESE *OTHER* PSYCHO ZAKUS?

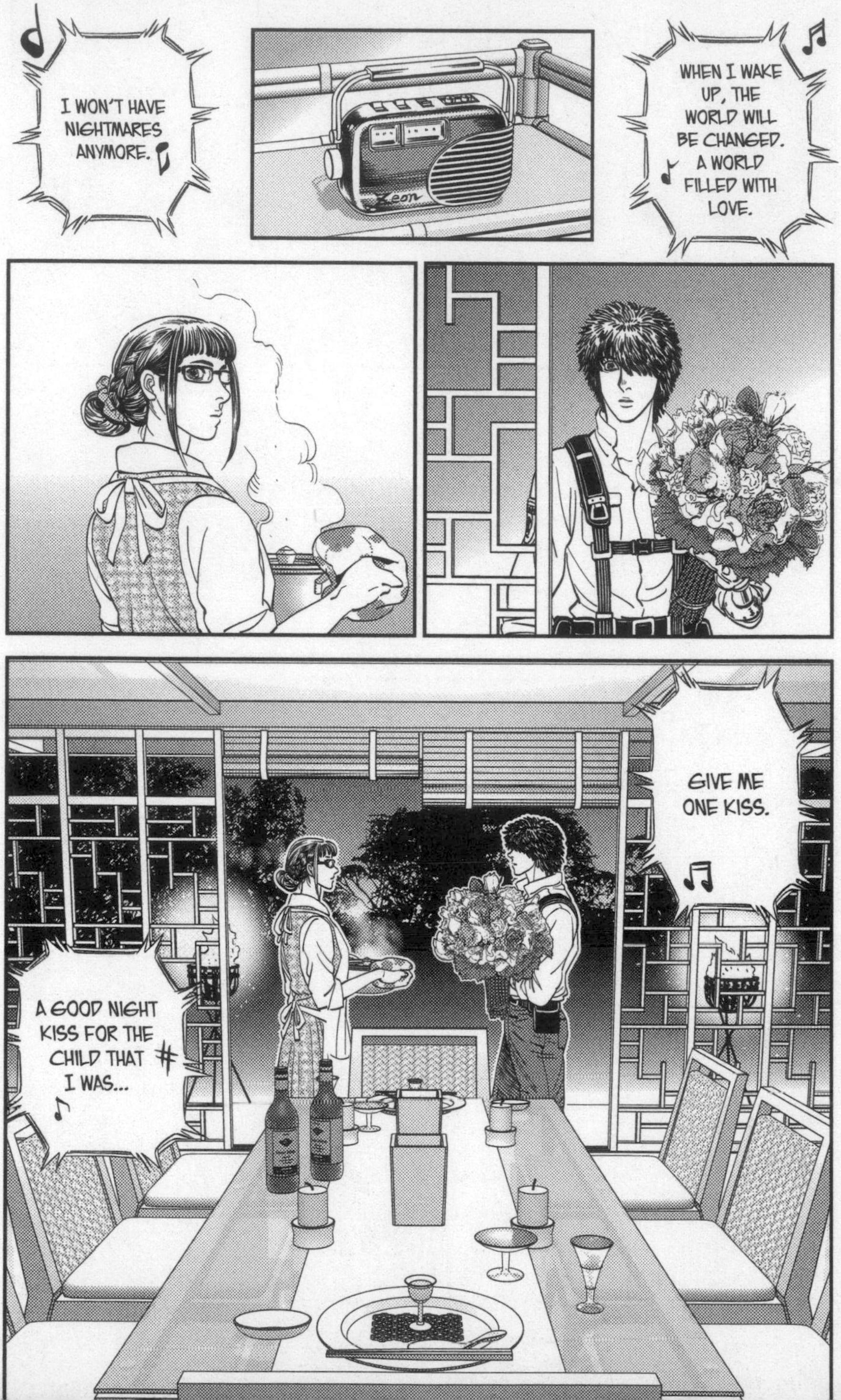
WHEN I WAKE UP, THE WORLD WILL BE CHANGED. A WORLD FILLED WITH LOVE.
I WON'T HAVE NIGHTMARES ANYMORE.
GIVE ME ONE KISS.
A GOOD NIGHT KISS FOR THE CHILD THAT I WAS...

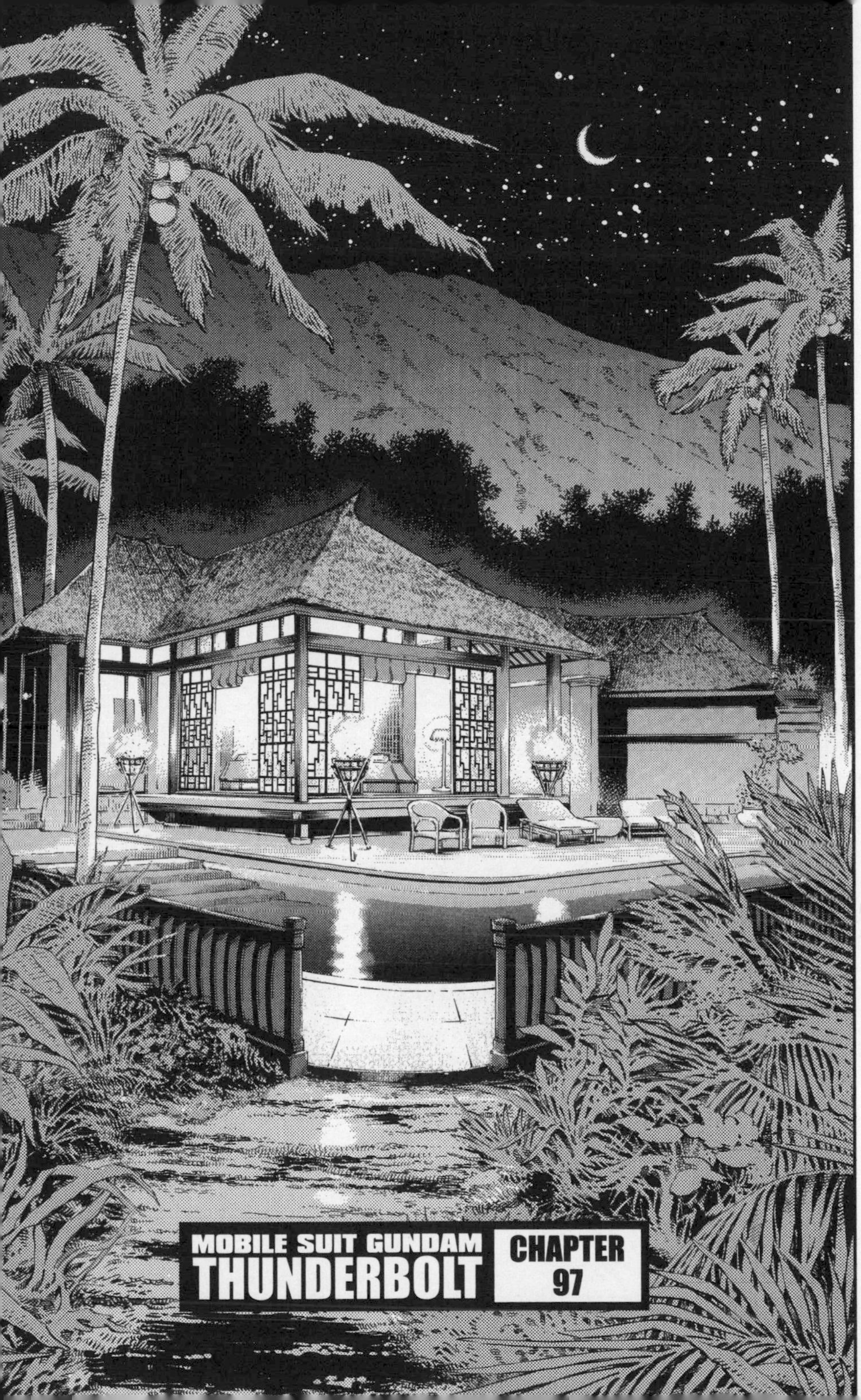
MOBILE SUIT GUNDAM
THUNDERBOLT
CHAPTER
97

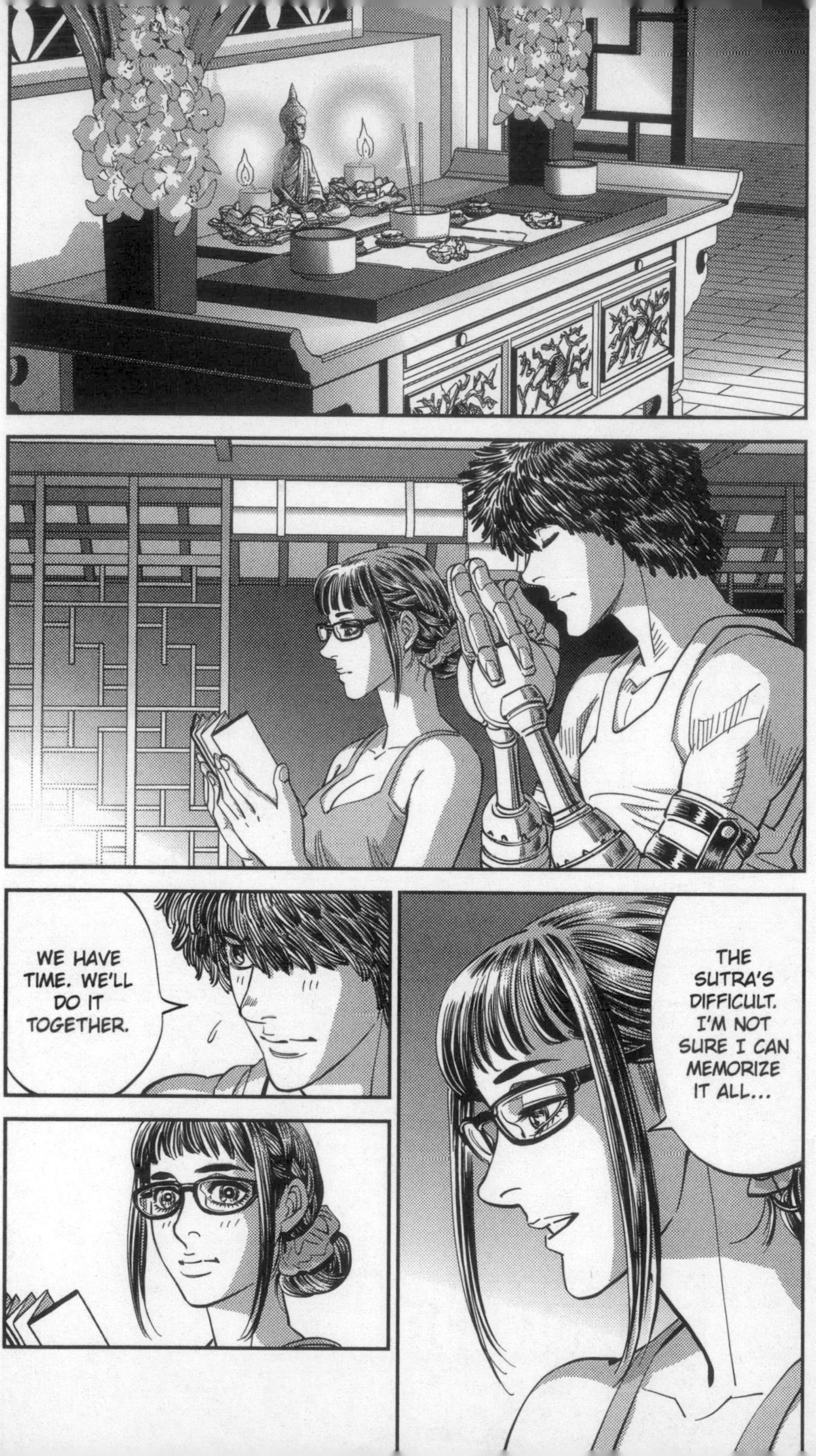
THE SUTRA'S DIFFICULT. I'M NOT SURE I CAN MEMORIZE IT ALL...
WE HAVE TIME. WE'LL DO IT TOGETHER.

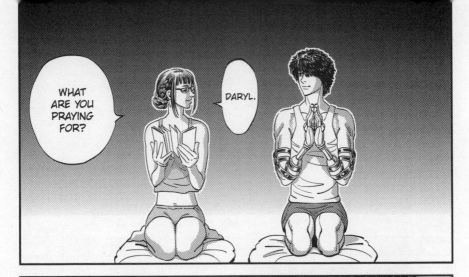

DARYL.
WHAT ARE YOU PRAYING FOR?
THE GUYS WE'VE LOST. AND... THE ENEMIES I'VE KILLED ON THE BATTLEFIELD.
I'VE NEVER KNOWN HOW TO PRAY BEFORE.
I'M PRAYING...
...FOR THEIR FORGIVENESS.

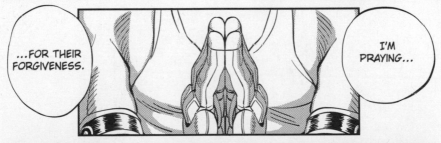

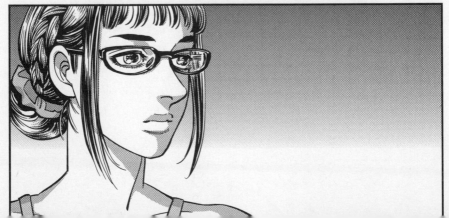

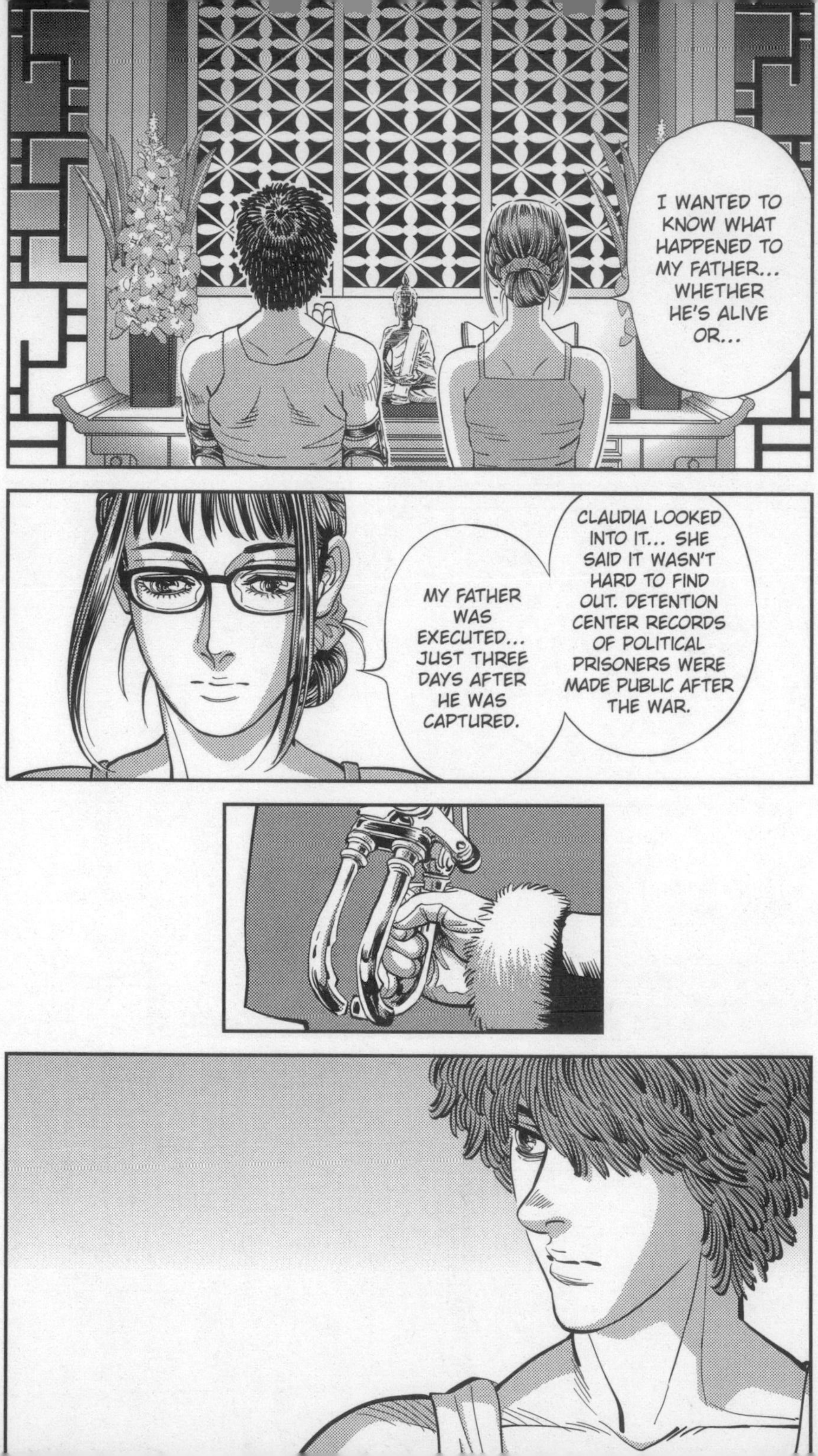
I WANTED TO KNOW WHAT HAPPENED TO MY FATHER... WHETHER HE'S ALIVE OR...
CLAUDIA LOOKED INTO IT... SHE SAID IT WASN'T HARD TO FIND OUT. DETENTION CENTER RECORDS OF POLITICAL PRISONERS WERE MADE PUBLIC AFTER THE WAR.
MY FATHER WAS EXECUTED... JUST THREE DAYS AFTER HE WAS CAPTURED.

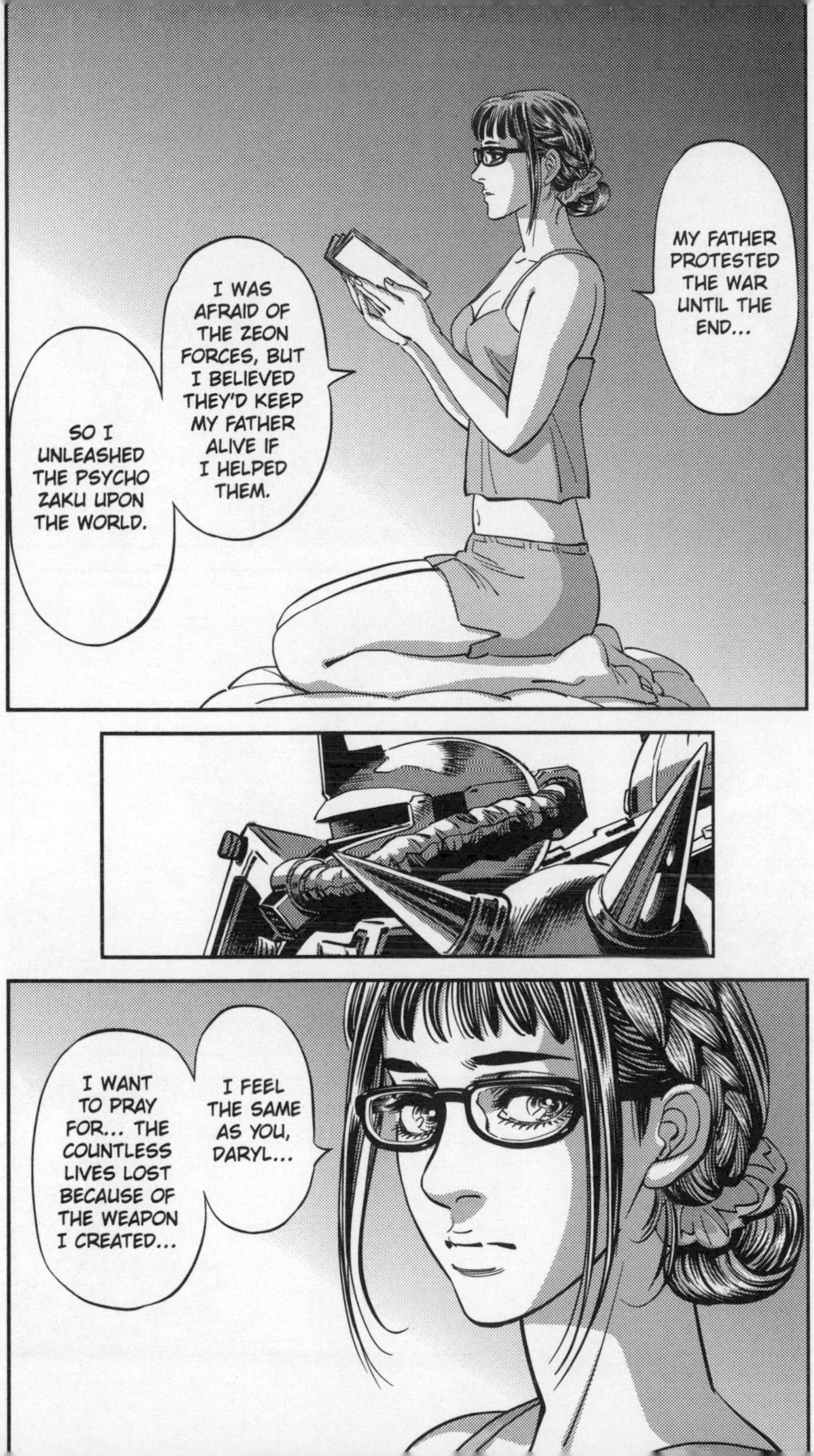
MY FATHER PROTESTED THE WAR UNTIL THE END...
I WAS AFRAID OF THE ZEON FORCES, BUT I BELIEVED THEY'D KEEP MY FATHER ALIVE IF I HELPED THEM.
SO I UNLEASHED THE PSYCHO ZAKU UPON THE WORLD.
I FEEL THE SAME AS YOU, DARYL...
I WANT TO PRAY FOR... THE COUNTLESS LIVES LOST BECAUSE OF THE WEAPON I CREATED...

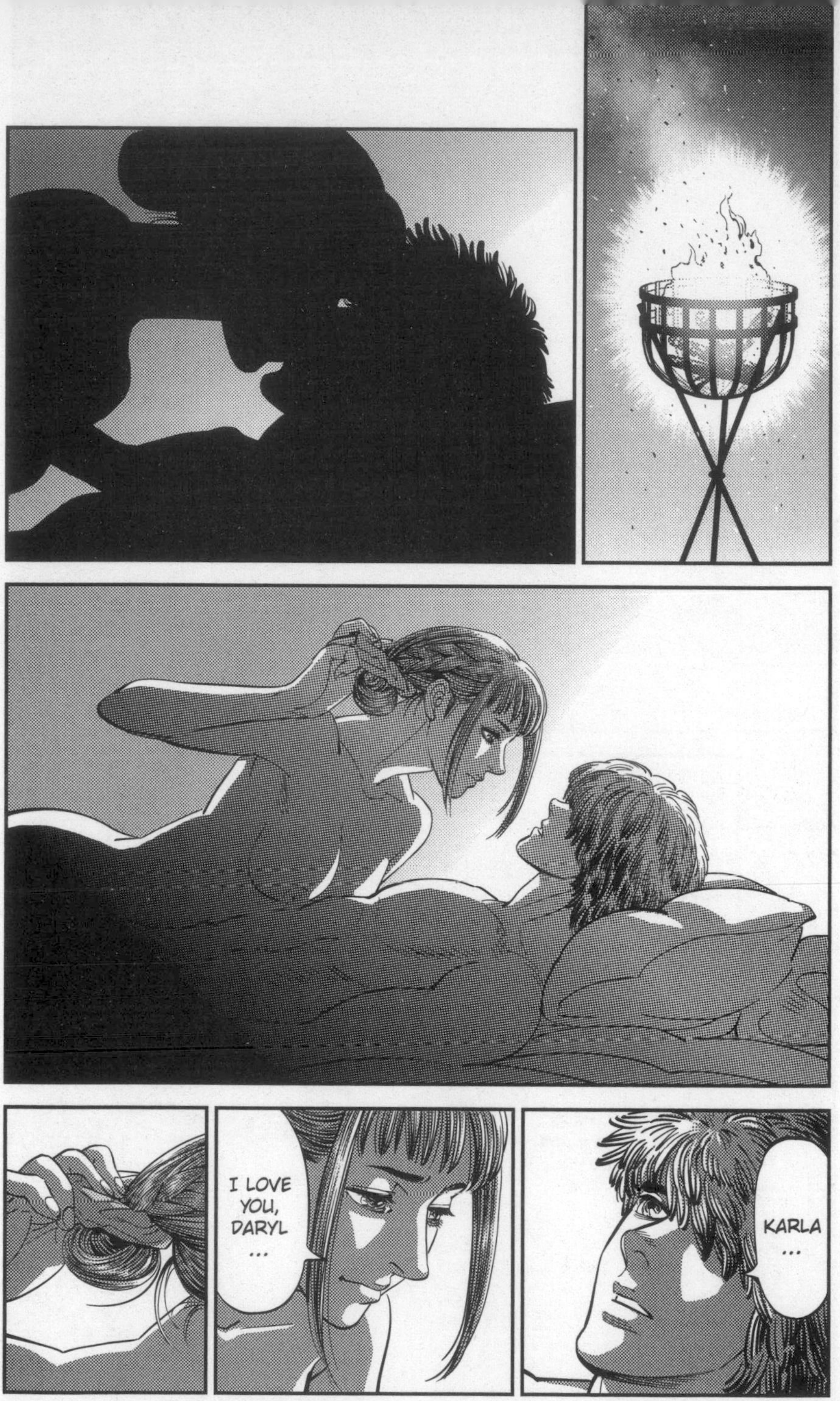
KARLA ...
I LOVE YOU, DARYL ...

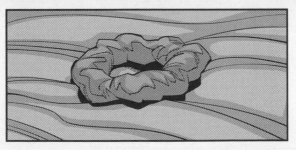

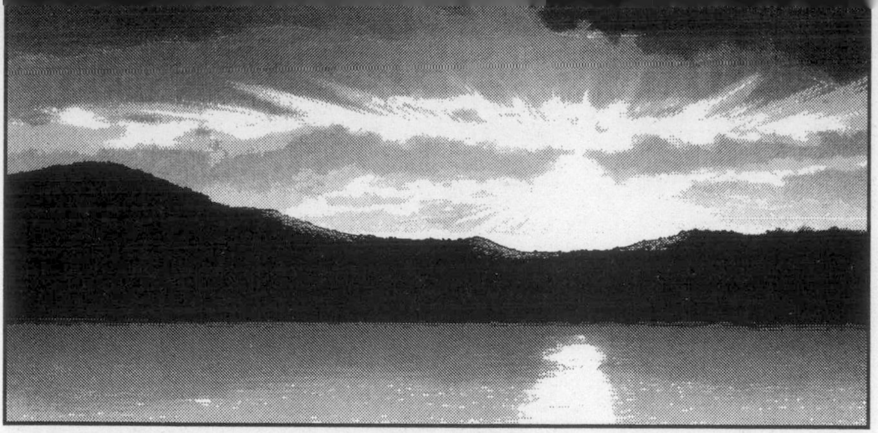
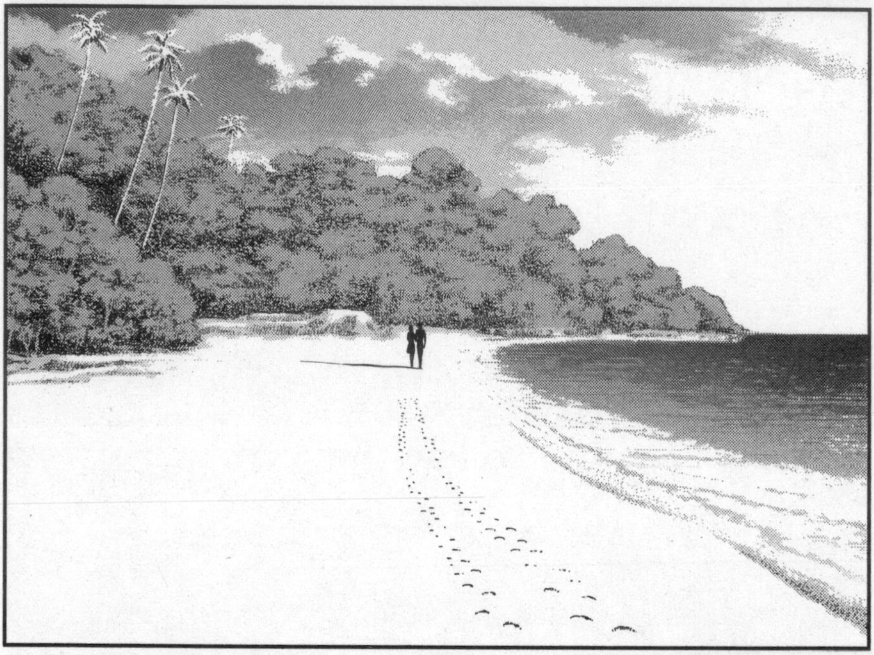
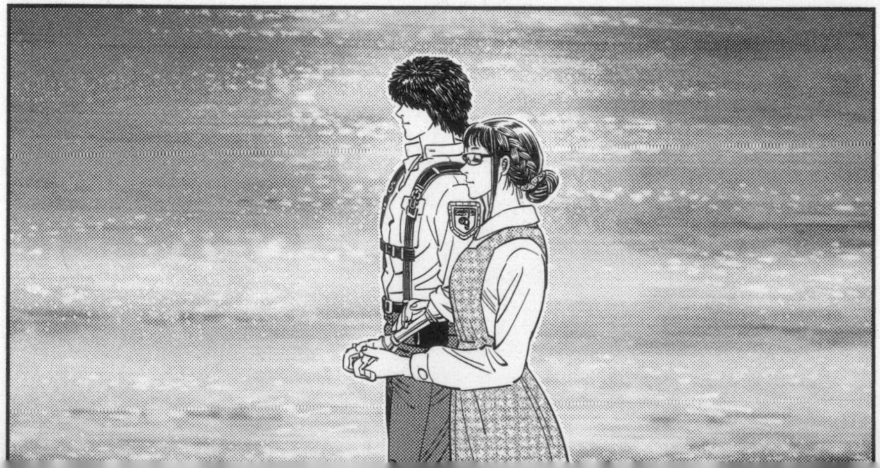

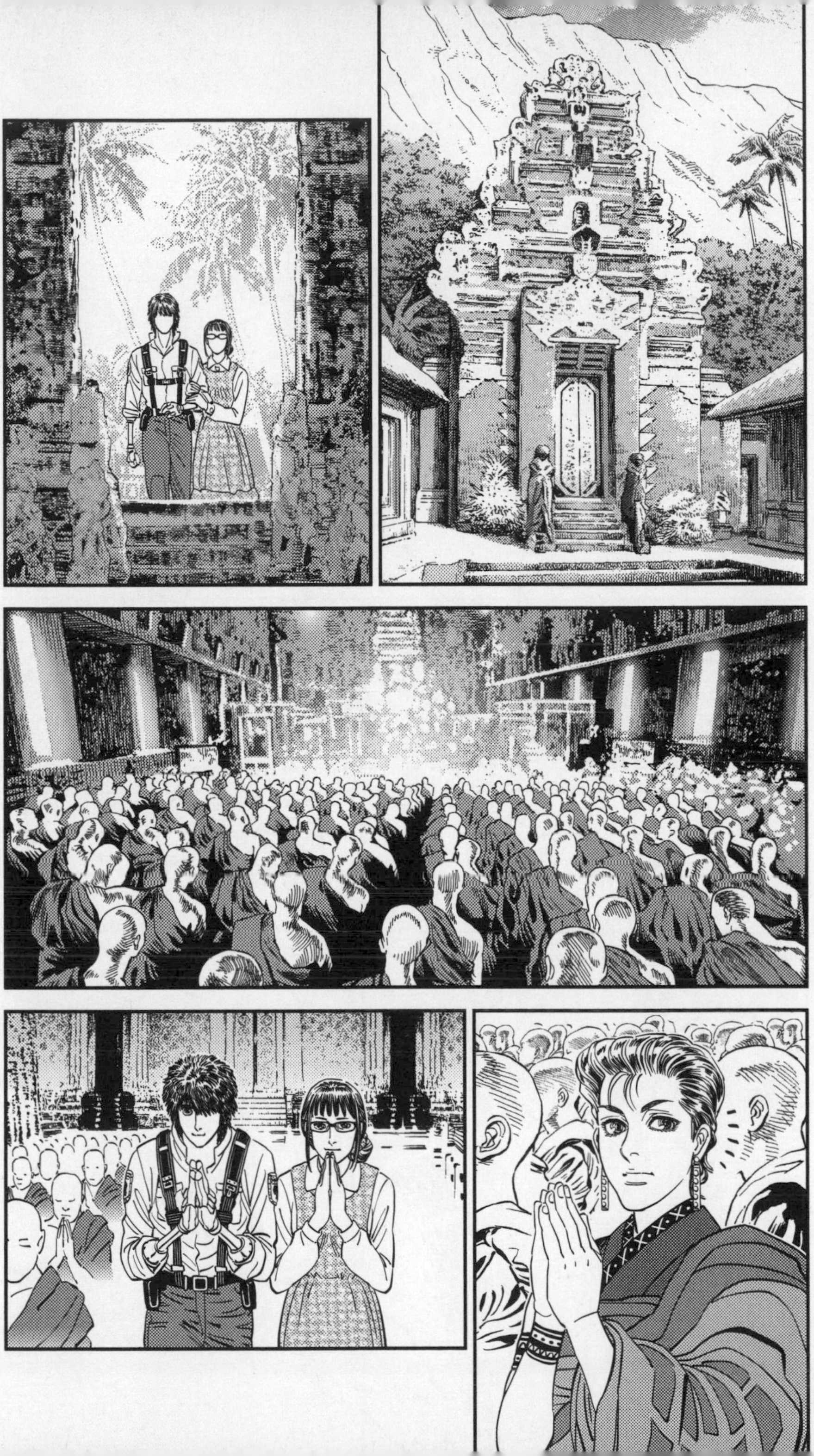

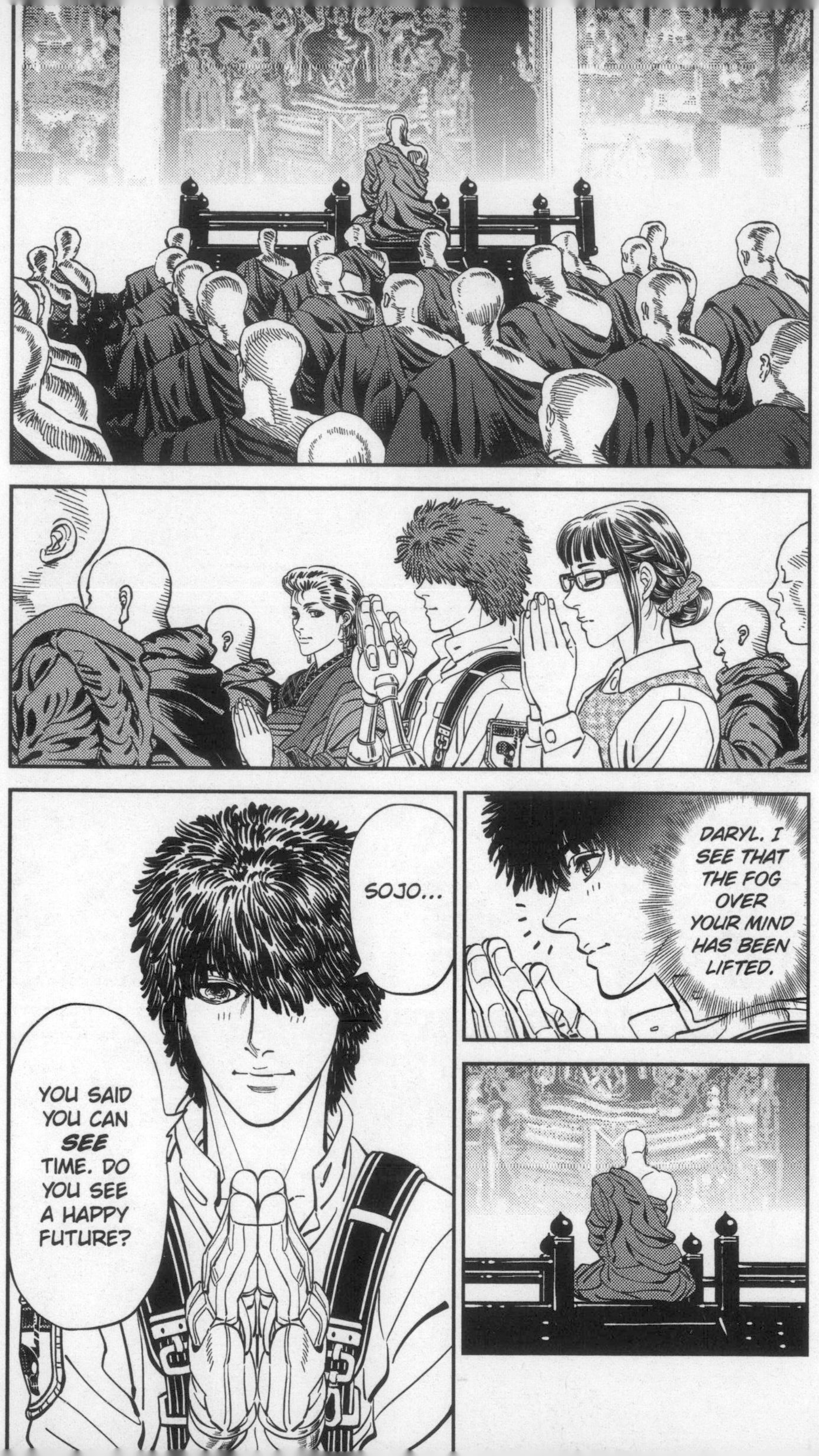
DARYL. I SEE THAT THE FOG OVER YOUR MIND HAS BEEN LIFTED.
SOJO...
YOU SAID YOU CAN SEE TIME. DO YOU SEE A HAPPY FUTURE?

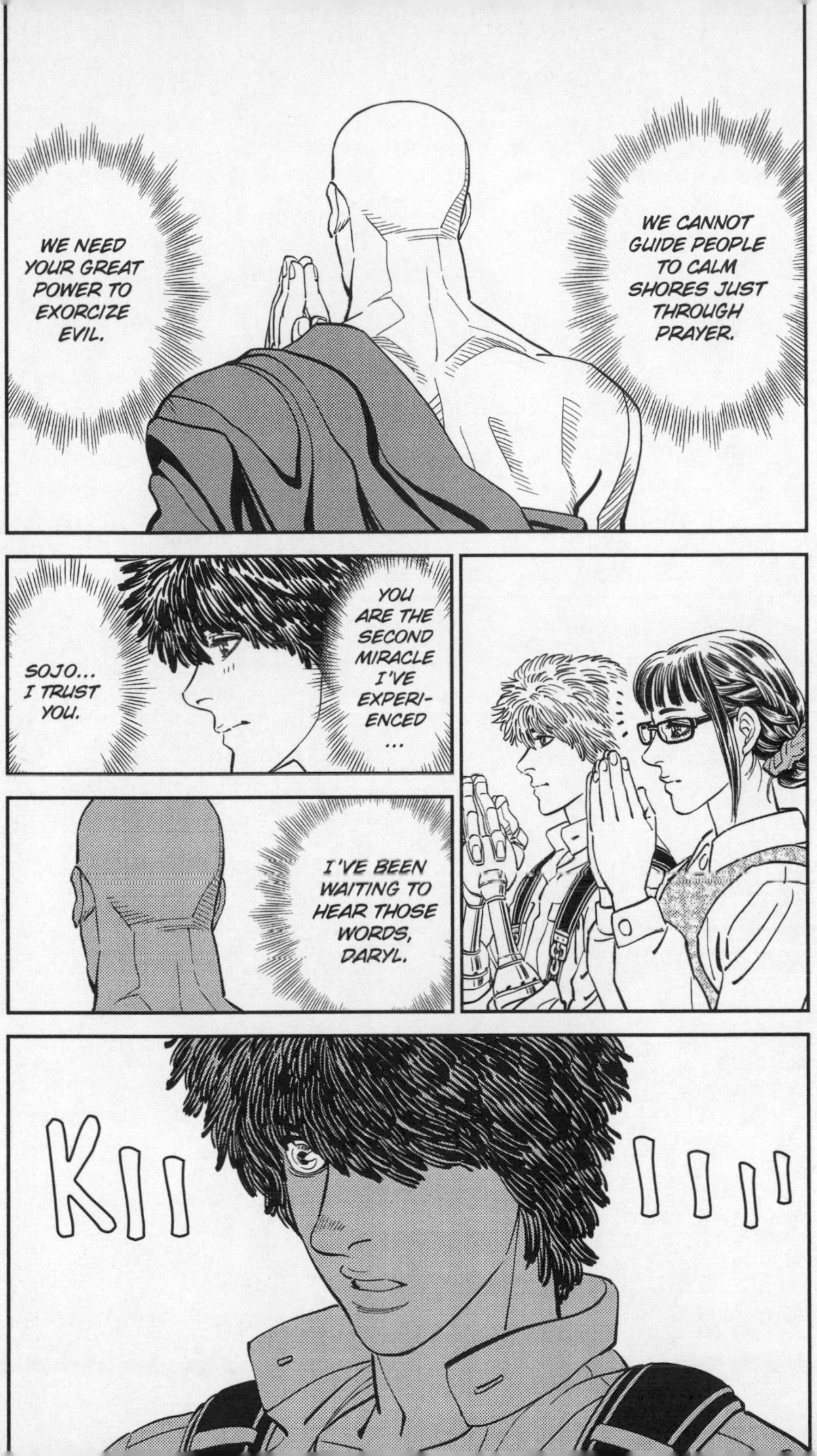
WE CANNOT GUIDE PEOPLE TO CALM SHORES JUST THROUGH PRAYER.
WE NEED YOUR GREAT POWER TO EXORCIZE EVIL.
YOU ARE THE SECOND MIRACLE I'VE EXPERIENCED...
SOJO... I TRUST YOU.
I'VE BEEN WAITING TO HEAR THOSE WORDS, DARYL.
KIIIIIII

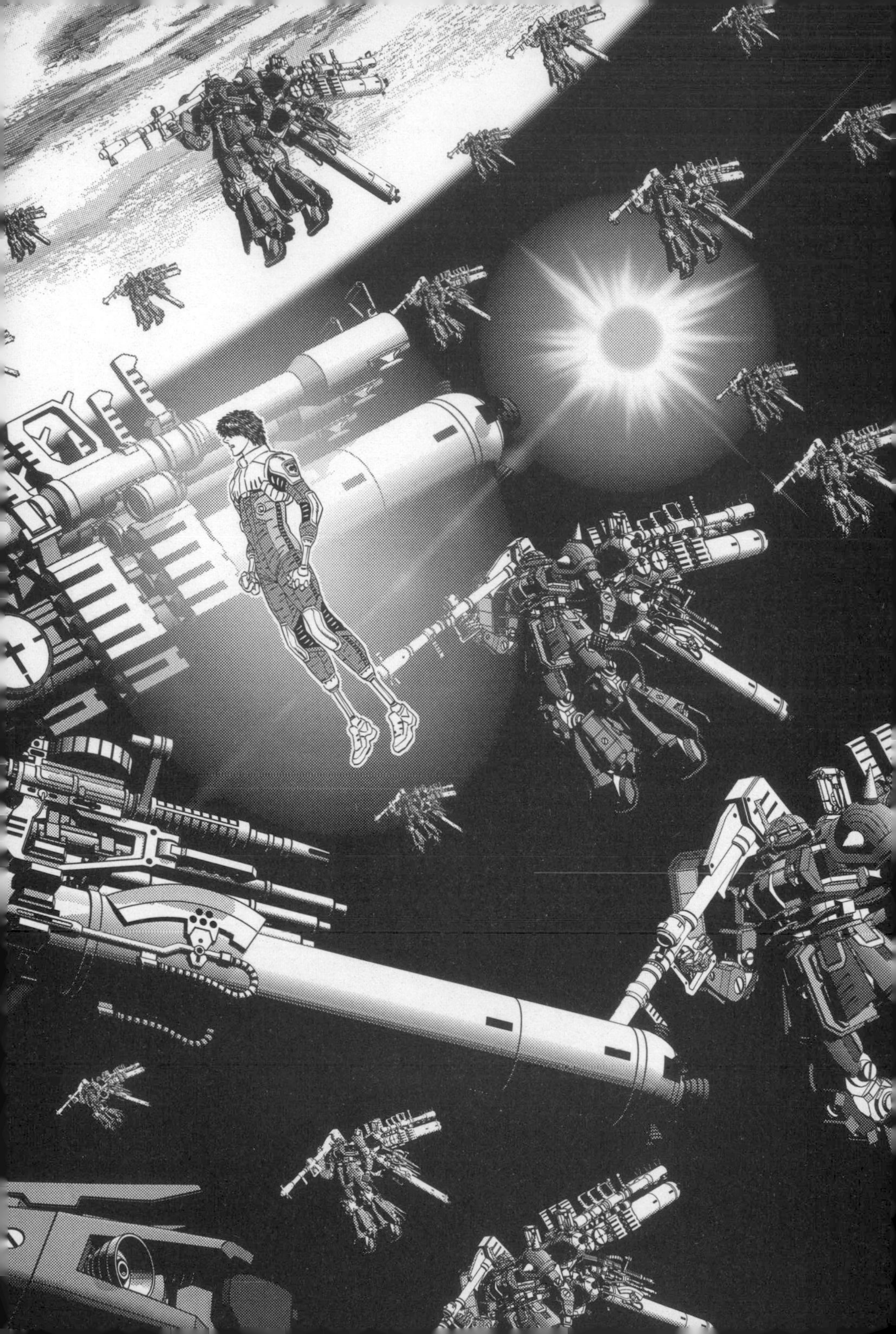

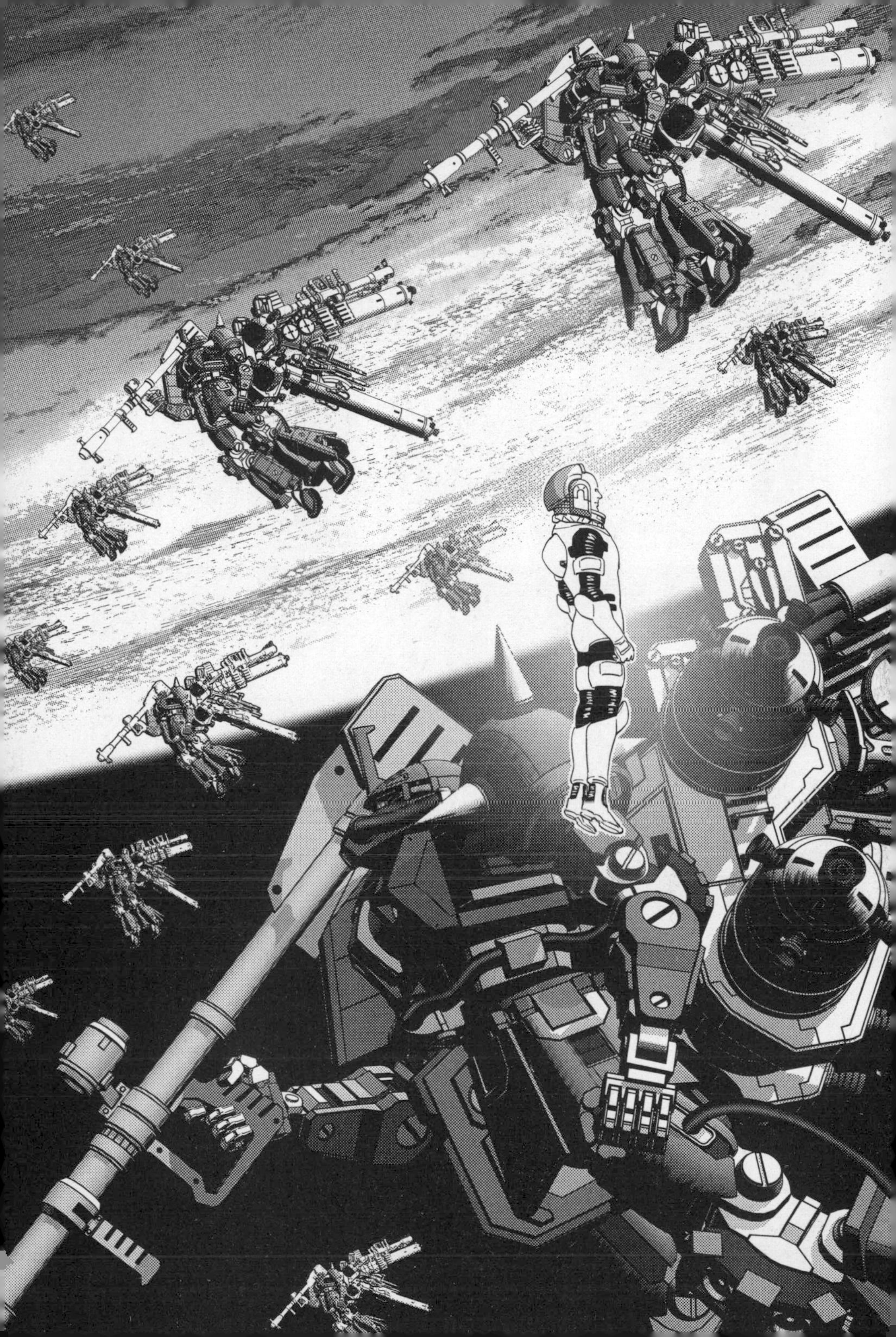

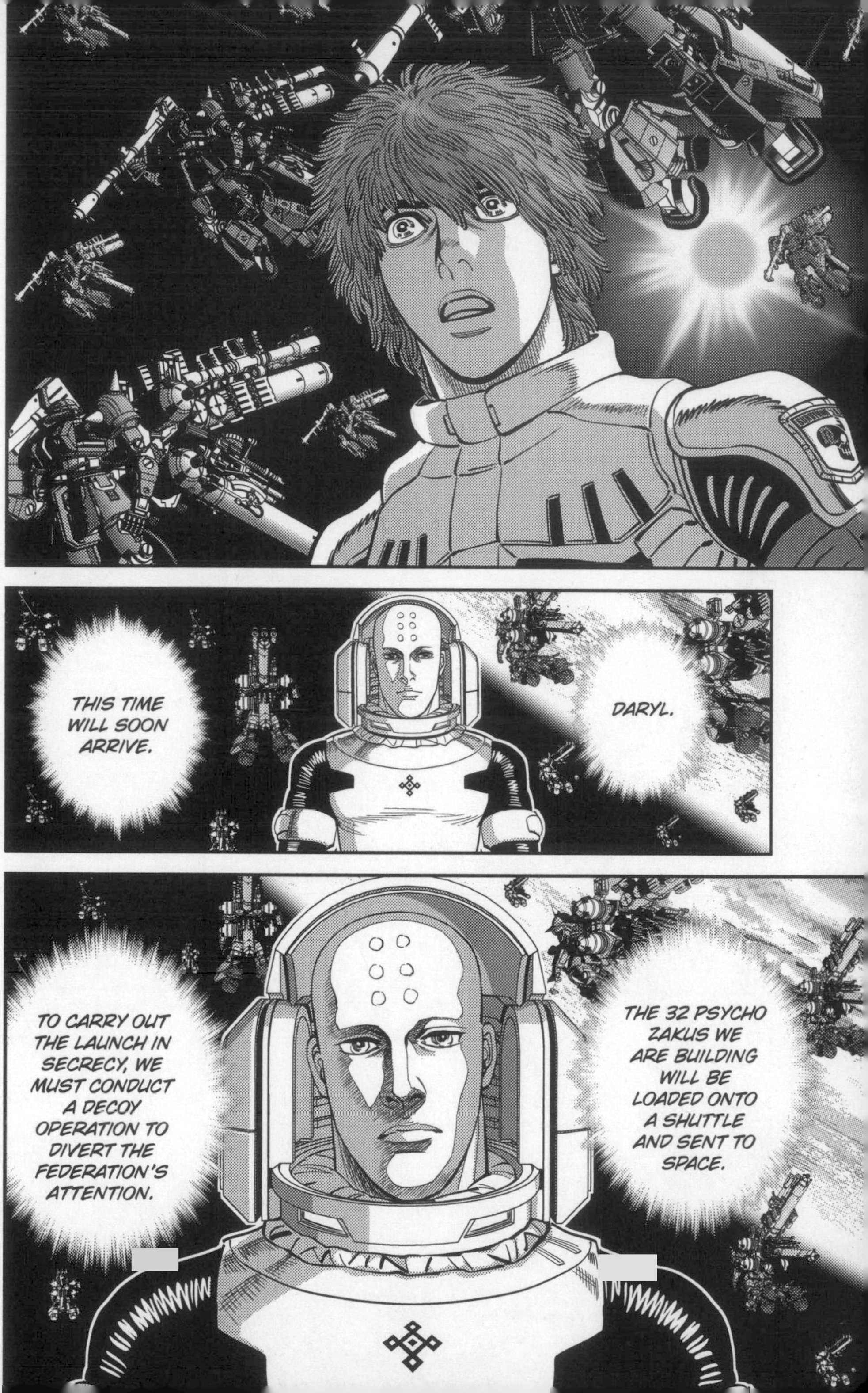
DARYL.
THIS TIME WILL SOON ARRIVE.
THE 32 PSYCHO ZAKUS WE ARE BUILDING WILL BE LOADED ONTO A SHUTTLE AND SENT TO SPACE.
TO CARRY OUT THE LAUNCH IN SECRECY, WE MUST CONDUCT A DECOY OPERATION TO DIVERT THE FEDERATION'S ATTENTION.

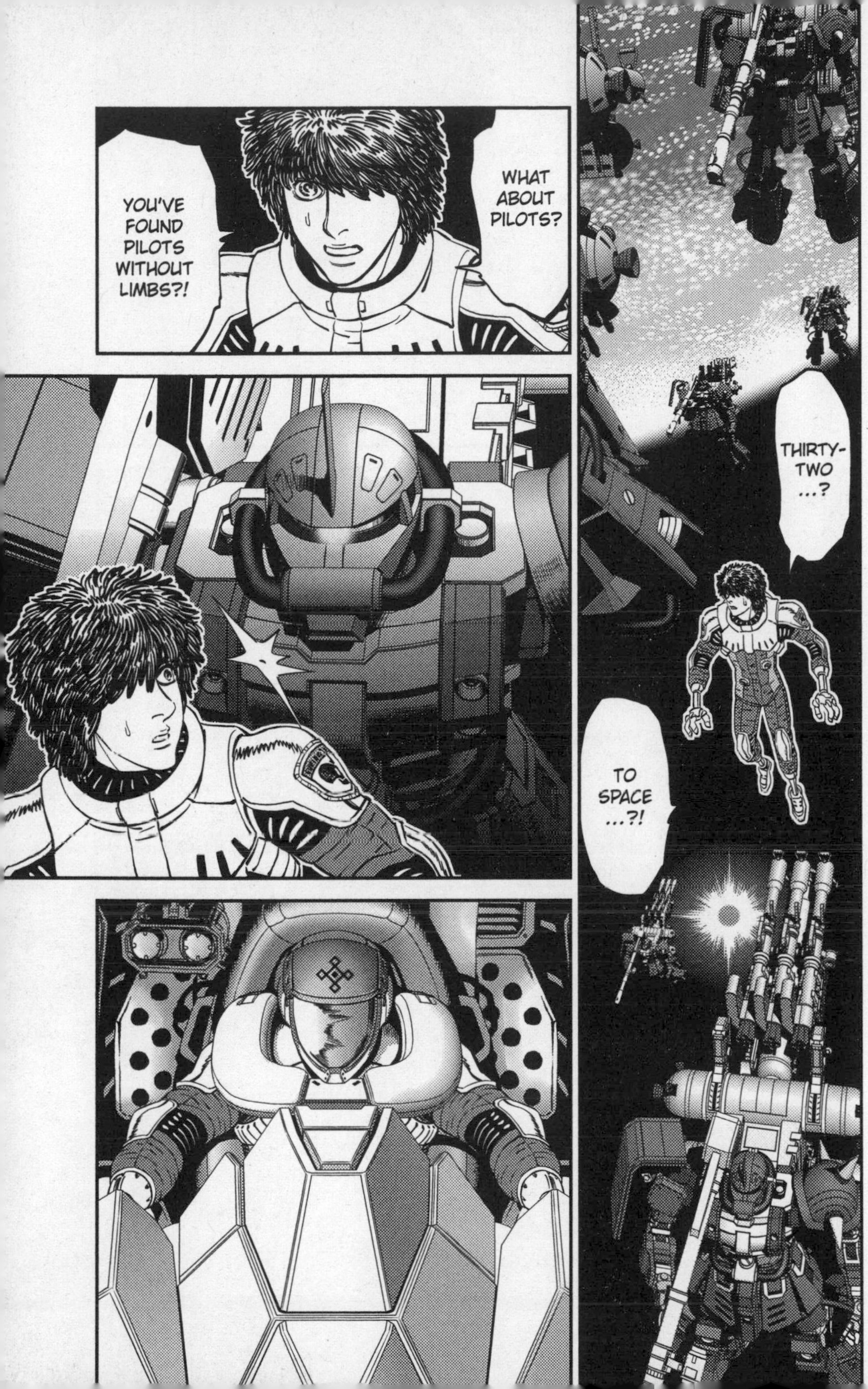
THIRTY-TWO ...?
TO SPACE ...?!
WHAT ABOUT PILOTS?
YOU'VE FOUND PILOTS WITHOUT LIMBS?!

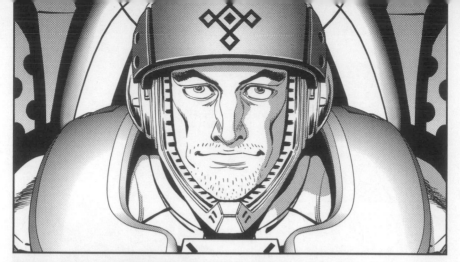

YOU'RE A PSYCHO ZAKU PILOT...?!

FISHER?

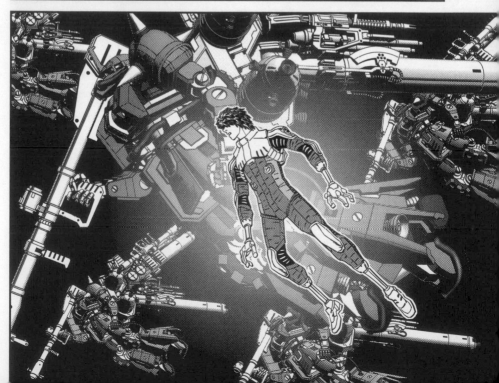

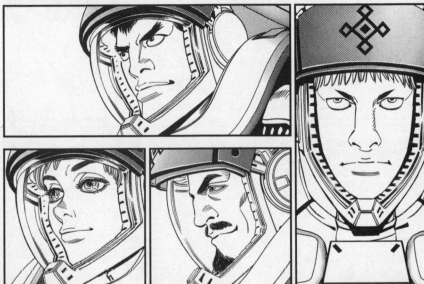

THEY ALL VOLUN-TEERED...

...FOR THE SAME CAUSE.

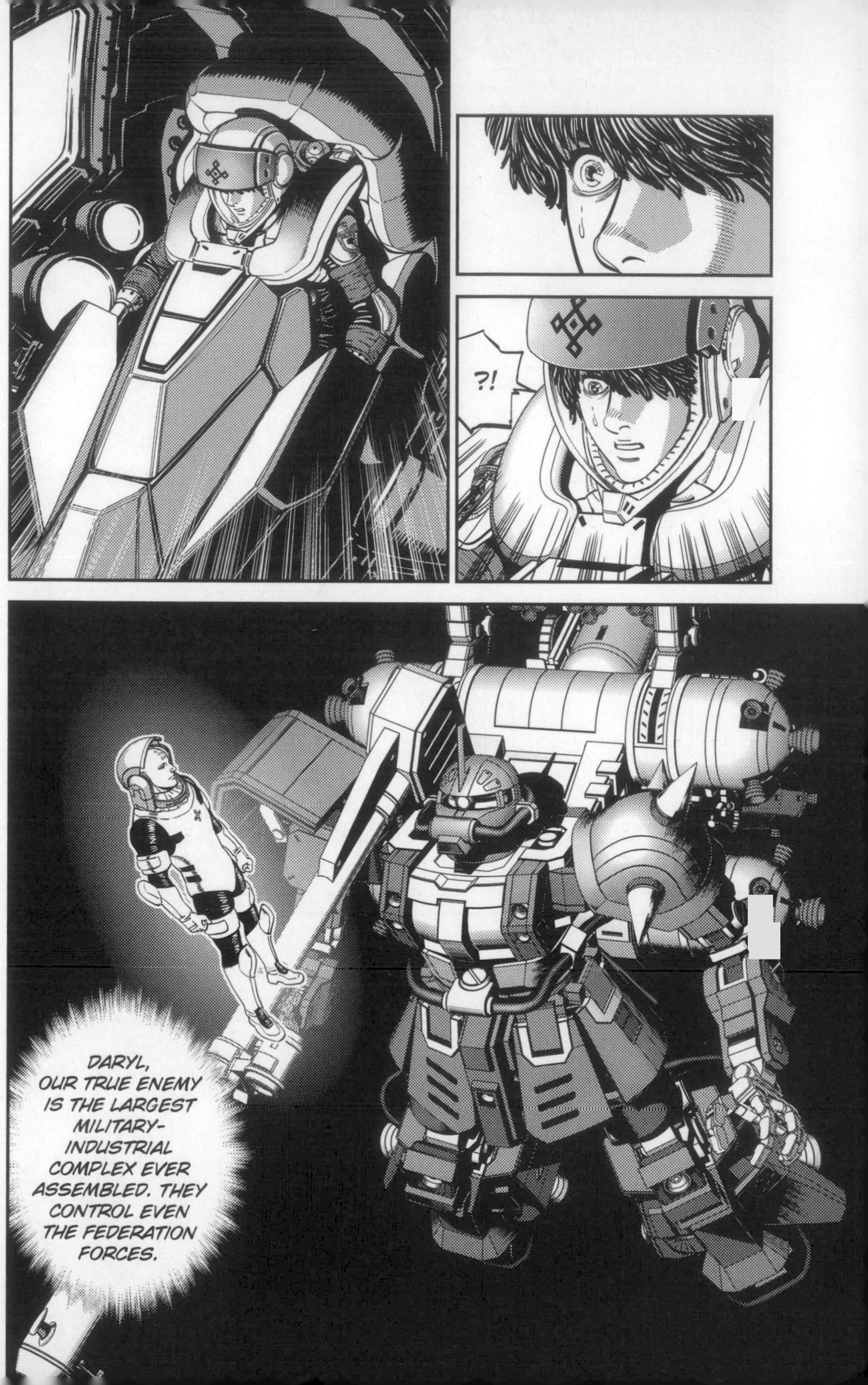
?!
DARYL, OUR TRUE ENEMY IS THE LARGEST MILITARY-INDUSTRIAL COMPLEX EVER ASSEMBLED. THEY CONTROL EVEN THE FEDERATION FORCES.

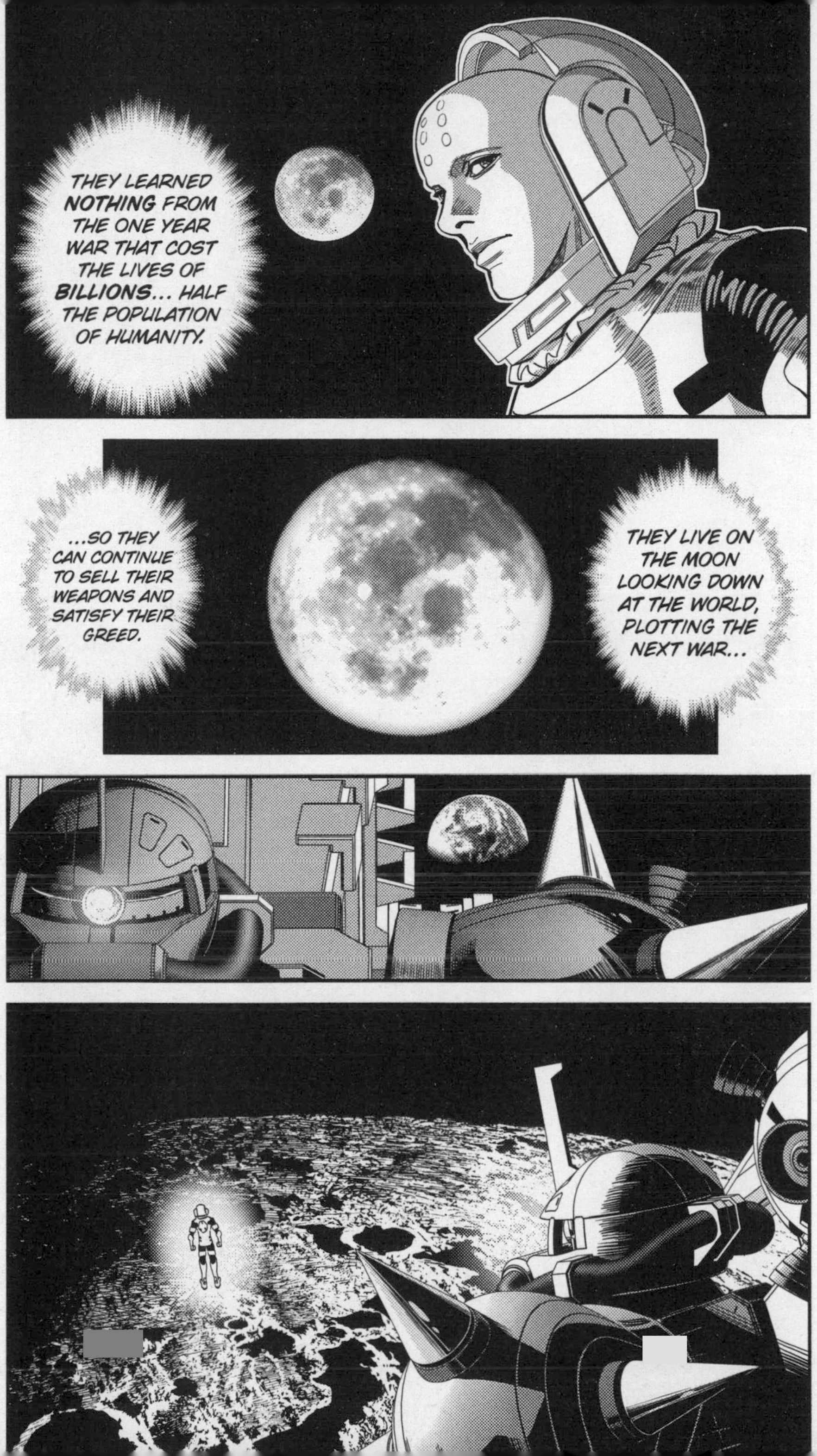
THEY LEARNED **NOTHING** FROM THE ONE YEAR WAR THAT COST THE LIVES OF **BILLIONS**... HALF THE POPULATION OF HUMANITY.
THEY LIVE ON THE MOON LOOKING DOWN AT THE WORLD, PLOTTING THE NEXT WAR...
...SO THEY CAN CONTINUE TO SELL THEIR WEAPONS AND SATISFY THEIR GREED.

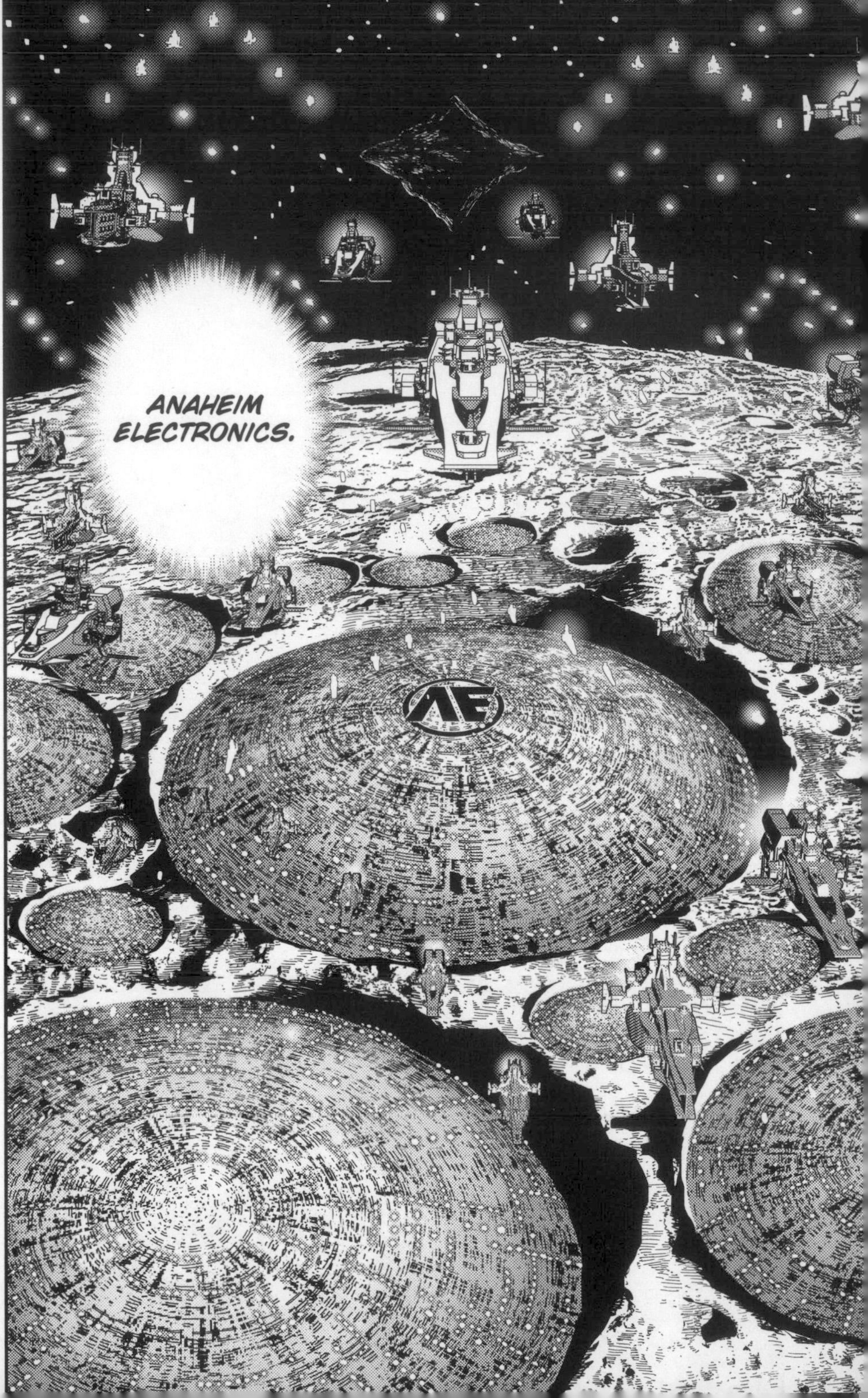
ANAHEIM ELECTRONICS.

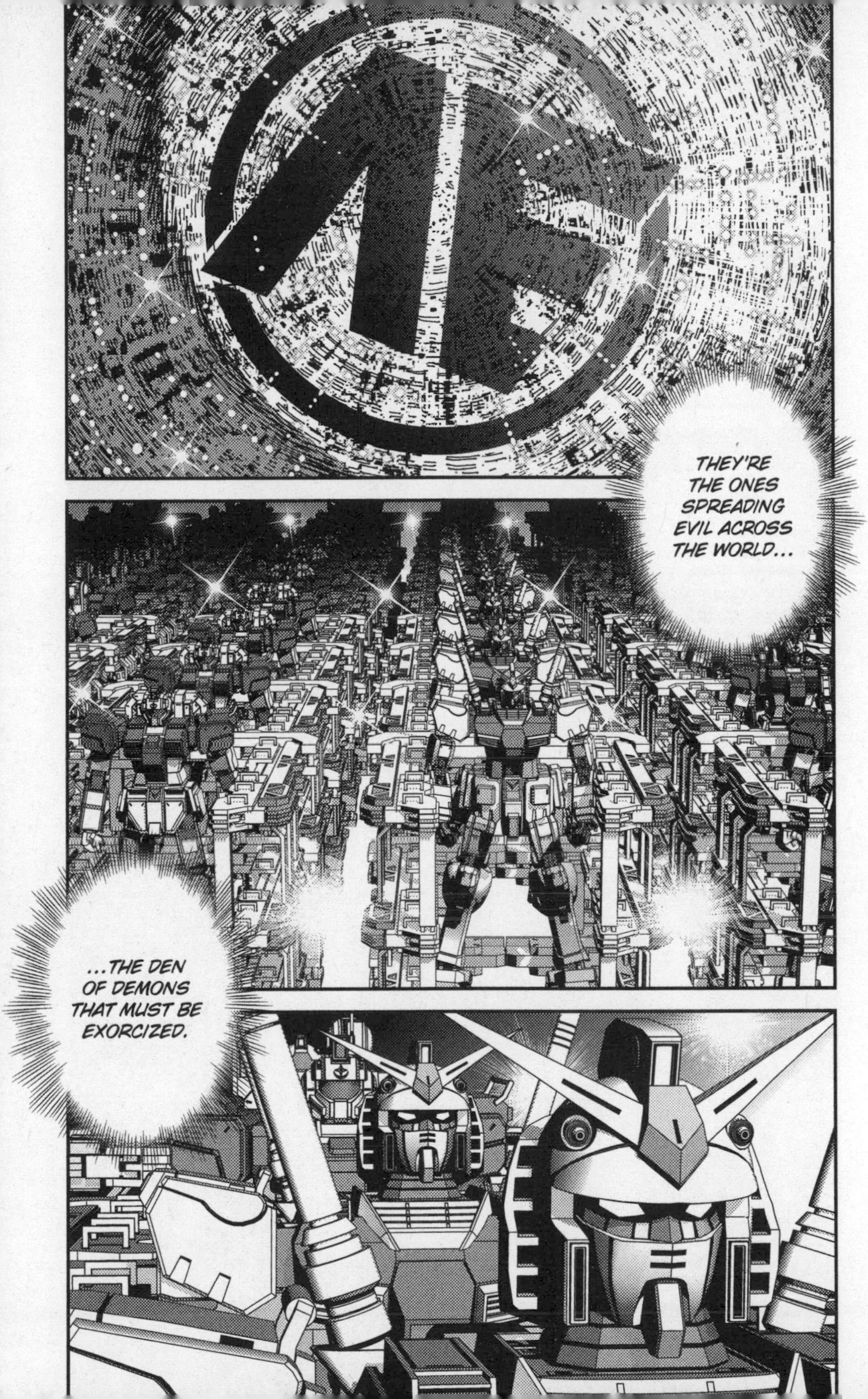
THEY'RE THE ONES SPREADING EVIL ACROSS THE WORLD...
...THE DEN OF DEMONS THAT MUST BE EXORCIZED.

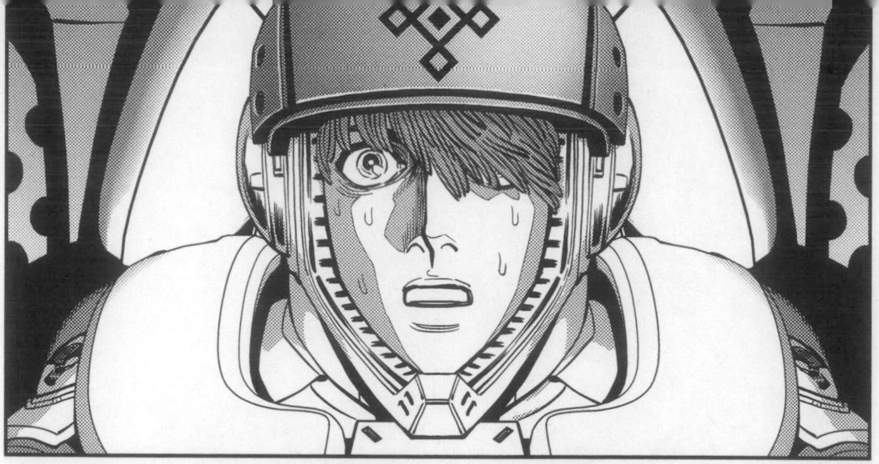

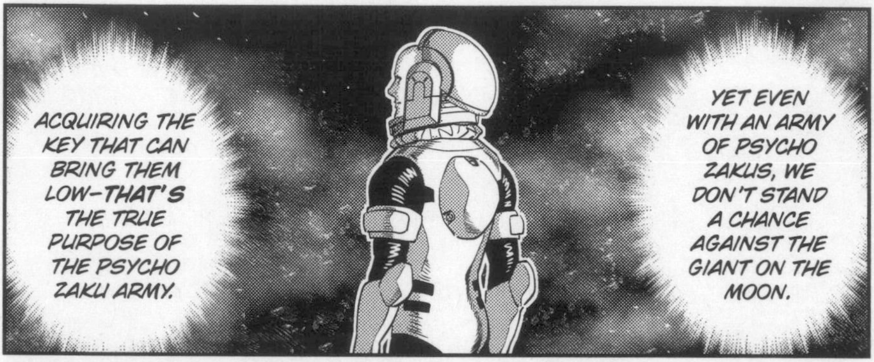
YET EVEN WITH AN ARMY OF PSYCHO ZAKUS, WE DON'T STAND A CHANCE AGAINST THE GIANT ON THE MOON.
ACQUIRING THE KEY THAT CAN BRING THEM LOW—THAT'S THE TRUE PURPOSE OF THE PSYCHO ZAKU ARMY.

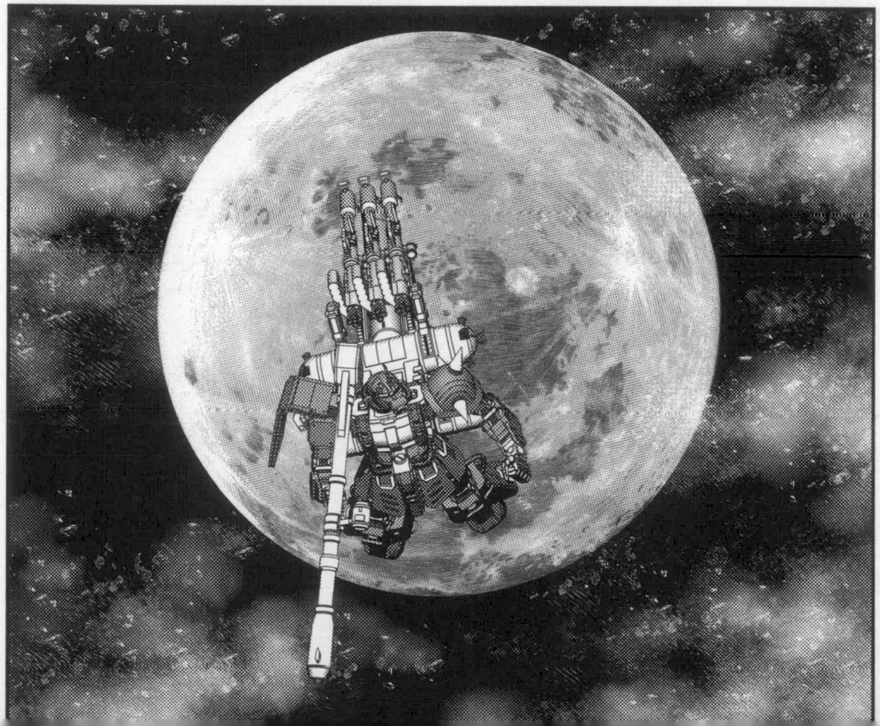

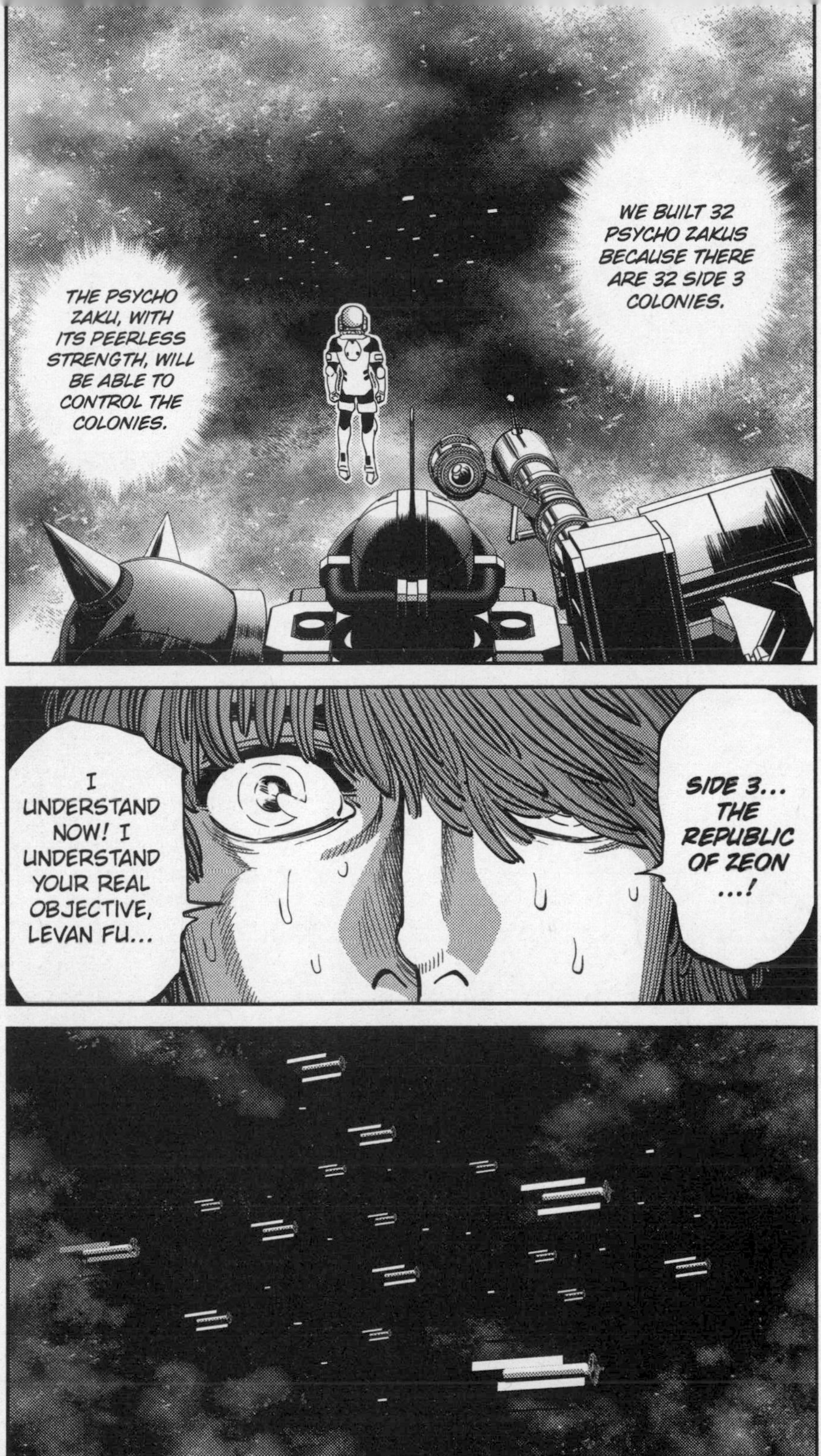
WE BUILT 32 PSYCHO ZAKUS BECAUSE THERE ARE 32 SIDE 3 COLONIES.
THE PSYCHO ZAKU, WITH ITS PEERLESS STRENGTH, WILL BE ABLE TO CONTROL THE COLONIES.
SIDE 3... THE REPUBLIC OF ZEON ...!
I UNDERSTAND NOW! I UNDERSTAND YOUR REAL OBJECTIVE, LEVAN FU...

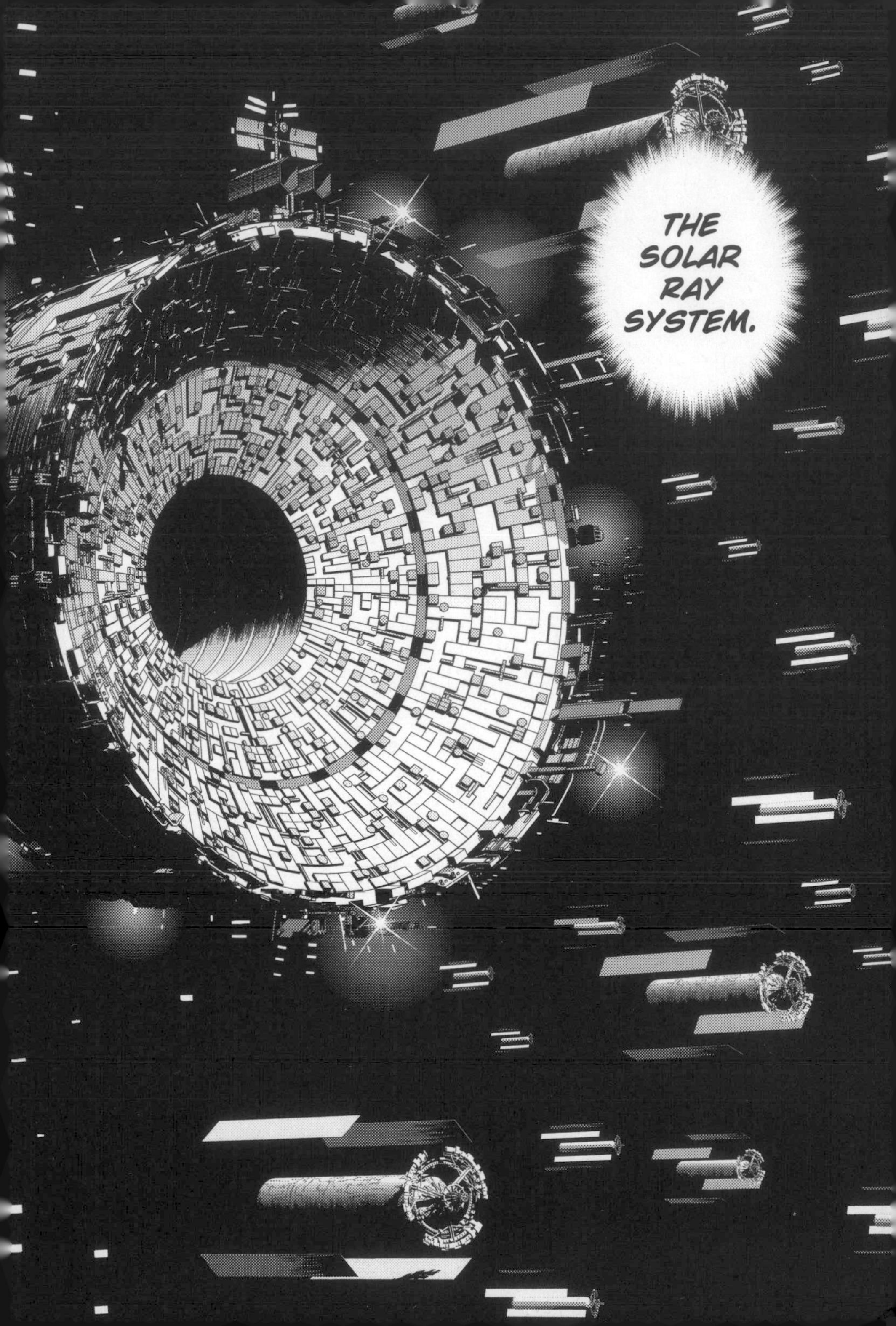
THE SOLAR RAY SYSTEM.

A GIANT BEAM WEAPON THAT WAS USED JUST ONCE NEAR THE END OF THE GREAT WAR. WE'LL USE IT TO SCOUR A.E. FROM THE MOON... AND THIS WORLD!

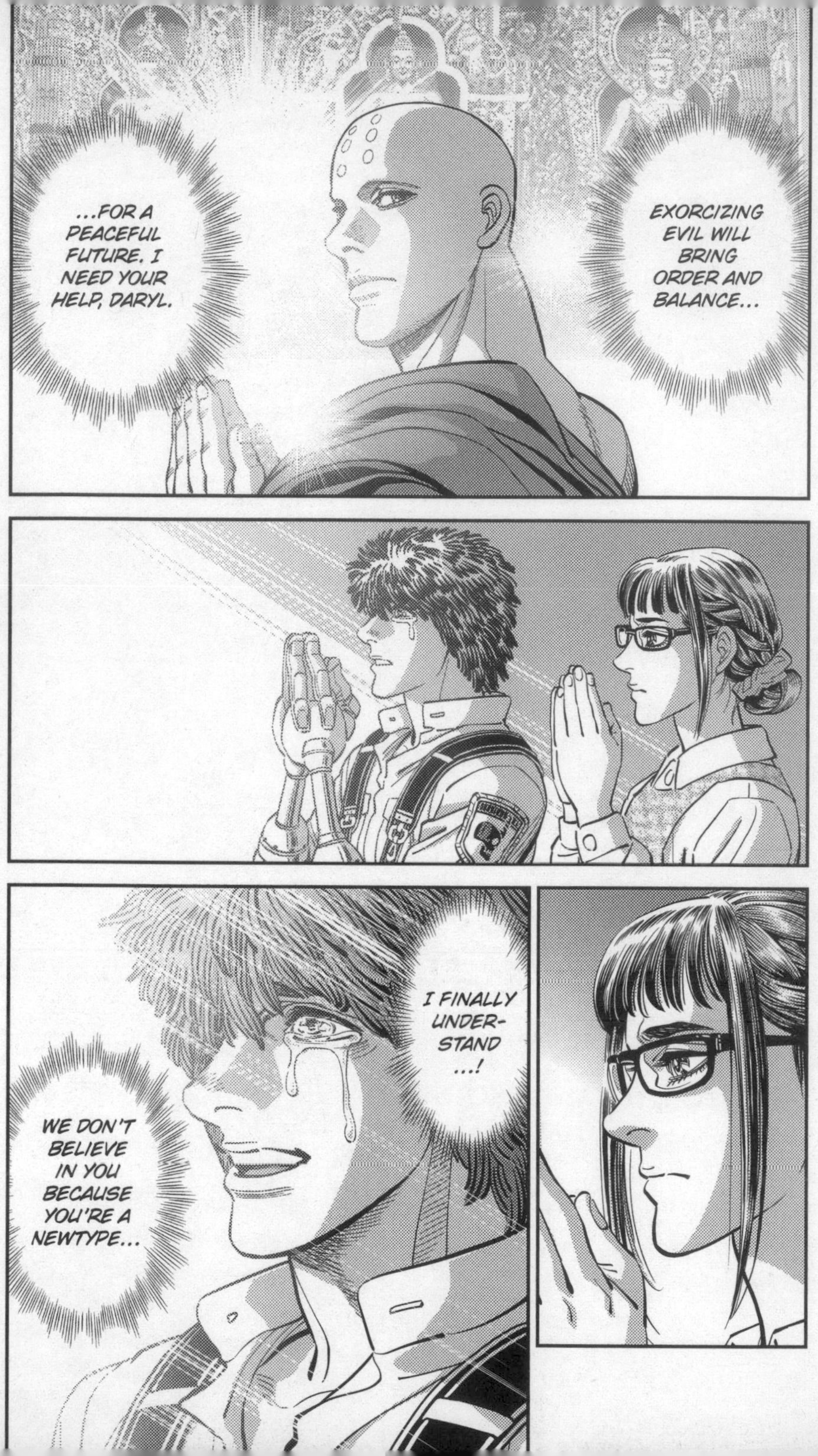
EXORCIZING EVIL WILL BRING ORDER AND BALANCE...
...FOR A PEACEFUL FUTURE. I NEED YOUR HELP, DARYL.
I FINALLY UNDER-STAND ...!
WE DON'T BELIEVE IN YOU BECAUSE YOU'RE A NEWTYPE...

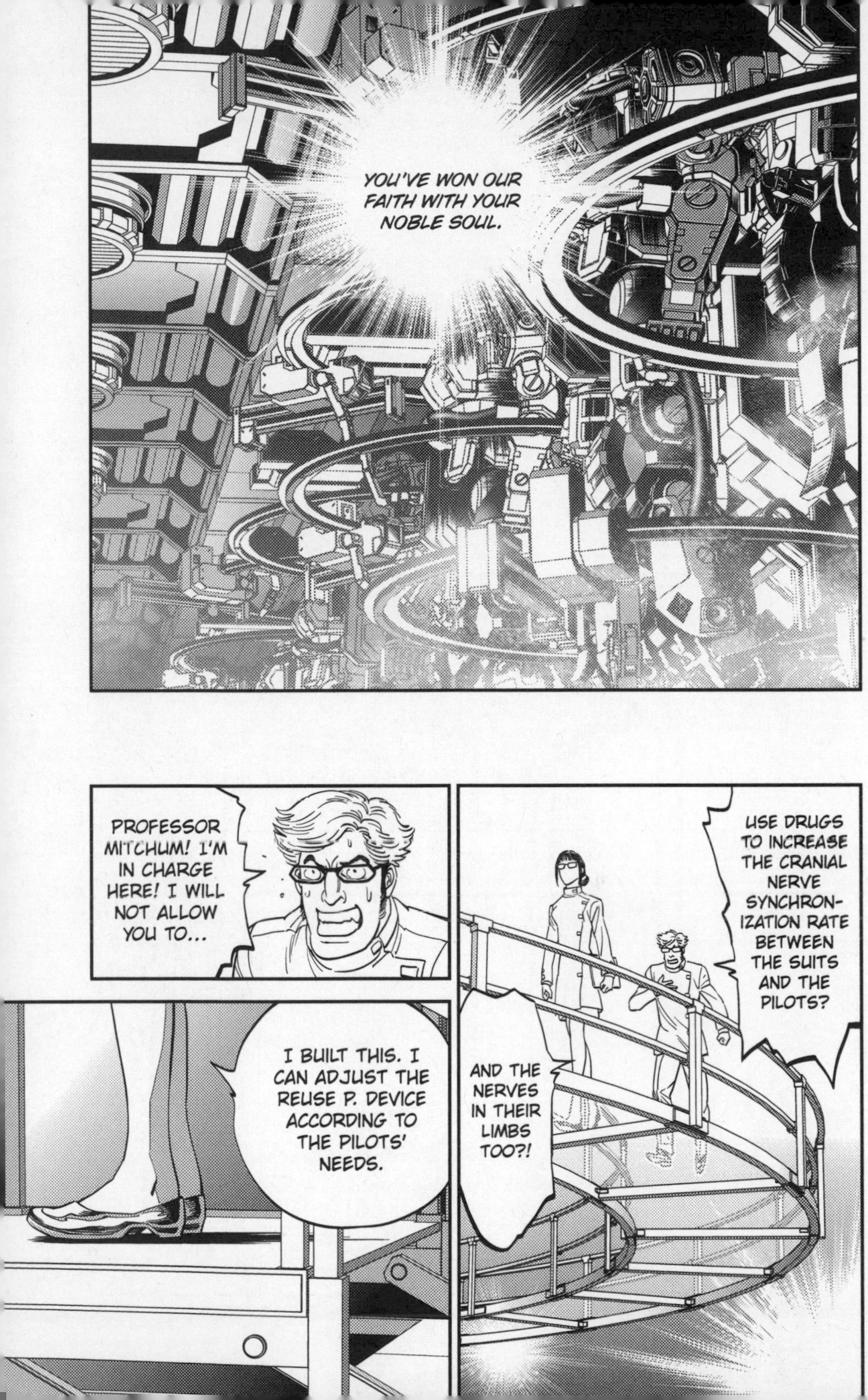
YOU'VE WON OUR FAITH WITH YOUR NOBLE SOUL.
USE DRUGS TO INCREASE THE CRANIAL NERVE SYNCHRON-IZATION RATE BETWEEN THE SUITS AND THE PILOTS?
AND THE NERVES IN THEIR LIMBS TOO?!
PROFESSOR MITCHUM! I'M IN CHARGE HERE! I WILL NOT ALLOW YOU TO...
I BUILT THIS. I CAN ADJUST THE REUSE P. DEVICE ACCORDING TO THE PILOTS' NEEDS.

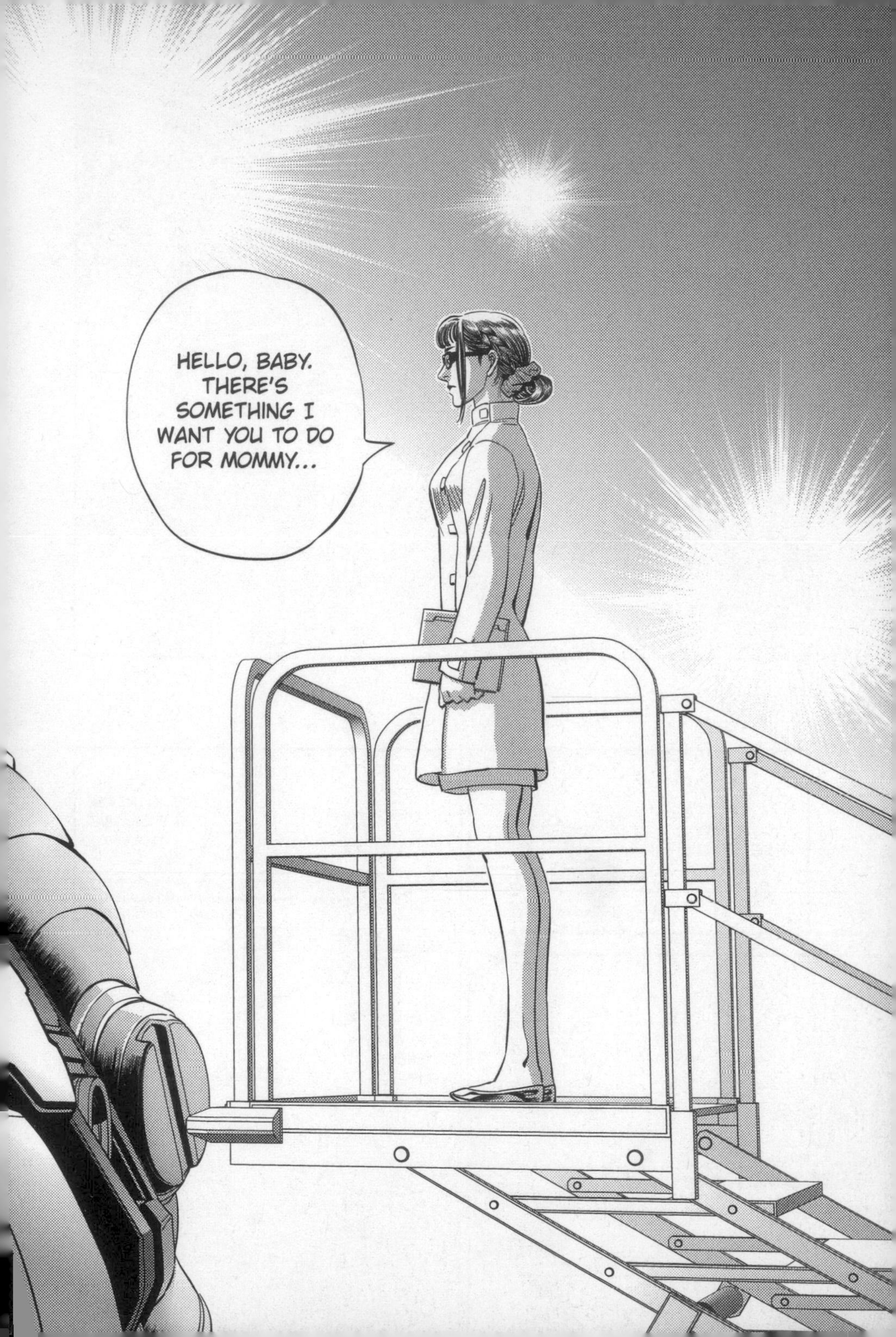
HELLO, BABY. THERE'S SOMETHING I WANT YOU TO DO FOR MOMMY...

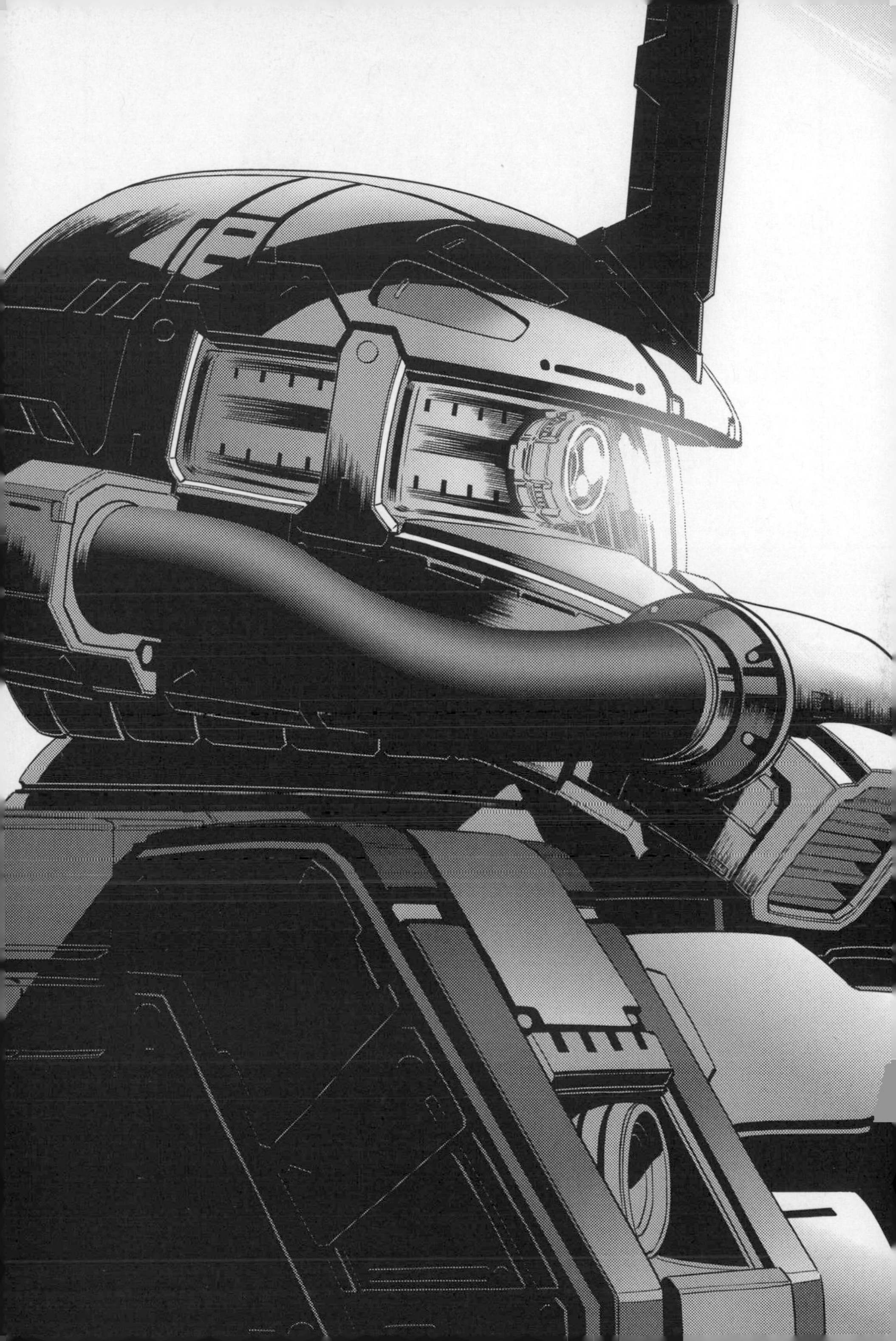

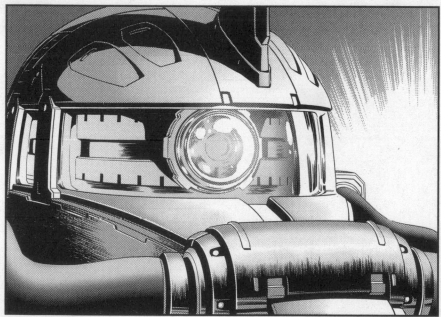

MOBILE SUIT GUNDAM - THUNDERBOLT - VOL. 11 - END

TO BE CONTINUED

STUDIO TOA S.P.A

Executive Director	**Yasuo Ohtagaki**
Chief	**Sayaka Ohtagaki**
Drawing Staff Lead	**Ju Ishiguchi**
Background Art	**Hikaru Kanefusa**
Drawing Staff	**Ryosuke Sugiyama**
	Izumi Yamada
	Shota Sugawa
	Rikuka Furusawa
	Tomomi Sawada
Production Manager	**Hideki Yamamoto**
Guest Designer	**Takuya Io**
Special Thanks	**Digital Noise Ltd.**

MOBILE SUIT GUNDAM THUNDERBOLT 11

VIZ Signature Edition

STORY AND ART **YASUO OHTAGAKI**
Original Concept by **HAJIME YATATE** and **YOSHIYUKI TOMINO**

Translation **JOE YAMAZAKI**
English Adaptation **STAN!**
Touch-up Art & Lettering **EVAN WALDINGER**
Cover & Design **SHAWN CARRICO**
Editor **MIKE MONTESA**

ORIGINAL COVER DESIGN / Yoshiyuki SEKI for VOLARE inc.

EDITORIAL COOPERATION / Shinsuke HIRAIWA (Digitalpaint.jp)

Printed in the U.S.A.

Published by VIZ Media, LLC
P.O. Box 77010
San Francisco, CA 94107

10 9 8 7 6 5 4 3 2 1
First printing, May 2019

VIZ MEDIA
viz.com

VIZ SIGNATURE
vizsignature.com

ratings.viz.com RATED T+ OLDER TEEN

PARENTAL ADVISORY
MOBILE SUIT GUNDAM THUNDERBOLT is rated T+ for Older Teen and is recommended for ages 16 and up. This volume contains realistic violence, strong language, mild nudity and some adult themes.

Hey! You're Reading in the Wrong Direction!

This is the *end* of this graphic novel!

To properly enjoy this VIZ graphic novel, please turn it around and begin reading from *right to left.* Unlike English, Japanese is read right to left, so Japanese comics are read in reverse order from the way English comics are typically read.

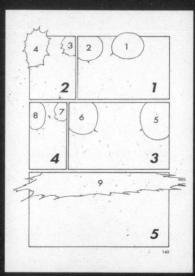

Follow the action this way

This book has been printed in the original Japanese format in order to preserve the orientation of the original artwork. Have fun with it!